Modernism, Music and the Politics of Aesthetics

Modernism, Music and the Politics of Aesthetics

Gemma Moss

EDINBURGH
University Press

Edinburgh University Press is one of the leading university presses in the UK. We publish academic books and journals in our selected subject areas across the humanities and social sciences, combining cutting-edge scholarship with high editorial and production values to produce academic works of lasting importance. For more information visit our website: edinburghuniversitypress.com

© Gemma Moss, 2021, 2023

Edinburgh University Press Ltd
The Tun – Holyrood Road
12(2f) Jackson's Entry
Edinburgh EH8 8PJ

First published in hardback by Edinburgh University Press 2021

Typeset in 10.5/13 Adobe Sabon by Servis
Filmsetting Ltd, Stockport, Cheshire

A CIP record for this book is available from the British Library

ISBN 978 1 4744 2990 0 (hardback)
ISBN 978 1 4744 2991 7 (paperback)
ISBN 978 1 4744 2992 4 (webready PDF)
ISBN 978 1 4744 2993 1 (epub)

The right of Gemma Moss to be identified as the author of this work has been asserted in accordance with the Copyright, Designs and Patents Act 1988, and the Copyright and Related Rights Regulations 2003 (SI No. 2498).

Contents

Acknowledgements vi
Permissions viii
List of Abbreviations and Editions Used in the Text ix
Preface x

Introduction 1
1. On Music and Modernism: Philosophies, Histories, Approaches 22
2. James Joyce, *Ulysses* and the Politics of Musical Form 49
3. Ezra Pound, Music and Fascism: Towards Canto LXXV 88
4. Sylvia Townsend Warner, Ideology and Marxist Aesthetics 137
5. Music and Twenty-first-century Modernism 179

Bibliography 231
Index 253

Acknowledgements

Many people have contributed to this book, which began as a PhD thesis at the University of Manchester, funded by the AHRC. Howard J. Booth has guided this project from start to finish, and he has been a wonderful mentor, friend and expert advisor. I'm grateful to everyone who taught me at Manchester, but especially Robert Spencer, for his kind encouragement and inspiring insights on modernism and theory. Thanks are due to many colleagues, mentors and friends who have taught me, helped me or otherwise shaped this book: Emma Sutton, David Alderson, Daniela Caselli, Kaye Mitchell, Anastasia Valassopoulos, Iain Bailey, J. T. Welsch, Matt Whittle, Neil Griffiths, Tom Whyman and Matthew Porto. Special thanks go to Jade Munslow Ong, Andrew Frayn, Sean Mark and Finn Fordham, who were particularly generous with their time, and to Nathan Waddell, whose careful feedback on the whole book and advice about the final chapter is greatly appreciated. Vincent Sherry's wisdom on Ezra Pound, the bigger picture and the writing process was indispensable. Benefiting from his remarkable ideas and careful commentary has been a privilege and a pleasure. I'm fortunate to have had wonderful colleagues during the final years of this project, so thank you to everyone at BCU, but particularly Soudabeh Ananisarab, Joseph Anderton, Islam Issa and Mark McGlashan, and Sarah Wood for being such a thoughtful and effective Head of School.

I'm grateful to Jackie Jones at Edinburgh University Press for agreeing to take on this book, and to Ersev Ersoy and Anna Stevenson for their help in the final stages. Thanks to the Estate of Sylvia Townsend Warner, Faber & Faber and New Directions for permission to reproduce material by Sylvia Townsend Warner, T. S. Eliot and Ezra Pound.

Finally, thank you to friends – especially Andy, Beth, Charlotte, Claire, Jack and Shaila – for the countless ways you've all helped. Special thanks to Christopher Moss, for your belief, infectious enthusiasm and friendship; Graham and Pauline West, not least for the musical education that might have been the start of this work; to Owen, for making daily life better; and most of all to my parents, Paul and Kate.

Permissions

'Burnt Norton' by T. S. Eliot, from *Four Quartets*, © 1943 T. S. Eliot. Reprinted by permission of Faber & Faber.
'Canto LXXV' by Ezra Pound, from *The Cantos of Ezra Pound*, © 1948 Ezra Pound. Reprinted by permission of New Directions Publishing Corp and Faber & Faber.
Mr Fortune's Maggot by Sylvia Townsend Warner, © 1927. Reprinted by permission of The Estate of Sylvia Townsend Warner.
The Corner That Held Them by Sylvia Townsend Warner, © 1948. Reprinted by permission of The Estate of Sylvia Townsend Warner.
The Music at Long Verney by Sylvia Townsend Warner, © 2001. Reprinted by permission of The Estate of Sylvia Townsend Warner.

List of Abbreviations and Editions Used in the Text

C   Ezra Pound, *The Cantos of Ezra Pound* (New York: New Directions, 1996).
CH   Sylvia Townsend Warner, *The Corner That Held Them* ([1945] London: Virago, 2012).
EPM   Ezra Pound, *Ezra Pound and Music: The Complete Criticism*, ed. R. Murray Schafer (London: Faber & Faber, 1978).
GK   Ezra Pound, *Guide to Kulchur* ([1938] New York: New Directions, 1970).
LE   Ezra Pound, *Literary Essays*, ed. T.S. Eliot (London: Faber & Faber, 1954).
MFM   Sylvia Townsend Warner, *Mr Fortune's Maggot* ([1927] London: Virago, 2000).
MLV   Sylvia Townsend Warner, *The Music at Long Verney* (London: Counterpoint, 2001).
T   Ezra Pound, *The Translations of Ezra Pound*, ed. Hugh Kenner (London: Faber & Faber, 1953).
U   James Joyce, *Ulysses: A Critical and Synoptic Edition*, prepared by Hans Walter Gabler, with Wolfhard Steppe and Claus Melchior, 3 vols (New York and London: Garland Publishing, 1984).

Preface

Music has a communicative capacity that can be compared with language: it seems laden with meaning and able to express emotion. How it does so is still the subject of much debate.[1] Although musical utterances cannot always be translated into words, what music 'says' can feel profound, truthful and accurate. The idea that music provides a valuable, non-linguistic form of communication is prominent in modernist writing, especially in T. S. Eliot, James Joyce, Ezra Pound, Marcel Proust, Thomas Mann, Dorothy Richardson, Virginia Woolf, E. M. Forster and D. H. Lawrence. Their work has driven extensive investigations into the interactions between modernist literature and music.[2] But why did so many modernists – writers who were deeply invested in producing social change through literature because of the many problems they saw in contemporary life – turn to an abstract art form like music?

Music and words have a long history of being combined in song. In 1691, Henry Purcell claimed that 'Musick and Poetry have ever been acknowledg'd Sisters. As Poetry is the harmony of Words, so Musick is that of Notes'.[3] Purcell demonstrates an idealised and long-held view of music as beautiful sound; a view shared by John Milton, for whom singing and poetry are 'Sphere-born harmonious Sisters, Voice, and Vers'.[4] The modernist engagement with music is different. Modernists are not always seeking harmonious combinations of words and music: instead, their acknowledgement of music's usefulness for literary form implies that language lacks something, and they often draw on musical rhythms and structures to achieve unusual forms that contribute to the aesthetic complexity of their literature. With these issues as our focus, we could find aesthetic and philosophical explanations for the use of music in modernist literature. But these writers also wanted their work to have an impact in the world, and many were deeply influenced by the newly dissonant music of the early twentieth century that registered the sounds of material existence: industrial machinery, city life and mechanised warfare. Since the project of modernist literature was both aesthetic (to experiment with literary forms) and social (to have an impact on people's thinking that might affect their actions in the world), locating music's value centrally in its aesthetic qualities, or centrally in its social production and functions, seems insufficient to me. This book seeks to bring aesthetic and social analyses of music in modernist literature into a productive tension, drawing out the political relevance of aesthetic judgements, and the ways in which aesthetic experiences inform social and political life. What, then, might be the real-world significance of the modernist search for new literary aesthetics, informed by music? And how might the pursuit of musically inspired forms of communication have been rooted in social and political experience?

Appeals to music in literary modernism signal anxieties, not simply about language or forms of art, but about the limitations of post-Enlightenment rationality and the ways of living it makes possible. Rational thought had brought about an advanced society, but one still laden with political, social and economic problems, in which the possibility of articulating resistance to 'the march of events' (as Ezra Pound wrote) seemed to be closing.[5] Writers sought methods of formal innovation that might provide alternative ways of thinking and generating meaning, fresh ways of conceptualising the value of art and ultimately new methods of addressing social problems. The political significance of literary engagements with music's ability to produce meaning non-linguistically can be accessed by reframing modernist uses of music as part of ongoing investigations of rational thought. This makes music a crucial aspect of modernist literature.

Literary modernism is overwhelmingly conceptualised as the aesthetic response to a crisis of language, thought and perception. Contributing to this crisis were questions about the kinds of progress produced by liberal democracy and scientific development: were science and rational thought simply helping people to understand the world, or might the way these were employed sometimes be restraining thought, understanding and action? It is commonly held that modernists questioned established notions of progress. 'In the new century progress could seem a cruel myth', writes Tim Armstrong. 'How can 20,000 dead in a morning at the Somme or the genocide of a million Armenians be fitted into a progressive world-view? Was moral, cultural, even biological degeneration intrinsic to modernity?'[6] These concerns, articulated formally by writers who often used music to try to break with established representational practices, also drove Frankfurt School philosophers during the 1930s and 1940s, whose status as the archetypal theorists of modernism has been cemented by Tyrus Miller's *Modernism and the*

Frankfurt School.[7] In *Dialectic of Enlightenment*, Theodor W. Adorno and Max Horkheimer rewrote the Enlightenment narrative – of greater knowledge and better technologies bringing humanity out of darkness and into light – into a narrative of disaster, in which reason's regression into instrumental rationality has enslaved rather than liberated humanity, culminating in fascism and the Second World War.

A discussion of what reason is and what is at stake in how we use it can be found in the voice of Elizabeth Costello, J. M. Coetzee's fictional novelist in *The Lives of Animals*.[8] Reason, she says, seems to be the way we understand the world: 'the fact that through the application of reason we can come to understand the rules by which the universe works proves that the universe and reason are of the same being'. However, Costello suspects that 'reason may not be the being of the universe but on the contrary merely the being of the human brain'.[9] Perhaps reason is not how humanity operates at its best, in a way that is deeply in tune with the world. Perhaps reason has been given undeserved precedence by focusing on the improvements to human life associated with the Enlightenment, otherwise known as the Age of Reason, rather than all the times reason has been used to limit and harm others. Costello argues that since René Descartes declared 'cogito, ergo sum', thinking has taken over, leaving little room for feeling. The ability to coldly rationalise cruelty – her example is towards animals farmed for meat, but there are many others such as slavery, colonisation, genocide and war – shows that reason can be used for unethical ends; to justify actions that people may *feel* are wrong. For Costello, and arguably for Coetzee, individualistic and utilitarian forms of rationalism too often quell people's capacities for imagination and empathy.

The fallibility and restrictiveness of rationalism is a lens through which modernists' radical and reactionary politics are now often analysed. For Mark Antliff, the rise of fascism in Europe leading up to the Second World War 'responded to a widespread search for spiritual values and "organic" institutions capable of counteracting what was considered the corrosive effects of rationalism (and capitalism) on the body politic'.[10] Michael North writes that by the beginning of the twentieth century, 'aesthetic modernism could be defined by its antagonism to the other elements of modernity: rationalism, material progress, liberal democracy'.[11] Rationalism had produced the technology for material progress and justified liberal democracy, but its legacy was not entirely positive, since material progress had failed to provide adequate living standards for everyone. Liberalism is premised on the notion of individual freedom – the state's role is to guarantee the conditions under which people can exercise their free will without encroaching on the freedom of others –

but modernist writers often express doubts about the degree to which the individual is autonomous, and able to make free choices. For Marx, the autonomous subject was a myth: under liberalism, he wrote, 'the State built itself up into an apparently independent force', claiming to be an impartial adjudicator that expressed theoretically the needs of the workers, but 'these theoretical ideas of the bourgeoisie had as their basis material interests and a *will* that was conditioned and determined by the material relations of production'.[12] Marx argued that people's actions and choices are affected by laws and structures that are often invisible and beyond an individual's control.

Why, then, was music so prominent in modernist writing? Corresponding with that suspicion of reason, liberal politics, language and established representational forms was a fascination with the non-linguistic way music creates meaning. Music had value to these writers because it is not without comprehensible meaning, but those meanings are not directly explainable in language, or in terms of rationality, logic or the empirical sciences that were partly responsible for the unsatisfactory aspects of contemporary existence. Music works on the body through sound waves and vibrations, and seems to affect the emotions and imagination rather than logic or common sense. Although music takes part in a process of signification, its meanings are contained within its form and it seems to transmit them with a directness impossible for signifying language. Language was freighted with worn-out phrases, terms from political discourse and rational meaning, but at the same time modernist writers were newly estranged from it: they used it with care and self-consciousness, aware that it not only described but constructed the world. Inspired by music's non-linguistic meanings that might be accessed by attending to sound or employing unusual forms influenced by music, writers were testing language's limitations, questioning how far rational thought can help us and investigating the possibility of new ways of thinking.

Ideas about music's ability to communicate without words are indebted to German Idealism and Romanticism, which came to inform British Aestheticism. These were typified respectively by Arthur Schopenhauer's claims about music's capacity to express the 'thing-in-itself' – the will, or the unmediated essence of life itself – and Walter Pater's writing about music as the art to which all others 'constantly aspire' because of its unification of content and form.[13] Instrumental music without narrative or reference to the material world seemed to transcend language and daily concerns, while still communicating concepts and emotions of distinctly human importance. These ideas become formalised in the discourse of 'absolute music', which refers to instrumental music considered purified by an absence of narrative and referent.[14] Throughout this book, I use the phrase 'musical transcendence' to refer to a range of approaches to music that have a long history – beginning with Pythagoras and the music of the spheres – but share an overwhelmingly positive conceptualisation of the non-referential way music creates meanings that have the potential to be timeless, universal and able to communicate human, emotional truths. 'Musical transcendence' includes discourses of 'absolute music' and more, because it refers to more general and widespread ideas about music's mysterious qualities, emotional impact and circumvention of language that persist today.[15] It is distinct from the Burkean sublime, which understands music's sensory impact on the body and elision of logic as potentially dangerous, rather than a beneficial escape from the rational.[16]

At the turn of the twentieth century, notions of musical transcendence were coming under pressure. Josh Epstein has examined writers and composers who tested the boundary between music and noise, attempting to inject music with political and social relevance in the wake of the *art pour l'art* adherents who had championed aesthetic contemplation as an end in itself. 'Pater, Stéphane Mallarmé, or any number of nineteenth-century aesthetes had idealized music's pleasurable unification of form and content', writes Epstein, while in the twentieth century Cecil Barber claimed that far from being a transcendent art form, music was just 'expensive noise': the material product of wealth and education.[17] For Epstein, by the modernist period musical philosophies and compositions had moved away from the transcendence associated with it during Aestheticism, towards dissonance, rhythm and noise, so that it 'no longer makes sense to critique literary treatments of music through Paterian eyes'.[18] Yet ideas about music that came to be typified by Pater had a long history and strong cultural purchase. They remained a presence in modernist texts, and still inform literature and popular understandings of music today.[19] In any case, they had never existed unchallenged, but alongside competing ideas about music as dangerous – especially in the thought of French *idéologues*, as Vincent Sherry has shown, for whom music had the potential to overpower the listener: to assault the senses and stir the emotions.[20]

Even Aestheticism always involved a political dimension when it was supposedly eschewing the real world and claiming music as a space apart. According to Carl Dahlhaus, the notion of 'absolute music' 'originated in German romanticism' as a reaction against moral philosophising about art's social purpose.[21] Music without words did not appear to police social and moral codes, so that 'the lack of a concept or concrete topic, hitherto seen as a deficiency of instrumental music, was now deemed an advantage'.[22] German Romantic philosophers began to use music to investigate rationalism. Dahlhaus claims Friedrich Schlegel mounted an 'attack on rationalism' by suggesting that instead of trying to understand music through logic, music and art should be used to investigate mathematics.[23] 'One has tried for so long', wrote Schlegel, 'to apply mathematics to music and painting; now try it the other way around'.[24] For Schlegel, it is usual to look to mathematics to decode the mystery of art's emotional impact, but the opposite is required: rational thought epitomised by the mathematical is in need of investigation. Music was a tool of understanding for many philosophers in the continental tradition, and this was reaffirmed by Jacques Attali in 1985 when he claimed, 'Music is much more than an object of study: it is a way of perceiving the world'.[25] In other words, music is not just something to be analysed or explained with tools and methodologies: it can provide ways of engaging with the world that might not otherwise be possible.

Andrew Bowie has argued for the enduring importance of music and continental philosophy for understanding how meaning is generated from signs, sounds and phenomena. Music is valuable for Bowie because it resists purely technical or empirical explanations, since its meaning and even its status as music depends on context: music is differentiated from sound when it is perceived as music, rather than by adhering to a set of rules. This means that there is no fundamental characteristic – no essence, in philosophical terms – to music that can be uncovered. Bowie argues that music therefore has a 'resistance to philosophy', since philosophy is traditionally concerned with metaphysical exploration and explanation, and aims to identify truths about concepts or objects.[26] Music frustrates the philosophical goal to determine the essence of music, because what is considered music is a matter of perspective and interpretation, which are affected by complex and non-homogeneous modes of human understanding, environments, education and experiences. Bowie challenges how philosophies of music usually operate by asking how the abstract and sensory thinking music beseeches might inform philosophy, rather than expecting the philosophical pursuit of essences to arrive at an explanation of music. He rejects methodologies of observation and classification used by analytic philosophers and natural scientists, arguing instead for the relevance of the German Romantic tradition's sensitivity to the complexities of individual perception, and for the value of ways of thinking about music made possible through literature. He asks, 'why is it, for example, that people may be convinced they gain a deeper understanding of music when it plays a role in a literary text like Proust's *In Search of Lost Time* or Mann's *Doktor Faustus* than when it is discussed in philosophical texts?'[27] Technical explanations of harmonic structure or the physics of wavelengths often fail to explain what music means to people, while accounts of music in literature or poetry can articulate things that people find meaningful.

If literary and philosophical interests in musical transcendence of language are driven by a suspicion of closed forms of rational and empirical thought, then modernist writers who engage with music are not merely retreating into high art, and musical transcendence does not become irrelevant with the advent of noise music or the twentieth century's increasing preoccupation with material conditions of music production. Modernists who refer to music in this way are participating in a tradition that questions restrictive uses of reason – rather than simply carrying with them the residues of an outdated nineteenth-century Aestheticism – and are motivated by the desire for social change. This means that their work is considering similar issues to Frankfurt School critical theory. Max Horkheimer, who gave critical theory its name, explained his aim for it to 'be a critical, promotive factor in the development of the masses' by analysing what appears normal or rational.[28] For Horkheimer, 'the real social function of philosophy lies in its criticism of what is prevalent', and the goal of critical theory is social transformation.[29] Throughout this book I argue that James Joyce, Ezra Pound and Sylvia Townsend Warner all saw music as a medium that can be used to investigate entrenched ways of thinking.

For similar reasons music was a topic returned to again and again by Adorno, for whom 'music resembles a language. Expressions such as musical idiom, musical intonation, are not simply metaphors. But music is not identical with language. The resemblance points to something essential, but vague'.[30] Music is not without discernible sense or meanings, but those meanings cannot be precisely translated into language. To identify that music has a signifying capacity related to but distinct from language is to acknowledge the possibility of ways of thinking that require different kinds of work and interpretation. Joyce, Pound and Warner each use music to alter literary form and investigate language and ideology, which they found necessary because rational thought had produced a world in which much seemed wrong. In this sense, they identify and try to remedy a similar problem to Adorno, who claims:

> When men are forbidden to think, their thinking sanctions what simply exists. The genuinely critical need of thought to awaken from the cultural phantasmagoria is trapped, channelled, steers into the wrong consciousness. The culture of its environment has broken thought of the habit to ask what all this may be, and to what end.[31]

Adorno saw contemporary life dominated by practices that prohibited independent thought. He argued that simple and repetitive forms of popular culture encouraged passive consumption, and that even certain styles of academic research simplified and standardised human behaviour. Adorno found this was the case with the questionnaires organised by his former colleague, sociologist Paul Lazarsfeld, who wanted to understand how people reacted to radio broadcasts but gave respondents only a small set of options to choose from, effectively silencing or denying the full range of human experience.[32] David Jenemen sees a complex subjectivity that resists standardisation as an integral part of modernist literature such as Joyce's *Ulysses* and Proust's *À la recherché du temps perdu* – 'the modernist subject utterly resists the logic of a social science that reduces human qualities to data points' – which is something important that he argues literary modernism shares with Adorno.[33]

Music could be valuable to Adorno because it requires human interpretation to arrive at meaning, so that what it says is not direct, definite or fixed: 'In contrast to philosophy and sciences, which impart knowledge, the elements of art which come together for the purpose of knowledge never culminate in a decision'.[34] Music's ambiguity works dialectically with its claim to communicate the absolute: to say what it says directly, without the mediation of language through its form, which is also the reason for its abstractness. Intentional language, on the other hand, is more overtly subject to the 'coercion of logic'.[35] Modernists show an acute awareness of this, as they actively seek to break away from quotidian meanings and ways of using language in their experiments with form, often turning to music for ideas and inspiration.

Notes

1. Chapter 1 provides a detailed exploration of these debates.
2. Brad Bucknell, *Literary Modernism and Musical Aesthetics: Pater, Pound, Joyce, Stein* (Cambridge: Cambridge University Press, 2001). John Xiros Cooper, ed., *T.S. Eliot's Orchestra: Critical Essays on Poetry and Music* (London: Garland, 2000). Josh Epstein, *Sublime Noise: Musical Culture and the Modernist Writer* (Baltimore: Johns Hopkins University Press, 2015). Michelle Fillion, *Difficult Rhythm: Music and the Word in E. M. Forster* (Chicago: University of Illinois Press, 2010). Timothy Peter Martin, *Joyce and Wagner: A Study of Influence* (Cambridge: Cambridge University Press, 1991). Susan Reid, *D.H. Lawrence, Music and Modernism* (Basingstoke: Palgrave Macmillan, 2019). Emma Sutton, *Virginia Woolf and Classical Music: Politics, Aesthetics, Form* (Edinburgh: Edinburgh University Press, 2013). Nathan Waddell, *Moonlighting: Beethoven and Literary Modernism* (Oxford: Oxford University Press, 2019). Michelle Witen, *James Joyce and Absolute Music* (London: Bloomsbury, 2018).

3. Henry Purcell (1691) cited in A. Ellis, ed., *The Cambridge Cultural History*, vol. 1 (Cambridge: Cambridge University Press, 1991), p. 47.
4. John Milton, 'At A Solemn Musick', in *The Poetical Works of John Milton*, vol. 2, ed. H. Darbishire (Oxford: Clarendon Press, 1955), p. 132.
5. Ezra Pound, 'Hugh Selwyn Mauberley', in *Selected Poems 1908–1969* (London: Faber & Faber, 1977), p. 98.
6. Tim Armstrong, *Modernism: A Cultural History* (Cambridge: Polity, 2005), p. 1.
7. Tyrus Miller, *Modernism and the Frankfurt School* (Edinburgh: Edinburgh University Press, 2014).
8. See also J. M. Coeztzee, *Elizabeth Costello* (London: Vintage, 2004).
9. J. M. Coetzee, *The Lives of Animals* (Princeton, NJ: Princeton University Press, 1999), p. 23.
10. Mark Antliff, *Avant-Garde Fascism: The Mobilization of Myth, Art, and Culture in France, 1909–1939* (Durham, NC and London: Duke University Press, 2007), p. 19.
11. Michael North, *The Political Aesthetic of Yeats, Eliot and Pound* (Cambridge: Cambridge University Press, 1991), p. 2.
12. Karl Marx and Friedrich Engels, 'Kant and Liberalism', in *The German Ideology* (London: Lawrence & Wishart, 1965), p. 207.
13. Arthur Schopenhauer, *The World as Will and Representation*, vol. 1, ed. Judith Norman, Alistair Welchman and Christopher Janaway (Cambridge: Cambridge University Press, 2011), p. 285. Walter Pater, *The Renaissance: Studies in Art and Poetry*, ed. Donald L. Hill (Berkley, CA: University of California Press, 1980), p. 106.
14. Carl Dahlhaus, *The Idea of Absolute Music*, trans. Roger Lustig (Chicago and London: University of Chicago Press, 1991). Witen, *James Joyce and Absolute Music*, pp. 17–82.
15. See Susan McClary's claims about the mystifying qualities of music in Chapter 1, 'New musicology, sociology and analytic philosophy', p. 23. See also the discussions of *Orfeo* and the 2016 Grawemeyer Award in Chapter 5, pp. 181, 206.
16. Kiene Brillenburg Wurth, *The Musically Sublime: Indeterminacy, Infinity, Irresolvability* (New York: Fordham University Press, 2009).
17. Epstein, *Sublime Noise*, pp. xvi–xvii. Cecil Barber, 'Battle Music', *The Musical Times* 59.899 (1918), 25, cited in Epstein, *Sublime Noise*, p. xvi.
18. Epstein, *Sublime Noise*, p. xix.
19. See Chapter 5, where I show how crucial notions of musical transcendence are in Richard Powers's *Orfeo* (2014), p. 181.
20. Vincent Sherry, *Ezra Pound, Wyndham Lewis and Radical Modernism* (Oxford: Oxford University Press, 1993).
21. Dahlhaus, *The Idea of Absolute Music*, p. 3.
22. Ibid. p. 7.
23. Ibid. p. 70.
24. Friedrich Schlegel, *Kritische Schriften und Fragmente*, vol. 5 (Paderborn: Schöningh, 1988), p. 41, cited and translated in Andrew Bowie, *Music, Philosophy and Modernity* (Cambridge: Cambridge University Press, 2009), p. 11.

25. Jacques Attali, *Noise: The Political Economy of Music*, trans. Brian Massumi (Manchester: Manchester University Press, 1985), p. 4.
26. Bowie, *Music, Philosophy and Modernity*, p. 13.
27. Ibid. p. 30.
28. Max Horkheimer, 'Traditional and Critical Theory', in *Critical Theory: Selected Essays*, trans. Matthew O'Connell (New York: Continuum, 1986), pp. 213–14 (188–243).
29. Max Horkheimer, 'The Social Function of Philosophy', in *Critical Theory: Selected Essays*, p. 264 (253–72).
30. Theodor W. Adorno, 'Music and Language: A Fragment', in *Quasi Una Fantasia*, trans. Rodney Livingstone ([1963] London: Verso, 1998), p. 1.
31. Theodor W. Adorno, *Negative Dialectics*, trans. E. B. Ashton (New York: Seabury Press, 1973), pp. 85–6.
32. David Jeneman, *Adorno in America* (London and Minneapolis: University of Minnesota Press, 2007), pp. 52–3, 72.
33. Ibid. p. 6.
34. Adorno, 'Music and Language: A Fragment', in *Quasi Una Fantasia*, p. 4.
35. Theodor W. Adorno, *Minima Moralia*, trans. Edmund Jephcott ([1948] London: Verso, 2005), p. 150.

Introduction

> I know that a poem, or a passage of a poem, may tend to realise itself first as a particular rhythm before it reaches expression in words, and that this rhythm may bring to birth the idea and the image; and I do not believe that this is an experience peculiar to myself. The use of recurrent themes is as natural to poetry as to music.
>
> T. S. Eliot, 'The Music of Poetry'[1]

In 'The Music of Poetry' Eliot writes that musical rhythms can drive poetic form, rather than the desire to communicate a specific idea.[2] This reverses a common way of thinking about writing and language: as a tool for making oneself understood or communicating preconceived thoughts. Eliot claims that some important non-linguistic thinking can happen through music, which can 'bring to birth' ideas and images that would not otherwise be thought. This gets to the heart of what this book argues is at stake in the modernist preoccupation with music: closely connected to the crisis of language, the ideas and formal innovations driven by music participate in longstanding investigations of commonsense thinking and rational thought. Music can create meaning without referring to anything outside itself and it also works directly on the body: it vibrates the organism and seems to affect the senses without the mediation of language, or even before a response to it has been rationalised. Music in modernist literature is often used to re-energise and reshape language, or bring individual perception and interpretation into the foreground. Because of this, there is a need to attend closely to modernist negotiations with music, which take part in projects to contest existing ways of thinking and understanding, to begin imagining new ways of living and interacting.

'The Music of Poetry' was delivered as a lecture in 1942, shortly after Eliot had published the final poems that would appear together as *Four Quartets* in 1943.[3] Eliot's interest in music can be seen at work in the form and thematic development of the opening lines from part II of *Burnt Norton*:

> Garlic and sapphires in the mud
> Clot the bedded axle-tree.
> The trilling wire in the blood
> Sings below inveterate scars
> Appeasing long forgotten wars.
> The dance along the artery
> The circulation of the lymph
> Are figured in the drift of stars
> Ascend to summer in the tree[4]

The plant, animal and mineral imagery – garlic and tree; blood, artery and lymph; sapphire – are connected through the theme of blood, with its circulating and clotting. In three sentences, each getting longer and more capacious like the objects they describe, we move from substances in the ground, into the body, up to the sky and into outer space. Different temporalities are connected: the past is figured in the roots of the tree because of the association between roots, origins and histories; the present through the 'trilling wire' in blood that has a relationship with the past – the 'long forgotten wars' that, although 'forgotten', have congealed into 'inveterate scars' that are like habits created from history, which is 'appeased' by the present tense blood that defers to that history by 'sing[ing] below' it, in an intricate interaction between past and present. The final sentence sees the present tense 'dance along the artery' predicted in the 'drift of stars' that are in the future, light years away, but also signify the past, since the starlight perceptible from Earth was emitted long ago. The irregular rhymes traverse these stages another way: from 'mud' to 'blood', 'scars' to 'stars', 'axle-tree' to 'artery' and back to 'tree'. The disparate items described are connected by blood, as though they are kin. Weaving connections through the structure of the lines to evoke a unity between its themes, this poem demonstrates an effect Eliot describes in 'Tradition and the Individual Talent': we see 'impressions and experiences combine in peculiar and unexpected ways' to evoke a 'substantial unity of the soul'.[5] Eliot's form, which he claims in 'The Music of Poetry' is driven by music, is used to explore the possibility of connections that transcend time and space.

This poem reaches towards the expression of essences and unity of form and content that has long been considered particular to music. As Carl Dahlhaus explains in *The Idea of Absolute Music*, since music does not have to refer to anything outside itself, for many writers and theorists of the nineteenth century, including Schopenhauer, Wagner, Nietzsche, Baudelaire, Mallarmé and Pater, 'music was considered to be an expression of the "essence" of things, as opposed to the language of concepts that cleaved to mere "appearances"'.[6] For Alex Aaronson, the 'concern with musical form' among early-twentieth-century novelists, such as 'Proust, Forster, Virginia Woolf and Thomas Mann', was integral to their attempts to communicate the 'inwardness of experience' – in other words, the essence of emotion and perception.[7] Brad Bucknell similarly sees modernists' use of musical aesthetics as driving formal innovations that investigate the possibilities for 'the representation of consciousness'.[8]

This book seeks to complicate accounts of engagements with music's non-referentiality in literary modernism, which are usually understood in the following ways: as part of strategies to communicate inner thoughts; as primarily aesthetic attempts to bring form and content closer in writing; and as appealing to older ideas – rooted in German Romanticism and British Aestheticism – about music as a pure and transcendent art form, separate from the social world. Josh Epstein has already contested these lines of inquiry, arguing that 'What needs more scrutiny is how these writers turned to music of their own time – music often infiltrated with noise'. 'Embracing music's power to shock or appeal to the body', Epstein writes, 'modernist art constantly recalls the material pressures of modernity' so that we must reconfigure understandings of music around the dissonance and noises that were contemporary with modernist writers, which they used to explore the political and social issues of the early twentieth century.[9] Yet the 'emancipation of dissonance' (a phrase used by Arnold Schoenberg in his 1926 essay 'Opinion or Insight?') that reached its peak with the atonal and serialist compositions of the Second Viennese School is widely considered to have begun in the mid-nineteenth century, with Richard Wagner, whose influence on literary modernism is extremely well documented.[10] When *Tristan und Isolde* was first performed in 1865, its dissonant, unresolved opening chord challenged established notions of aesthetic beauty – a challenge that the unusual forms, colours and sounds of modernist literature, art and music can be seen as taking up and extending. Wagner's dissonance was part of his operatic project designed to combat worn-out aesthetics and 'the logic of the understanding', or a restrictive rationalism.[11] Friedrich Nietzsche built on Wagner's conviction about the utopian potential of the aesthetic in *The Birth of Tragedy Out of the Spirit of Music*.[12] Douglas K. Smith notes that Nietzsche's 'hopes for German cultural renewal look to Wagnerian opera for their fulfilment', drawing on Wagner's close engagement with music as a non-representational art and his eschewal of certain longstanding notions of beauty.[13] For Nietzsche, music could aid cultural regeneration to combat a society that had become excessively rational and had long neglected the aesthetic and spiritual life.

Eliot's claim to use music to 'bring to birth' an idea must be understood in the context of a history of thought in which music, in the face of crises perceived to be caused by overreliance on logic and lack of attention to the senses and emotional life, has been drawn upon to produce new ideas and inject vitality into art forms and societies. I am using Eliot here as representative of a broader trend among literary modernists – without, of course, claiming they are all the same, and ultimately with a view to opening out definitions of modernism to include less well-known early-twentieth-century writers Sylvia Townsend Warner and contemporary writers like Paul Griffiths, whom I discuss in Chapter 5. Eliot, resisting rational explanations of poetry, does not articulate in technical terms why 'a particular rhythm' realises itself before a poem 'reaches expression in words'. This is typical of a modernist suspicion of technical description that also characterises much of Ezra Pound's writing, which Leon Surette relates to an interest in the occult that Eliot and Pound inherited from W. B. Yeats. For Surette, the occult is 'metaphysical speculation – speculation about the nature of ultimate reality and our relation to it'.[14] It is connected to an interest in the mythical and non-rational as a route to knowledge about the world and has at its core scepticism of closed logic, objectivism and empiricism. These scepticisms, Surette argues, drive the modernist engagement with the occult, where myth offers something distinct from scientific and religious ways of understanding history and making sense of the world. Such scepticisms also drive modernists' engagements with music, and are indebted to Nietzsche and Wagner for whom myth and music have a utopian potential that it is becoming increasingly important to harness: music might help to open up ways of thinking that could produce a better society.[15]

Music in literary modernism appears in a variety of ways, but very often it is used when logic, empiricism and rational thought will not do; when writers question gendered binaries, engage with the trauma of – and attempts to rationalise – war, or contest the linear nature of time by exploring how memory brings the past into the present.[16] In Dorothy Richardson's novel series *Pilgrimage*, music has the capacity to change how an individual understands their relationship to the rest of the world. When Miriam Henderson experiences music, 'she seemed to grow larger and stronger and easier as the thoughtful chords came musing out into the night and hovered amongst the dark trees'.[17] Miriam seems to experience a physical, bodily change on hearing the music that can also be understood as a metaphor for an intellectual or emotional change. Feeling as though she becomes 'stronger' in body suggests an increase in self-confidence and capability, while 'larger' implies a change in how she experiences herself in relation to her surroundings: she is becoming more significant and taking up more space in the world. Thomas Fahy writes that when Miriam plays Beethoven she 'experiences an emotional freedom that teaching doesn't offer her' and an 'outlet for genuine expression'.[18] These claims suggest that music merely allows Miriam to experience repressed emotions, but I see this as more than just a freedom to feel emotions stifled by teaching and the conventions of daily life: music has the capacity to alter how Miriam perceives herself and her place in the world, with the consequence that her beliefs about what she can do are also enlarged.

Music has a similar capacity for Lucy Honeychurch in E. M. Forster's *A Room with a View*. Forster's narrator tells us that 'Lucy, who found daily life rather chaotic, entered a more solid world when she opened the piano. She was then no longer deferential or patronizing; no longer either a rebel or a slave'.[19] For Lucy, music is a world apart where the restrictions of daily life do not apply. It gives her access to another realm of understanding that Mr Beebe guesses she will one day use in her daily life: 'Does it seem reasonable that she should play so wonderfully, and live so quietly? I suspect that one day she will be wonderful in both'.[20] Mr Beebe's prediction about Lucy's potential to be extraordinary comes to fruition when she rejects a financially advantageous marriage with the narrow-minded Cecil Vyse, who treats her as little more than an attractive object. Instead, Lucy chooses George Emerson, who is of a lower social class but shares the broader perspective that music has given her. Still, Lucy's access to music relies on her education, as does Miriam's in Richardson's novels. Lucy's family can afford piano lessons to nurture her talent, and this allows her to 'pass' as belonging to a higher social class, so that Forster shows access to music's perceived transcendence of material concerns relies on money.[21] Similarly, Miriam has enough education to become a teacher and gain a post in Germany, where she experiences a different culture that broadens her worldview. While Forster and Richardson acknowledge that their characters' musical educations depend on their wealth and class, music has the positive potential to enable people to think about how issues beyond money and status – such as cultural exchange and shared intellectual pursuits – can improve their lives.

Music also informs Richardson's work at the level of form, and is explicitly connected to gender. For Fahy, 'the structural importance of classical music' in *Pilgrimage* contributes to Richardson's 'attempts to reject masculine, heterosexist narratives'.[22] In this view, we can align Richardson with Virginia Woolf, whose considered departure from literary realism and naturalism rebelled against literary forms that had been complicit in sustaining a 'realist' worldview intricately bound up with patriarchal hierarchies and social practices.[23] Richardson's writing, too, rejects what she called 'masculine realism', referring to what she considered to be rigid narrative forms that were patriarchal in that they failed to question the status quo.[24] For Fahy, classical music 'functions both as an outlet for self-reflection – a way to transcend the boundaries of speech – and as a means to reject the various roles for women (teacher, secretary, wife, socialist) that tend to stifle artistic and social autonomy'.[25] Yet music is more than an 'outlet', since it helps Miriam to evaluate her position in the world, rather than just uncovering something that was already there. Experiencing music in Germany helps Miriam to see differently her life and the gendered choices available to her; to explore how to live and come to decisions that depart from what she has been told is rational. Towards the end of *Pointed Roofs*, in fragmented sentences Miriam considers her life if she were to remain a teacher: 'always alone, and just cancer coming . . . I shall be like that one day . . . an old teacher, and cancer coming'.[26] Partly because of her experience of music, Miriam eventually sees the teaching profession as taking over her identity, limiting possibilities in her life and ultimately as a form of death.

It is specifically German musical culture that changes Miriam, which gestures to the significance of German composers and philosophical thought – Schelling, Schopenhauer, Beethoven and Wagner – in creating a culture in which people engage with music in a way that adds to their lives. German composers were important reference points for other modernists, too: there are allusions to Wagner in Ford Madox Ford's *Parade's End*, and Chapter 5 of *Howards End* features a performance of Beethoven's Fifth Symphony attended by the Schlegels, who share the name – but not the philosophy – of German philosopher Friedrich Schlegel. Stoddard Martin has identified numerous Wagnerian allusions in the work of Eliot and several other writers, while Timothy Martin and Emma Sutton have shown how Wagner informed Joyce and Woolf respectively at the level of form and content.[27] More recently, Nathan Waddell has extended our understanding of the significance of German music and thought by exploring Beethoven's presence in the work of a variety of literary modernists, including Richardson.[28]

Richardson's shift towards a different form of musically inspired narrative suitable for female experience could be seen to reinforce binary categories associated with men and women (the rationality, solidity and presence associated with masculinity, versus the irrationality, fluidity and absence associated with femininity), but she made it clear that such writing was not only produced by women. In a Foreword to *Pilgrimage*,

Richardson wrote that 'feminine prose, as Charles Dickens and James Joyce have delightfully shown themselves to be aware, should properly be unpunctuated, moving from point to point without formal obstructions'.[29] For Richardson, 'feminine prose' is an alternative to dominant, often patriarchal, ways of writing and seeing the world. Its fluid and continuous nature – for which it withstands comparisons with flowing water and with music – resists standardised grammar and logical sentence structures, so that for Richardson a commitment to the anti-rational is conceptualised as a commitment to the feminine (but as a subservient part of a binary, rather than an essential truth about women) and the musical (as an art form that has associations with emotion rather than logic, where emotion is another subservient part of a binary).

Modernist writing attempts to recover those aspects of existence that have been rendered subservient, marginalised or invisible by rational, binary thought. Modernist literature is so often the work of outsiders: of exiles and émigrés like Joyce and Pound, women like Richardson, Warner and Woolf, people whose writing and thought were considered immoral and censored like Lawrence, or people whose sexuality was criminalised, like Forster. There is an anti-bourgeois, anti-establishment character to much modernist writing that sought out readerships of a variety of genders, sexualities, classes and nationalities (even though much of it was, as Raymond Williams notes, quickly integrated into the market and the class system by universities after the Second World War).[30]

The non-rational and non-linguistic has a special place among many modernist writers. Ford Madox Ford's insistent use of the ellipsis in the *Parade's End* tetralogy shows, as Sara Haslam writes, that 'Ford is often unsatisfied with the capacity of language to express the totality of thought or experience; speech constantly "gives out", to be replaced by his most characteristic grammatical tool: ellipsis'.[31] Ford makes use of these visual markers to do more than cue silence: they mark the absence of speech but not necessarily of thought or cognisance – just the absence of that which can be put into words. The novel narrates the difficulty Sylvia and Christopher Tietjens experience when trying to communicate with each other:

> They played that comedy occasionally, for it is impossible for two people to live in the same house and not have some common meeting ground. So they would each talk, sometimes talking at great lengths and with politeness, each thinking his or her thoughts until they drifted into silence . . .[32]

The ellipsis indicates the silence Sylvia and Christopher 'drifted into', figuring absence of verbal communication. But this is not the absence of thought, since both are thinking things they cannot express to one another. The breakdown in communication and personal relationships in the *Parade's End* tetralogy is the result of a decaying society in which critical thought and meaningful human interaction are increasingly difficult. In the second volume of the tetralogy, *No More Parades*, ellipses are markers of Tietjens's fragmented thought in the noise and pressure of war in the trenches: 'he was standing with his greasy, sticky hands held out from the flaps of his tunic ... Perhaps disgust! ... It was impossible to think in this row ....'.[33] Tietjens's thoughts shift from his clothes to a look he was given some time ago that was 'Perhaps disgust', to an acknowledgement of the difficulty of thinking during the noise of battle. Through Tietjens, who also struggles to navigate changing values as an administrative society replaces the feudal system, Ford constructs a damning account of the instrumental rationality that directs the decisions made during the First World War, which uses people as a means to a political end. As the novel progresses Tietjens's initial sense of being out of place intensifies into outright confusion due to his experiences in the trenches and his memory loss.

The novel's ellipses and fragmented structure register that words and linear narratives are not always enough to show the struggle to find meaning. On two occasions Sylvia and Tietjens turn to music, thinking about Wagner when trying to structure their thoughts during separate stressful experiences at the front line. Ford's use of music suggests the need for new ways of thinking, and the usefulness of literary form to try to explore a changing world. Rather than presenting music as straightforwardly positive, however, Ford shows that some music – specifically Wagner, in this case – is unsuitable for improving his characters' understanding of their circumstances. Tietjens interprets the noise of a strafe as Wagnerian opera during a scene in the trenches, and imagines the increasing din of shells and artillery as a musical crescendo that heralds the arrival of the Wagnerian Hero – as Rebekah Lockyer has argued.[34] The 'noise increased', which Tietjens finds 'comic to the extent that an operatic orchestra's crescendo is comic. Crescendo! ... C r e s c e n d o! C R R R R R E S C. ... The Hero must be coming! He didn't!'[35] The music gives Tietjens an idea about what ought to happen next that does not play out in reality. This, as I have argued elsewhere, is a failed attempt on Tietjens's part to use Wagner – who represents a major aesthetic tradition of the past – to navigate contemporary experiences, showing that new art is required to understand a new age.[36]

For Ford, music can shape expectations about what should or might happen in the world. He gestures to music's significance for helping individuals think, but stages a critique of Wagner as being unable to help his characters meaningfully interpret the violence and confusion of modernity. References to Wagner call up his idea of the *Gesamtkunstwerk*, which Wagner called 'the great and universal art-work of the future'.[37] The *Gesamtkunstwerk* aimed to unite the different branches of art to provide an absorbing aesthetic experience that would educate the audience and ultimately produce a better society. His thought, in this way, was utopian. At the start of the twentieth century, German artistic traditions fall under the shadow of deteriorating British-German relations, then the First World War, and then the Second World War. Where Wagner was interested in totality and grand narratives, Ford is interested in recovering something from the confusion and detritus of the First World War, after which a positive future is difficult to imagine. Robert Green claims that 'character and episode in *Parade's End* are fashioned by imperatives that lie outside the boundaries of the text, by the author's desire to construct a work of fiction that will modify human behaviour'. Ford's writing, he implies, is impressionist, offering us 'less factual veracity than the truthfulness of mood and personality'.[38] Green intends the first comment, at least, as negative criticism of *Parade's End*. Saying that Ford wishes to 'modify human behaviour' suggests didacticism; it is a less optimistic way of suggesting that Ford wishes fiction to educate people about alternative ways of seeing the world – to succeed, perhaps, where he thinks Wagner's utopian musical project has failed. With his suspicion of Wagner, elliptical emphasis on silence, and the fragmentation and non-linearity of the novel's structure, Ford reaches towards things that have not yet been, and cannot directly be, expressed, paying attention to form and music in order to do so.

Ford provides no solutions to the problems he identifies: all that can be done is to point out what is wrong. He is less optimistic than Pound, who thinks the traditions of the past can be recovered to build a better society. D. H. Lawrence, too, is more pessimistic: the possibility for articulating and mounting resistance to the conditions of modernity are closing in *St. Mawr*, which is critical of popular culture and especially popular music as a force that limits people's capacity for independent thought.[39] Lawrence thought that popular culture, like Rico's 'fashionable' paintings in *St. Mawr*, was acting like a harmful drug, producing people intent only on 'having a good time' in proscribed and ultimately unfulfilling ways.[40] The novella is structured so that the climax appears in the middle, when St Mawr violently rebels against the intrusion of vacuous popular culture – specifically a 'new dance tune' – onto a site of ancient spirituality in the Shropshire hills.[41] The dramatic climactic scene is followed by an essay-cum-soliloquy narrating Lou's terrifying vision of the world's appalling rottenness and unstoppable trajectory towards self-destruction. The disruption to the narrative's progress challenges traditional notions of social improvement produced by rationality through its form. Elsewhere I have argued that changes in the novel form can be productively compared with how Theodor W. Adorno explains the effects of the Second Viennese School's changes to musical form, which also sought to break out of established aesthetic patterns and associated ways of thinking.[42]

For Lawrence, you cannot simply tell people that their notion of progress might be wrong: one must come to an understanding about the rottenness of the world gradually. Writing about the need for social change in 1915, Lawrence thought that 'perhaps, in a little while, I can unite with the very young people to do something. But first let them try their teeth in the world, let them taste it thoroughly as it is, so that they shall be ready to reject it'.[43] Lawrence suggests that people must fully perceive and understand the problems in the world to be motivated to act. *St. Mawr* attempts this by offering immersion in a fictive world, only to reveal and frustrate normative expectations about narrative trajectory: a reader might be shocked into an awareness that aesthetic and narrative conventions, which also shape the ways people understand and live their lives, are shaping ideas about what is possible in the world.

Lawrence's alternative to 'the march of events' is bleak: Lou becomes disgusted with modern life and rejects it, but there is no better life available for her. Realising all that is rotten about the world leaves her unable to interact with others, and she chooses to live in isolation in the hostile natural environment of a Mexican ranch. While Lawrence seems to share with Adorno a conviction that art must work on people through its form, Lawrence is more optimistic, because he keeps open the possibility that individuals like Lou can resist and reject modernity.[44] For Adorno resistance can only happen unconsciously, at the level of form.[45] This is one reason why modernist texts, and the ways they draw on music to develop literary form, are worth studying: they are part of a window of time – one that Frankfurt School philosophers worried had almost closed – when artists were formally resisting the negative aspects of modernity and modern life.

Joyce, Pound and Warner

Many modernist writers are deeply influenced by music, but the very different politics of Joyce, Pound and Warner provide fertile ground to consider how aesthetics and politics interact. Warner joined the Communist Party of Great Britain in 1935, and her writing explores material culture and the economic conditions of music production as well as its expressive potential. The nationalist discourses with which Joyce engages in *Ulysses* rely on symbols, motifs and narratives, from Irish myths and songs to newspapers. Pound turns to fascism in the 1930s because he believes that urgent change is needed to stop the deterioration he sees happening in society and the arts, which he believes are interdependent. Despite their political differences, Joyce, Pound and Warner all think that studying music and including it in their work is crucial. Music helps them to work out new forms of writing and thinking, even though they have very different ideas about how the world ought to be organised. Their political positions – degrees of socialism, nationalism and fascism – are born out of dissatisfaction with the status quo, to which their use of music is intimately connected. Their politics and artistic choices react against objectionable aspects of modernity, from alienation in the metropolis to the commodification of art and fetishisation of technology; from political violence in Europe to the difficulty of analytically reflecting on learned behaviours and ways of understanding the world.

One of the questions this book will consider is how the politics of these different writers are pressuring the aesthetic. Their politics certainly affect their writing and how they handle music, from how they interpret it conceptually to how they use in their writing. Equally, though, music and the existent ideas about it that they inherit develops their cultural politics. Joyce, Pound and Warner all studied music, albeit to different degrees and under different conditions. Joyce had a background in choral church music in Ireland, where religion and culture are markers of difference that have been used to justify the political violence of colonialism. Warner's study of music was informal because women could not attend the Harrow school where her father taught, yet she became an expert musicologist, working for ten years on Tudor notation and the material history and production of early choral music for Oxford University Press. Pound's well-noted rejection of the educational establishment comes through in his antagonistic treatment of contemporary music theorists in *Antheil and the Treatise on Harmony*, demonstrating his belief in the connected decline of civilisation, education and the arts that contributes to his anti-Semitic fascism. These writers' politics work on and through their writing, including their use of music, but what they know about music and the conditions in which they acquired that knowledge also informs their politics.

The reason for approaching Joyce, Pound and Warner in that order is because of the questions their work and related criticism ask of music. Those questions are: (1) how, or how far, can music and literature be compared, and what can music productively offer literature (in *Ulysses* we see how music can inspire literary investigation of the complex workings of the mind)? (2) what is music, why is it important and how can it be recruited to serve fascist political thought (through Pound's writing we can think through some of the key debates about music as transcendent of language versus its effects on the body)? (3) how is music made and what has it done in the world (for which I explore Warner's musicological expertise and her conviction about the importance of reassessing, in the present, the history of how music has been produced and used)?

Each chapter also has a different target. In Chapter 2 the targets are Joyce's critics, who have sought to verify his claims that the 'Sirens' chapter of *Ulysses* is based on fugal structure, and who argue that this is an entirely positive thing in itself. Such arguments uncritically reproduce ideas about music as a pure and progressive art form, and miss some of the complexity of Joyce's engagement with music, which holds positive imaginative and problematic introspective musical effects in tension. I look to deepen ideas about how music can inform literature by showing how Joyce uses music to add new dimensions to literature and communicate the pre-verbal and pre-rational through form. In Chapter 3, the target is Pound's fascist and hierarchical thought. I explore the limitations of Pound's attempts to explain music mathematically and technically, and show that his approach to music is linked to an excessively rational mode of thought that also underpins his fascist elitism, because it elides complexity to arrive at straightforward answers to multifaceted social problems. Alongside this, Pound also maintains a paradoxical belief in the value of music's non-referentiality and the effect of sound on the body, so that his work provides rich ground to investigate the competing and contradictory schools of thought regarding music that modernists inherited.

Warner turned to literary writing when Joyce and Pound were already well known, publishing her first novel, *Lolly Willowes*, in 1926. I approach Warner last, in Chapter 4, because her work shows that it is still possible to produce complex, political literary writing after the formalism of high modernism. The target in this chapter is narrow definitions of modernism and the relative neglect of Warner by the critical establishment. The abstraction and difficulty that differentiates Joyce and Pound from Warner is the result of formal innovations often inspired by music, yet the ideas about music the high modernists drew on were far from new, which troubles assertions about modernism as fresh and breaking with the past. Noticing the archaic attitudes to music often employed by Joyce's critics and by Pound reveals that Warner's handling of music is fresh and innovative: a place where her texts offer newness – and a modernist newness – although not one traditionally accepted as such. Contrasting the high modernists' indebtedness to aesthetic traditions with Warner's critical evaluation of the same reveals the understated complexity of Warner's texts, which critically handle ideology and provide a detailed, Marxist-informed aesthetic.

Although this book is not centrally about gender or canonisation, the importance of addressing these issues has shaped my selection of authors and texts. Next to Joyce and Pound, Warner is now comparatively unknown. This is despite her having published, during her lifetime, seven novels,[46] six books of verse,[47] twelve collections of short stories,[48] a critical biography of T. H. White,[49] translations of Marcel Proust's *Contre Sainte-Beauve* and Jean René Huguenin's *La Côte sauvage*,[50] more than one hundred and fifty stories in the *New Yorker*, as well as her work on *Tudor Church Music*. Being a Communist, a woman and a lesbian does not appear to have endeared Warner to the critical establishment, and her writing remains relatively neglected. Warner was a qualified musicologist, widely read by a broad demographic of people during her lifetime, successful in achieving financial independence as a writer while producing intelligent and valuable writing full of intrigue, depth, darkness and joy – yet she is much less celebrated than Joyce and Pound. She is increasingly recognised as an important writer on issues of colonialism, gender, class and history. Her fiction considers the effects of ideology and the utopian potential of art – issues that come to be theorised extensively by Adorno.

Adorno and Modernist Literature

Adorno is particularly useful for analysing music because his approach to musicology brings together two branches of analysis that rarely meet: the aesthetic and the social. To arrive at a defence of Adorno's methodology, Chapter 1 offers a history of how music has been conceptualised and examines the benefits and limitations of aesthetic and social modes of analysis. By drawing on Adorno's dialectical method we can make a fresh case for the value of literary modernism's musically influenced aesthetic innovations. We can also identify further arguments for reading Joyce, Pound and Warner together by revisiting their literature (and critical approaches to it) in relation to Adorno's arguments about the limitations of modernism.

Adorno explicates the negative dialectic of modernist art as not just asserting its newness through innovation, but negating what went before it:

> The experience of the modern says more, even though its concept, however qualitative it may be, labours under its own abstractness. Its concept is privative; since its origins it is more the negation of what no longer holds than a positive slogan.[51]

In other words, if modern art is the necessarily failed attempt to master the experience of modernity because it recognises the failure of language to sufficiently communicate meaning, modernism becomes a negative category as primarily a negation of tradition. As Fredric Jameson understands this:

> what drives modernism to innovate is not some vision of the future or the new, but rather the deep conviction that certain forms and expression, procedures and techniques, can no longer be used, are worn out . . . and must be creatively avoided.[52]

The use of musically inspired language and form by Joyce and Pound is part of innovative attempts to communicate the experience of modernity, because music, as Bucknell notes, appears to offer a medium for non-lexical communication of 'deeper significance'.[53] I do not negate those observations about the new and creative forms modernists achieved by referring to music. However, by analysing music using Adorno's methodology, we can see that texts by Joyce, Pound and Warner are informed by longstanding notions of musical transcendence and non-referentiality, without needing to claim that texts drawing on these ideas do in fact achieve separation from the material and social world. By acknowledging the value of the established discourses of musical transcendence on which modernists often rely, we can see that the use of music in modernist literature does not necessarily attempt a problematic separation from history, but in fact responds to the dominance of cold, restrictive forms of rationality that had long been seen by philosophers such as Schopenhauer, Schlegel and Nietzsche, and continue to be seen in the twentieth and twenty-first centuries by Adorno and Andrew Bowie.

Analysing music also reveals how these authors' texts avoid the pitfalls of Adorno's critique of modernist formal innovation as becoming limited by its own abstraction and negation of traditions. Modernism, for Adorno, does not 'negate previous artistic practices, as styles have done throughout the ages, but rather tradition itself'.[54] He continues,

> given that the category of the new was a result of historical process that destroyed a specific tradition and then tradition as such, modern art cannot be an aberration susceptible to correction by returning to foundations that no longer should or do exist.[55]

Narratives that assert their novelty and difference place themselves outside history as the 'new' and reject their foundations in the history of thought. The wish to enact a complete separation means modernism risks becoming nothing but a denial, with no positive content. Martin Jay explains Adorno's argument as follows:

> Although he applauds the modernist intent to abandon exhausted models of universalizing aesthetic normativity, Adorno accuses the fetish of newness for its own sake, the need always to innovate and leave behind the past, of complicity with the very forces it tries to negate.[56]

By focusing on the aesthetic, specifically musical, traditions Joyce and Pound are engaging with and developing, I show that their writing is fraught with complications and contradictions rather than a break with tradition that situates the work above and beyond history.

Music thus offers an avenue to re-evaluate and re-historicise the work of Joyce and Pound. When analysing music, authors and critics alike have at times been unable to see the historicity and political significance of the musical ideas to which they refer. This is the case when critics make assumptions about the positive potential and democratic nature of music in *Ulysses*, or when they fail to see the connection between Pound's cold rationalisation of music and the instrumental rationality that contributes to fascist thought. Analysing music, combined with Adorno's critique of modernist formal innovation in *Aesthetic Theory*, offers a way to examine where modernism's claims to newness obscure older ideas about musical transcendence that remain significant, and indeed have utopian potential, in Warner's work. For Adorno, 'the new is a blind spot, as empty as the indexical gesture "look here"'.[57] Longstanding ideas about music's non-referential communication of emotions and essences have inspired Joyce's and Pound's formal innovations, and these have produced the 'blind spot' that Adorno describes. In Chapters 2 and 3 we will see where critics have been unable or unwilling to see Joyce and Pound engaging with well-established ideas in order to celebrate them as radical and new, and how music has helped to obscure the historicity of Joyce's and Pound's texts by contributing to radical forms that appear to get beyond historicisation.

Malcolm Bradbury found that the difficulty of historicising modernism was itself historically constituted: conceptualising modernism and post-modernism as that which is at the forefront of and beyond the modern began when modernism

> took on meaning towards the end of the period, and above all after it, when we began to historicise what (since so much of the modern movement

perceived itself as "new" and ahistorical) was never meant to be historicised at all.[58]

During the Cold War, modernist art was held up as proof of the superior creativity enabled by the greater intellectual freedom afforded in the West, with one of the most obvious examples being the use of abstract expressionism as propaganda.[59] In line with post-Cold War reappraisals of modernism, it is no longer necessary or accurate to see modernism as entirely radical or ahistorical. This also makes it possible to reconsider writers like Warner, whose membership of the Communist Party might account for her critical neglect. Bradbury claims that the end of the Cold War led people to 'reconsider the nature of traditions and cultures, the bases of personal and collective identity, the value of our institutions, our long-term social direction and prospects'.[60] Leo Bersani's *The Culture of Redemption*, for example, reassesses modernism to reveal where critics have been invested in achieving affirmations of the positive values we have been accustomed to consider inherent in literary modernism, with *Ulysses* used as a key example.[61] Pound, meanwhile, received a literary award whilst charged with treason as New Critics sought to defend art from politically motivated censorship.

Writing by Joyce and Pound is valuable, but not only as a transcendent aesthetic achievement. Their writing, like Warner's, uses music to attend to the senses and emotions as well as the intellect in a world where utilitarian approaches to reason has resulted in social inequalities, economic problems and wars. Now that high modernism has been demythologised, establishing the complexity of Warner's work is essential to think about other ways that writing can be new and radical. We can begin to see the value of Warner's handling of music, and what she has in common with the utopian Marxism of Adorno and the Frankfurt School. For Warner, music is always materially and historically situated, can be experienced as transcendent and has the potential to inspire positive social change.

Scope and Structure

In scale and organisation, this book seeks to fit somewhere between expansive studies (Josh Epstein's *Sublime Noise: Musical Culture and the Modernist Writer*; Daniel Albright's *Untwisting the Serpent: Modernism in Music, Literature and Other Arts*) and single-author studies (Emma Sutton's *Virginia Woolf and Classical Music: Politics, Aesthetics, Form*; Michelle Fillion's *Difficult Rhythm: Music and the*

Word in E. M. Forster). Overall this book is most like Brad Bucknell's *Literary Modernism and Musical Aesthetics: Pater, Pound, Joyce and Stein*, since I give a detailed account of music's philosophical and literary history, followed by chapters centred on three authors. I also draw on Epstein's approach by including the state of play in two key areas (contemporary musicology, and literary criticism on music) in Chapter 1, to which I add examples of music analysis in contemporary sociology, analytic philosophy and continental philosophy. I explore these areas to justify my decision to make Adorno central to my way of reading music in modernist literature. This means that I begin with a premise with which Bucknell ends: he notes that Adorno offers 'a completely new set of ideas' for thinking about music.[62] If I pick up where Bucknell leaves off, I also double back on Epstein's use of new musicology and sound studies by returning to centre stage the issues of meaning and perception debated in the longer German tradition that Adorno inherits.

This book undertakes the 'two significant enterprises' important to the New Modernist Studies: to apply 'new approaches and methodologies to "modernist" works', and to reconsider the 'definitions, locations and producers of "modernism"'.[63] I do the first by applying Adornian continental philosophy to renderings of music in literary modernism. I make more room for Warner in modernist studies by showing that she asks questions about music that are often specifically modernist, and that her work is no less complex than that of Joyce and Pound. Overall, this book seeks to expand the categories of modernism by arguing that questioning the limits of utilitarian rationality is something modernist texts have in common. I retain the idea that modernism responds to aesthetic, political and social conditions, but do not limit modernism to a narrow temporality or aesthetic category. In my final chapter, I argue that modernism remains relevant and is still being produced today by discussing two twenty-first-century texts: Richard Powers's *Orfeo* (2014), which demonstrates an enduring fascination with modernist music and discourses of musical transcendence, and *let me tell you* (2008) by musicologist Paul Griffiths, which I argue is a modernist text. Contemporary writers continue to see much of value to be extracted from literary-musical interactions, and my methodology provides a nuanced approach to music that can help us to understand the political implications of the way music is used in twenty-first- century texts.

Using an approach informed by Adorno to analyse music in Joyce, Pound, Warner, Powers and Griffiths, I argue that modernist writers are those who rigorously investigate rational thought as they respond to a world where automation, standardisation and ideologies of domination, mastery and control have become naturalised. Music plays a key role in modernist efforts to construct writing that facilitates critical, imaginative thought by combining rational thinking and linguistic sense with the attention to feeling that comes from engaging with music.

Notes

1. T. S. Eliot, 'The Music of Poetry', in *Selected Prose of T. S. Eliot*, ed. Frank Kermode (London: Harcourt Brace Jovanovich, 1975), p. 114.
2. Ibid. p. 110.
3. T. S. Eliot, *The Music of Poetry: The Third W.P. Ker Memorial Lecture, 24th February 1942* (Glasgow: Jackson, Son & Co., 1942). In 1943, previously published poems – *Burnt Norton, East Coker, The Dry Salvages* and *Little Gidding* – were collected and published as *Four Quartets*. See T. S. Eliot, *The Poems of T. S. Eliot: Collected and Uncollected Poems*, vol. 1, ed. Christopher Ricks and Jim McCue (London: Faber & Faber, 2015), p. 881.
4. T. S. Eliot, *Four Quartets*, in *The Poems of T. S. Eliot: Collected and Uncollected Poems*, vol. 1, p. 180.
5. T. S. Eliot, 'Tradition and the Individual Talent', in *The Sacred Wood and Major Early Essays* (New York: Dover, 1998), p. 32.
6. Carl Dahlhaus, *The Idea of Absolute Music*, trans. Roger Lustig (Chicago and London: University of Chicago Press, 1991), p. 10.
7. Alex Aronson, *Music and the Novel: A Study in Twentieth-Century Fiction* (Totowa, NJ: Rowman and Littlefield, 1980), p. 32.
8. Brad Bucknell, *Literary Modernism and Musical Aesthetics: Pater, Pound, Joyce, Stein* (Cambridge: Cambridge University Press, 2001), p. 3.
9. Josh Epstein, *Sublime Noise: Musical Culture and the Modernist Writer* (Baltimore: Johns Hopkins University Press, 2015), pp. xiv, xxxix.
10. Arnold Schoenberg, 'Opinion or Insight', in *Style and Idea: Selected Writings of Arnold Schoenberg*, ed. Leonard Stein, trans. Leo Black (London: Faber & Faber, 1975), pp. 258–64. Carl Dahlhaus, *Richard Wagner's Music Dramas*, trans. Mary Whittall (Cambridge: Cambridge University Press, 1992), p. 64.
11. Richard Wagner, *Wagner on Music and Drama*, trans. H. Ashton Ellis (New York: Da Capo Press, 1988), p. 152.
12. Friedrich Nietzsche, *The Birth of Tragedy Out of the Spirit of Music*, ed. Michael Tanner, trans. Shaun Whiteside (London: Penguin, 2003). In the second edition, issued in 1886, Nietzsche changed the title to *The Birth of Tragedy. Or: Hellenism and Pessimism*. See 'Introduction' to *The Birth of Tragedy Out of the Spirit of Music*, p. vii. Despite the change in title, the centrality of Wagner and music to the text are not contested. In the Oxford World's Classics edition, simply titled *The Birth of Tragedy*, Douglas K. Smith writes that 'Nietzsche is conducting a double argument in *The Birth of Tragedy*. On the one hand, he is advancing a controversial academic argument about the origin and decline of Greek tragedy. On the other hand, he is also writing an impassioned manifesto for the regeneration of contemporary German culture. What links the two is the role

ascribed to music – as the title of the first edition makes clear from the outset'. Douglas K. Smith, 'Introduction', in Friedrich Nietzsche, *The Birth of Tragedy*, trans. Douglas K. Smith, Oxford's World Classics (Oxford: Oxford University Press, 2000), p. xvi.
13. Smith, 'Introduction', in Nietzsche, *The Birth of Tragedy*, p. xvi.
14. Leon Surette, *The Birth of Modernism: Ezra Pound, T. S. Eliot, W. B. Yeats and the Occult* (Montreal and London: McGill-Queens University Press, 1993), p. 13.
15. Surette, 'Nietzsche, Wagner and Myth', in *The Birth of Modernism*, pp. 157–230.
16. I have made this argument in an analysis of memory, sensation and consciousness in Virginia Woolf's *Mrs Dalloway* and Wagnerian leitmotif. See Gemma Moss, 'Classical Music and Literature', in Anna Snaith, ed., *Literature and Sound* (Cambridge: Cambridge University Press, 2020), pp. 92–113.
17. Dorothy Richardson, *Pilgrimage 1: Pointed Roofs, Backwater, Honeycomb* ([1921] London: Virago, 1979), p. 205. *Pointed Roofs* was first published in 1915, *Backwater* in 1916 and *Honeycomb* in 1917. They were collected as the first volume of the *Pilgrimage* series and published together for the first time in 1921.
18. Thomas Fahy, 'The Cultivation of Incompatibility: Music as a Leitmotif in Dorothy Richardson's *Pilgrimage*', *Women's Studies* 29.2 (2000), 134, 135.
19. E. M. Forster, *A Room With a View* ([1908] London: Penguin Classics, 2000), p. 50.
20. Ibid. p. 111.
21. For a more detailed discussion of this, see my article, 'Music in E. M. Forster's *A Room With a View* and *Howards End*: The Conflicting Presentation of Nineteenth-Century Aesthetics', *English Literature in Transition* 59.4 (2016), 493–509.
22. Fahy, 'The Cultivation of Incompatibility', 131.
23. Toril Moi, *Sexual/Textual Politics* (Abingdon: Routledge, 1992), pp. 1–20.
24. Richardson, 'Foreword', *Pilgrimage 1*, p. 9.
25. Fahy, 'The Cultivation of Incompatibility', 132.
26. Richardson, *Pilgrimage 1*, p. 172.
27. Timothy Peter Martin, *Joyce and Wagner: A Study of Influence* (Cambridge: Cambridge University Press, 1991). Emma Sutton, *Virginia Woolf and Classical Music: Politics, Aesthetics, Form* (Edinburgh: Edinburgh University Press, 2013).
28. Nathan Waddell, *Moonlighting: Beethoven and Literary Modernism* (Oxford: Oxford University Press, 2019).
29. Richardson, 'Foreword', *Pilgrimage 1*, p. 12.
30. Raymond Williams, 'When Was Modernism?', in *The Politics of Modernism: Against the New Conformists*, ed. Tony Pinkney ([1989] London: Verso, 2007), p. 35.
31. Sara Haslam, *Fragmenting Modernism: Ford Madox Ford, the Novel and the Great War* (Manchester: Manchester University Press, 2002), p. 86.
32. Ford Madox Ford, *Parade's End* ([1924] London: Penguin, 2002), p. 164.
33. Ibid. p. 308.

34. Rebekah Lockyer, 'Ford Madox Ford's Musical Legacy: *Parade's End* and Wagner', *Forum for Modern Language Studies* 50.4 (2014), 439.
35. Ford, *Parade's End*, p. 559.
36. Gemma Moss, 'Music, Noise and the First World War in Ford Madox Ford's *Parade's End*', *Modernist Cultures* 12.1 (2017), 59–77.
37. Richard Wagner, *Richard Wagner's Prose Works*, vol. 1, *The Art-Work of the Future and other Works*, trans. William Ashton Ellis (Lincoln, NE: University of Nebraska Press, 1993), p. 90.
38. Robert Green, *Ford Madox Ford: Prose and Politics* (Cambridge: Cambridge University Press, 1981), p. 130.
39. For a thorough discussion of Lawrence's negotiations with music, see Susan Reid, *D.H. Lawrence, Music and Modernism* (Basingstoke: Palgrave Macmillan, 2019).
40. D. H. Lawrence, *St. Mawr and Other Stories*, ed. Brian Finney (Cambridge: Cambridge University Press, 1983), pp. 23, 74.
41. Ibid. p. 74. See also Gemma Moss, '"A Beginning Rather Than an End": Popular Culture and Modernity in D. H. Lawrence's *St. Mawr*', *Journal of D. H. Lawrence Studies* 4.1 (December 2015), 128–9.
42. Moss, '"A Beginning Rather Than an End"', 119–39.
43. D. H. Lawrence, *The Letters of D. H. Lawrence*, vol. 2, ed. George J. Zytaruk and James T. Boulton, 8 vols (Cambridge: Cambridge University Press, 1981), p. 468.
44. Moss, '"A Beginning Rather Than an End"', 135–9.
45. Discussions of form are central to the analyses of literature in this book, but I return to this particular issue in Chapter 2, 'Cyclops', p. 72.
46. Sylvia Townsend Warner, *Lolly Willowes* ([1926] London: Virago, 2012); *Mr Fortune's Maggot* ([1927] London: Virago, 2000); *The True Heart* ([1929] London: Virago, 2012); *Summer Will Show* ([1936] New York: New York Review of Books, 2009); *After the Death of Don Juan* ([1938] London: Virago, 1989); *The Corner That Held Them* ([1945] London: Virago, 2012); *The Flint Anchor* ([1954] London: Virago, 2011).
47. Sylvia Townsend Warner, *The Espalier* (London: Chatto & Windus, 1925); *Time Importuned* (New York: Viking Press, 1928); *Opus 7* (London: Chatto & Windus, 1931); *King Duffus and Other Poems* (Wells: Clare, Son & Co, 1968). Sylvia Townsend Warner and Valentine Ackland, *Whether a Dove or a Seagull* (London: Chatto & Windus, 1934). Sylvia Townsend Warner and Alan Reynolds Stone, *Boxwood* ([1957] London: Chatto & Windus, 1960).
48. Sylvia Townsend Warner, *Some World Far From Ours and Stay Corydon, Thou Swain* (London: Elkin Matthews, 1929); *Elinor Barley* (London: Cresset Press, 1930); *A Moral Ending and Other Stories* (London: William Jackson, 1931); *The Salutation* ([1932] Horam: Tartarus, 2000); *More Joy in Heaven* (London: Cresset Press, 1935); *A Garland of Straw* ([1943] Freeport, NY: Books for Libraries Press, 1972); *Museum of Cheats* (London: Chatto & Windus, 1947); *Winter in the Air* ([1955] London: Faber & Faber, 2013); *The Cat's Cradle Book* (London: Chatto & Windus, 1960); *A Spirit Rises* ([1962] London: Faber & Faber, 2011); *A Stranger with a Bag* ([1966] London: Faber & Faber, 2011); *The Innocent and the*

Guilty (London: Chatto & Windus, 1971); *Kingdoms of Elfin* ([1977] Harmondsworth: Penguin, 1979).
49. Sylvia Townsend Warner, *T. H. White: A Biography* ([1967] Oxford and New York: Oxford University Press, 1989).
50. Marcel Proust, *By Way of Saint-Beuve*, trans. Sylvia Townsend Warner ([1958] London: Hogarth Press, 1984). Jean René Huguenin, *A Place of Shipwreck*, trans. Sylvia Townsend Warner (London: Chatto & Windus, 1963).
51. Theodor W. Adorno, *Aesthetic Theory*, ed. Gretel Adorno and Rolf Tiedemann, trans. Robert Hullot-Kentor (Minneapolis: University of Minnesota Press, 1997), p. 21.
52. Fredric Jameson, *The Modernist Papers* (London: Verso, 2007), p. 5.
53. Bucknell, *Literary Modernism and Musical Aesthetics*, p. 1.
54. Adorno, *Aesthetic Theory*, p. 21.
55. Ibid. p. 23.
56. Martin Jay, 'What's New? On Adorno and the Modernist Aesthetics of Novelty', in Stephen Ross, ed., *Modernism and Theory: a Critical Debate* (London: Routledge, 2009), p. 171.
57. Adorno, *Aesthetic Theory*, p. 20.
58. Malcolm Bradbury, 'What Was Post-Modernism? The Arts in and after the Cold War', *International Affairs* 71.4 (October 1995), 765.
59. See the following essays in Francis Frascina, ed., *Pollock and After: the Critical Debate* (London: Psychology Press, 1985); Eva Cockroft, 'Abstract Expressionism, Weapon of the Cold War', pp. 125–35; Max Kozloff, 'American Painting during the Cold War', pp. 107–25; David Shapiro and Cecile Shapiro, 'Abstract Expressionism: the Politics of Apolitical Painting', pp. 135–53.
60. Bradbury, 'What Was Post-Modernism?', 774.
61. Leo Bersani, *The Culture of Redemption* (Cambridge, MA: Harvard University Press, 1990), pp. 158–9.
62. Bucknell, *Literary Modernism and Musical Aesthetics*, p. 223.
63. Douglas Mao and Rebecca L. Walkowitz, eds, *Bad Modernisms* (Durham, NC and London: Duke University Press 2006), p. 1.

Chapter 1

On Music and Modernism: Philosophies, Histories, Approaches

Modernist writers inherited a long history of debates about what music is, why it is valuable and why we find it aesthetically pleasing. Philosophers have long tried to account for how music can contain meanings and the difficulty of translating those meanings into words. New as their techniques may have been, the modernist fascination with music is part of longstanding attempts to understand beauty, individual experience and the search for truths that underlie questions of metaphysics. Since the early Neo-Platonists – who rationalised pleasant musical sounds as the work of God, and appropriated Pythagorean observations about pitch and ratio as evidence of divine coherence in the natural world – music has seemed to offer a pure form of communication transcendent of language. Its apparent transcendence of language and human understanding has been explored in German Romanticism, French Symbolism and British Aestheticism. Modernists take part in those inherited discourses when they attempt to use music to reach beyond the ordinary signifying capacities of everyday language.

Claims about music as a transcendent art from are now broadly considered outdated by contemporary musicologists, sociologists and analytic philosophers, having been strongly contested since the 1980s – and rightly so. Even assertions about music's separation from the material world were always rooted in the politically motivated desire to get beyond conceptualisations of art as a means to promote moral codes and social norms. Yet contemporary studies of music that use observation and data analysis can sometimes lack an appreciation of the cultural, historical and experiential significance of musical transcendence. As they try to dismantle and disprove these ideas, they can also fail to address the questions of rationality and signification that musical philosophies – especially the German Romantic tradition – have engaged in the past.

For this reason, this chapter begins by evaluating contemporary approaches to music, before showing what is missing from the contemporary that can be supplied by German Romantic, French Symbolist and British Aesthetic thinkers. While these eighteenth- and nineteenth-century negotiations with music are largely concerned with aesthetics, contemporary methodologies seek to situate music in its social context. An approach is needed that mediates between the aesthetic and the social, and so this chapter finishes by considering Theodor W. Adorno's musicology, which does just this. Adorno is attentive to form and the material conditions of music production, and provides a way of thinking about music that is useful for examining modernist writers who were navigating inherited discourses of musical transcendence in connection with ideas about music as socially and materially produced.

New Musicology, Sociology and Analytic Philosophy

Since the 1980s efforts have been made to 'free' studies of music from ideas about transcendence and the non-conceptual. New musicology has used cultural theories of gender, race and politics to explore the composition and listening processes as inseparable from historically specific ideologies and subjectivities. Work by Susan McClary, Richard Leppert and Lawrence Kramer has been important in establishing the field.[1] As part of the essential social grounding they give to analyses of music, it is sometimes argued that contemporary performers and listeners – especially non-experts – are falsely invested in the idea of musical transcendence. Music's 'mysterious' quality is considered an illusion that is wilfully perpetuated but possible to be rid of. For McClary, 'both musician and layperson collude in this mystification, both resist establishing connections between the outside, social world and the mysterious inner world of music'.[2] Janet Wolff's foreword to McClary's and Leppert's *Music and Society* traces the concept of art's aesthetic autonomy mainly back to nineteenth-century Britain, arguing that it is illusory since 'contemporary art education originated in a close relationship with industry'. Wolff briefly cites Vasari's *The Lives of Painters* (1550) as 'the most important early example' of a tradition that sees 'fine art as transcending the social and the historical'.[3] While explaining the material basis for the formation of aesthetics as a discipline is important, the approach risks neglecting the epistemological and discursive significance, and the philosophical depth of ideas specifically about music's transcendence, as well as the complex ways these interact with music as materially produced. Music's history of 'transcending the social and historical' dates back much further than 1550, and the use among Neo-Platonists of classical and mathematical knowledge to justify religious truth points to a longstanding relationship between materiality and transcendence.[4] Neither has existed independently. A consideration of their interaction is necessary, instead of simply rejecting notions of aesthetic purity and replacing them with factual or material observations. Framing the idea that music is or ever was an aesthetically pure realm as 'mystification' – a trick or illusion, in other words – attempts to negate the validity of a long and complex philosophical engagement with metaphysics and meaning through music that dates back to Ancient Greek philosophy.

New musicologists also had a great deal of work to do overcoming the dominance of Schenkerian formal analyses, which neglected social and historical contexts. Robert Snarrenburg describes Schenker's formalism succinctly: 'Whatever the experience or meaning of music is believed to be, it must be traced back to composed arrangements of tones and their effects'.[5] For Schenker, the beauty of a musical work was the product of genius – a transhistorical, transcultural essence that it was the responsibility of the recipient to perceive and appreciate: 'each and every content', Schenker wrote, 'retains the power which it had originally, and it is up to us to perceive this vitality anew'.[6] (Not all formalists agreed on this: Nicholas Cook notes that for Eduard Hanslick, author of *On the Musically Beautiful*, musical forms could lose their power, become old fashioned, out of date: they may 'wear out, so that what was once beautiful may with the passage of time cease to be so'.)[7] The problems with pure formalism became impossible to ignore after it became common knowledge that musical compositions were politically directed, censored and analysed in Soviet Russia and Nazi Germany, where governments reacted strongly against art and art criticism they considered formalist and elitist. In the longer term, the legacy of this environment was to make impossible purely formal analyses of compositions that were produced under duress, with directives, by composers at risk of censorship and death, because it became impossible to deny that the conditions in which music is produced affect its form.

Purely formal analyses and uncritical assertions of music's transcendence of the material world have become obsolete. Now, scholarship argues that music is socially produced and that other ways of explaining it are therefore false and problematic. Leppert and McClary's *Music and Society* is a direct and necessary challenge to Schenkerian formal analysis. In the foreword, Wolff rejects 'the idea of "Art" as comprehensible in terms which are purely intrinsic'. 'The notion that Art – at least Great Art – transcends the social, the political and the everyday has been under attack for fifteen years or so', Wolff writes, and explains the need to add musicology to this trend by 'challenging the notion of music as autonomous'. She describes the social and cultural production of notions of artistic purity in order to rid such ideas of their power: 'the individualism of the liberal-humanist thought associated with mercantile capitalism and with the bourgeoisie confirmed and reinforced the aesthetic ideology of the artist as sole and privileged originator of the cultural work'.[8] While pointing this history out is important and accurate, it does not negate the fact that musical transcendence had strong cultural purchase in the past, and continued to do so in the work of the modernist writers that this book considers.

Issues of context, reception and illuminating comparisons are, of course, crucial to any detailed study of music, and need to be approached alongside a critical awareness of the ways ideas about music as transcendent of language are at work in texts. Jean-Jacques Nattiez has explained the variety of material conditions that need to be considered: 'the [musical] work is also constituted by the procedures that have engendered it (acts of composition), and the procedures to which it gives rise: acts of interpretation and perception'.[9] This position is widely reflected in ethnomusicology, which is described by Bruno Nettl as:

(1) [the] comparative study (of musical systems and cultures) ...; (2) comprehensive analysis of the music and musical culture of one society – essentially anthropological; (3) the study of musics as systems, perhaps systems of signs, an activity related to linguistics or semiotics; (4) the study of music in or as culture, or perhaps music in its cultural context, with techniques derived from anthropology, often called "anthropology of music"; and (5) historical study of musics outside the realm of Western classical music, using approaches of historians, area studies specialist, and folklorists.[10]

Ethnomusicology is also often understood as the study of world music and world cultures (which usually signifies that they go beyond the Northern American and Western European), acknowledging culture-specific understandings of music. For Ted Solis, ethnomusicologists who teach the study of non-Western musical cultures often ask, 'How do we represent the rich cultures we revere while we acknowledge and deal with the cultural distance between us and our students, and between both of us and these cultures?'[11] New musicologists now pay careful attention to the interaction between historical conditions and musical form.

Sociologists, however, often argue against the idea that music contains any meanings at all, other than those attributed to it in specific social contexts. This often means that the usefulness and validity of close attention to musical form is rejected entirely, as well as approaches that counter music as straightforwardly a product of its environment. For Peter J. Martin, 'a sociological concern with the uses of music seeks to return such cultural objects to the social contexts in which they are produced and experienced'.[12] Martin suggests that other ways of analysing music are divorcing it from its rightful contexts. But what contexts are these? What about when a piece of music's context of production and reception include people who analyse form, or think of music as transcendent or mystical? What about when music is received in contexts that Martin does not know about, that it might be difficult to imagine and even more difficult to access? Further, since music is produced and consumed in so many different social contexts, with what tools is it appropriate to analyse so many different musics, people and conditions of production?

Analysing music's effect on people is important for ascertaining its human value, but this can result in simplistic approaches that fail to take into account the problems of translating signification and meaning from a non-lexical form into language. John Shepherd considers musical form, but suggests a very simple theory of form as straightforwardly reflective of the society and individual through whom the music was produced, so that art and culture risk being considered a mirror for understanding people and the world:

> because people create music, they reproduce in the basic structure of their music the basic structure of their own thought processes. If it is accepted that people's thought processes are socially mediated, then it could be said that the basic structures of different styles of music are likewise socially mediated and socially significant.[13]

This implies that the 'thought processes' of socially produced individuals are easily readable and directly communicable through music, which neglects the complexity of the mediation that occurs during artistic production, as well as the full range of multifaceted, opaque and contradictory ideas that often comprise human thought. Martin places the emphasis on empirical observations: 'sociological interest is in *actual* associations between music and meaning, and the use of music in real situations, rather than in philosophical speculation about its potential significations for hypothetical "subjects"'.[14] For Martin, associations made by certain people are 'actual', while others (theoretical interpretations which he calls 'speculation') are not. He does not acknowledge that associations made in 'real situations' by '*actual*' people could be contradictory, or based on simple error. Although these can become common currency among certain social groups in a given culture, it is unclear why Martin implies these should carry more weight than an interpretation rooted in formal analysis. After all, these are also associations made by *actual* people in real situations. Presumably, by Martin's standard, fiction is also an unsuitable medium for thinking about music, or indeed anything, since the people in it are not real. As part of an attempt to bring studies of music down from a perceived ivory tower, Martin accidentally suggests that philosophers are not real people, and do not do things in real situations. Martin may be differentiating between expert and lay interpretations of music, but his language fails to make this clear. While he criticises the ideological motivations of formal analysis, his own use of language is ideologically motivated by a desire to make judgements about whose interpretations of music are valid.

Claiming certain situations are not real, or that musical transcendence is a false ideology, does nothing to divest the ideology of its power for those who work with, experience, or believe in it. Martin claims the special ability to see illusions from a clear, unclouded vantage point, which implies a very crude way of thinking about ideology, as false consciousness.[15] If those invested in music as a transcendent art form were wrong and influenced by bourgeois or religious ideologies, it follows that contemporary researchers are also ideologically driven: for example, by the shift towards prioritising empirical observation and data analysis that has overtaken academia because of an increased interest in using simple metrics to judge standards and drive competition in the education market. As universities increasingly function as the research tool of businesses, research outputs are designed to respond to the market-driven need for simple data, eliciting straightforward and limited responses that are easily measured to provide manageable and implementable recommendations for policy, consumer products and services. Stefan Collini has explored this at length in his book *What are Universities for?*[16]

The empirical study of music and desires to ground it in 'actual' social observations are indicative of a shift towards affect and empiricism in the humanities and social sciences, which in its worst manifestations rejects things that are abstract and difficult to define. Simple applications of affect theory and empirical data analysis can fail to historically situate the knowledge available in a given moment. 'Actual' observations of affective responses are often treated as unmediated data that can be unproblematically communicated and apprehended. Affect theorists engage ontological questions about the nature of being and existing in the world, but work from the assumption of a firm ontological foundation from which questions can be asked and data can be analysed. For Ruth Leys, affect theorists are united in 'the belief that affect is independent of signification and meaning', and affect theory is motivated by a desire to ground understanding in observations of affective emotions that are biologically fundamental, universally applicable and not conditioned by the intervention or interpretation of reason or a learned system of rational thinking.[17] Since specific, intentioned language must be used to describe and categorise phenomena – even if those phenomena appear to exist independently in the world – the articulation of 'facts' or 'actual observations' is always complicated by the historical concepts, knowledge and epistemologies that are inscribed within a particular language system, since what it is possible to think, as well as 'actual' permissions and impossibilities in daily life, are informed by what can be thought and articulated at a given moment. Affect theory and the refusal of the aesthetic and immaterial does not get away from questions of signification and meaning. In the case of music, the operation of discourses of transcendence needs to be addressed, as concepts that have and continue to contribute to how we can think about the world.

A similar argument can be made about empirical approaches to music in analytic philosophy. For example, in *Music Alone* Peter Kivy wants to find out why people find music so rich and expressive, and investigates why 'people sit for protracted periods of time doing nothing but listening to meaningless – yes, meaningless – strings of sounds'.[18] Before he begins he has already decided music is meaningless, because his idea of a meaning is something that exists in the world of tangible objects that can be accurately assessed and reliably described. For Kivy, sounds are just frequencies: attributing any more meaning to them is obfuscation, and the fact that people find meaning in music is a useless and inexplicable by-product of evolution. His approach, coming out of the natural sciences, sees value only in processing data gathered from the world through our senses and accurately describing phenomena in language.

As with affect theory, sciences of observation can fail to address open questions of what perception is, and how it is mediated. For John McDowell, the data used by the physical sciences are 'bare presences that are supposed to constitute the ultimate grounds of empirical judgement',[19] but those 'ultimate grounds' are questionable, as Andrew Bowie explains:

> There are, though, as McDowell and others argue in the wake of German Idealist and Romantic philosophy, good reasons for suggesting that we don't have access to any such ultimate grounds because we don't apprehend pure sense-data anyway, but rather apprehend tables, trees, chemical elements, notes, etc. Separating the conceptual from the non-conceptual content in perception is seen as involving a misapprehension of what perception is, because perception is of a world which is always already intelligible, not of some intermediary between us and reality, such as sense-data.[20]

For Bowie, music is valuable because many questions about what meaning is remain unanswered by analytic philosophy, which seeks concrete truths and connects language to objects and reality, aiming to make knowledge more precise, accurate and secure. Music frustrates this process, because there is no agreed definition of what it is or how it contains meanings. Its meaning (and indeed its very status as music) depends on context and interpretation, rather than a specific, consistent observation about its physical manifestation.[21] Bowie uses McDowell to critique analytical philosophies of music, of which Peter Kivy's work is a case in point. For Bowie, studying music through natural history, the physical sciences or analytic philosophy has not produced sufficient results. This is nowhere more evident than in Kivy's approach, which decides even before he has begun his investigation that music is meaning*less*. Kivy demonstrates some interest in music, claiming he wants to retain a 'sense of wonder and mystery about the whole enterprise' of a philosophy of music.[22] Yet for Kivy, experiencing such wonder can only be explained as an accident of evolution: he can find no clear biological purpose for the human capacity to enjoy music, so that it remains merely a mystery, or bizarre evolutionary by-product.

In the face of analytic approaches to music, Bowie reasserts the importance of European (or 'continental') philosophies as methodologies for considering questions about music and non-referential meaning, saying that we need to return to ways of thinking associated with German Romantic traditions. While we need to revisit these strains of thought, this is not to say they are entirely right. They are, however, interested in music's potential to contain meanings in a way that doesn't seek to objectively explain or rationalise it in the same way as the natural sciences, analytic philosophy or sociology.

At this moment, when the a priori refusal of the transcendent is dominant, we are able to see the dogmatism of this position. We need to revisit anew why the potential for non-conceptual understanding available in the non-referential way music inspires meaning and emotion is significant. Although it is always produced and received in a social context, any attribution of political or social meaning by analysing music's effects involves interpretation of what it says or does via language. In this way, both aesthetic and social analyses of music, or music in literary texts, are instances of the interpretation of a non-linguistic medium with the language available. This makes considering the role of rationality, signification and meaning essential. Modernist writers often contemplate how far language can communicate experience, and use music to do so. Their attempts cannot be adequately addressed if the metaphysical exploration of music is rejected outright. The modernist exploration of the material and metaphysical through music also needs to be seen historically.

Histories of Musical Transcendence

There is a well-established precedent in philosophy, religious discourses, literature, and among composers for considering music a purely aesthetic art form: one that does not refer to the social due to the apparently non-conceptual way it creates meaning without language or re-presenting the material world. While music is no longer thought of in this way, these ideas were still influencing modernist writers. The idea of music as a transcendent art form has a long and complex history in Western thought, and has been visible at different times and in conjunction with competing ideas. Neo-Platonist philosophy, appropriated by early Christians, claimed proof of God's existence can be seen through the natural structure and organisation in the world which could only occur through intelligent design, and used Pythagorean observations about correspondence between pitch and ratio as evidence.[23] Pythagoras is credited with discovering that two strings of the same material and tautness with a length ratio 2:1 (one half as long as the other) will produce sounds an octave apart when they vibrate. As Eli Maor explains, 'this was an important discovery, the first time a natural phenomenon was described in terms of precise quantitative expression'. Maor describes Pythagoras's subsequent discovery that

> more complicated ratios correspond to less pleasing chords; for example, the ratio 9:8 produces a second, a distinctly dissonant chord. Pythagoras therefore concluded that numerical ratios rule the laws of musical harmony – and, by extension, the entire universe. It was to become an idée fixe with the Pythagoreans, the cornerstone of their world picture.[24]

For the Pythagoreans there was a connection between logic and aesthetics, since intervals produced by simple ratios, such as the third, fifth, fourth and octave, sound most aesthetically pleasing. Aristotle noted that Pythagoreans saw music and the number as the key to understanding the universe:

> the attributes and the ratios of musical scales were expressible in numbers; since, then, all other things seemed in their whole nature to be modelled after numbers, and numbers seemed to be the first things in the whole of nature, they supposed the elements of numbers to be the elements of all things, and the whole heaven to be a musical scale and a number.[25]

Aristotle was unconvinced by the Pythagoreans' belief, as he understood it, that matter was created out of number, and noticed that there was a big leap from identifying the mathematical basis of sound to the conviction that this underpins the universe. Despite this, the belief in a rational order to the natural world retained its appeal into the Middle Ages and beyond, into literary modernism. Franchino Gaffurio's *Practica Musicae* (1496), for example, contains a chapter on 'Mode and the correlation of music with the universal order'. For Gaffurio, following Pythagoras, mathematical proportions and aesthetic beauty were connected with the divine source of universal order, meaning that art and music abiding by mathematical laws were adhering to structures that transcended the social and everyday.[26]

Music's non-referential manner of communication became increasingly significant as a way of accessing non-conceptual understanding during German Romantic philosophy's negotiations with how it is possible to discern meaning in the world, which moved away from trying to access the objective or enduring truth of an object. Kant and the German Romantics stressed the importance of aesthetic contemplation, placing the emphasis on the way the object is experienced. T. J. Reed notices the emphasis placed on aesthetics by German Romantics, but also notes that Schiller and Goethe wrote extensively on the aesthetic in the 1790s.[27] Kant's transcendental idealism claims that we can experience only the appearance of the thing, rather than the thing-in-itself (*Ding-an-Sich*):

> We have therefore wanted to say that all our intuition is nothing but the representation of appearance; that the things that we intuit are not in themselves what we intuit them to be, nor are their relations so constituted in themselves as they appear to us; and that if we remove our own subject or even only the subjective constitution of the senses in general, then all constitution, all relations of objects in space and time, indeed space and time themselves would disappear, and as appearances they cannot exist in themselves, but only in us.[28]

While for Plato, order in the world was the result of a divine creator and serves the purpose given to it, or for Aristotle, the organism fulfils only its own purpose, Kant changed the discussion by claiming there is a gap between reality and perception. Kant thus distinguishes between two classes of object (or two aspects of the same object): appearances and the thing-in-itself. The order that Neo-Platonists and Pythagoreans saw in the world becomes, for Kant, notions with which they approach phenomena instead of truths: purpose, order, design or logic are conferred onto objects by those experiencing or explaining them, rather than being innate. The way this relates to music, and to art in general, is that aesthetic contemplation becomes prioritised, instead of attempts to access something immutable about the world.

Carl Dahlhaus describes how notions of instrumental music's transcendence 'originated in German Romanticism' where music without words and referents began to derive special status as 'absolute music'.[29] Moral philosophy, which thought of 'art as a means of discourse about problems of morality' had rendered instrumental music superfluous because it could not be used to promote social or moral codes.[30] During the eighteenth century instrumental music began to be seen differently: with no vocal parts and therefore no narratives that could be used to reinforce dominant ideologies, it appeared to offer a pure form of communication, distinct from language or reasoning which usually mediates experience. Dahlhaus cites Karl Philip Moritz as reacting against art as something that should be socially useful as a way of maintaining bourgeois ideologies. Moritz, Dahlhaus claims

> proclaimed the principle of *art pour l'art* with a bluntness attributable to his disgust with moral philosophy's rationalizations about art, and to the urge to escape into esthetic contemplation from the world of bourgeois work and life that he found oppressive.[31]

Bowie notes that before the Romantic era music 'generally did not become an object of pleasurable contemplation for its own sake', but the 'emergence of philosophical aesthetics and nature's new importance for music are closely connected: both involve the idea of relationships between humankind and nature that transcend what can be understood in conceptual terms'.[32] Aesthetic contemplation through art and music seemed to offer opportunities to explore different ways of thinking about, living in and understanding the world.

Arthur Schopenhauer's writing on music developed in response to Kant's arguments about the importance of aesthetic contemplation. Since music does not signify in the same way as language, or imitate in the same ways as certain kinds of visual art, it becomes an area ripe for aesthetic contemplation and interpretation. It has special status in Schopenhauer's thought as the absolute communication of essences:

> it [music] does not express this or that individual or particular joy, this or that sorrow or pain or horror or exaltation or cheerfulness or peace of mind, but rather joy, sorrow, pain, horror, exaltation, cheerfulness and peace of mind as such in themselves, abstractly.[33]

What music communicates, according to Schopenhauer, is not a particular instance of an emotion, but the abstract emotion itself. Music becomes the key to metaphysics, since for Schopenhauer 'the purpose of all art is the communication of the apprehended Idea', where the Idea is the Platonic Idea (that the abstract and not the material thing is the highest form of reality).[34] Schopenhauer knew his claim that music represents the thing-in-itself is difficult to support with evidence:

> I recognize, however, that it is essentially impossible to demonstrate this explanation, for it assumes and establishes a relation of music as a representation to that which of its essence can never be representation, and claims to regard music as the copy of an original that can itself never be directly represented.[35]

Schopenhauer's philosophy can be thought of as Kantian as far as he agrees that the subject/object distinction is the primary condition for knowledge, but Schopenhauer critiques the notion that the thing exists independently of the mind.[36] While there are numerous criticisms of Schopenhauer's ideas, he significantly influenced many composers such as Brahms, Wagner, Mahler and Schoenberg.[37]

Wagner read Schopenhauer in 1854 and was profoundly influenced by his descriptions of music's ability to communicate the 'will'. Wagner wrote to Liszt on 29 September that year: 'I have of late occupied myself exclusively with a man who has come like a gift from heaven, although only a literary one, into my solitude. This is Arthur Schopenhauer, the greatest philosopher since Kant'.[38] For Wagner, if Schopenhauer's claim about music's capacity to communicate, without mediation, something true about the nature of human existence is correct, it becomes necessary to harness this capacity and use it for social good. Wagner becomes a key influence among modernist writers partly because of his belief in the capacity of art to address social problems. Wagner argued that art had become atomised and fragmented under capitalism, and his *Gesamtkunstwerk* sought to combine music, words, gesture and set design to provide aesthetic education and cultural revival in response to a related crisis – that of the health of the German nation, and what he perceived to be the connected decline of art and society. For Wagner, music had been devoid of value until Beethoven, subject to the whims and fashions of a market economy instead of containing any valuable, spiritual content.[39] He saw problems, too, with the language of the present: it was 'a language whose usages and claims, based on the logic of the understanding we must unconditionally obey' and 'we cannot discourse on this language according to our innermost emotion'.[40] For Wagner, language enforced logical ways of thinking, but was a failure for communicating emotions and issues of enduring, trans-historical importance.

For Nietzsche, too, music might provide a way to oppose the tyranny of logic that was the root of social problems. He claimed that certain strands of thought, developed out of 'the logical nature' of the Socratic, had resulted in a 'logical drive' that 'developed itself to excess'.[41] Nietzsche frames this as the domination of the Apollonian (the logical, moderate and visible, connected with the plastic arts of representation) over the Dionysian (formlessness, excess and mysticism, to which the art of music belonged). In *The Birth of Tragedy*, drawing on Wagner's conviction about the necessity of myth, art and especially music for spiritual growth, Nietzsche argued that music, being 'devoid of image and concept', could be used to combat the excessive rationalism and logic that he believed was damaging society.[42]

Both Nietzsche and Wagner are hugely indebted to the writing of Schopenhauer, who opens up a strand of thought around the benefits of music's abstraction. Lydia Goehr describes Schopenhauer as a 'central reference point' in the most significant historical debates about the nature of music and musical aesthetics.[43] The development of his ideas can be traced through French Symbolism and late-Victorian British Aestheticism into modernist thought and art. French Symbolism's interest in musical-literary relations is also related to music's potential for absolute, non-linguistic communication. Baudelaire thought that writers had often aimed towards musicality, and claimed that poetry looks to music not just in attempts to sound aesthetically pleasing, but also in its desire to communicate in a way that is somehow true and beyond the capacity of ordinary language:

> Which of us has not, in his ambitious days, dreamt the miracle of a poetic prose, musical without rhythm or rhyme, supple enough and striking enough to suit lyrical moments of the soul, undulations of reverie, the flip-flops of consciousness.[44]

For Baudelaire, something can be musical 'without rhythm or rhyme' because of the communicative ideal that music represents, as something that is suitable for representing both sides, or 'flip-flops of consciousness'. Many of the same ideas are present here as in philosophical discussions of music, such as music's connection to the abstract world of emotions, but also to the 'soul', which suggests its capacity for communicating a fundamentally human truth that cannot be put into words. Brad Bucknell and Peter Dayan have explored French Symbolism as a significant precursor to the modernist preoccupation with music's aesthetic potential. For Bucknell, Mallarmé's use of music is in line with the 'idealism in aesthetic thought concerning music' during the nineteenth century, and he explores the extent to which modernism is indebted to French Symbolism's negotiations with music as a way of transcending quotidian linguistic communication through attention to sound and sensation.[45] For Dayan, Baudelaire and Mallarmé exemplify 'a style of writing that refused to recognise clear boundaries between the literary, the critical, and the musical' and he argues that this continues to be relevant into the twentieth century, seeing parallels between Derrida's metaphysical discussion of 'presence' and the attempt in French Symbolism to use music's potential for communicating the thing-in-itself.[46] Helen Abbott has explored how Baudelaire and Mallarmé 'exploit the precarious balance between music and poetry' as she investigates how their shift away from 'straightforward representational language, to more elusive, indirect, suggestive language' affects reading practices.[47] From the nineteenth century onwards, the potential for music and attention to sound to shape literature in a way that affects the sense of language and the meanings it contains becomes central to the work of many writers. This continues into modernist literature, where it takes on a new impetus as writers examine and resist the flawed rationality that has contributed to constructing the circumstances with which they are dissatisfied.

The influence of German Romanticism, particularly Kant's emphasis on the importance of aesthetic contemplation, can also be seen in British thought: most famously in that of Walter Pater, among the leading figures of the British Aesthetic movement, who argued for 'the love of art for its own sake', and famously wrote that 'all art constantly aspires to the condition of music', positioning music as the highest form of art.[48] Primarily concerned with aesthetic beauty and the separation of aesthetic concerns from social and moral life, in British Aestheticism we can see the reception of German Romantic thought as well as responses to the French *art pour l'art* movement and reactions against Victorian materialism and the bourgeoisie. Jonathan Freedman describes the British Aesthetic movement as 'valorizing art in general and visual art in particular as a means of provoking intense experience in a society that seems able to deaden the senses and the spirit alike'.[49] William Hamilton's *The British Aesthetic Movement* defined the movement and included sections on such significant figures as John Ruskin and Oscar Wilde.[50] Ruskin emphasised and popularised the importance of the aesthetic contemplation of art in Britain, but as a way of creating a moral society: good art, he said, excites 'the best of the moral feelings'.[51] Ruskin's use of pre-determined religious doctrines as a moral guide is something that Pater and Wilde moved away from. Pater claimed that 'to the modern spirit nothing is, or can be rightly known, except relatively and under conditions', so that his writing exhibits a philosophical scepticism and relativism that shares much with Kant's conviction that subjective experience ought to be the focus of philosophical inquiry.[52]

Pater argued that music is the highest form of art because it is non-referential, while he considered literature, art and architecture limited in their ability to achieve pure expression by their lexical or pictorial reference to the material world.[53] Pater's famous, often-quoted dictum about music states:

> All art constantly aspires to the condition of music. For while in all other kinds of art it is possible to distinguish the matter from the form, and the understanding can always make this distinction, yet it is the constant effort of art to obliterate it.[54]

For Pater, music's unique and transcendent capacity is derived from the unity between form and content, in addition to its apparent separation from material concerns. Art represents the world and can never be the thing that it represents. In saying that art wants to 'obliterate' the distinction between form and content, Pater notices how the artistic impression points towards the thing that it represents, attempting to bridge the gap between the artwork-as-representation and the object itself, but is unable to do so. Because music, however, points to nothing outside itself, yet still appears to mean something, Pater considered it the supreme form of art.

Purely aesthetic contemplation is a recurring theme in the traditions that precede and influence the modernists. Its importance stems from a shared conviction about the need to nurture ways of thinking that can get beyond social and moral codes, because of a suspicion that there are problems with rationality and established ways of thinking. For Schopenhauer, Baudelaire, Mallarmé and Pater, music's capacity to create a powerful sense of meaning that was difficult to translate into language seemed to be opening up new avenues of thought. Joyce's early work is heavily indebted to Paterian ideas about music, as Richard Poirer, Alan D. Perils and Robert M. Scotto have shown.[55] Pound's early conceptualisation of music's value shares striking similarities with that of Mallarmé, while Warner engages closely and critically with the connection between religious and musical notions of transcendence. For many modernist writers, the way music seemed to stretch rational thought was positive, because they felt there was a need for new ways of thinking. In this sense, they draw on aesthetic traditions that view music as having a uniquely positive potential.

There was an alternative strain of thought about music operating in Europe. For others, the way music affected the body instantly, physically, seeming to bypass reason, was dangerous. Although Kant's conviction about the importance of aesthetic contemplation deeply influenced Schopenhauer and Pater, Kant considered music to have the 'lowest place' among the arts because it 'merely plays with the sensations' instead of the critical faculties. For Kant, music 'moves the mind in a greater variety of ways and more intensely' than other arts, 'although only transitorily'.[56] Kant's criticism that music primarily affects the nervous system prefigures a number of French thinkers who drew different conclusions from music's bodily affects. Vincent Sherry has explored the history of these discourses at length, showing how their influence on strands of British modernism, mainly Pound and Wyndham Lewis. For Henri Bergson, Sherry says, 'sound stirs the restive fibres of the biological soul' and 'the movements of sound are heard to correspond to the motions of the vital spirit'.[57] Conversely, others found the physical affects of sound regressive and primitive, appealing to the body rather than the mind. Sherry identifies influential thinkers who disapproved of the affective power of sound, including Julien Benda, Remy de Gourmont and José Ortega Y Gasset, and writes that 'the wonders those other writers praised in this sympathetic expansion through sound strike Benda as dangerous political delusions'.[58] For these writers, who – like Kivy – were interested in how the rational mind can be used to make accurate judgements about the world around them, music appeared to affect the senses without the intervention of reason, which made it a dangerous, populist art form. There are positive and negative strands of thought about music in Pound's writing, while Lewis shared with Julien Benda the conviction that the eye is a superior organ to the ear, and painting a superior art form to music. In Chapter 3 I track Pound's digestion of these ideas through Remy de Gourmont, who was a significant influence on Pound. Concerns about music's potential to incite mass empathy and arouse primitive emotions ran alongside notions of musical transcendence.

Adorno's Musicological Method

Adorno's musicology builds on the German Romantic tradition, but he also connects musical form to the material and social conditions of its production without seeing music as a simple reflection of those conditions. His approach combines aesthetic and social analyses of music, and draws on the traditions that modernists were negotiating. By considering the musical composition as a product of the consciousness of an individual which is itself produced by social relations, Adorno draws conclusions from music that have political relevance, without disregarding the complexity of music's social mediation or the difficulty of putting musical experience into words. His writing does not provide a straightforward methodology that can be transferred onto particular texts, but encourages close reading with attention to form that also takes into account social and historical contexts.

Musical material, Adorno suggests, 'is itself a crystallization of the creative impulse, an element socially predetermined through the consciousness of man ... the material is of the same origin as the social process'.[59] This is distinct from methods that expect the basic reproduction of 'thought processes' in the structure of music.[60] For Adorno, although musical material is 'of the same origin', this does not mean that identifiable social structures will be mirrored in musical structures, and he also acknowledges the difficulty of speaking about music since lexical meaning cannot be directly extracted:

> Music resembles language in the sense that it is a temporal sequence of articulated sounds which are more than just sounds. They say something, often something human ... But what has said cannot be detached from the music. Music creates no semiotic system.[61]

Music seems to say something 'human', since it is produced by people and can profoundly affect the emotions – it entreats us to decipher it. Yet the process of comprehending our response must be carried out through language, and because the gap between music and language is unbridgeable it must always be kept in sight: 'Music resembles a language ... But music is not identical with language. The resemblance points to something essential, but vague'.[62] In other words, music's power to 'say' things that are socially relevant is central to Adorno's analyses, but the abstract manner of its saying is not something to be overcome with social or empirical analyses; it is a crucial aspect of music's distinctive communicative capacity.

In Adorno's philosophy, the fascination with music as something that is what it describes – or in the Paterian terms I discussed earlier, achieves the ideal union between form and content – is placed in the broader context of Western philosophy's contemplation of the metaphysical, to which music relates as a form of 'absolute' signification. Adorno describes metaphysics as the search for 'the "last things" on account of which human beings first began to philosophize', so that metaphysics is the search for origins, essences or the study of things that do not change.[63] Discussions of metaphysics and universals date back to Ancient Greece, particularly Plato's theory of forms (not a self-contained theory but an explanation of Plato's ideas found throughout his writing, particularly the middle period). In the *Phaedro* Plato differentiates between particular material forms and universal, unchanging forms which include concepts.[64] Metaphysics enters religious discourses when God acts as the guarantor of the sign. For example, in Descartes's *Meditations*, he describes God as 'a substance that is infinite, independent, supremely intelligent, supremely powerful' which allows Descartes to believe in a notion of verification that exists transcendent of human-level discourse.[65] Words are not things but signs, meaning that investment in the accuracy of the sign requires belief in a verifying or guaranteeing principle independent of human discursivity. Derrida explains this by writing that 'the sign and divinity have the same place and time of birth. The age of the sign is essentially theological'. According to Derrida, the understanding of the sign assumes an 'ideal' of pure intelligibility – a form of immediate knowledge of the world, such as we experience in the present – and this, as with Descartes, is derived from the idea of God as the unmediated face of intelligibility: 'the intelligible face of the sign remains turned toward the word and the face of God'.[66]

Music's theological or metaphysical aspect lies in its direct communication, Adorno argues, rather than in being a system of signifiers:

> The language of music is quite different from the language of intentionality. It contains a theological dimension. What it has to say is simultaneously revealed and concealed. Its Idea is the divine Name which has been given shape. It is demythologized prayer, rid of efficacious magic. It is the human attempt, doomed as ever, to name the Name, not to communicate meanings.[67]

Since music does not rely upon an external guaranteeing principle, it appears to offer an instance of absolute signification: 'the identity of these musical concepts [lies] in their own nature and not in a signified outside them'.[68] Yet musical meaning is never absolutely apprehended because it can only be discussed in language. This is why, in both language and music, the human attempt to 'name the Name, not to communicate meanings' is 'doomed'. As Adorno explains: 'music finds the absolute immediately, but at the moment of discovery it becomes obscured, just as too powerful a light dazzles the eyes, preventing them from seeing things which are perfectly visible'.[69] Music engages questions of metaphysics by appearing to offer a pure, unmediated way of saying something or knowledge of the world, but it also frustrates questions of metaphysics because its discussion and comprehension must always be mediated through language.

While new musicology and sociology tends to approach musical transcendence as an illusion from which we need to be freed, for Adorno it is part of a longstanding Western philosophical engagement with questions of metaphysics. Equally, however, music is not an aesthetically pure realm for Adorno. It is not without meaning or 'intention', despite that meaning being difficult to apprehend:

> Music aspires to be a language without intention. But the demarcation line between itself and the language of intentions is not absolute; we are not confronted by two wholly separate realms. There is a dialectic at work. Music is permeated through and through with intentionality.[70]

The meanings or intentions available in music are informed by social contexts, so that musical forms derive significance from the environment of their formation. Music can contain 'concepts' in a manner similar to language, since it 'makes use of recurring ciphers ... established by tonality' such as 'cadential progressions ... stock melodic figures which are associated with the harmony'. The abstract nature of these musical structures has been given meaning 'by the context in which they were located'.[71]

Adorno's ideas are a strong presence in work by some of the most influential new musicologists. McClary's analysis of the relationship between musical form and society is decidedly Adornian, reiterating claims about the association between functional harmony and the bourgeois subject:

> The values it [functional tonality] articulates are those held most dear by the middle class: beliefs in progress, in expansion, in the ability to attain ultimate goals through rational striving, in the ingenuity of the individual strategist operating both within and in defiance of the norm.[72]

What Adorno offers musicologists is the ability to claim that music constructs, maintains or questions social order rather than just participating in social life through the ways certain people are able to articulate their understanding of it – as sociologists maintain. Adorno's methodology looks for relationships between art and society based on form and structure, rather than only on what individuals are able to articulate about art from a particular subject position, and this enables musicologists to connect formal and social analyses. This becomes very useful if we want to say anything about the way modernist writers engage with formal aspects of music.

Despite mediating between two ways of studying music that are frequently opposed, Adorno is still often neglected or condemned – especially in musico-literary studies. For example, Alan Shockley demonstrates that novels can use musical forms by selecting 'prose works that use musical structures and techniques', yet he is concerned with success or failure in purely aesthetic terms divorced from the social or moral attribution of value such as we find in Adorno's analyses. Shockley's strategy is recuperative and explanatory as he seeks to justify attributing value to texts based on their incorporation of musical forms, such as the 'musical brilliance' of Joyce's 'Sirens' chapter in *Ulysses*. He acknowledges Adornian analysis only indirectly in a single footnote, referring to it as 'a quite different mode of writing'. The footnote does not, in fact, directly reference any of Adorno's texts, but reads: 'for an approach to a quite different mode of writing, see Lydia Goehr's work on Theodor W. Adorno's basis for his philosophies in the music of Schoenberg'.[73] There have been frequent charges of elitism for the sweeping negativity of Adorno's statements about 'mass culture', with Bruce Baugh showing the potential problems of Adorno's critique but also a way of positively reading parts of mass culture through critical theory.[74] David Jeneman is particularly thorough in answering charges that Adorno is an 'anti-American intellectual elitist' by showing that 'Adorno was thoroughly engrossed by the day-to-day life of radio networks and studio filmmaking' during his time in the USA and thus 'comes by his criticism – no matter how biting – honestly and with sensitivity for its material conditions'.[75]

Musicologists have usefully critiqued Adorno's judgements about specific musical works. Rose Rosengard Subotnik writes about Adorno's listening strategies as prioritising 'structural values and concepts that originated in Viennese Classicism' and criticises his 'inability to imagine alternative, equally honest, stylistic definitions of or solutions to the social problems surrounding music'.[76] Parts of Subotnik's study are centred on deconstructing Adorno's ideas, and her criticism does come close to accusing him of 'not doing enough', but her thorough engagement with the complexity of Adorno's thought attests to the extent to which the ideas are considered worth engaging with. A similar argument could be made about Adorno's extensive engagement with 'mass culture' as a way of answering basic charges of elitism – the fact that he engages so closely with it, even though what he says is not positive, means that it has an important place in his thought. For Andreas Huyssen, Adorno's theories rely on 'certain strategies of exclusion which relegate realism, naturalism, reportage literature and political art to an inferior realm', but he still maintains that 'any critique of the culture industry theory must be grounded to Adorno's modernist aesthetic'.[77]

While Huyssen and Subotnik critically engage with Adorno's writing, others offer minimal engagement with his texts and exhibit poorly justified ill-feeling towards his ideas. Alex Aronson makes an unfavourable comparison between Adorno and Thomas Mann's Adrian Leverkühn, but he offers no analysis of Adorno's ideas or any explanation for his hostility. Aronson praises Mann but likens Adorno to the fictional syphilitic composer who sells his soul to the devil:

> Adorno's interpretation of Schoenberg's musical innovation is put into Leverkühn's mouth as if it were his own discovery, while Mann, surely, could not have helped realising that the 'tragically cerebral relentlessness of [Adorno's] critique of the contemporary musical situation' related him intellectually to his fictitious composer.[78]

Aronson is referring to Mann's correspondence with Adorno in which he asks for advice on musical theory for including in *Doctor Faustus*.

The novel's description of Leverkühn's work is based on Adorno's analysis of Schoenberg's twelve-tone row, but Aronson mysteriously argues that there is a connection between Leverkühn and Adorno, but not between Leverkühn and Schoenberg.[79] Aronson quotes from Mann's *The Story of a Novel* which describes the genesis of *Doctor Faustus*, but his appropriation of Mann's words is piecemeal and obscuring; the full quotation reads: 'his [Adorno's] rigorous manner of veneration, the tragically cerebral relentlessness of his criticism of the contemporary musical situation, was precisely what I needed'.[80] When cited in full, we can see that the quotation is complimentary, which is how Mann usually refers to his collaborator.

Edward Said finds Adorno's methods valuable and offers a possible explanation for his neglect:

> And while I am very far from rejecting all, or even a significant portion, of what musicologists do by way of analysis or evaluation, I am struck by how much does not receive their critical attention, and by how little is actually done by fine scholars who, for example, in studying a composer's notebooks or the structure of classical form, fail to connect those things to ideology, or social space, or power, or the formulation of an individual (and by no means sovereign) ego. Theodor Adorno may have been the last thinker about Western classical music to attempt many of these bigger things. I have little idea what his influence or status is in musicology today but I suspect that his intransigent theorising, complicated philosophical language, and vast speculative pessimism do not endear him to busy professionals.[81]

For Said, Adorno's writing style and dialectical approach are too impenetrable for many to engage with substantially. This is apparent in the way he is dealt with, even in discussions of music and literature where his ideas would seem to be most relevant. Daniel Albright's reference to Adorno reveals the attitude Said notices most explicitly, and his defensive condescension to Adorno's ideas shows unjustified and unexplained hostility that validates Said's assessment that the difficulty of Adorno's writing creates a negative response to his work among scholars. Albright claims that the 'intellectual dazzle of Adorno's prose tends to disguise the simplicity of some of his assumptions about art'.[82] Instead of seeing the density and complexity of Adorno's writing as a marker of the dialectical thinking he undertakes, Albright characterises it as unnecessarily difficult so that he can undermine its relevance. The word 'assumptions' is telling, as it claims for Adorno some ill-arrived at conclusions about what art actually is, rather than approaching Adorno's writing as a methodological choice designed to draw out complexities and contradictions through the dialectical use of language – a technique that Adorno explains succinctly in *Minima Moralia*: 'Dialectical thought is an attempt to break through the coercion of logic by its own means. But since it must use these means, it is at every moment in danger of itself acquiring a coercive character'.[83] Adorno's critique of Stravinsky is an obstacle to Albright's positive aesthetic analysis. Albright attempts to discredit Adorno's style since he apparently cannot discredit the ideas themselves, but he does not explain himself fully enough for the critique to be thoroughly convincing, since he gives no examples of how Adorno's technique manages to make simple ideas look complicated. Adorno's first discussion of Stravinsky was in 'Stravinsky and Restoration' in *Philosophy of Modern Music*, and he explains how that piece has been misread in *Quasi Una Fantasia*.[84] The misreading he describes is the same one that Albright is guilty of, despite the fact that Albright had access to this explanatory text. Adorno claims:

> that chapter on Stravinsky has been more misunderstood than any other. It began with the accusation that I had no feeling for order, for ontology, in music – whereas what I objected to in Stravinsky was not order but the illusion of order. At the other extreme I was rebuked for calling him a schizophrenic, whereas what I repeatedly insisted on was that the complexion of his music was derived from the lesson of obsessional neurosis and schizophrenia – that is, that he had chosen this method as a stylistic principle, or had constructed schizophrenic models . . . It never occurred to me to treat Stravinsky himself as a pathological case or to diagnose him with the aid of some intrusive psychological theory . . . It is the act of a philistine to confuse the objective form of a work of art with the psyche of the man who created it.[85]

Disregarding the political aspect of Adorno's critique, Albright refocuses it as a personal aversion to the aesthetic qualities *Untwisting the Serpent* prizes. Stravinsky is a good example of the 'convergent' art forms Albright praises because the relationship between dance and music in *The Rite of Spring* supposedly 'asks the eye to do the work of hearing'.[86] Adorno, however, is described as motivated by a 'complex of hatreds' for Albright, who completely misses the fact that the philosopher is critiquing the music, rather than the person, and fails to see the utopian potential of Adorno's thinking.[87] Yvonne Sherratt's *Adorno's Positive Dialectic* is able to see this potential: she argues that Adorno's philosophy often appears negative because it engages in a sustained critique of Western rationality, its genesis and its cultural products, but despite this his philosophy actually contains a model for a fully enlightened mode of thought, and is fundamentally utopian, because its goal is social transformation.[88]

Adorno shares with Pound, Joyce and Warner the conviction that music can be used to contemplate different, non-lexical and anti-rationalist ways of thinking. Through critical and evaluative use of Adorno's musicology and formal analysis, throughout this book I attempt to bring into productive opposition two approaches to music that rarely meet in literary criticism: the aesthetic and the social, by retaining understanding of the cultural and non-referential power of music, whilst connecting formal developments to ideology and political intentionality.

Notes

1. Lawrence Kramer, *Music as Cultural Practice, 1800–1900* (Berkeley, CA: University of California Press, 1990). For feminist musicology, see Susan McClary, *Feminine Endings* (Minneapolis: University of Minnesota Press, 1991).
2. Susan McClary, 'The Blasphemy of Talking Politics during Bach Year', in Richard Leppert and Susan McClary, eds, *Music and Society: the Politics of Composition, Performance and Reception* (Cambridge: Cambridge University Press, 1987), p. 17.
3. Janet Wolff, 'Foreword', in Leppert and McClary, eds, *Music and Society*, pp. 2, 4.
4. I return to this issue later in this chapter, in the section entitled 'Histories of Musical Transcendence', pp. 30–7.
5. Robert Snarrenburg, *Schenker's Interpretive Practice* (Cambridge: Cambridge University Press, 2005), p. 5.
6. Heinrich Schenker quoted in Nicholas Cook, *The Schenker Project: Culture, Race, and Music Theory in Fin-de-siècle Vienna* (Oxford: Oxford University Press, 2007), p. 48.
7. Ibid. See also Eduard Hanslick, *On the Musically Beautiful: A Contribution Towards the Revision of the Aesthetics of Music*, trans. and ed. Geoffrey Payzant from the 8th edn (1891) of *Vom Musikalisch-Schönen: ein Beitrag zur Revision der Ästhetik der Tonkunst* (Indianapolis: Hackett Publishing, 1986).
8. Wolff, 'Foreword', in Leppert and McClary, eds, *Music and Society*, pp. 4, 1, 3.
9. Jean-Jacques Nattiez, *Music and Discourse: Towards a Semiology of Music*, trans. Carolyn Abbate (Princeton, NJ: Princeton University Press, 1990), p. ix.
10. Bruno Nettl, *The Study of Ethnomusicology: Thirty-one Issues and Concepts* (Champaign, IL: University of Illinois Press, 2005), pp. 4–5.
11. Ted Solis, 'Teaching What Cannot Be Taught: An Optimistic Overview', in Ted Solis, ed., *Performing Ethnomusicology: Teaching and Representation in World Music Ensembles* (Berkeley, CA: University of California Press, 2004), pp. 1–2.
12. Peter J. Martin, *Music and the Sociological Gaze* (Manchester: Manchester University Press, 2006), p. 2.
13. John Shepherd, 'Towards a Sociology of Music Styles', in Avron Levine White, ed., *Lost in Music Culture: Style and the Musical Event* (London: Routledge, 1987), p. 57.
14. Martin, *Music and the Sociological Gaze*, p. 5 (his emphasis).

15. For more detail about the problems with this view, see my discussion of Warner's handling of ideology operating through music in Chapter 4, 'The Music at Long Verney', pp. 142–8.
16. Stefan Collini, *What Are Universities For?* (London: Penguin, 2012).
17. Leys also notes that this is connected to a belief that 'most philosophers and critics in the past (Kantians, neo-Kantians, Habermasians) have overvalued the role of reason and rationality in politics, ethics, and aesthetics'. See Ruth Leys, 'The Turn to Affect: A Critique', *Critical Inquiry* 37.3 (Spring 2011), 443, 436.
18. Peter Kivy, *Music Alone: Philosophical Reflections on the Purely Musical Experience* (London and Ithaca, NY: Cornell University Press, 1990), p. 12.
19. John McDowell, *Mind and World* (Oxford: Oxford University Press, 1994), p. 24.
20. Andrew Bowie, *Music, Philosophy and Modernity* (Cambridge: Cambridge University Press, 2009), p. 8.
21. Ibid. pp. 7–8.
22. Kivy, *Music Alone*, p. 13.
23. Pauliina Remes, *Neoplatonism* (Berkeley, CA: University of California Press, 2008), p. 2.
24. Eli Maor, *The Pythagorean Theorem: A 4,000-Year History* (Princeton, NJ: Princeton University Press, 2007), p. 19.
25. Aristotle, *Complete Works of Aristotle, Vol. 2: The Revised Oxford Translation*, ed. Jonathan Barnes (Princeton, NJ: Princeton University Press, 1984), p. 1559.
26. See Leslie Blasius, 'Mapping the Terrain', in Thomas Christensen, ed., *The Cambridge History of Western Music Theory* (Cambridge: Cambridge University Press, 2002), p. 31.
27. T. J. Reed, 'The "Goethezeit" and its Aftermath', in Malcolm Pasley, ed., *Germany: A Companion to German Studies* (London: Methuen, 1972), p. 517.
28. Immanuel Kant, *Critique of Pure Reason*, ed. and trans. Paul Guyer and Allen W. Wood (Cambridge: Cambridge University Press, 1998), p. 168. Kant focuses on aesthetics in the 'Critique of the Aesthetic Power of Judgement', discussing what aesthetic beauty is and how it can be characterised. See Immanuel Kant, *Critique of the Power of Judgement*, ed. Paul Guyer, trans. Paul Guyer and Eric Matthews (Cambridge: Cambridge University Press, 2000), pp. 96, 104, 120.
29. Dahlhaus, *The Idea of Absolute Music*, p. 4.
30. Ibid. p. 4.
31. Ibid. p. 4.
32. Andrew Bowie, 'Romanticism and Music', in Nicholas Saul, ed., *The Cambridge Companion to German Romanticism* (Cambridge: Cambridge University Press, 2009), p. 250.
33. Schopenhauer, *The World as Will and Representation*, Vol. 1, p. 289.
34. Ibid. p. 257. For Plato's theory of forms and its place in metaphysics, see n. 64 below.
35. Schopenhauer, *The World as Will and Representation*, Vol. 1, p. 257.
36. Schopenhauer, 'Appendix: Criticism of the Kantian Philosophy', in *The World as Will and Representation*, Vol. 1, pp. 441–566.

37. Lydia Goehr, 'Schopenhauer and the Musicians: an Inquiry into the Sounds of Silence and the Limits of Philosophizing about Music', in Dale Jacquette, ed., *Schopenhauer, Philosophy and the Arts* (Cambridge: Cambridge University Press, 1996), p. 200.
38. Letter from Wagner to Liszt, 29 September 1854, in Richard Wagner and Franz Liszt, *Correspondence of Wagner and Liszt*, ed. Francis Hueffer (New York: Haskell House, 1897), p. 53.
39. Richard Wagner, 'Beethoven', in *Music in European Thought: 1851–1912*, ed. Bojan Bujic (Cambridge: Cambridge University Press, 1988), pp. 65–6.
40. Wagner, *Wagner on Music and Drama*, p. 152.
41. Friedrich Nietzsche, *The Birth of Tragedy*, trans. Douglas Smith (Oxford: Oxford World's Classics, 2000), p. 75.
42. Ibid. p. 34.
43. For Schopenhauer's influence on composers, see Goehr, 'Schopenhauer and the Musicians', pp. 200–28; Bryan Magee, *The Philosophy of Schopenhauer* (Oxford: Oxford University Press, 1997), pp. 350–402. For criticisms of Schopenhauer's ideas about music, see Malcolm Budd, *Music and the Emotions* (London: Routledge, 1992), p. 96; Magee, *The Philosophy of Schopenhauer*, pp. 240–3.
44. Charles Baudelaire, *Paris Spleen: Little Poems in Prose*, trans. Keith Waldrop (Middletown, CT: Wesleyan University Press, 2009), p. 3.
45. Brad Bucknell, *Literary Modernism and Musical Aesthetics* (Cambridge: Cambridge University Press, 2001), p. 17.
46. Peter Dayan, *Music Writing Literature: From Sand to Debussy via Derrida* (Aldershot: Ashgate, 2006), p. ix.
47. Helen Abbott, *Between Baudelaire and Mallarmé: Voice, Conversation and Music* (Farnham: Ashgate, 2009), pp. 3, 9, 183–222.
48. Pater, *The Renaissance*, pp. 117, 106. Walter Pater's ideas were deeply influenced by both Hegel and Kant. See William F. Shuter, 'Heraclitus, Hegel and Plato', in *Rereading Walter Pater* (Cambridge: Cambridge University Press, 1997), pp. 61–77. See also Pater, *The Renaissance*, p. 386.
49. Jonathan Freedman, *Professions of Taste: Henry James, British Aestheticism, and Commodity Culture* (Stanford, CA: Stanford University Press, 1992), p. 2.
50. William Hamilton, *The British Aesthetic Movement* (London: Reeves & Tucker, 1882).
51. John Ruskin, *Modern Painters*, vol. 1 (London: Smith, Elder & Co., 1843), p. 14.
52. Walter Pater, 'Coleridge', in *Appreciations: With an Essay on Style* ([1901] London: Macmillan, 1924), p. 66.
53. Pater's ideas were not universally accepted. John Addington Symonds disagrees with Pater's attribution of special status to music. In his essay 'Is Music the Type or Measure of All Art?' Symonds claims Pater's assertion is either 'personal partiality' or an 'inconclusive, aesthetical hypothesis': 'beauty is the sensuous manifestation of the idea – that is, of the spiritual element in man and in the world – and that the arts, each in its own way, conveys this beauty to our percipient self. We have to abstain on the one hand from any theory which emphasizes the didactic function of art ... fine and liberal art, as distinguished from mechanical art or the arts of the kitchen and

millinery, exists for the embodiment of thought and emotion in forms of various delightfulness'. John Addington Symonds, *Essays Speculative and Suggestive* (London: Chapman and Hall, 1893), p. 367.
54. Pater, *The Renaissance*, p. 106. For Pater's influence on Pound, see Richard Read, 'Art Criticism versus Poetry: an Introduction to Adrian Stokes's "Pisanello"', in E. S. Shaffer, ed., *Comparative Criticism Volume 17: Walter Pater and the Culture of the Fin-de-Siècle* (Cambridge: Cambridge University Press, 1995), p. 145. For Baudelaire's influence on Pater, see David Carrier, *High Art: Charles Baudelaire and the Origins of Modernist Painting* (Philadelphia: Pennsylvania State University Press, 1996), p. 70.
55. Richard Poirier, 'Pater, Joyce, Eliot', *James Joyce Quarterly* 26.1 (1988), 21–35; Alan D. Perils, 'Beyond Epiphany: Pater's Aesthetic Hero in the Works of Joyce', *James Joyce Quarterly* 17.3 (1980), 272–9; Robert M. Scotto, '"Visions" and "Epiphanies": Fictional Technique in Pater's *Marius* and Joyce's *Portrait*', *James Joyce Quarterly* 11.1 (1973), 41–50.
56. Kant, *Critique of the Power of Judgement*, pp. 174, 172.
57. Vincent Sherry, *Ezra Pound, Wyndham Lewis and Radical Modernism* (Oxford: Oxford University Press, 1993), pp. 12, 11.
58. Ibid. p. 16.
59. Theodor W. Adorno, *Philosophy of Modern Music*, trans. Anne G. Mitchell and Wesley V. Blomster ([1947] London: Continuum, 2007), p. 24.
60. I refer here to John Shepherd's methodology (see n. 13 above), 'because people create music, they reproduce in the basic structure of their music the basic structure of their own thought processes'. Shepherd, 'Towards a Sociology of Music Styles', p. 57.
61. Adorno, *Quasi Una Fantasia*, p. 1.
62. Ibid. p. 1.
63. Theodor W. Adorno, 'Lecture 1: What is Metaphysics?', in *Metaphysics: Concepts and Problems* (Stanford, CA: Stanford University Press, 2001), p. 1.
64. For Plato's theory of forms, see the argument from 'recollection' of forms in which he discusses abstract 'Justice' (72e–78b), and the argument from affinity of soul to forms (78b–84b). Plato, *Phaedro*, ed. and trans. David Gallop (Oxford: Oxford University Press, 1993).
65. René Descartes, 'Meditations on First Philosophy', in *The Philosophical Writings of Descartes*, trans. John Cottingham, Robert Stoothoff and Dugald Murdoch (Cambridge: Cambridge University Press, 1985), p. 31.
66. Jacques Derrida, *Of Grammatology*, trans. Gayatri Chakravorty Spivak (Baltimore: Johns Hopkins University Press, 1997), pp. 14, 13.
67. Adorno, *Quasi Una Fantasia*, p. 2.
68. Ibid. p. 2
69. Ibid. p. 4.
70. Ibid. p. 3.
71. Ibid. p. 2.
72. McClary, 'The Blasphemy of Talking Politics during Bach Year', in Leppert and McClary, eds, *Music and Society*, p. 22.
73. Alan Shockley, *Music in the Words: Musical Form and Counterpoint in the Twentieth-Century Novel* (Farnham: Ashgate, 2009), pp. 2, 7, n. 22.

74. Bruce Baugh, 'Left-Wing Elitism: Adorno on Popular Culture', *Philosophy and Literature* 14.1 (1990), 65–78.
75. Jeneman, *Adorno in America*, pp. xv, xviii.
76. Rose Rosengard Subotnik, *Deconstructive Variations: Music and Reason in Western Society* (Minneapolis: University of Minnesota Press, 1996), pp. 156, 167.
77. Andreas Huyssen, *After the Great Divide: Modernism, Mass Culture, Postmodernism* (Bloomington, IN: Indiana University Press, 1986), p. 25.
78. Aronson, *Music and the Novel*, p. 200.
79. Christopher Gödde and Thomas Sprecher, eds, *Correspondence 1943–1955: Theodor W. Adorno and Thomas Mann*, trans. Nick Walker (Cambridge: Polity, 2005).
80. Thomas Mann, *The Story of a Novel: The Genesis of 'Doctor Faustus'*, trans. H. T. Lowe-Porter ([1947] Harmondsworth: Penguin, 1971), p. 54.
81. Edward Said, *Musical Elaborations* (New York: Columbia University Press, 1991), p. 13.
82. Daniel Albright, *Untwisting the Serpent: Modernism in Music, Literature, and Other Arts* (Chicago: University of Chicago Press, 2000), p. 4.
83. Adorno, *Minima Moralia*, p. 150.
84. Adorno, *Philosophy of Modern Music*, pp. 100–57.
85. Adorno, 'Stravinsky', in *Quasi Una Fantasia*, p. 148.
86. Albright, *Untwisting the Serpent*, p. 18.
87. Ibid. p. 14.
88. Yvonne Sherratt, *Adorno's Positive Dialectic* (Cambridge: Cambridge University Press, 2002).

Chapter 2

James Joyce, *Ulysses* and the Politics of Musical Form

Joyce claimed, in a letter to Harriet Shaw Weaver in 1919, that the 'Sirens' chapter of *Ulysses* was modelled on a '*fuga per canonem*', and critics have debated what kind of classical musical form the chapter most resembles.[1] Readings of 'Sirens' that are based purely on Joyce's statement about its musicality are limited because they only aim to prove his intentions and radical artistry. Approaching the use of musical form as having purely aesthetic value that requires only schematic and technical explanation draws uncritically on nineteenth-century ideas about music's positive potential, and misses the competing arguments about music that are staged in the chapter. Music's positive capacity to encourage different ways of thinking is appealed to by the chapter's musically inspired form, which produces an ambiguous narrative that requires an enhanced degree of interpretation and promotes independent thought. On the other hand, the musical performance in the Ormond Bar is used to criticise music: the singing provokes Bloom's retreat into an emotional sentimentality that inhibits social interaction.

Joyce needs to be read with an awareness of a shift in his work away from the presentation of music as aesthetically pure, and towards an engagement with music's dual qualities of thought-provoking abstraction and propensity to encourage introspective sentimentality. In Joyce's early collection of poetry, *Chamber Music*, we can see the influence of British Aestheticism and the classical musical traditions in which he was schooled, since music is primarily associated with beauty and aesthetic purity.[2] He diverged from these traditions when writing his later works. This chapter begins by discussing the influence of Walter Pater and nineteenth-century aesthetics in *Chamber Music*, which helps to contextualise the following analysis of Joyce's very different approach to musicality and form in 'Sirens'. My approach reconstructs Joyce as someone who produced texts that were influenced by a particular education and traditions that became destabilised due to shifting social, economic and political conditions.

'Sirens' is not, in any case, musical because it replicates fugal or canonic form, but because it uses repetition as a formal device to give additional meanings to certain words that are entirely dependent on the form of and context created by the chapter. Joyce's language is musically informed because it conveys meaning formally – specifically, by repetition and association within the chapter – rather than through the established definitions and connotations of particular words. While debates between critics who have struggled to make the text fit a specific musical model can tell us much about the extent of the differences and similarities between literary and musical forms, instead of arguing for Joyce's intentional use of a specific musical form or attempting to produce a definitive reading of any part of his texts, I investigate 'Sirens' to show what happens to the way language produces meaning when a literary form is (reportedly) influenced by music.

The musical forms with which 'Sirens' is usually compared – the fugue, sonata and symphony – are not the most appropriate for analysis of Joyce's *Ulysses*. The fragmentation, dissonance and abstraction that are key characteristics of modernist writing are not available in the unified and totalising musical structures that it is claimed Joyce adopts in 'Sirens' – as David Herman has suggested when he reads 'Sirens' in relation to Arnold Schoenberg's twelve-tone row.[3] To advance on Herman's reading, and instead of referring back to musical forms that were being challenged at the time Joyce was writing, I consider how the formal innovations in *Ulysses* relate to changes in musical form in Europe at the start of the twentieth century by reading 'Cyclops' in relation to Theodor W. Adorno's analysis of twelve-tone technique's relationship to the social experience of modernity. The social meanings and functions in Schoenberg's music at a formal level enhance our understanding of the political content of 'Cyclops' by connecting the fragmentation techniques in Joyce's novel to the social conditions of the text's production. In discussions of 'Cyclops', critics have been keen to read the chapter as endorsing either Bloom's or the citizen's political opinions.[4] The narrative of 'Cyclops' does not prioritise one 'voice' in the episode as they claim: rather, like the twelve-tone row, it resists traditional development and resolution.

Chamber Music

Joyce's first published literary work was *Chamber Music* (1907), a collection of thirty-six lyric poems narrating the development and decline of a love affair.[5] Joyce is working within an established poetic form.

The lyric originated in Ancient Greece as verse usually accompanied by a lyre, and underwent a revival in German Romanticism: for Georg Lukács, the 'lyric poetry' of Joseph Eichendorff was 'the purest expression of the folk-song like strain in [German] Romantic poetry', which 'instinctively follows the line of reviving the folk song tradition which began with Herder and Goethe'.[6] Wordsworth and Coleridge popularised the genre in Britain, publishing *Lyrical Ballads* in 1798.[7] The lyric subsequently re-emerged in nineteenth-century Britain and France as the dominant poetic form. M. H. Abrams describes how the lyric became a 'poetic norm' towards the end of the eighteenth century, leading to its dominance among poetic forms during Romanticism and in the nineteenth century.[8] Joyce can be seen consciously working in this tradition, since he was keen for the poems to be considered as lyrics, claiming that 'the book is in fact a suite of songs and if I were a musician I suppose I should have set them to music myself'.[9]

His comment also shows his desire to claim an innate musical quality for the collection. That the poems aspire to be music calls up the elevated position of music in Pater's thought, whose influence is well noted in Joyce studies. Richard Ellmann claims that as a schoolboy Joyce attempted to imitate and improve on Pater's writing, choosing a 'highly adorned, rhythmical style'.[10] Vincent Sherry describes the 'shaping and stylizing of writing' that characterised Pater's practice, and Max Beerbohm famously described Pater's style as 'that sedulous ritual wherewith he laid out every sentence as in a shroud'.[11] David Weir has also argued for the influence of decadence and Aestheticism in modernist literature, exploring how Joyce is occupied with 'the same decadent interests that had preoccupied Pater and Moore'.[12] The influence of Pater in *A Portrait of the Artist as a Young Man* has been a recurring topic in *James Joyce Quarterly*.[13] Marguerite Harkness has discussed Joyce's engagement with Aestheticism, arguing that he develops a position on the relationship between art and life through characters – notably Stephen Dedalus in *A Portrait of the Artist as a Young Man* and Bloom in *Ulysses* – whose thinking is informed by Aesthetes like Pater and Ruskin.[14]

Joyce's statement about the musicality of *Chamber Music* shows how heavily his early thought draws on nineteenth-century aesthetics and discourses of transcendence associated with music and poetic form. Lyric poetry has an established relationship with subjective experience: Abrams notes that the lyric has been 'connected by critics to the state of mind of the author'.[15] The lyric is itself embedded in historical discourses of transcendence. It had an elevated position in Hegel's aesthetic thought:

therefore, in order to be the centre which holds the whole lyric work of art together, the poet must have achieved a specific mood or specific situation, while at the same time he must identify himself with this particularization of himself as with himself, so that in it he feels and envisages himself.[16]

Hegel considered the lyric the art form most fully able to express a unique and individual subjectivity. Joyce's poems are broadly in the lyric tradition, narrating a personal experience, and they are suitable as lyrics due to their regular rhyme and metre. Angela Leighton has discussed the importance given to the rhythms of sentences and verses in W. B. Yeats's poetry, and Yeats's influences extend back 'through Pater, Tennyson, and Hallam, to Keats'.[17] These are all writers who thought of rhyme and metre as able to produce, in Yeats's words, 'a beauty so preoccupied with itself that its contemplation is a kind of lingering trance'.[18] But while rhyme and metre are formal characteristics that can affect how meaning is produced, the poems of *Chamber Music* primarily create meaning linguistically, albeit with constant reference to sound and the visual.

Despite drawing heavily on traditions associated with aestheticism, *Chamber Music* is not a musical work in Pater's sense: it does not provide sustained engagement with the formal qualities of music that were significant in Pater's thought. For Pater, instrumental music's unique quality of transcendence is distinct from lyric poetry. It was derived from music's ability to create meaning without referring to the material world through language, combined with its 'ideal' fusion of form and content since music does not point to anything outside itself. As such, even if *Chamber Music* was set to music, the songs would not exhibit the non-lexical quality of instrumental music that is significant for Pater.

While poetry can certainly achieve musical effects, it is not necessary to police the boundaries between language and music to notice that overall *Chamber Music* is far more concerned with the visual than with music or the auditory, and the collection should be considered among the least musical of Joyce's writings, in the sense that it lacks an engagement with specifically musical forms and music as a non-referential, formal art. The first poem of the collection exemplifies this:

I
Strings in the earth and air
Make music sweet;
Strings by the river where
The willows meet.

There's music along the river
For Love wanders there,

Pale flowers on his mantle,
Dark leaves on his hair.

All softly playing,
With head to the music bent,
And fingers straying
Upon an instrument.[19]

The 'music sweet' heightens the atmospheric effect of the pastoral landscape imagery. In the final stanza the instrument is used alongside the visual image of the leaf-adorned Love bent over with 'fingers straying'. In poem XIV, the inclusion of music provides skill and craftsmanship to 'The odorous winds' that 'are weaving / A music of sighs', giving a visual, personified element to the otherwise invisible wind. Music is used to create a visual impact and contribute to the romantic atmosphere. These poems primarily appeal to the optical: musical instruments are used to emphasise the beauty of visual images. The poems refer to music but do not create meaning through their form alone; there is no sustained engagement with the idea of music or its formal qualities.

Joyce's later works have overshadowed the collection, which has received limited critical attention and mixed responses. Joyce engages with an established poetic form without irony, making it the work of a writer attempting to master a well-known style. *Chamber Music* exhibits a non-satirical use of cliché and old-fashioned language, such as in IX, where the allusion to the nursery rhyme 'Ring a ring o' roses' ('Dancing a ring-around in glee') is followed five lines later by the exclamations 'Welladay! Welladay!', a variation of 'wellaway', an interjection derived from the Old English *wei lá wei*.[20] The uncritical use of archaic phrases in *Chamber Music* does not sit easily beside the liberal use of parody and pastiche in *Ulysses* or the radical reforming of language in *Finnegans Wake*. Kenneth Grose finds the poems 'soft-centered', 'an empty exercise in factitious emotion-mongering'.[21] To make the poems 'fit' with Joyce's later, much more experimental work, William York Tindall tries to find precursors to aspects of *Ulysses* in *Chamber Music*: recalling Molly Bloom 'on her pot in the last chapter' of *Ulysses*, he argues 'Joyce never wasted anything so good on a single reference', so that 'we may take it ... as a clue to one of the meanings of his title'.[22] That *Chamber Music* is not generally considered a successful work of art on its own terms suggests the difficulty of writing a fictive lyric 'I' in modernity with conventional language. Joyce's departure from the lyric form is significant in showing how certain modes of expression are becoming unconvincing, however, and *Chamber Music* does not need to be reconciled with his later work, but can be seen as the work of a writer refining his craft by mastering established techniques from which he later departs.

According to Lee Spinks, the 'strengths and weaknesses of the collection come into relief when considered in the context of the Imagist movement with which his work was directly contemporary'.[23] One of Joyce's poems was included in the 1914 anthology *Des Imagistes*, edited by Ezra Pound, who had praised the 'delicate temperament' of the collection.[24] Joyce's directness, simplicity of phrase and limited use of adjectives aligns the work with Pound's Imagist requirements, which favoured economical language and clear visual representation. In 1912, Pound describes his admiration for poetry that is 'objective – no slither; direct – no excessive use of adjectives; no metaphors that won't permit examination'.[25] The extent to which the majority of *Chamber Music* is heavily indebted to lyric poetic traditions may explain why it was the final poem of the collection – one of the 'tailpieces', as Joyce called it, that the author of the 'make it new' slogan chose to publish.[26] The poem is markedly different in structure and tone to the rest of the collection:

XXXVI
I hear an army charging upon the land,
And the thunder of horses plunging, foam about their knees:
Arrogant, in black armour, behind them stand,
Disdaining the reins, with fluttering ships, the charioteers.
They cry unto the night their battle-name:
I moan in sleep when I hear afar their whirling laughter.
They cleave the gloom of dreams, a blinding flame,
Clanging, clanging upon the heart as upon an anvil.
They come shaking in triumph their long, green hair:
They come out of the sea and run shouting by the shore.
My heart, have you no wisdom thus to despair?
My love, my love, my love, why have you left me alone?[27]

While the auditory is subservient to the ocular in the majority of the collection, in the final two poems the auditory produces the visual. The speaker, appearing to recall troubled sleep, hears sounds to which they fix images of 'an army charging upon the land'. For the majority of the poetry collection, music is gentle and pleasant, but in the final poems noise torments: 'All day I hear the noise of waters / Making moan' (XXXV). The 'soft sweet music' (III) of the early poems is produced beside the river during leisure time, through instruments crafted from trees, but this gives way to 'noise' (XXXV), and loud, abrasive sound produces anguish and despair. Noise is the unharnessed natural world, and the result of man's violence exerted upon it for survival: the army is heard 'Clanging, clanging upon the heart as upon an anvil' (XXXVI).

Chamber Music presents a dichotomy: music is artfully constructed and pleasant, while noise is dangerous and sinister. By the time Joyce writes *Ulysses*, however, the way he deals with music is very different. In *Chamber Music* there is none of the attempted structural engagement with musical form that Joyce claims for the 'Sirens' chapter of *Ulysses*.

'Sirens' and Musical Form as Aesthetic Paradigm

The desire to test the validity of Joyce's claim that 'Sirens' contains 'all the eight regular parts of a *fuga per canonem*' means that analyses usually try to pin the chapter down to a specific musical form – even though the form Joyce is referring to is not entirely clear.[28] *Fuga per canonem* appears to mean 'fugue according to the rule' (from the Latin *canon* – rule). Brad Bucknell claims this is an early-sixteenth-century form, 'essentially what we would call today a canon', but provides no reference (and in any case he also explores the difficulties involved in ascribing any specific form to 'Sirens').[29] Susan Brown points out that 'no contemporaneous standard musical dictionary or encyclopedia in English or Italian offered a definition or entry for "fuga per canonem", "tela contrappuntistica" or "stretto maestrale"'.[30] On another occasion Joyce referred to the chapter simply as a 'fugue', claiming it is a 'fugue with all musical notations: *piano, forte, rallentando*, and so on'.[31] The dynamic markings he describes as 'musical notations' are not particular to a fugue, and neither does this form necessarily have to have eight parts.

The inconsistency and inaccuracy of Joyce's claims have not stopped critics from trying to corroborate them, or from going to great lengths to affirm his intelligence and genius. For Stuart Gilbert and David Cole the chapter successfully emulates the structure of a fugue.[32] A. Walton Litz, Stanley Sultan and Timothy Martin have claimed the chapter is modelled on an operatic overture.[33] For Don Noel Smith, 'Sirens' emulates part of a sonata, and Robert Boyle argues that *Ulysses* resembles a 'frustrated' sonata form.[34] Lawrence Levin decides that 'Sirens' achieves a polyphonic effect, but any discussion of what this musical appropriation does besides create 'many different moods' and provide an example of 'a virtuosic display of craftsmanship' is absent.[35] Margaret Rogers 'believe[s] Joyce used a variety of devices to encipher his music in "Sirens" including encoded notes based on a Renaissance model'.[36] Nadya Zimmerman is certain that Joyce manages to accurately emulate fugal form and provides a diagrammatic chart to 'illuminate the specific ways in which Joyce translates a *fuga per canonem* into an entire chapter of prose'.[37] Alan Shockley argues 'there is no denying Joyce's success with "Sirens." "Sirens" is an intensely contrapuntal work on many levels', because 'the text makes it clear that several streams of sound occur here simultaneously'.[38] Michelle Witen uses claims about Joyce's 'expert knowledge' to underpin her argument that 'Joyce has indeed succeeded' in creating a fugue in 'Sirens'.[39] All these critics approach 'Sirens' as succeeding or failing in aesthetic terms only, or in its accuracy of musical representation. Although they provide meticulous (if questionable) analyses of form and intention, addressing the politics of aesthetics is not a priority, so they offer no sense of why the things they notice matter.

While the musical form that 'Sirens' uses has been debated, most agree that the chapter attempts to evoke simultaneous events or voices using narrative techniques that are distinct from those used anywhere else in the novel. For Bucknell, 'Sirens' imitates music by evoking 'a simultaneity of various spaces' which is 'probably as close to a narrative counterpoint as Joyce can come'.[40] Yet those who argue for the achievement of polyphony or simultaneity are also aware of the limitations of their claim, because of the problems of translating between musical and literary forms. Writing about 'Sirens', Werner Wolf notes 'the difficulty language, the "monadic" medium of (narrative) literature, has in imitating musical polyphony'.[41] Zimmerman acknowledges that 'both the fugue and the canon depend upon a fundamental attribute – simultaneity. Clearly a prose rendering of any musical form will not be able to achieve such simultaneity; at any given moment, there is only a single line of narrative'.[42] In Zimmerman's reference to 'both the fugue and the canon', we can see how she tries to ensure her analysis matches Joyce's own claims about his work. Even though these are different forms, critics have such a strong desire to claim that Joyce is in control of his work that they claim he can successfully mediate or combine two different musical forms and translate them into text. Why not acknowledge the possibility that Joyce was incorrect, attempting to impress his patron (Harriet Shaw Weaver), or just trying to encourage readers to see a degree of musicality in his work? Shockley also agrees about the obvious ways in which 'Sirens' cannot replicate the simultaneity of polyphonic music: 'admittedly, Joyce writes a *constrained* polyphony. This is literature, after all, and the author does seem to accept the left-to-right, single-line-at-a-time limitations of his printed pages'.[43]

Linearity is often considered a limiting aspect of literature to which music can provide relief, and critics usually argue that musical form helps the text escape language's limitations to some degree. This type of criticism thus works with notions of music's aesthetic purity and transcendence, as though it has internalised Pater's famous statement about music. This is implicit in most discussions of 'Sirens' that claim it achieves polyphony, simultaneity or a contrapuntal effect, as Zimmerman states:

> The developmental narrative of events occurring in temporal succession has come to dominate the way in which we conceptualize life, the ways in which it proceeds, and in which we relate past, present, and future. By evoking a musical form, Joyce derails this linearity with the simultaneity that only music possesses.[44]

Zimmerman sets up a strict demarcation between what music alone can do, as opposed to literature, but then argues that 'Sirens' transcends its literary confines, doing the thing that 'only music' can do. She polices the boundaries between literature and music, whilst still arguing that Joyce escapes them.

Literature, however, can invoke simultaneity in different ways. A narrative, although it must usually be read one line at a time if we want to make sense of it, can evoke and describe many different characters, opinions, points of view, languages and cultures. Music may allow for the simultaneity of different sounds, but being non-lexical these cannot hold their own distinct viewpoint in the same way as language. Nor can they impart as much diverse information as a narrative is able to when it communicates, for example, the quality of light in a room, its smells, sounds, appearances or the emotions and aspirations of its characters. When music is notated the same imposition of linearity is afforded as we find in written literary text, and hearing music is always a passive act; we are obliged to hear the notes in the order they appear. In contrast, when reading a text, there is nothing (apart from our own desire to read in a way that allows us to understand the text) forcing us to read it in this way, in the same way that listening to the so-called correct order of notes in a musical performance is enforced. The idea of linearity being limiting, then, is only relevant if the text aspires to be like music, and even then a musical performance when our primary concern is hearing different sounds simultaneously (rather than a written musical text). Usually, music, its listeners and performers are 'bound' by many of the same so-called restrictions as literary texts.

Zimmerman and Shockley do not engage thoroughly with historical notions of musical transcendence, although they rely on the idea that music transcends language to claim that Joyce's use of musical form escapes language's limitations. In Paterian terms, of course, music's unique transcendence is rooted in the cohesion of form and content, and absence of reference to the material world – not in its ability to achieve simultaneity of sounds. If music were to be used as a model for elevating the communicative potential of language, then it would not be in order to achieve simultaneity, but to edge closer to that ideal union of form and content, which (for Pater and Schopenhauer, for example) means that music is the thing-in-itself, rather than a representation.[45] Critical writing on 'Sirens' overwhelmingly apportions a transcendent capacity to music which is figured only in terms of 'simultaneity' through the replication of fugal or polyphonic form, when this is not music's hallmark of transcendence, and literature can in fact represent simultaneity in different ways. In other words, simultaneity is not achieved, but it is suggested. It is communicated – not in a way that gets around the linearity of a written text, or by direct explanation – but by the inference that we glean from the repeated words and thematic material that tie events together. When a similarity to music is figured only in terms of simultaneity, and this is itself derailed due to the differences or limitations of linear text, then the pay-off of these analyses becomes unclear.

'Sirens' and Musical Form Reconsidered

Joyce attempts to emulate musical form through repeated words and phrases, which appear at the beginning of the chapter as a semi-nonsensical list. The chapter opens with sixty-three lines of short phrases that appear to have no relation to each other, the first three of which are:

> Bronze by gold heard the hoofirons, steelyringing
> Imperthnthn thnthnthn.
> Chips, picking chips off rocky thumbnails, chips. (*U* 11.1–3)

These phrases lack context and do not form a traditional narrative opening, which would typically introduce setting or character. As the chapter progresses the phrases return in a context through which they can be understood: the language of the opening section gains its significance from the context in which it reappears. 'Bronze' and 'gold' are quickly revealed to refer to Miss Douce and Miss Kennedy, who have bronze and gold hair, and the colours are frequently substituted for their names (*U* 11.64–5, 74, 83–4, 97, 112, 115). 'Imperthnthn thnthnthn' later returns as the phrase mumbled by Pat the waiter, mocking Miss Douce as he retreats from her criticism (*U* 11.100). 'Chips, picking chips' is Simon Dedalus picking his fingers, and his thematic material returns when 'into their bar strolled Mr Dedalus. Chips, picking chips off one of his rocky thumbnails' (*U* 11.192–3).

Over the course of 'Sirens' these words are revealed to refer to the appearance or actions of specific characters, or sounds heard in the

Ormond Bar. They are then endowed with a function additional to their standard denotations and connotations. They begin, similar to a musical leitmotif, to signify the return of a particular character, setting or point in time previously narrated. A leitmotif is generally understood as a short, recurrent musical phrase that has a representational function, and in this sense the opening words and phrases of Joyce's chapter work like leitmotifs. According to Barry Millington, a leitmotif's 'purpose is to represent or symbolize a person, object, place, idea, state of mind, supernatural force, or any other ingredient in a dramatic work'.[46] There is often more than one set of thematic or leitmotif-like material associated with each character. At the opening of the chapter the meaning of the initially nonsensical phrase 'Trilling, trilling: Idolores' (U 11.9) is eventually revealed to be Miss Douce's singing: 'Gaily Miss Douce polished a tumbler, trilling: – O, Idolores, queen of the eastern seas!' (U 11.225–6), so that variations on this phrase, as well as the word 'bronze', indicate Miss Douce's presence in the narrative.

Joyce's use of repeated words encourages the recollection of a moment in the narrative, as well as a character. The thematic words indicate a return to a point in time already narrated, and usually coincide with the narration of that moment from another character's perspective. For example, the reference to Miss Douce and Miss Kennedy hearing hooves on the road outside appears three times. This does not signify three separate occasions when they hear horses go past the Ormond Bar, but announces the return of the narrative to that specific point in time. The phrase is modified each time it appears, first of all in the opening thematic material – 'Bronze by gold heard the hoofirons, steelyringing' (U 11.1) – and then later on towards the end of the chapter: 'Bronze by a weary gold, anear, afar, they listened' (U 11.937). While similar to a musical leitmotif in some senses, in most cases in 'Sirens' the recurring words do not have the structural and psychological significance of the leitmotif, and are more akin to the reminiscence motif (*Reminiszenzmotiv*, *Erinnerungsmotiv*) – an earlier precursor signifying a character's recollection of the past. David Fanning explains that 'When earlier composers, such as Méhul, Cherubini, Marschner and Spohr, used motifs with character or situation associations but without Wagner's degree of thoroughness, those motifs have become generally known as "Erinnerungsmotive" – reminiscence motifs'.[47] In Wagner's later compositions, the leitmotif is intended to fully encompass an idea or concept in a musical phrase in a way that is exceptionally stimulating to the emotions, since the musical phrase has a particular connection to the concept it signifies.[48] Raymond Furness explains it as capable 'of compressing into a few bars the most profound emotional and psychological experience'.⁴⁹ This does not simply signify the return of a particular character, as the word 'bronze' signifies Miss Douce. While a reminiscence motif usually returns unaltered, the leitmotif returns in rhythmic or intervallic variations, so that Joyce's use of thematic words draws on features of the leitmotif and reminiscence motif.⁵⁰

The opening words and phrases come to signify characters and temporality, gaining this meaning through repetition in their particular context. This takes the prose closer to how meaning can be produced in music: through form and its own internal relations, rather than referentially. Adorno's discussions of music can help us consider how music creates meaning in greater critical detail than the scholarship on 'Sirens' so far discussed. Meaning can be inferred from music, but in music the meaning is contained within the form and its manner of implementation. What music communicates cannot be directly translated into language, but due to the repeated use of particular techniques and forms, over time traditions are produced to which it is possible to attach meaning. For Adorno:

> [Music] makes use of recurring symbols, insignia that bear the stamp of tonality ... But the identity of these musical concepts lies in their own existence and not in something to which they refer. Their invariance has become sedimented, a kind of second nature ... Music without any signification, the mere phenomenological coherence of the tones, would resemble an acoustical kaleidoscope. As absolute signification, on the other hand, it would cease to be music and pass, falsely, into language. Intentions are essential to it, but appear only intermittently. Music points to the true language as to a language in which the content itself is revealed, but for this it pays the price of unambiguousness, which has gone over to the signifying languages.⁵¹

Adorno points out that music functions differently from signifying, intentional language, which aims to be unambiguous. 'Sirens', however, is intentionally ambiguous to begin with, and the opening words only make sense later in the chapter. In this way, Joyce's use of language in 'Sirens' gets closer to the ambiguity of music, by producing meaning through its own formal structure, which is comparable with the internal, formal logic through which music creates meaning. In Western music, as Adorno identifies, this internal logic is 'tonality' – a longstanding musical system used among countless compositions. Unlike the sounds and their patterns of organisation that comprise Western tonality and its identifiable, recurring meanings, the words Joyce employs as thematic material do not have the same meanings outside 'Sirens', in the broader tradition of literature or language more generally. But they do derive meaning through form – through the manner of their arrangement and repetition, instead of purely through their linguistic denotations – which withstands comparison with music's formal production of meaning. Certain words in 'Sirens' are given additional, context-specific meanings in a manner that can be compared to how music produces meaning: through recurring words and patterns that must be interpreted via an engagement with the text in its own terms, not through external elements to which the words point.

'Sirens' requires careful reading to understand how the thematic material works throughout the text, promoting independent thought by simulating the ambiguity of a non-lexical form. The reader is recruited by this unusually demanding text as an active participant, to make sense of words for which the meaning is partially constructed in the text's own terms through its form. The function of these words is comparable to the way meanings can build up in a piece of music, but the words still refer to something outside themselves and have initial referential meanings, so that the way language functions is highlighted at the same time as those functions are stretched and challenged.

The significance that I have derived from considering the text as musical differs from the consequences noticed by critics so far. Zimmerman, for example, argues that the multiple layers of sound she identifies at work in 'Sirens' endow the chapter with a positive, implicitly democratic potential. In her formulation, 'Sirens' succeeds in emulating the simultaneity of music, which is 'closer to the reality' of everyday life:

> However, with the *fuga per canonem* structure, the reader can also experience the counterpoint shared by the characters. No one develops independently of the others because their actions and thoughts are interconnected by verbal simultaneity. And, perhaps, this is closer to the reality of the ways we live – we develop not in a vacuum, but in counterpoint with our surroundings, building life's narrative in each moment.[52]

In this reading, music's formation out of several separate parts (or lines, or voices) apes the social world, which also comprises multiple narratives and voices. Even this interpretation, though, can be considered idealistic. Multiple voices are not necessarily or exclusively evidence of something positive: to identify multiple voices does not account for what those voices might be saying, or the different volume, length, value or status of the utterances. Further, the use of music does not produce an unquestionably democratic text, since not everyone shares the ability to notice that this is what the chapter is doing, or to analyse it in a way that realises this democratic potential. The reference to counterpoint and the resulting connotations of harmony elide the conflict that is part of daily existence and which is demonstrated at the opening of the chapter, where words are divorced violently from their established context (*U* 11.1–63), so that they are initially conspicuously nonsensical, and afterwards new meanings are enforced upon the initial thematic words and phrases by the form of the chapter. This is not the kind of activity we might associate with a democratic plurality of voices.

The attempted fusion of musical and literary form – and the related critical discussions – reveals problems of interpretation and comparison that have much wider implications for criticism in general. Categories such as 'music' and 'literature' allow us to police boundaries and distinctions between phenomena in the world. Jacques Rancière argues that the construction of aesthetic categories is part of a political process that impacts thought and action: since an individual must have a role in society, forms of activity and the time and space in which they happen are differentiated and the boundaries between them are monitored, and this is the case for artistic work as well as monetised labour. Rancière calls this the 'distribution of the sensible', meaning the distribution of sense experience, so that 'there is thus an "aesthetics" at the core of politics' because 'politics revolves around what is seen and what can be said about it'.[53] Rancière is right to say that the policing of aesthetic categories contributes to the organisation of daily life, and affects other methods of policing activities to ensure productive citizens. As such, I do not wish to suggest that the distinctions between art forms ought to be policed or that comparisons between art forms are fundamentally problematic. Rather, I mean that these similarities and differences between music and literature are often expressed in ways that serve political purposes, but are articulated by literary critics through vague metaphors that do not stand up to intensive scrutiny. The similarities between spoken language, narrative and musical 'voice' can be strongly sustained by the language that is chosen, in terming the musical element to which we refer a 'voice' rather than a 'line' of music. Arguments sustained through stylistic use of language, or careful but non-interrogative use of particular words like 'voice', have been used to make connections that serve no purpose other than supporting claims about authorial intention. The equation of 'voice' in music and literature is utilised to support Joyce's claim that he uses fugal form to evoke multiple simultaneous 'voices', for example, and this has obstructed other ways of reading the text.

'Sirens' through Wagner

The way 'Sirens' engages with music is more complex than discussions of simultaneity allow for. Joyce refers to music specifically in 'Sirens' because he is communicating a complexity of mental function not yet put into words – not just engaging in intellectual point scoring and showing skill. Bucknell hints at this when he notes that:

> The linguistic practices of ['Sirens'] do require attention in terms of formal literary analysis; perhaps they even require *rational* explanation. But there is also no doubt that they point to an irrationality at the heart of musical experience, especially – and this is crucial – as this applies to the social context of hearing and interpreting: the social, the rational, the irrational, and the formal – musical or literary – cannot be separated here, nor one examined to the exclusion of the other.[54]

Bucknell makes several claims here: that the complexity of 'Sirens' beseeches attention to form; that this has resulted in attempts to explain it with rational ordering systems; but that 'Sirens' seems to ask for more than this because it also encourages us to be aware of the emotional complexity of music, and the way that responses to music can be immediate, bypassing rational thought. Bucknell concludes this potentially fascinating observation by saying that all of these things are in the mix. Bucknell's suggestion can be developed by attending to a claim Joyce made about 'Sirens' and Wagner, who theorised what music's emotive power could achieve when joined with words in opera.

Joyce reportedly asked a friend, 'Don't you find the musical effects of my *Sirens* better than Wagner?'[55] Wagner's ideas about music's communicative potential can help us to explore what is at stake in Joyce's claim. Wagner, like Schopenhauer, was convinced about music's unique capacity to represent (or arguably, just present, since music is an instance of the thing-in-itself for Schopenhauer) essential truths and human emotion. For Wagner, music was 'affect of the Will' which means 'we understand without any mediation by concepts what the shout for help, the cry of complaint, or the shout of joy says'.[56] Especially after he read Schopenhauer in 1854, Wagner attempted to represent the complexity of human psychology through leitmotifs.[57] Joyce's use of language can be read as a comparable attempt to communicate emotions and psychological complexity.

It is well known that Joyce's stream-of-consciousness technique was derived, indirectly, from Wagner. The term 'stream-of-consciousness' was first used by May Sinclair in her review of Dorothy Richardson's first volume of *Pilgrimage*, and is broadly understood to refer to a prose style that flows from one idea to another like a stream, similar to the way thoughts arise in the mind.[58] Timothy Martin identified a chain of influence whereby Wagner's impact on Eduard Dujardin contributed to Joyce's stylistic choices:

> Joyce did not make the personal acquaintance of Dujardin until shortly after he came to Paris in 1920. But he had bought *Les Lauriers sont coupés* at a

railway kiosk in 1903, and, after *Ulysses* had made the 'interior monologue' famous, he was always careful to credit Dujardin's book as its inspiration. Dujardin, it turns out, got the idea from Wagner's 'infinite melody'.[59]

Martin reminds us that Dujardin was a Wagner enthusiast who founded and edited the *Revue wagnérienne* in Paris.[60] He took from Wagner's infinite melody the idea of a continuous, flowing prose suitable for communicating the meanderings of the human mind. Wagner's influence, as I explain elsewhere, extends into Virginia Woolf's writing, who was in turn inspired by Joyce's focus on internal thoughts and issues of the spirit, rather than the external, material world.[61] Further explication of what is at stake in Wagner's 'infinite melody' and the leitmotif can help to deepen our understanding of the effect achieved by Joyce's leitmotif-like words and phrases. When explaining his 'infinite melody', Wagner writes that successful art is dependent upon not only what is included, but also what is left out:

> In truth, the measure of a poet's greatness is that which he does not say in order to let what is inexpressible silently speak to us for itself. It is in the musician who brings this great Unsaid to sounding life, and the unmistakable form of his resounding silence is infinite melody [*unendliche Melodie*].[62]

Wagner is interested in representing things that are 'Unsaid' – indeed, things that cannot be said. The 'infinite melody' on which it is claimed Joyce and Woolf drew is connected to Wagner's desire to express the inexpressible. Wagner shared something with modernist writers who wanted to investigate and represent the mind and emotions as they are felt, rather than linguistically expressed or rationalised. For Jeri Johnson, 'stream-of-consciousness' is a term suitable for describing both *Ulysses* and Woolf's *Mrs Dalloway*, because the term is not directly related to a specific narrative style, but is 'descriptive only of fictions which share a preoccupation with representing character through pre-verbal or unspoken "thoughts"'.[63]

Johnson's reference to 'pre-verbal' thoughts brings to mind the Freudian concepts of pre-conscious and repressed thoughts. Freud's considerable impact on modern culture and literature means that issues of consciousness and language are often filtered through his ideas. Richardson points out the established connection between Freudian ideas about consciousness and 'stream-of-consciousness' writing when she claims that *Pilgrimage* was accused of 'post-War Freudianity'.[64] Following Freud, the difference between interior monologue and stream-of-consciousness is usually couched in terms of the difference between the expression of the conscious mind (thoughts to which an individual has access) and the pre-conscious (that which is not immediately available to the conscious mind) or unconscious (the repressed) – to use the terms from Freud's first topography.⁶⁵ Stream-of-consciousness as the term is used today, then, has developed out of a Freudian conceptualisation of consciousness, and is useful to describe literary attempts to communicate things of which characters are not fully conscious, such as the way that past experiences, repressed thoughts or partially forgotten memories return to affect the present.

The representation of psychological complexity sought by stream-of-consciousness narratives is attempted in 'Sirens' by using language in a similar way to a leitmotif. The reasons why Wagner developed the leitmotif, which are connected to his ideas how music creates meaning, can illuminate Joyce's use of thematic material, which shows us matters that are affecting Bloom's thought, but about which Bloom is not fully conscious. Andrew Bowie explains how Wagner conceptualises musical meaning, writing that:

> music conveys its own kind of thought, because what is signified by the melody is not just an object which is referred to but also an affective relationship to whatever is at issue in the object, which depends on the object's relations to other aspects of the world in which it occurs.⁶⁶

In music, then, remembering the original instance of a melody and connecting it with past situations when that meaning arose helps to produce and develop its meaning. Music is able to have these affective meanings because people make connections based on context and memory. For Matthew Bribitzer-Stull, this conceptualisation of musical meaning informed Wagner's development of the leitmotif as he used it in his *Gesamtkunstwerk*: as part of his attempt to create a fully immersive aesthetic experience that could contribute to the audience's moral, spiritual and intellectual education. Bribitzer-Stull describes the leitmotif as 'developmental associative themes that comprise an integral part of the surrounding musical context'.⁶⁷ Rather than just a 'musical idea' (or 'leading musical ideas', as the term *leitmotif* might suggest) and the smallest component of a complete musical piece, the Wagnerian leitmotif is a significant idea in itself, and integral to the meaning of the musical piece. Bribitzer-Stull writes that the leitmotif has an 'evolving associative capacity': 'with each re-statement of a theme there exists the possibility that added perspective will colour the emotional associations we have with it, much like the experience of revisiting childhood haunts as an adult'.⁶⁸ The leitmotif, then, is intimately connected to issues of an individual's sensory response to sounds and sights, and is reliant on memory and context for its meaning. Wagner comes to use the leitmotif as the musical expression of a particular idea that is capable of an overwhelming mental and emotional effect. As Heath Lees explains, it is intended to function as the 'musical embodiment of a suggested but often unexpressed idea'.[69]

It is as an unexpressed, repressed idea that Blazes Boylan's thematic material eventually appears in 'Sirens'. Variations on the words 'jingle' and 'jaunt' indicate his presence both real and imagined at different points in the chapter. Boylan's opening thematic phrase is 'Jingle jingle jaunted jingling' (*U* 11.15), and the material returns later in the chapter, when 'With patience Lenehan waited for Boylan with impatience, for jingle jaunty blazes boy' (*U* 11.289–90). The jingling and jaunting refers to him driving around in his car, from the Ormond Bar to meet Molly at four o'clock. Bloom contemplates following Boylan, but remains in the Ormond Bar: 'Jingling on supple rubbers it jaunted from the bridge to Ormond quay. Follow. Risk it. Go quick. At four. Near now. Out' (*U* 11.304–5).

While some of the words in 'Sirens' simply function to indicate a character, place or setting, Boylan's thematic material is far more psychologically significant. The words come to indicate Bloom's repressed but very significant knowledge that Boylan is Molly's lover. After this, Boylan's 'jingle' theme returns in a different way, slipping into Bloom's inner monologue:

> Bloom bent Leopold ear, turning a fringe of doyley down under the vase. Order. Yes, I remember. Lovely air. In sleep she went to him. Innocence in the moon. Still hold her back. Brave, don't know their danger. Call name. Touch water. *Jingle Jaunty*. Too late. She longed to go. That's why. (*U* 11.637–41, emphasis added).

The words represent the sounds of Boylan's keys and car, showing how Bloom's memory is reliant upon an affective experience of hearing the keys jingle. As with Wagner's conceptualisation of a repeated musical motif, the original context in which the sound arose has a psychological effect on Bloom, and it is through an indication of this affective experience of hearing a sound associated with him that 'Sirens' communicates Boylan's presence in Bloom's thoughts. The memory of Boylan's jingling and jaunting, and the knowledge of where he is going, is a passing thought that Bloom tries to suppress but cannot. The passage recounts Bloom's disjointed thoughts, combining his actions at the table with the doyley, his memories of Molly and the painful knowledge of her meeting with Boylan that he is attempting to ignore. Boylan's presence in Bloom's thoughts is indicated in a very oblique way, through the repetition of the thematic material.

'Sirens' is particularly concerned with attempts to express things that cannot be said: these are things of which Bloom is not fully conscious. The musically inspired form communicates a truth of which Bloom is not yet fully cognisant:

> – Twopence, sir, the shopgirl dared to say.
> – Aha . . . I was forgetting . . . Excuse . . .
> – And four.
> At four she. (*U* 11.306–9)

Bloom's awareness of Molly and Boylan's impending meeting is communicated not through Bloom dwelling on it, but through significant words and phrases. He finds particular significance in the 'shopgirl' saying 'twopence . . . and four' because of Molly's meeting with Boylan at four. Bloom stops short of making the connection, not naming his 'she' (Molly). The sentence abruptly ends, but we are able to see what Bloom is not prepared to admit to himself directly. We see this again when he asks 'Who said four?' (*U* 11.352) when nobody has said four.

The significance of how Joyce refers to music in this chapter can also be productively compared with the way Adorno formulates how music produces meaning:

> Music . . . is a temporal succession of articulated sounds that are more than just sound. They say something, often something human . . . But what is said cannot be abstracted from the music; it does not form a system of signs.[70]

For Adorno, music has a capacity for communicating 'something human'. In 'Sirens', referring to music allows us to see a particularly human truth that cannot be communicated through words. We need the musically inspired form to communicate Bloom's pre-conscious, because it can allow us to see these things that Bloom is not fully prepared to acknowledge. The complex form requires a level of absorption and concentration from the reader, too, and this detracts attention away from our social world and into the text. The form of 'Sirens' is much more complex than the 'democratic plurality' of voice and perspective that has been claimed for it.

'Sirens' and the Critique of Musical Transcendence

'Sirens' stages two separate arguments about music, contemplating its positive and negative potential. While there has been much debate about whether Joyce successfully used musical form or not, the rest of the music in the chapter, which critiques music's capacity to stimulate the emotions, has not received as much critical attention. Like the song of the Sirens in the *Odyssey* that is alluring but devastatingly dangerous, the music in the Ormond Bar promotes an anti-social and potentially damaging self-absorption.

In the *Odyssey*, Circe warns Odysseus that nobody who hears the song of the Sirens can survive:

> Your next encounter will be with the Sirens, who bewitch everybody who approaches them. There is no homecoming for the man who draws near them . . . For with their high clear song the Sirens bewitch him, as they sit there in a meadow piled high with the mouldering skeletons of men, whose withered skin still hangs upon their bones.[71]

The threat of death associated with the magical allure of the Sirens of the *Odyssey* is also present in Joyce's 'Sirens'. In the Ormond Bar music is equated with danger, war and violence when Ben Dollard plays the piano: 'Boomed crashing chords. When love absorbs. War! War! The tympanum' (*U* 11.20). At one moment, the musical instrument is placed in its social context as an appendage to violent rituals when Bloom imagines the 'Hunter with a horn' (*U* 11.1240),[72] while Ben Dollard's musical performance is an 'attack, booming over bombarding chords' (*U* 11.528–9). He leaves the keyboard 'punished' afterwards (*U* 11.473). When Ben Dollard plays, he becomes 'the warrior' (*U* 11.532) according to Father Cowley, and the sound he produces is an assault on the ears; a physical affect that those nearby are powerless to do anything about: '– Sure, you'd burst the tympanum of her ear, man, Mr Dedalus said through smoke aroma, with an organ like yours' (*U* 11.536–7). Due to his huge size, Ben Dollard's voice and pounding on the keyboard involve real violence that carries (at least anecdotally) the threat of physical injury.

Music is also associated with another form of danger – that of extreme introspection and solitary reflection, which is the basis of Kant's critique of music in *Critique of the Power of Judgement*. For Kant, music was afforded the 'lowest place' among the arts because it 'merely plays with the sensations': although music 'moves the mind in a greater variety of ways and more intensely' than other arts, it does so 'only transitorily'.[73] Despite Miss Douce and Miss Kennedy apparently taking the place of the Sirens, their singing is not the Sirens' song. In 'Sirens' music appeals to the mind, rather than the body: the men are physically attracted to the barmaids – they are the 'sweets of sin', '[t]empting poor simple males' (*U* 11.202) – but it is Simon Dedalus's singing that flows 'over skin limbs human heart soul spine' (*U* 11.669) signifying not only a physical allure but one of the mind and soul. Likewise, in Homer's text, the Sirens' appeal is also not to the flesh or to physical gratification, but to the mind and the spirit: they know 'all that the Argives and Trojans suffered on the broad plain of Troy by the will of the gods, and we know whatever happens on this fruitful earth'.[74] The magnetism of the Sirens in the *Odyssey* is the promise of unmediated personal knowledge that appeals to the mind, constituted in the form of a song: the form and content of the Sirens' song comprises the dangerous totality. Since the Sirens know everything that has happened in Odysseus's and his crew's past, according to Adorno and Horkheimer, 'their allurement is that of losing themselves in the past'. Homer's Sirens, they write, prompt 'euphoria in which the self is suspended' and this is rooted in the desire for self-preservation but produces self-destruction.[75]

In Joyce's corresponding chapter, Simon Dedalus's song allows the possibility of retreat into the inwardness of personal remembrance that elides the social by inhibiting people's ability and wish to engage with one another. Immediately as the song begins the threat of loss of self appears: '– A beautiful air, said Bloom lost Leopold. I know it well' (*U* 11.642). The familiarity of the song for Bloom, like the familiarity of the past for Odysseus and his crew, prompts the recollection of a history that has been integral to the construction of the present self, and thus requires protection at all costs. Yet the reverie about the past (self) removes the individual from the present, acting out the destruction of the self in the present and threatening the destruction of the self as a whole.

The Sirens' song in the *Odyssey* is dangerous because it has not yet been, in Adorno's words, 'rendered powerless by reduction to the condition of art'.[76] In Homer's *Odyssey*, the song of the Sirens is 'divine': it is a form of absolute beauty and knowledge, rather than an imitation.[77] It is not a representation, but beauty and truth so undiluted and irresistible that listeners cannot bear to extract themselves from it once they have heard it. The reduction of music to the condition of art has taken place in *Ulysses*, making it less dangerous, although still able to produce a problematic emotional response that prohibits engagement with others. Bloom takes the place of Odysseus, but he does not need to tie himself to the mast: he gestures to Pat, the waiter (who is deaf and so does not require his ears to be stopped with wax like Odysseus's crew), to open the door. Pat replaces the sailors, who do the labour at Odysseus's bidding to enable him to hear the music. The door is a physical construction allowing or preventing movement like the mast that facilitates the sails. Odysseus uses the mast as a restrictive apparatus, while Bloom uses the door not to stop the music, but to let it in:

> Braintipped, cheek touched with flame, they listened feeling that flow endearing flow over skin limbs human heart soul spine. Bloom signed to Pat, bald

> Pat is a waiter hard of hearing, to set ajar the door of the bar. The door of the bar. So. That will do. Pat, waiter, waited, waiting to hear, for he was hard of hear by the door. (*U* 11.668–72)

With the door propped open, Bloom is susceptible to the inwardness and loss of self provoked by the music during its performance. His reminiscences about Molly culminate in a verbal description of emotional-physical surge or tumescence that corresponds with the musical crescendo: 'Tenderness it welled: slow, swelling. Full it throbbed. That's the chat. Ha, give! Take! Throb, a throb, a pulsing proud erect' (*U* 11.701–2). His mind and his body are entirely at the whim of the music, to which Bloom's emotional response is erotic and intimately personal, and excludes others. He takes no action in the Ormond Bar, sitting apart from Simon Dedalus and Ben Dollard, entirely consumed by his own thoughts. He takes no action in relation to Molly's impending meeting with her lover Boylan, either. Music performs a less deadly diversion than in the *Odyssey*, but it still encourages Bloom's retreat from action as he sinks into sentimental thought.

Stuart Allen argues that Bloom is uniquely capable of avoiding the dangerous emotional pull of music, while others in the Ormond Bar are transfixed by its spell. In Allen's reading, Bloom alone notices music's artifice and responds to it when he postulates, 'Words? Music? No: it's what's behind' (*U* 11.703). Allen claims that 'Bloom peers beyond the inward results of the affects of music (and poetic language) to the *original source of sensuality* – the material world and the people in it'.[78] He suggests that Bloom can access the physical world independently of the mediation of language, implying access to some kind of reality for which language and music are merely a veil: 'Bloom recognizes the bullying artifice, the commandment, that passes for natural and feeling relations'.[79] Herman also makes grand claims for Bloom's abilities, arguing that his musings about 'what's behind' words and music constitute 'an antiprogrammatic, even Pythagorean view of music. He absolutizes musical structures and deemphasizes the particular phonic substance in which those structures might be realized'.[80] Herman's reading constructs Bloom as the quotidian hero, uniquely able to resist the 'bullying artifice' of songs that inspire emotion.

Yet Bloom rather puzzles over the effect of music, rather than peering past its power. His response to the music is mixed and he adjusts it as he thinks it through:

> Numbers it is. All music when you come to think. Two multiplied by two divided by half is twice one. Vibrations: chords those are. One plus two plus six is seven. Do anything you like with figures juggling. Always find out this

equal to that. Symmetry under a cemetery wall. He doesn't see my wall. He doesn't see my mourning, Callous: all for his own gut. Musemathematics. And you think you're listening to the ethereal. But suppose you said it like: Martha, seven times nine minus x is thirtyfive thousand. Fall quite flat. It's on account of the sound it is.

Instance he's playing now. Improvising. Might be what you like til you hear the words [. . .] Time makes the tune. Question of mood you're in. Always nice to hear. (*U* 11.830–42)

Bloom recognises that music has mathematical underpinnings, but goes on to consider the problems of music-as-mathematics: music is made of 'sound it is', whereas maths is not. He wants to disarm music of its power, because you only '*think* you're listening to the ethereal', but his mathematical explanation is ultimately insufficient. It gets caught up in ideas about death and mourning: Bloom identifies the limitations of explaining what is in a cemetery through ideas like symmetry because the rational and the ordered cannot explain grief, nor death, nor music's ability to soothe or recall those emotions. Bloom attempts to, but does not succeed in, de-mythifying music: it may be partially 'numbers' yet this thought is not sufficient to explain music's allure – it is still 'Always nice to hear'. While Allen's and Herman's analyses want to see Bloom as uniquely able to extract himself from the dangers of music's artificially constructed inwardness, really Bloom is just as susceptible to the emotional impact of music, as his tumescent and reflective emotional response to it reveals.

The desire to see Bloom as contemplative and scholarly is another way that reverence for Joyce manifests itself in (and clouds) critical discussion. When Bloom thinks about mathematics and acoustics he doesn't follow his thoughts through to any conclusions, stopping when he muddles and confuses himself. Leo Bersani has noted this tendency to read for positive moral affirmations, either of Joyce or of Bloom, in Joyce studies. He argues that critics make contradictory claims about *Ulysses*: that it contains 'pure linguistic effects' and reaches towards a 'type of psychological and moral appreciation made obsolete by the New Criticism of half a century ago'. This moral appreciation also underpins readings of 'Cyclops' that attempt to claim a specific political position for Joyce and/or Bloom, exemplifying what Bersani terms 'the paranoid response to what might be called the irreducibility of voice in literature to locations and identities'. The desire to read Joyce positively and to find affirmative statements in writing that is 'perspectivally shifty' (to use Bersani's phrase) has also resulted in limited engagement with the complexity of the presentation of music in 'Sirens'.[81] Judging the 'success' of the chapter only by the extent to which it fuses musical and literary form assumes a positive potential in music that is only one aspect of how music is represented. Often, the purpose of readings that seek to evidence Joyce's claims about the musicality of the chapter are not immediately obvious, because the aim is simply to prove Joyce's assertions about the musicality of 'Sirens' to be true. The desire to read Bloom positively also elides appreciation of the limitations of his engagement with music.

How, then, can comparing music and literature be productive? By 'productive' I mean whether analysing music and literature together can produce a new reading that is contingent upon the knowledge arrived at through the interpretation of music, or by analysis of the differences and similarities that are illuminated when music and literature are read together. In addition, how can reading literature with music affect the way we interpret the political content of the text? This is particularly important for an analysis of 'Cyclops', which contains some of the most expressly political dialogue in the novel.

'Cyclops'

Dissonance, conflict and departure from established aesthetics are recognised as central to artistic responses to modernity. But forms such as the fugue and the sonata contain none of these characteristics. Joyce's *Ulysses* ought to be considered with the 'new music' that was being composed in the early twentieth century, which also rejected established artistic forms in favour of forms that embrace dissonance. Schoenberg's compositional techniques and *Ulysses* reject functional harmony and traditional narrative structures respectively, replacing them with highly organised, dissonant forms. Joyce's 'Cyclops' and Schoenberg's twelve-tone row employ fragmentation techniques to resist resolution and unity. Schoenberg achieves this by avoiding functional harmony, which is characterised by the dominant-tonic relationship, while *Ulysses* achieves this at the level of its narrative style, which changes from chapter to chapter, but also within the 'Cyclops' chapter itself, resisting forms of storytelling that have a consistent narrative voice.

'Cyclops' moves constantly between different styles of narration: John Nash has identified 'thirty-three parodies' in the chapter that 'parody general literary or newspaper styles'.[82] The different sections are of indeterminate length and can only be identified by the altering narrative styles: they are not separated in the text beyond the usual use of paragraph indentations. By moving through these thirty-three parodies, there is a systematic and considered erosion of any dominant narrative voice. This can be illuminated by comparing and contrasting it with the social conditions that Adorno argues are reflected in the formal structure of Schoenberg's twelve-tone row. Building on Nash's claim that 'it is by reading the form that the problem of voice can be answered',[83] I argue that a renewed focus on form is useful for reading 'Cyclops' because it enables us to read the political content differently, although I do not claim to provide a final reading or an 'answer' to the problem posed by the 'perspectival shiftiness' or ambiguity of the text.

'Sirens' (although not 'Cyclops') has previously been compared to Schoenberg's music and twelve-tone compositional technique. The Italian serialist composer Luigi Dallapiccola discussed Joyce's influence on his own compositional style, and Herman argues that both Schoenberg's compositions and 'Sirens' are best understood as concerned with the relation between 'structures of elements, on the one hand, and rules or principles for ordering' on the other.[84] These writers focus on patterns and structures within the text. Instead, I want to discuss 'Sirens' and Schoenberg's compositions in their broader social context.

There is some evidence that Joyce took an interest in avant-garde music whilst in Paris and Zurich, and that he was aware of Schoenberg's compositions. Jack W. Weaver cites Otto Luening as recalling Joyce stating: 'For me there are only two composers. One is Palestrina and the other is Schoenberg'.[85] Weaver notes that Joyce attended the premiere of Georges Antheil's 'Ballet Mécanique' in Paris, and claims that by the time Joyce had finished writing *Ulysses* he greatly admired Schoenberg's 'experimental atonal music'.[86] While it is useful to know Joyce was aware of Schoenberg, I do not claim that he intentionally appropriated or was influenced by the composer's musical style. Schoenberg announced in a letter to the composer Joseph Matthias Hauer, dated 1 December 1923, that his method of 'twelve-note composition' is 'now more precise than it has ever been', although '[a]dmittedly I have not yet taught this method'.[87] Since the twelve-tone method was not made public until 1923, Joyce's text could not have been modelled on the technique. Rather, Joyce and Schoenberg can be compared using Adorno's texts and his version of Frankfurt School Marxism, whereby composition and any artistic endeavour is considered to be intricately bound up with historical subjectivity, so that an Adornian reading would see comparable structural elements in their work as the formal registration of the social conditions in Western Europe during the First World War, when their work was produced.

Both Joyce and Schoenberg produced work that expresses dissonance not only through structure, but also by referencing and departing from classical art forms. *Ulysses* references the classical epic the *Odyssey* in its name, the titles of its chapters and their structures, but diverges from it in narrative form, setting and subject matter.[88] While the *Odyssey* is an epic of homecoming and years of grand adventures, the narrative of *Ulysses* is about one day in Dublin, ending with a homeless Stephen Dedalus and without the promise of stronger social relationships. The novel both calls up the *Odyssey* and distances itself from it, the result being the juxtaposition of the old form and the new. Similarly, Schoenberg's twelve-tone row expresses dissonance at the level of form in a radical departure from functional harmony. The music works referentially with the classical music it eschews: its stark difference due to its atonality can be identified only in relation to the functional harmony it departs from. Joyce's and Schoenberg's fiction and music are radical because there is a previous, historically established precedent for linear narratives and tonal music.

It is specifically in the form of Joyce's and Schoenberg's work that the rejection of previously used modes of expression can be found. For Adorno and Horkheimer, artistic responses cannot consciously resist systems of domination, but can only do so through their formal structure. A rejection of established forms is broadly considered to respond to the social conditions of modernity, which has rendered traditional modes of expression insufficient for communicating the true condition of the individual in society. According to Adorno and Horkheimer, economic and industrial modernity has produced an alienated subject: the increasing efficiency of modes of production results in the division of labour which both alienates the individual from the object produced and allows more standardised, efficient production.[89] The continuing success of society's domination over itself is dependent on the imperceptibility of its systems of control to the individual: 'concentration and control in our culture hide themselves in their very manifestation. Unhidden they would provoke resistance. Therefore the illusion . . . must be maintained'.[90]

Adorno's rejection of synthesis can be seen in the aphorism 'the whole is the false' – an inversion of Hegel's dictum 'the whole is the true'.[91] Adorno challenges Hegel, who considered the arrival at truth possible through the synthesis of the whole. Hegel's truth is the Absolute, or universal totality, which he argues can only be arrived at through engagement with negative and positive concepts in a developmental process:

> only this self-restoring sameness, or this reflection in otherness within itself – not an original or immediate unity as such – is the True. It is the process of its own becoming, the circle that presupposes its end as its goal, having its end also as its beginning; and only by being worked out to its end, is it actual.[92]

Adorno, on the other hand, rejects synthesis entirely and shows an active interest in difference and fragmentation. His aphorism asserts that there is no such thing as a complete truth, history or discipline. The totalitarian nature of the systems of material and cultural production profess a wholeness and unity that is rather a veil for reality – something that is opposed by the assertion that wholeness is false, and by the nature of aphoristic thinking. Conceptual wholeness is further opposed in *Minima Moralia* by the 'disconnected and non-binding character of the form'.[93] Sara Haslam, who sees fragmentation recurring in the literature of modernism and the historical discourses of the early twentieth century, has comprehensively noted the absence of wholeness and unity from modernist texts: 'Where modernism is credited with a pattern, and it usually is', she writes, 'it is more than likely that the concept of fragmentation is prominent in it'.[94]

The 'truth-content' of an artwork, for Adorno, lies in its ability to reveal at the unconscious level of form the dissonance and fragmentation that remains hidden but is the true condition of society.[95] Since society has been atomised through the micro-division of labour, and the meaningful interactions surrounding the production of the necessary staples of life have been removed, the individual exists in a relatively new state of isolation. The use of the word 'isolation' is slightly different from the previous term 'alienation' (*Entfremdung*). While the term 'alienation' is heavily indebted to Marx's use of the term, the words 'isolation' (*Isolierung*) and 'loneliness' are used to describe the conditions that the fragmentation of society, through the alienation of the subject, has produced. Adorno refers to a 'formula of loneliness' (*die Formel des Stils der Einsamkeit*) that is present in the music of Schoenberg.[96] For Adorno, the only art that has truth-value is that which internalises the fractured nature of the social fabric, reproducing and reflecting it through the work of art, which displays at the level of its form similar dislocation, fragmentariness and mutilation. These formal devices are the tools by which the opacity of modernity's reality is exposed, and the result of the exposure is fragmentation that can be perceived as disordered or chaotic, but is nonetheless controlled at the level of form through ordered structures. Modern music, he says 'sees absolute oblivion as its goal. It is the surviving message of despair from the shipwrecked'.[97] These highly structured forms betray nostalgia for a pre-modern transparency that only reinforces the extent of separation from it.

For Adorno, composition and any artistic endeavour is intricately bound up with historical subjectivity. Composers write in direct relation to both their experience of contemporary society and the compositional language that had been built up historically before them. Twelve-tone compositional technique is a response to functional harmony, not a complete negation of music. It has a relationship with tradition, but becomes restricted by its own form and internal relations. Schoenberg inherited a musical language of tonality, tempered tuning and particular precedents of harmonic progression, such as modulations through the circle of fifths, or to the relative minor. These principles, Adorno says, 'inscribe the (hi)story of subjectivity. They are the congealed residues of past subjectivity', in the sense that these forms of artistic expression convey the state of an individual's existence in the time they were written.[98] The result is that the existing music and historical precedent that a composer works with is 'the critically reflected objective state of the technical productive forces of an age in which any given composer is inevitably confronted'.[99] The rise of dissonance in the music of the early twentieth century, like the comparable shift away from narrative traditions in *Ulysses*, shows that certain composers no longer felt traditional tonal approaches to music sufficient to express contemporary subjectivity.

The twelve-tone technique was developed by Schoenberg as a way of tightly structuring music to ensure total escape from any suggestion of functional harmony, and the meanings or 'intentions' that had become inscribed within it. It uses a then-new method of extreme organisation to obliterate traditional harmonic relationships. Functional harmony is characterised by the dominant-tonic relationship and is audible in particular cadences used in classical music. Even in atonal music, it would be possible to hear vestiges of this if a certain note were audibly dominant. This would mirror a piece of tonal music as a dominant note could be audibly perceived as the tonic. If a dominant note or chord can be heard, cadential relationships may be audible in the music, lending it the (even fleeting) appearance of tonality. The organisation of the notes into a row of twelve tones allowed Schoenberg to ensure that none was repeated more times than any other, so that no note would appear dominant. Adorno explains this in the following terms:

> That the row uses no more than twelve tones is a result of the endeavour to give none of the notes, by means of greater frequency, any emphasis which might render it a 'fundamental tone' and thereby evoke tonal relationships ... With every new pitch the choice of remaining pitches diminishes, and when the last one is reached there is no longer any choice at all. The force exerted by the process is unmistakeable.[100]

The aim was to eliminate hierarchical tonal relationships. With the dominance of any note avoided through the rigid structure of the twelve-tone system, any attempt to navigate the music through traditional chord relationships, cadences or modulations is impossible.

Figure 2.1   Arnold Schoenberg, *Wind Quintet Op. 26* (1923–4).

Schoenberg's system ensures the absence of tonal relationships and chord progressions associated with functional harmony. Serialism thus avoids the totality that a piece of tonal music has by virtue of it beginning and ending on the tonic note, and the music also resists progression in the ordinary sense, since harmonic relationships, chord sequences and modulations do not occur, and it is these that give the sense of traditional development, or moving through time. Adorno did also note some problems with twelve-tone technique: it subjects the composer and musical material to strict governing rules that are just as limiting as the functional harmony from which it seeks to escape, so that for Adorno the technique was not an improvement on free atonality. Additionally, 'the row, valid for one work only, does not possess the comprehensive universality that would, on the basis of schema, assign a function to the repeated event, which as a reiterated individual phenomenon it does not have'.[101] In other words, the row creates works that are rigidly structured and characterised by repetition, and which are ultimately isolated.

In the extract from Schoenberg's score above, the numbers of the twelve-tone row have been added to the score so that it is possible to see how the construction of the row avoids traditional harmonic relationships.[102] In the top line of the music (the flute part) the first interval between notes one and two is a minor sixth. With the absence of an interval of a fifth, this is instead an interval through which it is not possible to discern a tonic or dominant relationship. Both notes, G natural and E flat, could be found in the scale of E flat major. However, any possible relation to this key is immediately dispelled by note three of the row (A natural), which is not present in the E flat major scale. This is in fact a sharpened fourth, the key accidental in the Lydian mode, noted for its mystical sound which blurs the sense of major-minor tonality. The notes in the row are carefully arranged in such a way as to avoid intervals (particularly the fifth and major or minor third) that would imply tonic-dominant relationships that form the basis for functional harmony.

Joyce's 'Cyclops' similarly resists traditional methods of textual navigation by moving through different styles of narration. 'Cyclops' is a series of parodies that systematically eradicates continuity in the narrative, and the reliability of the narrator is continuously undermined as the chapter appropriates different voices and parodies different styles of discourse. An unidentified narrator begins 'Cyclops', saying, 'I was just passing the time of day with the old Troy of the D.M.P. at the corner of Arbour hill there and be damned but a bloody sweep came along and he near drove his gear into my eye' (U 12.1–3). The first-person narrator recounts events in which they participate but is never officially identified, and the narrative switches without explanation from a conversation with 'Joe Hynes' (U 12.5) to detailing a list of 'nonperishable goods' and the rules of their purchase (U 12.33), before changing style once more to a monologue of pastoral pastiche, beginning with a reference to the poem 'Prince Alfrid's Itinerary through Ireland', translated by James Clarence Mangan: 'In Inisfail the fair there lies a land' (U 12.68).[103] After moving back into dialogue between the anonymous narrator, an unidentified 'he' and the citizen, the narrative launches into a long list of the names of 'Irish heroes and heroines of antiquity' (U 12.176).

The alterations in the narrative that fluctuate between dialogue and hyperbolic description mean it is not possible to perceive events or conversations as a series of events happening in real time in a specified location. The conversation between the characters, from whom the reader is alienated because there is no indication of who they are, is regularly suspended and punctuated by narrative changes in tone, subject matter and apparent location, causing a disruption in the reading experience that prohibits a clear sense of moving through linear time. Changes in tone are continuous, from the banal observations of daily life such as 'I was just passing the time of day', to hyperbole of a magical and mythical scale in the description of 'widewinged nostrils . . . of such capaciousness that within their cavernous obscurity the fieldlark might easily have lodged her nest' (U 12.159–61). These changes in tone make it difficult to navigate the chapter in terms of voice, space and direction; the narrative shifts from the streets of Dublin to rural Ireland, from Barney Kiernen's Tavern to a mythical land. Any degree of reliability in the narrative is weakened further by the descriptive passages, which often reproduce the same events previously explained by the anonymous narrator in a way that contradicts the previous account. These continuous twists and turns in the structure of the chapter perform an assault on conventional senses of time and place, since the banal and the mythical, as well as different versions of events, exist in the same narrative space.

By moving through these different narrative styles and parodies there is a systematic and considered erosion of any central or dominant narrative voice or linear narrative trajectory, and the force exerted by the process is as unmistakable as the eradication of tonal centre achieved by Schoenberg's twelve-tone row. Both Joyce and Schoenberg use tightly ordered structures to methodically destroy a sense of key, centre or dominant. The listener's or reader's attempt to map that which they are experiencing, via the tools used to understand the language of diatonic music and linear narrative respectively, is made impossible by the fragmentation techniques that divorce parts of the composition from each other, resisting traditional senses of narrative or harmonic progression.

Despite this, critics have tried to resolve the tensions in 'Cyclops', which features a political disagreement between Bloom and the citizen. Nash has connected this with the difficulties posed by the form of the chapter, saying that 'one of the principal problems facing the reader of *Ulysses* lies in identifying the relative authority of the different narrative positions'.[104] The 'winner' of the argument and overall meaning of the chapter has been much debated because there is no clear victor, which is in keeping with the discontinuity and disconnect in the narrative. Yet critics have been keen to decide who is dominant in the debate between Bloom and the citizen. The initial tendency has been to affiliate Joyce's own position with Bloom's liberal humanism, and therefore to declare Bloom the dominant voice in the chapter. For Philip Herring, 'Joyce abhorred the "Citizen's" political stance and recognized the nobility of the liberal humanitarian sentiments in Bloom'. Yet Herring also qualifies his position, noting that because of 'Joyce's use of exaggeration ("gigantism" is the technique here) and irony ... it is impossible in this episode to take anything seriously'.[105] Vincent J. Cheng describes Bloom as being able to step outside the narrow view of his 'xenophobic fellow Irishmen', resulting in an oversimplification which assigns Bloom a dominant, liberal humanist voice and the citizen racism and xenophobia.[106] Emer Nolan has moved away from the default position of finding ways to prioritise Bloom's position, arguing that his liberal voice is not in fact dominant. He asserts that 'the language of the individuals who constitute its primary focus are implicated in a practice of verbal or symbolic violence'.[107] However, as John Nash has noted, this argument merely assigns the dominant voice to another individual, 'placing greater authority and credibility in the [voice] of the citizen'.[108] Despite many critics giving prominence to Bloom's tolerant humanism (as they see it), the unidentified narrator mocks his sentimentality, sarcastically cutting in with 'Love loves to love love' (*U* 12.1493) after Bloom's assertion that 'love' will solve the problems (serious problems, such as imperial violence and corporal punishment) they are discussing.

Ulysses and Schoenberg's twelve-tone compositions convey dissonance through formal devices that exile their writing from traditional modes of narrative or tonality. These in turn exile the receiver, as the experience of communication between medium and reader or listener is strained. The constantly shifting narrative of *Ulysses* elides a passive reading, requiring active interpretation. That so much is required of the reader works against an increasingly industrial society in which products are standardised and the consumer response is presupposed. The exile from traditional forms of narrative, by which the reader enters a foreign space, is what gives the novel comparable truth-value to that which is present in Schoenberg's atonal music. As David Clarke has noted, Schoenberg's music 'denies its bourgeois consumers illusory solace from reality',[109] and the effect of the music for Adorno is that 'when confronted with utterly unleashed sound that defies the net of organised culture, such culture is revealed as fraud'.[110] Joyce, meanwhile, unleashes a variety of voices in 'Cyclops', using a fragmented narrative comprised of dissonant styles and views to reveal the artificiality of the way more limited narrative perspectives represent the world and discourses.

Reading 'Cyclops' with music allows us to avoid the binaries that have been constructed by critics through a renewed attention to form. Parts of 'Cyclops' demonstrate a back and forth between the competing politics of the citizen and Bloom, but in the form of the chapter and its narrative styles there are no direct opposites, only perpetual change. Yet critics responding to 'Cyclops' (and 'Sirens' too) have sought to organise and explain through established frameworks of classical musical forms or radical versus reactionary politics. Joyce, according to Bersani, has become 'one of the darlings of that branch of narratology obsessed with origins, with determining where narrators are located, over whose shoulder they may be speaking, from what temporal perspective and from whose voice they address us'.[111] Critics often read the texts with ordering methodologies: replacing the scaffolding of Homeric myth with fugal form in 'Sirens', or trying to find evidence of the endorsement of one side of a binary politics displayed in 'Cyclops'.

Exile and loneliness are treated as structural laws in *Ulysses*. Removing the traditional means of textual navigation and understanding of the narrative, *Ulysses* places the reader in a position of loneliness that is the true experience of contemporary subjectivity. The individual parodies in 'Cyclops' inherently undercut each other, so that its form reproduces the fragmented structure of society where traditional social relationships have been removed and individuals now exist in dissonant relation to each other, apparent here through the fragments of different parodies. The whole novel is the sum total of the chapters which work together (and against each other) to destabilise traditional methods of textual navigation. This works in a way that bears comparison with a twelve-tone composition: the sum total of many twelve-tone rows, it destabilises historical notions of subjectivity concerned with unity and totality. What it presents instead is a fragmentary, fractured experience, where parts of the whole exist in dissonant relation to each other, yet just about hang together.

Joyce's refusal to straightforwardly advocate any specific political position in 'Cyclops' can be understood against the background of his own writing about politics in Ireland. Joyce's early essays show that he considered modern politics to be oppressive, self-serving and lacking morality. He was particularly critical of the English Liberal Party, and the kind of politics he felt they represented. After the promise of cooperation in the 1886 Home Rule Bill, Joyce wrote that by 1907, 'The English Liberals have forgotten their commitments' and 'the most powerful weapons that England may use against Ireland are no longer those of Conservatism, but of Liberalism and the Vatican. Conservatism, for all that it may be tyrannical, is a frank and openly hostile doctrine'.[112] Liberals, he felt, concealed their immorality and used covert tactics of oppression, which were harder to see and respond to. He found that, as a result, opposition to colonial rule in Ireland shifted its focus from politics to culture.[113] Joyce began *Ulysses* the same year the Third Home Rule Bill was postponed due to the outbreak of the First World War in 1914.

Like the twelve-tone compositional method, *Ulysses* performs and celebrates dissonance. Discussing Joyce's *Work in Progress* in 1929, Samuel Beckett wrote that 'Here form is content, content is form . . . His writing is not about something; it is that something itself' – words are drunk when the characters are drunk; at other times words go to sleep with the characters.[114] Conversely, in *Chamber Music*, although Joyce claimed for it a sort of musicality it is noticeably absent in Paterian terms comparable with the musicality that Beckett here claims for Joyce's later work. In 'Sirens', a kind of musicality is present because by reading it with attention to form and how music produces meaning, we can see that it explores the possibilities and limitations of music through both form and content. Both 'Sirens' and 'Cyclops' show the difficulty of taking a position on how music can function within literature, because texts and forms, like the world and its representation in art, are sites of unsettling and often paradoxical obscurity. In each case, analysing the music in the text, or analysing the text with attention to the abstract way music creates meaning, can illuminate but also give political significance to the tensions and dissonances that it can be tempting to try to resolve.

Notes

1. James Joyce to Harriet Shaw Weaver, 6 August 1919. James Joyce, *Selected Letters of James Joyce*, ed. Richard Ellmann (London: Faber & Faber, 1975), p. 242. It is unclear what Joyce meant by adding 'per canonem' after 'fuga'; this could mean 'by the rule' or it could be a reference to a 'canon'.
2. Richard Ellmann, *James Joyce* (Oxford: Oxford University Press, 1983), p. 95; Stanislaus Joyce, *My Brother's Keeper: James Joyce's Early Years*, ed. Richard Ellmann ([1953] Boston: Da Capo Press, 2003), pp. 100, 164–5, 216.
3. David Herman, '"Sirens" after Schönberg', *James Joyce Quarterly* 31.4 (1994), 473–94.
4. Emer Nolan, *James Joyce and Nationalism* (London: Routledge, 2002), p. 118. Philip Herring, *Joyce's Ulysses Notesheets in the British Museum* (Charlottesville, VA: University Press of Virginia, 1972), p. 14. Vincent J. Cheng, *Joyce, Race and Empire* (Cambridge: Cambridge University Press, 1995), pp. 177, 178–84.
5. James Joyce, *Chamber Music* (London: Elkin Matthews, 1907).
6. For the history of the lyric form, see the following: Andrew Miller, *Greek Lyric: An Anthology in Translation* (Indianapolis: Hackett Publishing, 1996), pp. xii–xiii; Cecil Bowra, *Greek Lyric Poetry: From Alcman to Simonides* (Oxford: Oxford University Press, 1961), pp. 1–3; Georg Lukács, *German Realists in the Nineteenth Century*, ed. Rodney Livingstone, trans. Jeremy Gaines and Paul Keast (Cambridge, MA: MIT Press, 1993), p. 55.
7. William Wordsworth and Samuel Taylor Coleridge, *Lyrical Ballads and Other Poems* (Hertfordshire: Wordsworth Editions, 2003).
8. M. H. Abrams, 'The Lyric as Poetic Norm', in *The Mirror and the Lamp: Romantic Theory and the Critical Tradition* (Oxford: Oxford University Press, 1953), p. 76.
9. Joyce, *Selected Letters of James Joyce*, p. 167.
10. Ellmann, *James Joyce*, p. 95.
11. Vincent Sherry, *Modernism and the Reinvention of Decadence* (Cambridge: Cambridge University Press, 2014), p. 163. See also Max Beerbohm, 'Diminuendo', in *The Works of Max Beerbohm* (London: John Lane, The Bodley Head, 1896), p. 150.
12. David Weir, *Decadence and the Making of Modernism* (Amherst, MA: University of Massachusetts Press, 1995), p. 120.
13. Richard Poirier, 'Pater, Joyce, Eliot', *James Joyce Quarterly* 26.1 (1988), 21–35. Perils, 'Beyond Epiphany'. Scotto, '"Visions" and "Epiphanies"'.
14. Marguerite Harkness, *The Aesthetics of Dedalus and Bloom* (London: Associated University Presses, 1984).
15. Abrams, *The Mirror and the Lamp*, p. 76.
16. G. W. F. Hegel, *Aesthetics: Lectures on Fine Art*, vol. 2, trans. T. M. Knox (Oxford: Clarendon Press, 1975), p. 1133.
17. Angela Leighton, *On Form: Poetry, Aestheticism, and the Legacy of a Word* (Oxford: Oxford University Press, 2007), p. 150.

18. W. B. Yeats, 'Edmund Spenser', in *Essays and Introductions* (London: Macmillan, 1961), p. 378.
19. Joyce, *Chamber Music*, I.
20. See Hans Kurath, Sherman McAllister Kuhn and Robert E. Lewis, *Middle English Dictionary*, vol. 18 (Ann Arbor, MI: University of Michigan Press, 2001), p. 806.
21. Kenneth H. Grose, *James Joyce* (London: Evans Bros., 1975), p. 45.
22. William York Tindall, 'Joyce's Chambermade Music', *Poetry* 80.2 (1952), 112.
23. Lee Spinks, *James Joyce: A Critical Guide* (Edinburgh: Edinburgh University Press, 2009), p. 46.
24. Ezra Pound, *The Letters of Ezra Pound to James Joyce*, ed. Forrest Read (London: New Directions, 1967), p. 178.
25. Ezra Pound, *The Letters of Ezra Pound: 1907–1941*, ed. D. D. Paige (London: Faber & Faber, 1951), p. 11.
26. James Joyce, *Letters of James Joyce*, vol. 1, ed. Stuart Gilbert (London: Faber & Faber, 1966), p. 67.
27. Joyce, *Chamber Music*, p. xxxvi.
28. Letter from James Joyce to Harriet Shaw Weaver, 6 August 1919. Joyce, *Selected Letters of James Joyce*, p. 242.
29. Bucknell, *Literary Modernism and Musical Aesthetics*, pp. 122, 124.
30. Susan Brown, 'The Mystery of the *Fuga per Canonem* Solved', *Genetic Joyce Studies* 7 (Spring 2007), https://www.geneticjoycestudies.org/articles/GJS7/GJS7brown (last accessed 7 August 2020).
31. Ellmann, *James Joyce*, p. 459.
32. Stuart Gilbert, *James Joyce's 'Ulysses': A Study* (New York: Vintage Books, 1958), p. 242. David W. Cole, 'Fugal Structure in the Sirens Episode of *Ulysses*', *Modern Fiction Studies* 19.2 (1973), 221–6.
33. A. Walton Litz, *The Art of James Joyce: Method and Design in 'Ulysses' and 'Finnegans Wake'* (London: Oxford University Press, 1961), pp. 66–70. Stanley Sultan, 'The Sirens at the Ormond Bar: "Ulysses"', *University of Kansas City Review* 26.2 (1959), 91. Timothy Martin, 'Joyce, Wagner, and Literary Wagnerism', in Ruth H. Bauerle, ed., *Picking up Airs: Hearing the Music in Joyce's Text* (Urbana, IL: University of Illinois Press, 1993), p. 107.
34. Don Noel Smith, 'Musical Form and Principles in the Scheme of *Ulysses*', *Twentieth Century Literature* 18.2 (1972), 79–92. Robert Boyle, '*Ulysses* as Frustrated Sonata Form', *James Joyce Quarterly* 2.4 (1965), 247–54.
35. Lawrence Levin, 'The Sirens Episode as Music: Joyce's Experiment with Prose Polyphony', *James Joyce Quarterly* 3.1 (1965), 23, 24.
36. Margaret Rogers, 'Mining the Ore of "Sirens": An Investigation of Structural Components', in Sebastian D. G. Knowles, ed., *Bronze by Gold: The Music of Joyce* (London: Routledge, 1999), p. 263.
37. Nadya Zimmerman, 'Musical Form as Narrator: The Fugue of the Sirens in James Joyce's *Ulysses*', *Journal of Modern Literature* 26.1 (2002), 113.
38. Shockley, *Music in the Words*, p. 73.
39. Witen, *James Joyce and Absolute Music*, pp. 3, 9.
40. Bucknell, *Literary Modernism and Musical Aesthetics*, p. 144.

41. Werner Wolf, *The Musicalization of Fiction: A Study in the Theory and History of Intermediality* (Amsterdam: Rodopi, 1999), p. 134.
42. Zimmerman, 'Musical Form as Narrator', 110.
43. Shockley, *Music in the Words*, p. 54. Emphasis added.
44. Zimmerman, 'Musical Form as Narrator', 117.
45. Pater, *The Renaissance*, p. 106. Schopenhauer, *The World as Will and Representation*, p. 289.
46. Barry Millington, *The New Grove Guide to Wagner and His Operas* (Oxford: Oxford University Press, 2006), p. 153.
47. David Fanning, 'Leitmotif in *Lady Macbeth*', in David Fanning, ed., *Shostakovich Studies* (Cambridge: Cambridge University Press, 2006), p. 151.
48. This use of the leitmotif is not available in all Wagner's works, but is a technique that he developed during his career. Barry Millington points out that 'a leitmotif is to be distinguished from a reminiscence motif (*Erinnerungsmotif*), which, in earlier operas and in Wagner's works up to and including *Lohengrin*, tends to punctuate the musical design rather than provide the principal, "leading" thematic premises for that design'. Millington, *The New Grove Guide to Wagner and His Operas*, p. 153.
49. Raymond Furness, *Wagner and Literature* (Manchester: Manchester University Press, 1982), p. 7.
50. See Arnold Whittall, 'Leitmotif', in *The New Grove Dictionary of Opera*, ed. Stanley Sadie, 2nd edn (London: Oxford University Press, 1992), p. 1137.
51. Theodor W. Adorno, 'Music, Language, and Composition', trans. Susan Gillespie, *The Musical Quarterly* 77.3 (1993), 401.
52. Zimmerman, 'Musical Form as Narrator', 118.
53. Jacques Rancière, *The Politics of Aesthetics*, ed. and trans. Gabriel Rockhill (London: Bloomsbury, 2013), p. 8. For a deeper discussion of how Rancière can help us to think through the politics of aesthetics, see the final section of Chapter 5, 'Politics, Aesthetics and Music', pp. 217–21.
54. Bucknell, *Literary Modernism and Musical Aesthetics*, pp. 130–1.
55. Ellmann, *James Joyce*, p. 460.
56. Richard Wagner, *Gesammelte Schriften und Dichtungen*, vol. 9 (Leipzig: Siegel, 1907), pp. 71, 100. Cited in and translated by Bowie, *Music, Philosophy and Modernity*, p. 227.
57. Wagner wrote to Liszt, 'I have of late occupied myself exclusively with a man who has come like a gift from heaven, although only a literary one, into my solitude. This is Arthur Schopenhauer, the greatest philosopher since Kant'. Richard Wagner to Franz Liszt, 29 September 1854. Wagner and Liszt, *Correspondence of Wagner and Liszt*, p. 53.
58. May Sinclair, 'The Novels of Dorothy Richardson', *The Egoist* 5.4 (1918), 57, https://modjourn.org/issue/bdr522839/ (last accessed 7 August 2020).
59. Timothy Peter Martin, *Joyce and Wagner: A Study of Influence* (Cambridge: Cambridge University Press, 1991), p. 9. See also Raymond Furness, *Wagner and Literature* (Manchester: Manchester University Press, 1982), p. 16.
60. Martin, *Joyce and Wagner*, p. 8.

61. See Moss, 'Classical Music and Literature'. See also Virginia Woolf, 'Modern Fiction', in *The Essays of Virginia Woolf, Vol 4: 1915–28*, ed. Andrew McNeille (London: Hogarth Press, 1984), p. 161.
62. Richard Wagner, *Three Wagner Essays*, trans. Robert L. Jacobs (London: Eulenburg Books, 1979), p. 40.
63. Jeri Johnson, 'Introduction', in James Joyce, *Ulysses* (Oxford: Oxford University Press, 1993), pp. xx–xxi.
64. Dorothy Richardson, 'Foreword', in *Pilgrimage 1*, p. 12.
65. Jean Laplanche and Jean-Bertrand Pontalis, *The Language of Psycho-Analysis*, trans. Donald Nicholson-Smith (London: Karnac Books, 1988), pp. 138, 197. M. Guy Thompson, 'The Role of Being and Experience in Freud's Unconscious Ontology', in John Mills, ed., *Psychoanalysis at the Limit: Epistemology, Mind, and the Question of Science* (Albany, NY: SUNY Press, 2004), pp. 3, 9.
66. Bowie, *Music, Philosophy and Modernity*, p. 224.
67. Matthew Bribitzer-Stull, *Understanding the Leitmotif: From Wagner to Hollywood Film Music* (Cambridge: Cambridge University Press, 2015), p. 7.
68. Ibid. p. 4.
69. Heath Lees, *Mallarmé and Wagner: Music and Poetic Language* (Aldershot: Ashgate, 2007), p. xvi.
70. Theodor W. Adorno, *Essays on Music*, ed. Richard Leppert, trans. Henry W. Pickford (New York: Columbia University Press, 2002), p. 113.
71. Homer, *Odyssey*, book XII, trans. E. V. Rieu (London: Penguin, 1991), p. 180.
72. There is a sexual pun on the word 'horn': thoughts of 'Molly in her shift in Lombard street west, hair down' are followed with the sexually suggestive 'Wet night in the lane. Horn. Who had the?' (11.1240, 1253). Both references to the 'horn' here refer back to Lenehan's comment to Boylan early in the chapter, 'Got the horn or what?' (11.432), which produces anxious echoes in Bloom's consciousness: 'Horn. Have you got the? Horn. Have you the? Haw haw horn' (11.526–7).
73. Kant, *Critique of the Power of Judgement*, pp. 174, 172.
74. Homer, *Odyssey*, p. 184.
75. Theodor W. Adorno and Max Horkheimer, *Dialectic of Enlightenment*, trans. John Cumming ([1944] London: Verso, 1997), p. 32.
76. Ibid. p. 32.
77. Homer, *Odyssey*, p. 183.
78. Stuart Allen, 'Thinking Strictly Prohibited: Music, Language and Thought in "Sirens"', *Twentieth-Century Literature* 53.4 (2007), 452. Emphasis added.
79. Ibid. p. 453.
80. Herman, '"Sirens" after Schönberg', 478.
81. Bersani, *The Culture of Redemption*, pp. 158, 159.
82. John Nash, 'Newspapers and Imperialism', in Howard J. Booth and Nigel Rigby, eds, *Modernism and Empire* (Manchester: Manchester University Press, 2000), p. 176.
83. Ibid. p. 192.
84. Luigi Dallapiccola, 'On the Twelve-Note Road', trans. Deryck Cook,

Music Survey 4.1 (1951), 318–32; David Herman, 'Sirens after Schönberg', 473.
85. Jack W. Weaver, *Joyce's Music and Noise: Theme and Variation in his Writings* (Gainesville, FL: University of Florida Press, 1998), pp. 193–4.
86. Ibid. p. 92.
87. Arnold Schoenberg, *Letters*, ed. Erwin Stein, trans. Eithne Wilkins and Ernst Kaiser (Berkeley, CA: University of California Press, 1964), p. 104.
88. For a thorough discussion of the correspondences between *Ulysses* and the *Odyssey* see Gilbert, *James Joyce's 'Ulysses'*, pp. 93–344.
89. Adorno and Horkheimer, *Dialectic of Enlightenment*, p. 22.
90. Theodor W. Adorno, 'On Popular Music', in Simon Frith and Andrew Godwin, eds, *On Record: Rock, Pop and the Written Word* (London: Routledge, 1990), p. 308. This essay first appeared as Theodor W. Adorno, 'On Popular Music', *Studies in Philosophy and Social Science* 9 (1941), 17–48.
91. Adorno, *Minima Moralia*, p. 50. Hegel's aphorism is otherwise translated as 'the True is the whole'. G. W. F. Hegel, *The Phenomenology of Spirit*, trans. A. V. Miller (Oxford: Oxford University Press, 1977), p. 20.
92. Hegel, *The Phenomenology of Spirit*, p. 18.
93. Adorno, *Minima Moralia*, p. 18.
94. Haslam, *Fragmenting Modernism*, p. 1. Peter Childs also gives key importance to the 'principles of fragmentation and discontinuity' in modernist literature. See Peter Childs, *Modernism* (Abingdon: Routledge, 2008), p. 14.
95. Adorno, *Aesthetic Theory*, p. 169.
96. Adorno, *Philosophy of New Music*, pp. 45–6. See also Theodor W. Adorno, *Alban Berg*, trans. Juliane Brand and Christopher Hailey (Cambridge: Cambridge University Press, 1994), p. 300.
97. Adorno, *Philosophy of New Music*, p. 133.
98. Robert W. Witkin, *Adorno on Music* (London: Routledge, 1998), p. 130.
99. Theodor W. Adorno, 'Vers une musique informelle', in *Quasi Una Fantasia*, p. 281.
100. Adorno, *Philosophy of New Music*, pp. 72–3.
101. Ibid. p. 73.
102. See Arnold Whittall, *Serialism* (Cambridge: Cambridge University Press, 2008), p. 52.
103. Weldon Thornton, *Allusions in Ulysses: An Annotated List* (Chapel Hill, NC: University of North Carolina Press, 1968), pp. 256–7.
104. Nash, 'Newspapers and Imperialism', p. 175.
105. Herring, *Joyce's Ulysses Notesheets in the British Museum*, p. 14.
106. Cheng, *Joyce, Race and Empire*, pp. 177, 178–84.
107. Nolan, *James Joyce and Nationalism*, pp. 118, 120.
108. Nash, 'Newspapers and Imperialism', p. 178.
109. David Clarke, 'Musical Autonomy Revisited', in Martin Clayton, Trevor Herbert and Richard Middleton, eds, *The Cultural Study of Music* (London: Routledge, 2003), p. 165.
110. Adorno, *Philosophy of New Music*, p. 29.
111. Bersani, *The Culture of Redemption*, p. 159.
112. James Joyce, 'Home Rule Comes of Age', in *Occasional, Critical, and*

Political Writing (Oxford: Oxford University Press, 2003), pp. 143, 144.
113. Joyce, 'The Irish Literary Renaissance', in *Occasional, Critical, and Political Writing*, p. 137.
114. Samuel Beckett, 'Dante ... Bruno. Vico ... Joyce', in *Disjecta: Miscellaneous Writings and a Dramatic Fragment*, ed. Ruby Cohn (New York: Grove Press, 1984), p. 27.

Chapter 3

Ezra Pound, Music and Fascism: Towards Canto LXXV

Canto LXXV combines words and music, featuring seven lines of verse followed by two pages of a musical score. The second of *The Pisan Cantos* – often thought of as Pound's greatest work, an aesthetic achievement marking the culmination of his lifetime dedication to poetry and the arts – the poem was written during his incarceration at a military detention centre in Pisa in 1945. If Pound's conviction about the need to study poetry, music and art had brought him to the 'genius' of *The Pisan Cantos*, his political opinions broadcast over Radio Rome had brought him to incarceration, awaiting extradition to the USA to stand trial for treason. When the verses in Canto LXXV metamorphose into a musical score, in an apparent poetic demonstration of Pater's claim that 'all art constantly aspires to the condition of music', this aesthetic sits uneasily beside the politically charged circumstances of the text's production at the end of the Second World War. When the 1949 Bollingen Prize was awarded to *The Pisan Cantos*, two articles by Robert Hillyer in *The Saturday Review* claimed that arguments for the autonomy of art were being used as cover to promote totalitarianism: the poetry could not help but communicate Pound's politics, meaning an endorsement of *The Pisan Cantos* was an endorsement of fascism.[1]

This brings us to the question considered so often in relation to Pound's poetry: how are his politics and aesthetics connected? In this chapter, I consider what Pound's study and use of music – an art form so often considered a domain apart from daily life and politics – can tell us about how his politics inform his aesthetic judgements, and how his aesthetics affect his politics. By beginning with Canto LXXV and reading back into Pound's then-forty-year engagement with music and its relation to poetry, we can see the constellation of artistic, historical, mathematical, political, racial and scientific ideas that crystallise in Canto LXXV, to see why music appears when words will not do, and why he uses the visual shock of a handwritten score on the page to communicate the aural art.

Canto LXXV sits on a double-page spread in the New Directions edition, so that we see it complete and contained, from beginning to end. But the material in this Canto, as in all others, is tentacular, gaining its meaning – and in this case its form and the marks on the page – from other texts, artworks and people. The score is an extended quotation: Gerhart Münch's violin adaptation of Clément Janequin's choral work *Le chant des oiseaux*. While many Cantos contain unusual visual elements such as diagrams, Chinese characters, uneven line spacing, and different languages and alphabets, Canto LXXV is perhaps the most striking to look at. When the Latin text gives way without closing punctuation to musical notation gesturing to musical sound, inviting us to hear the birdsong, the arresting visuals of the score signal that a different kind of reading is required. The ciphers point towards music, but they cannot make the sound of the birds alone. Their transformation into music requires interpretation: performance, or sight-reading ability to imagine the music. The tools are there, if we can use them, so that the text gives us potential and possibility: an unheard music that is offered and withheld.

On one hand, Canto LXXV encourages active participation to convert the notation into sound. On the other, it may goad a reader about their lack of ability to read the score and hear the music. The poem is fruitful ground for considering some of the questions often asked of modernism more broadly: is its unusual form bafflingly exclusionary in the knowledge it assumes and requires, or optimistically inclusive in liberating us from established reading practices? Is its approach encouragingly educational or condescendingly alienating? Canto LXXV is all of these things, and in further ways holds multiple ideas and possibilities in tension. The verses claim a natural hierarchy based on aesthetic achievement, as men of genius – Buxtehude, Klages, Münch and finally Pound – transmit the essence of birdsong, and thus a message of artistic purity, across history. Yet the score, and the absence of aural music, locates the completion of the artwork in the recipient, rather than the artwork's essence. The visual difference of the handwritten score requires that we acknowledge the collaboration and labour behind the artefact, working against the notion of art as autonomous or the work of a lone genius.

That these competing ideas coexist in Canto LXXV needs to be understood as hard won in Pound's thought. Over the years, he struggles to define and explain music. How he describes it and where he places its value shifts and changes. The early Pound prized the attention paid by troubadour and Provençal poets to the sounds of verses, arguing that musical rhythms were a formal route to the direct treatment of abstractions and emotions that he advocated in the 1912 Imagist principles. In the 1920s, however, he prefers the 'hard bits' of rhythm he finds in

George Antheil's music, and in his musical theories – 'absolute rhythm' in *Antheil and the Treatise on Harmony* (1924) and its elaboration, 'Great Bass', in *Guide to Kulchur* (1938) – he tries to reduce music to manageable rules, arguing that the value of musical compositions can be worked out with mathematical formulae. Yet Pound's musical theories do not engage with music in terms that are useful to explain what he feels it offers poetry. Writing in *The Delphinian Quarterly* in 1936 about Münch's version of *Le chant des oiseaux*, Pound values its accurate imitation of 'natural sound' (*EPM* 379) – specifically birdsong, which is markedly different from Antheil's mechanical rhythms that he valued in the previous decade.

A change in Pound's approach to music tracks a change in his politics. He wants music to do the work of thinking and feeling in his early writing, but ends up describing it in cold and technical terms in *Antheil and the Treatise on Harmony*. To understand the political significance of Pound's attempts to rationalise music and bring it under control, we must consider the influence of Rémy de Gourmont, whom Pound had been writing about since 1915 and whose *Natural History of Love* he translated from French in 1922. The summary of Gourmont's ideas in this chapter is deeply indebted to Vincent Sherry's *Ezra Pound, Wyndham Lewis and Radical Modernism*, which does not feature in other work on Pound and music, even though it provides an invaluable account of Gourmont's politicisation of music and the aesthetic more broadly. For Gourmont, music had no positive potential: it was not a route to abstract, higher thought. Music's vibrations and affects were base, immediate forms of stimulation, to which the optical sense was superior because it was capable of judgement and intelligent discrimination. Pound's study of Gourmont contributes to an increasingly hierarchical and discriminatory mode of thought, and to an increasingly visual conceptualisation of music that culminates in the score in Canto LXXV, which is Pound's attempt at a solution to the problem of music, as he tries to navigate his desire to write poetry informed by musical sounds to achieve the formal expression of emotions, but not to capitulate to music's bodily affect or its tendency towards abstraction.

Direct Presentation: Imagism, the Troubadours and *Vers Libre*

Pound never departs from his poetics of clarity and direct presentation outlined in the 1912 Imagist principles, in which musical rhythm has a key role:

1. Direct treatment of the 'thing' either subjective or objective.
2. To use absolutely no word that does not contribute to the presentation.
3. As regarding rhythm: to compose in the sequence of the musical phrase, not in sequence of a metronome. (*LE* 3)

While the first two conditions are related to the object, the third seems to stand alone: Pound does not specify straight away what relation composing in the sequence of the musical phrase bears to the 'thing'. This is because it is difficult to describe briefly: rhythm, he explains later, should 'correspond exactly to the emotion or shade of emotion to be expressed' (*LE* 9). In Pound's early thought, musical rhythms are for the formal communication of abstract emotions: things that cannot be adequately put into words. The problems of reconciling music's formal abstraction with his desire for clarity and specificity will be a recurrent feature of Pound's writing on music, and will affect his developing poetics.

Pound's interest in music began with his study of the Provençal and troubadour poets at Hamilton College in New York in 1903–4.[2] Rachel Blau DuPlessis and Helen Carr attribute Pound's continued interest to his acquaintance with the actress, writer, polemicist and singer Florence Farr, who worked with W. B. Yeats on the connection of music and poetry, applying tones to specific words in his poems to give some musical direction to the way they should be spoken. DuPlessis describes how 'Yeats and Farr gave lecture-demonstrations in a number of cities to showcase her "extraordinarily impressive and poetical" method of *Sprechstimme* [speech-voice]; in 1907 she toured America giving lectures on music and poetry'.[3] Farr's book *The Music of Speech* (1909) was dedicated to Yeats, and also to Arnold Dolmetsch, about whose writing Pound would publish several articles between 1915 and 1917 (*EPM* 35–50).[4]

Pound forges a link between poets and musicians in the introduction to his translations of Guido Cavalcanti's sonnets in 1910, where he refers to the troubadours and other major classical poets as songwriters:

> For if he [Cavalcanti] is not among the major prophets, he has at least his place in the canon, in the second book of The Arts, with Sappho and Theocritus; with all those who have *sung*, not all the *modes* of life, but some of them, unsurpassedly. (*T* 17, emphasis added)

The metaphor 'modes of life' proposes a strong correspondence between music and being alive. 'Mode' can mean 'manner' or 'type', but coming straight after a reference to song, the musical meaning of the word is called up: groupings of pitch organised around a tonic note, which can be played as scales and form the harmonic basis for tonal compositions.

The seven Western musical modes – Ionian, Dorian, Phrygian, Lydian, Mixolydian, Aeolian and Lochrian – each suggest a distinctive atmosphere or mood, and Pound's metaphor discloses his conviction that there is something particular about music that is suitable for expressing human emotion. Since some of these modes date back to the Gregorian chants of central Europe in the ninth and tenth centuries, which were influenced by the music of the Byzantine Empire, there is a historical, cross-cultural precedent for the modal-emotional connections to which Pound gestures. In *The Republic,* Plato commented on the suitability of different modes for representing different emotions.[5] The most obvious example is the attribution of positive and negative emotional content to major and minor modes respectively. In the sixteenth century, Italian Renaissance music theorist Gioseffo Zarlino's treatise *Istitutioni harmoniche* (1558) paid attention to major and minor triads, describing them respectively as 'gay and lively' and 'sad and languid'.[6] This is still an area of academic inquiry: much more recently Bruno Nettl has documented the affective connotations of Persian modes.[7]

The early Pound is working with these longstanding ideas to ask philosophical questions about how to navigate the necessary mediation of language during the search for philosophical truths. This search is often taking place in his writing on music, because he suspects music to be particularly suitable for communicating nuances of human emotion. In Cavalcanti's musical writing Pound finds the direct expression of emotion, like that which Schopenhauer found in music: the essence of pain, or joy, or sadness.[8]

> Than Guido Cavalcanti no psychologist of the emotions is more keen in his understanding, more precise in his expression; we have in him no rhetoric, but always true description, whether it be of pain itself, or of the apathy that comes when the emotions and possibilities of emotion are exhausted. (*T* 18)

Pound believes that Cavalcanti's innately musical writing can be used to recuperate a direct and meaningful way of using language. Since Cavalcanti, 'six centuries of derivative convention and loose usage have obscured the exact significances of such phrases as: "The death of the heart" and "The departure of the soul"' (*T* 18). Through careless or thoughtless usage, words and phrases have lost the force of their meaning, and the desire to repair language motivates Pound's 1912 Imagist principles, which must follow Cavalcanti's example, incorporating music by paying attention to musical sounds, cadences and rhythms. Pound is convinced here about the capacity of art – and specifically poetry that is like music – to communicate the emotions. This is not retained in his later writing, in which he grows increasingly suspicious of art that affects the nerves, senses and passions. Eventually, in 'absolute rhythm' and 'Great Bass', Pound attempts to avoid music's emotive qualities by rationalising its effects through physics and mathematics.

In Pound's contributions to little magazines between 1911 and 1918 he makes many references to music's necessity for poetry, especially in his series on poetic technique in *The New Age*, 'I Gather the Limbs of Osiris', the tenth instalment of which was subtitled 'On Music' (*EPM* 30–5).[9] In this series, Pound describes his desire to use music to get 'close to the thing', meaning poetry's subject and anything mediated by language.[10] He hoped to achieve musical rhythms through *vers libre* (free verse) to give poetry additional, non-linguistic meanings. Pound's interest in the technique was intimately connected to his study of music, particularly Arnold Dolmetsch, on whom he wrote several articles in *The Egoist* (*EPM* 42–50). In *The Interpretation of the Music of the XVIIth and XVIIIth Centuries*, Dolmetsch refers to a time when notated music did not include bar lines, which, for Pound, enforce a regular metre and limit individual expression. Pound argued that Dolmetsch's citations of seventeenth- and eighteenth-century authors contained 'proof' of 'the recognition of *vers libre* in music – and this during the "classical period"' (*EPM* 44). Pound considered bar lines the musical equivalent of the restrictive iambic pentameter in poetry, and he looked back to music to theorise and inform his use of *vers libre*. Dolmetsch's musical history offered Pound a methodology for incorporating music into poetry, yet the reference point is an old one. Daniel Katz's comment about Arnaut Daniel's influence on Pound is also true of *vers libre*: it is 'one of the most important of the typically if counterintuitively archaic sources' on which Pound relied to 'make it new'.[11]

Pound wants to describe with precision, but often finds it difficult to articulate, what music brings to poetry. His writing about music is full of tensions and competing claims: he wants music to help him communicate abstractions through form, but when he describes its qualities he must always put something abstract into words. *Vers libre*, he writes, is for 'when the "thing" builds up a rhythm more beautiful than a set of metres, or more real, more a part of the emotion of the "thing", more germane, intimate' (*LE* 3). He makes multiple attempts to explain this – 'more real, more a part of the emotion ... more germane' – so that in trying to articulate those things to which music corresponds he resorts to the verbosity and abstraction he dislikes in poetry. In his 1917 article 'Vers Libre and Arnold Dolmetsch' in *The Egoist*, Pound claims that 'poetry withers or "dries out" when it leaves music' (*EPM* 42). Here, music becomes the bodily fluid of poetry: something entirely essential that animates it. Yet the essence that Pound attempts to extract from music is abstract and he struggles to explain it, reverting to a visual metaphor. The insufficiency of the metaphor is indicated by the quotation marks around 'dries out', and it is inadequate because there is something that Pound feels music gives to poetry that he cannot express in words. Music seems to offer him something important but withholds straightforward articulation of what it offers.

Pound was putting these aims and ideas into practice in his verse, experimenting with rhyme and metre. In 'The Encounter' the rhythms of the verses communicate the changing intensity of what is described. Though set in a social context, an intimate interaction is the focus of the poem:

> All the while they were talking the new morality
> Her eyes explored me.[12]

The thirteen-syllable opening line does not conform to a regular metrical pattern, but the double unstressed syllables of its anapaests and closing dactyl generate a sense of movement, like conversation flowing between multiple participants. The scene that is conjured suggests a room with multiple people discussing 'the new morality', but no description of place or participants is given, so a distinct image cannot be formed. The slower rhythm of the next line introduces a new subject: the gaze. The two iambs of 'Her eyes explored' reduce the pace and contrast with the movement of the first line, enacting the steady, slowly moving gaze of the exploring eyes that rest on the pause after the final syllable of the considerably shorter second line. The distinctive rhythms and lengths of the lines mark the contrast between what is being communicated: their different expression gestures to the difference between the content, so that compared with 'the new morality' of the conversation there is something sensual and potentially corrupt about the exploring, probing gaze. Even this is partially visual: the absence after the period visually signals a long pause. Pound's pace works to show the rhythms relevant to the images he presents, and these are not perfect metrical rhythms but contain the incongruities and fluctuations of action, as in 'Image from D'Orléans':

> Young men riding in the street
> In the bright new season
> Spur without reason
> Causing their steeds to leap.
>
> And at the pace they keep
> Their horses' armoured feet
> Strike sparks from the cobbled street
> In the bright new season.[13]

K. K. Ruthven identifies this poem as a translation of 'a fifteenth century chanson by Charles D'Orléans'.[14] It is one of Pound's unconventional translations: as with 'The Seafarer', he chooses to recreate the poem's original rhythms, preferring to retain the affective qualities of sounds over the original linguistic sense of the words. Repetition which mimics footfalls is generated from the sounds of the words in the first stanza: the repeated vowels in 'street', 'season', 'reason', 'steeds' and 'leap' create an intensifying rhyming recurrence, while the 'i' of 'riding' is repeated in 'bright'; its vowel closed by the 't' is echoed by 'without'. An irregular syllabic structure and uneven rhythms mimic the spurring that causes the horses to 'leap' rather than maintain a steady pace. Regular syllabic rhythms do not begin until the iambic trimester of the second stanza's first two lines, mimicking regular footfalls of horses settled into a even pace. The introduction of the seven-syllable third line interrupts the rhythm that has been established, drawing attention to the sparks that fly from the cobbles on contact with the horseshoes. Pound's rhythms, adapted from the French *chanson*, play with regularity only to depart from it to produce tension and vibrancy, drawing attention to words and images by frustrating regular rhythmic patterns, and creating sounds and rhythms that work towards the aural communication of what is being described.

Pound's poetics develop considerably after this point: these early verses did not fulfil his ambitions for poetic musicality or rhythm. Pound was seeking not just musical rhythms appropriate for what he describes, but rhythms that are an essential part of the object or emotion. The '"thing" builds up a rhythm' because objects and ideas have a rhythm of their own. In his enduring preoccupation with 'absolute rhythm', which is first mentioned in 1910, Pound considers how to create the perfect work of art by combining rationality (through language) with the abstract (through musical expression and absolute rhythm). He is seeking a form of totality, or an absolute and infallible form of expression:

> I believe in an ultimate and absolute rhythm as I believe in an absolute symbol or metaphor. The perception of the intellect is given in the word, that of the emotions in the cadence. It is only then, in the perfect rhythm joined to the perfect word, that the twofold vision can be recorded. (*T* 23–4)

To understand the significance of absolute rhythm, the word 'presentation' from the second Imagist principle needs to be differentiated from 'representation'. 'The artist', he wrote, 'seeks out the luminous detail and presents it. He does not comment'.[15] Pound is not after a copy or mimesis, but a fresh object made from musically inspired language that allows something new to be seen, getting directly to the truth of the subject matter. He appreciates that language is a system of symbols: he writes that poetry 'is an art of pure sound bound in through an art of arbitrary and conventional symbols'.[16] Pound's Imagism connects sound and rhythm to linguistic expression, combining an attitude to the object ('direct treatment'), a presentation of the object that is made from sparse language ('no word that does not contribute') and an attention to the sound of language that communicates the real 'rhythm' of the subject matter, rather than an established poetic rhythm or meter, to present a 'luminous detail' through language.

There are striking similarities between Pound's introduction to his Cavalcanti translations and Mallarmé's 'Crisis in Poetry' (1896), showing that although Pound wished to appear radically new, his aesthetic and musical concerns were far from new. Seeing how heavily Pound drew on *fin-de-siècle* French Symbolism enables us to recast his later break with these ideas as part of his drive to modernise his aesthetic approach, for which he moves towards mathematics and the natural sciences. Stanley Coffman and Vincent Sherry have shown that claims about the musical essences of poetry made by Verlaine and Mallarmé were a significant influence on Imagism.[17] For Pound 'the science of the music of words and their musical powers has fallen away' (*T* 23) while for Mallarmé musical abilities have been 'broken up and scattered':

> Our present task, precisely (now that the great literary rhythms I spoke of are being broken up and scattered in a series of distinct and almost orchestrated shiverings), is to find a way of transposing the symphony to the Book: in short, to regain our rightful due. For, undeniably, the true source of Music must not be the elemental sound of brasses, strings, or wood winds, but the intellectual and written word in all its glory – Music of the perfect fullness and clarity, the totality of universal relationships.[18]

Mallarmé and Pound both believe in a historical trajectory in which literary technique is being eroded. For Mallarmé music must be put back into writing, but he also locates the 'true' source of music in the written word, proposing an interdependent relationship. We can see that Pound subscribes to this view when he claims that 'the perception of the intellect is given in the word, that of the emotions in the cadence' (*T* 23). Both writers stress the need for a verbal narrative and an emotive musical aspect to art, and Pound's poetic project is to achieve the ideal combination of these concepts. The poets also share an interest in achieving indivisible unity through art: Pound refers to the 'absolute', Mallarmé to the 'totality of universal relationships', and they both aim for 'perfection'. Pound argues that symbolism fails to achieve this unity, while his symbol is a way of using language that takes it closer to the thing-in-itself. 'The symbolists', Pound wrote, 'dealt in "association", that is, in a sort of allusion, almost of allegory. They degraded the symbol to the status of a word'.[19] To put it another way, Pound found the symbolists' use of language vague and imprecise – a failed attempt to make meaning, rather than a direct presentation of the object or idea.

Pound believes that truth, wholeness and totality can be achieved in successful art forms. This is apparent when he discusses Cavalcanti's sonnets, describing how his translations try 'to bring over the qualities of Guido's rhythm, not line for line, but to embody in the whole of my English some trace of that power which implies the man' (*T* 24). As apparent as Pound's interest in music here is his tendency to conceive of ideas in terms of universals and absolutes: it is in the *whole* of Pound's English that the truth or accuracy of his translations can be found. Pound has a degree of surety in his own judgement: Cavalcanti's lines have a power that Pound is sure he can identify and translate. Pound acknowledges that language mediates experience and is an imperfect medium – this is why he must join music and language – but he believes in a world of things that can be directly experienced and accurately captured in language. This is because Pound sees 'reality' as something that exists entirely independently and that can be accessed and communicated, rather than something that is always mediated by language and perception.

Rémy de Gourmont

Discourses connected to natural history and the objective study of human physiology inform Pound's conviction that the external world can be correctly apprehended. He comes to these ideas through Rémy de Gourmont, who had a profound impact on Pound's approach to music and his politics.[20] Pound's translation of Gourmont's *Natural Philosophy of Love* was published in 1922, and it helps us to see the significance of Pound's confidence in his judgements about the external world and his ability to correctly present luminous details in art.[21] *Natural Philosophy of Love* seeks to explain human love and sex by comparing behaviours and concepts with those found among animals, but more broadly it argues that instinct and aesthetic ability are innate and the marker of superior individuals:

> But if one considers the different instincts of animal species one will scarcely find any which are not also human. The great human activities are instinctive. Doubtless man may refrain from building a palace, but he can not dispense

with a cabin, a nest in a cave, or in the fork of a tree, like the great apes, many mammals, birds, and most insects ... Song, dance, strife, and, for the group, war; human instincts are not unknown to all animals. The taste for brilliant things, another human instinct is frequent enough in birds; it is true that birds have not yet made anything of it, and that man has evolved the sumptuary arts. There remains love, but I think this supreme instinct is the consecrated limit of the objections.[22]

For Gourmont, instinct is a type of intelligence, and civilisation does not bypass 'natural' physiological characteristics, but accentuates them. Animal instincts ('song, dance, strife ... war') still motivate humans, and these sensory experiences are things we can really know. Some individuals have more developed senses and understanding: a greater 'taste for brilliant things', and the ability (unlike birds) to 'make something of it'. The 'sumptuary arts' are therefore the pinnacle of human evolution, and those capable of artistic greatness are those with superior physiology, instincts and senses, meaning they can make the best judgements. Gourmont uses conversational observations – that all humans have their basic needs, such as shelter, but not all will build palaces – to justify social hierarchy based on physical capability, without taking into account economic or environmental variables. Gourmont also argues that physiological differences are racial: 'Dimorphism of men and women varies according to race or rather according to species. Very feeble in most blacks and reds it is accentuated among Semites, Aryans, and Finns.'[23] The argument that physical differences between men and women are differently pronounced in different races is a mode of thought designed, or at the very least makes it possible, to argue for the supremacy of certain people and races. Pound's own belief in 'natural' characteristics associated with race underpins his anti-Semitism, as we know. What is less well known is that the intellectual traditions informing his anti-Semitism are connected to his developing attitude to music. For Gourmont, racial and biological differences made individuals more or less accomplished at aesthetic appreciation, and the senses, too, were in a hierarchy: Gourmont prioritised the visual over the aural.

Pound's advocacy of music was being questioned by his reading of Gourmont, for whom music was an inferior art form. Gourmont criticised contemporary pedagogy, claiming that aural learning, rote learning and memorisation were wrongly prioritised at the expense of visual learning that required active, intelligent engagement:

the principle is to encourage verbal memory at the expense of visual memory. One is encouraged, not to look but to listen ... The ear is the foundation they stress, the Holy Spirit enters always through the ear, but under the form of words and phrases that inscribe themselves on the brain exactly as they are pronounced ... That which enters through the eye, however, can leave through the lips only after the original work of transposition; to relate what one has seen, that is, to analyse an image, is an operation complex and laborious; to tell what one has heard, however, is to repeat sounds, perhaps like a wall.[24]

For Gourmont, while the eye can come to reasoned judgements by identifying difference and discriminating between things, the aural immediately affects the body before responses can be processed by the intellect. Sherry has traced a history of approaches to music that are derived from its ability to instil 'feelings of group empathy' that originated in 'the 1780s, in France, [where] it entered into easy alliance with the protorevolutionary doctrine of mesmerism ... music drew the auditor into physical union, first with acoustic stimulus, then with other listeners'.[25] There is an explicitly political aspect to this interpretation of music, which sees its potential to create group empathy as a problem. Music's capacity for bringing disparate individuals together through shared aesthetic experiences can, of course, be interpreted positively. But for Gourmont, and others such as Julien Benda and José Ortega y Gasset, it was problematic: stimulating the emotions means that faculties of reason and discrimination are bypassed.[26] Sherry writes that:

> the physiology of ear and eye offered them [Benda and Gourmont] a pseudo-scientific language, one in which they could advance arguments for the political ideas of servitude and mastery, emphasizing in turn the mass mergings of aural empathy and the ascendency of visual discrimination.[27]

The ability to create mass feeling meant that it was – literally – music for 'the masses': the uneducated, or those incapable of discernment. For these writers, far from bypassing lexical communication to arrive at a higher form of communication – as music did for Pater, Schopenhauer, Baudelaire and Mallarmé – it stimulated only base, animal emotions.

Gourmont used pseudoscientific language to give authority to his statements about music, sound, the visual and natural hierarchies. As Sherry explains:

> Silencing the old myth of cosmic consonances, Benda and Gourmont relocated its idea of authority in a new, sensory register. Whereas the democratic ear merges, the aristocratic eye divides. Separating the viewer from the object of sight, the eye also achieves the distinctions on which clear conceptual intelligence relies; it thus provides the emblem and instrument of a ruling intellectual elite. Returning the musical myth of social hierarchy to the more severe measures of the eye, Benda and Gourmont represent a significant, intentionally scientific, characteristically modern attempt to reconstitute the aesthetic basis of political dominance.[28]

The 'myth of cosmic consonances' that these thinkers depart from is the Pythagorean music of the spheres, and associated connections between music and divine order in the material world.[29] For Benda and Gourmont, if forms of art are superior and inferior, so are individuals, who are capable of different degrees of judgement and production. Sherry notes that contributors to these discussions included 'Henri Bergson, Georges Sorel, and Gustave LeBon in France, Wilhelm Worringer and Theodor Lipps in Germany, the Futurists in Italy, and José Ortega y Gasset in Spain'. While they shared a methodology of linking aesthetic judgement with physiology, they did not all agree about the superiority of the eye and inferiority of the ear. Some writers 'see individual images as the unintellectual (nonverbal) language of intense sensation' and 'such variations remind us that these writers are all offering an imaginative hermeneutic of the senses, not the findings of hard science'. Still, these commentators shared 'an inquiry into aesthetics [that] verged ever on social statement'.[30] If an individual's capacity for understanding was biologically determined, rather than affected by economic, social and cultural variables, they could imagine social models based on notions of 'natural' difference which justified structures of domination, mastery and servitude in which individuals fit 'naturally' into different roles. The artist, as an individual capable of superior aesthetic judgement using the detached objectivity of the eye, belongs to the top echelon of society. This is a claim made, according to Sherry, obliquely by Gourmont and more clearly by Benda, while Gasset 'links this act of optical severance with the idea of a natural hierarchy in ways more literal, radical and historically specific than his French colleagues'.[31]

These narratives find their way into Anglophone modernism through Pound and Wyndham Lewis, who were influenced by Gourmont and Benda respectively.[32] In a 1905 essay, 'Le Vers populaire', Gourmont criticised contemporary musical poetry that sought to arouse the emotions of the masses without exercising their mental faculties. For Gourmont, Sherry explains, 'the music of public poetry typically commits "la synérèse", drawing together in one sound two vowels normally kept separate; it obliterates specifically the distinctions proper to visual intelligence'.[33] This conflation of two vowel sounds is not typically a feature of English language poetry, and since Pound did not abandon music it is clear that he did not entirely agree with Gourmont's aesthetic hierarchy: he continues to use music as a central component of his poetics. Pound does, though, begin to recognise some of the issues with music that Gourmont and Benda identified. Julien Benda writes that 'the sensations of hearing . . . cause vibrations in a nervous system connected with a vital organism which lies deeper than that affected by sight'.[34] For Benda, only the lower classes who are incapable of discernment are susceptible to the thrall of music and sound.[35] Lewis echoes Benda's and Gourmont's critique of music in *Time and Western Man* when he dismisses Gertrude Stein's 'thick, monotonous prose-song' that gets 'inside the reader's head' in a way that bypasses their own intellectual involvement and overtakes their senses.[36]

During the 1920s Pound moves away from discussing music in connection with the emotions. The political aspects of Gourmont's critique of music help to reveal the significance of the language Pound uses to describe music, artists and aesthetics. Pound's claim in 1917 that 'poets who will not study music are defective' (*EPM* 42) uses language associated with genetics to claim that individuals who produce poor poetry are innately biologically flawed. The influence of Gourmont's and Lewis's suspicion of affective emotional art can be seen as early as 1915 in Pound's rejection of music which assaults the body:

> That is the whole flaw of impressionist or 'emotional' music as opposed to pattern music. It is like a drug, you must have more drug, and more noise each time, or this effect, this impression which works from the outside, in from the nerves and sensorium upon the self – is no use, its effect is constantly weaker and weaker. (*EPM* 38)

The complexity of Pound's position on music becomes apparent here. As we have seen, Pound approved of Guido Cavalcanti's precise rendering of the abstract emotions through intrinsically musical poetry. Yet here Pound claims certain 'impressionist or "emotional"' music affects the 'nerves and sensorium' like a drug, taking over the body and weakening its defences. Pound was also critical of decadent writing, which he also describes as a drug that hampers perceptive abilities. To Louis Berman in 1919, he writes: 'the term decadent (dee-kay-d'nt) conveys the impression of young man doped with opium in the act of dyeing his finger nails with green ink'.[37] The phonetic spelling provides a critique that associates decadence with decline and includes an imperative not to take part: the first syllables sound out 'decay' and the last syllable almost adds 'don't'. The mistreatment (as Pound saw it) of the body with opium, which dulls the senses and thus aesthetic perception, combined with indulgent but worthless decoration of the fingernails, was a metaphor for the mistreatment of language that he saw in decadent writing. Writing in his memoir of Gaudier-Brzeska, Pound rejected the 'mushy technique' and 'impressionism' of the symbolists, voicing opposition to anything that contained 'sentimental aesthetics' and worked primarily upon the emotions.[38]

Gourmont's prioritisation of the visual also influences Pound's poetics as he shifts from Imagism to Vorticism. Pound had been led to Imagism, as Ethan Lewis claims, 'through his study of Arnaut Daniel, Guido Cavalcanti, and Dante, writers of precision and detail'.[39] These were also very musical writers, for Pound, as we have seen. Sherry and Sieburth have shown that Pound's Imagist principles were also derived from Gourmont, whose prioritisation of image and eye comes through in Pound's desire for direct presentation, which belongs to the optical sense.[40] Imagism was a poetics of minute detail, risking, as Reed Way Dasenbrock says, 'a poetics of stasis',[41] and by 1915 Pound had moved past it to the layered images and movement of Vorticism, through which he and Wyndham Lewis converged. It was a movement known primarily for its painting: *Blast* (the movement's 1914–15 magazine) used striking and forceful visuals, with the first issue featuring a bright magenta cover and large bold typefaces. Vorticism, Pound wrote in 1914, is the 'one image poem': 'a form of super-position, that is to say it is one idea set on top of another'.[42] The emphasis on the visual poses a problem for poets, because even when poetry is presenting images it must do so through language. With Pound's existent anxieties about the mediation of language already hampering his desire for precision and specificity, music poses a further problem: its abstractness is difficult to reconcile with his poetics of directness, visuality and objectivity. Pound develops a new approach to music that focuses on visual, objective analysis and movement.

Théophile Gautier and 'Hugh Selwyn Mauberley'

Pound finds a language through which to approach music as a visual art of precision through Parnassian poet Théophile Gautier, who was exempted from Pound's mistrust of the symbolists. Pound makes use of Gautier's quatrains from *Emaux et Camées* in 'Hugh Selwyn Mauberley'. David Weir explains that Gautier's famous poem 'L'art' 'says that the most beautiful art emerges from material that is difficult to work with and offers resistance': Gautier's comparison of 'the poet's art to the sculptor's or the enameller's makes the point that the struggle with difficult materials (such as Carrara marble) pays off in precision, in the "pure contour" of form'.[43]

> Oui, l'œuvre sort plus belle
> D'une forme au travail
> Rebelle,
> Vers, marbre, onyx, émail[44]

Gautier's verses compare the poet to a sculptor: art is more beautiful when it comes from working in a difficult medium, such as verse, marble, onyx or enamel. In 'The Hard and the Soft in French Poetry', Pound refers to this poem in his claim that Gautier 'exhorts us to cut in hard substance, to cut, metaphorically, in hard stone'.[45] He uses this language to favourably review Joyce's *A Portrait of the Artist as a Young Man*: 'Mr. Joyce's realism', he writes, is 'hard, clear-cut, with no waste of words, no bundling up of useless phrases, no filling in with pages of slosh'.[46] The idea of mediums that offer resistance is useful to Pound as he tries to reconceptualise music to avoid its overwhelming qualities in line with Lewis's and Gourmont's warnings about capitulation to its dangerous emotional pull.

In *The Cantos*, Pound uses a visual conceptualisation of music when he recasts Gautier's comparison between the sculptor and the poet, imagining music sculpted into stone. Music's most significant element for Pound is rhythm – music is 'rhythm, pure rhythm and nothing else' (*EPM* 469) – which he represents in the Canto XXIX as 'waves':

> So Arnaut turned there
> Above him the wave pattern cut in the stone
> Spire-top alevel with the well-curb
> And the tower cut with stone above that, saying:
>   "I am afraid of the life after death." (*C* 145)

In this poem, Pound gives us an Arnaut Daniel inspired by visual, not aural, renderings of music, cut in hard stone. The description of music as 'waves' – combining the visuality of Imagism with the movement of Vorticism – recurs in *The Cantos*, where music is often made into something solid: it is carved into stone and seen, not heard or sung. In Canto XXV the musician is, like Gautier's poet, a 'sculptor', seeing 'form in the air': 'the waves taking form as crystal, / notes as facets of air' (*C* 119). Music is described for the optical sense as sound waves, which then physically harden into crystal. The transformed, crystallised 'notes' are no longer sounds, but 'facets', many-sided objects – again an entirely visual way of describing music and sound.

Still conceiving of music in visual terms, Pound becomes preoccupied with 'hard bits' of rhythm in *Antheil and the Treatise on Harmony*: 'Stravinsky's merit lies very largely in taking hard bits of rhythm and noting them with great care. Antheil continues this' (*EPM* 258). This is a strategy to bypass the claim that music affects the nervous system and arouses sentiment, and bring it into the realm of the optical. For Epstein and Albright, these 'hard bits' of rhythm are Antheil's influence, but this writes out the influence of Gautier and the reasons why the phrase is so useful for Pound:

If, as Daniel Albright suggests, Pound began around 1924 to deemphasise the fluid yet 'absolute' rhythmic arcs of *vers libre* and to prefer discrete, isolatable 'hard bits' of rhythm, concurrent with this shift is the entrance of Antheil, who helped with Pound's operatic setting of Villon's *Testament* (1923), who inspired Pound's *Antheil* monograph (1924), and who premiered *Ballet Mécanique* the same year.[47]

Pound's advocacy of 'hard bits' predates Antheil. Further, limiting the phrase to Pound's approach to music fails to account for this as a visual technique, closely linked to the prioritisation of the optical by Gourmont, Benda and Lewis. The phrase 'hard bits' comes directly from Gautier, whom Pound admires because of his reaction against the sentimentality of romantic and symbolist poetry – a reaction that is informed by Gourmont's suspicion of affective art. That Gautier's quatrains are used in 'Hugh Selwyn Mauberley', which is as much a poem about past failure as it is about new beginnings, shows how pivotal these ideas were in changing the direction and crux of Pound's poetics, and music's place therein.

The shift away from *vers libre* in Pound's and Eliot's poetry, which happens around the same time, was not, then, informed purely by Antheil. In 'Hugh Selwyn Mauberley' (1920), Pound replicates the rhymes and regular strophes of Gautier's quatrains. The poem is Pound's self-conscious attempt to modernise his thought and poetics, beginning with the death of the 'old' Ezra to make way for the new. The poem encourages the 'he' of the opening to be read as Pound's earlier self by titling the section with his own initials: 'E.P. Ode Pour L'Election De Son Sepulchre' (E.P. Ode for the selection of his tomb). Eliot remembers Pound recommending Gautier at this time: he wrote that the poems in his second volume (1920) 'were largely influenced by Ezra Pound's suggestion that one should study Théophile Gautier and take a rest from *vers libre* in regular quatrains'.[48] Pound's dissatisfaction with contemporary culture is framed in Gautier's language:

> The 'age demanded' chiefly a mould in plaster,
> Made with no loss of time,
> A prose kinema, not, not assuredly alabaster
> Or the 'sculpture' of rhyme.[49]

The time-intensive arts of sculpting in alabaster and careful rhyme are compared to the cheap moulds that can be produced quickly in plaster, or cinema for the masses. For Rebecca Beasley:

> in the use of Gautier's metaphor we can discern aspects of Pound's individualism: not only is the plaster mould quick to produce and sell, it is a copy of something else, rather than the original produce of an individual artist. It can therefore present no new data about human nature.[50]

This final stanza of part two leads in to the unfavourable comparison between old and new forms of art and culture in part three, in which the modern 'tea-rose, tea-gown' sadly 'Supplants the mousseline of Cos', while the 'pianola "replaces"' (in other words, entirely fails to adequately live up to) 'Sappho's barbitos'. 'Hugh Selwyn Mauberley' is frequently anthologised, known to mark a turning point in Pound's poetic practice. It is the last major poem Pound writes before he gives his entire focus to *The Cantos*, and it asks how one should write poetry appropriate for the modern age. It criticises simple, mass-produced art; the modern age demands more than 'the classics in paraphrase': made easy enough for anyone to understand, but with their form and artistry removed. This emphasis on difficulty, showing that creating and understanding art ought to be a matter of effort and application, is derived from Gautier's claim that art should be difficult: that crafting poetry ought to be akin to working in hard stone. Complexity and difficulty come to dominate *The Cantos*, with its encyclopedic references to Chinese, American, Italian, Greek, Ancient and Renaissance histories, languages, images and symbols. This is particularly so in Canto LXXV, where the knowledge required from us is historical, musical and interpretative on an unprecedented level.

'Hugh Selwyn Mauberley' also points forward to 'absolute rhythm' and 'Great Bass', where Pound considers how one could be in key with a time by attempting to arrive at one rule governing pitch frequency and time.

> For three years, out of key with his time,
> He strove to resuscitate the dead art
> Of poetry; to maintain 'the sublime'
> In the old sense. Wrong from the start—[51]

The younger Pound, interested in '"the sublime" / In the old sense' is dead, while the 'the obscure reveries / Of the inward gaze' are out of date, paving the way for a change in approach and methodology – moving away from aestheticism and its interest in the sublime – which is exemplified in *Antheil and the Treatise on Harmony*. That he is 'out of key with his time' suggests that the 'dead' poet's approach was wrong for the moment in which he lived, stressing the need for change. In another sense, however, since there is no necessarily correct key for a particular time signature, it suggests confusion and the impossibility of ever being correct. Looking forward from these lines to *Antheil and the Treatise on Harmony* also shows 'Mauberley' to be articulating Pound's developing ideas about pitch and time, but in the context of a post-First World War moment of crisis. The poem asks how one should write poetry today, at a time in which everything has been called into question. 'Mauberley' signals the end of Pound's time in London, prompted by his disillusionment with Britain and the political elite after the devastation of the First World War, and the personal losses he suffered as well as the needless loss to the arts – which have the potential to heal society – that he saw embodied in the death of Henri Gaudier-Brzeska.

Next to Pound's signal that there is something wrong about the time in which he lives, in which he is 'out of key', the musical theories of 'absolute rhythm' and 'Great Bass' can be read as evidence of anxiety about the capacity of language and modern rationality to articulate and understand the value of the arts. In the face of this crisis, music becomes more important as the vehicle for non-rational expression, since language is damaged and bound up in the sedimented ways of thinking that have contributed to a decaying society. The need to understand music so that its unique communicative capacity can be harnessed and used in poetry to combat a failing society becomes urgent, but it goes hand in hand with Pound's anxiety about the capacity of language to articulate adequately that value. Rather than abandon it, Pound reconceptualises music itself, and shifts to empirical and mathematical laws to verify his aesthetic judgements.

Pound's Musical Theories

Pound produced two musical theories. 'Absolute rhythm' had been in development since 1910 in the introduction to the Cavalcanti sonnets, was continued in his essays in *The New Age* and is most fully explained in *Antheil and the Treatise on Harmony* (1924). Its various manifestations are collected in R. Murray Schafer's *Ezra Pound and Music* (*EPM* 467–75). 'Great Bass' can be found in *Guide to Kulchur* (1938). Both theories devalue melody and traditional Western harmony, and assert the significance of rhythm in an attempt to approach music 'scientifically' in a broad sense, by focusing on the fact that music can be described as combinations of sound frequencies.

The theories serve several purposes. Arguing that music's important aspect is rhythm allows Pound to sidestep the affective qualities of melody and harmony, which Gourmont criticises. Attempting to discuss music mathematically means Pound avoids having to use metaphors and abstract language. Claiming that musical 'greatness' is dependent on mathematical precision means that musical achievement is reliant on a form of exactitude that relates to Gautier's exhortation to work in 'hard bits'. The theories also argue that innately superior individuals can attain musical greatness, bringing musical achievement in line with Gourmont's ideas about natural hierarchy: the finest art is produced by the most discerning individuals with the greatest sensory perception and accuracy. Neither theory, however, makes illuminating references to how music can be used in poetry, showing that in his attempts to manage music, Pound loses his focus on the study of music to inform troubadour-like verses with attention to sound, rhythm and tone.

A thorough investigation of these theories' viability has not yet been undertaken: they are confident and assertive but also confusing and highly vague. *Antheil and the Treatise on Harmony*, as Erin E. Templeton acknowledges, is 'difficult even for musicians to understand' due to the 'abstract and fanciful' nature of Pound's claims.[52] The influences driving Pound's new approach to music are crucial: the politicisation of the aesthetic by Gourmont informs Pound's reformulation of what music is in these two theories, meaning the aesthetic judgements Pound makes in his writing about music have political implications that can be accessed by the language he uses, and how it engages in further ideas about rhythm that influenced the modernists.

'Absolute rhythm'

'Absolute rhythm' claims that music is primarily rhythmic, comprising sound waves; that this fact has been neglected; and that it is important because musical 'greatness' results when compositions adhere to mathematical laws that mean the rhythms of frequencies are perfectly blended. Pound proposes (or imagines) a law or ordering principle as a hypothetical justification as to why certain poetic and musical compositions are 'masterpieces':

> I believe in an ultimate and absolute rhythm . . . Rhythm is perhaps the most primal of all things known to us. It is basic in poetry and music mutually, their melodies depending on a variation of tone quality and of pitch respectively, as is commonly said, but if we look more closely we will see that music is, by further analysis, pure rhythm: rhythm and nothing else, for the variation of pitch is the variation in rhythms of the individual notes, and harmony the blending of these varied rhythms. When we know more of overtones we will see that the tempo of every masterpiece is absolute, and is exactly set by some further law of rhythmic accord. (*T* 23–4)

This quotation is from Pound's 1910 introduction to his translations of Cavalcanti, where he imagines that the troubadour's rhythms must adhere to some natural, immutable 'law of rhythmic accord', which explains why the verses are so beautiful and powerful. 'Absolute rhythm' imagines rules and structures that are inherent in the material world and in acoustic vibrations, explaining the aesthetic beauty of certain artworks as the result of natural consonances achieved by 'great' artists and superior individuals who are capable of discerning 'absolute' tempos.

Explaining the limitations of Pound's theory shows the aspects of music that are left unexplained through his excessively rational approach. Pound offers no criteria through which music can be differentiated from sound. When he says music is 'pure rhythm', what he notices is relevant to all sound, and not music specifically – it is the 'further law of rhythmic accord' to which they adhere that marks out 'masterpieces', so that aesthetic beauty is dependent on order and form, not just the observation that music comprises frequencies. When Pound refers to pitch as 'the variation in rhythms of the individual notes' he notices that sounds are produced by vibrating objects which produce sound waves. What we experience as sounds and refer to as 'sound waves' are variations in the air pressure, caused by an instrument or object vibrating and disturbing the surrounding air molecules. Sound consists of vibrations at different frequencies. For example, A4 is 440Hz and A3 (one octave lower) is 220Hz. Hertz is a measurement of the frequency of vibrations, so an A4 is the sound of 440 vibrations per second. (For an A4, the note referred to is A, and the number designates the pitch relative to the sound frequency, i.e. 440Hz. In music, pitches are referred to not through their frequencies, i.e. 440Hz, but by the names A, B, C# and so on.) As Dmitri Tymoczko explains, sound waves are 'small fluctuations in air pressure, akin to changes in barometric pressure. These fluctuations are heard as having a definite pitch when they repeat themselves (at least approximately) after some period of time'.[53] The ear hears these sound waves, not individually since there are too many per second, but as a particular pitch. The sounds that we hear as musical notes are thus produced by vibrating objects which create fluctuations in air pressure, meaning that sound comprises vibration, pressure and the movement of molecules, and is also dependent upon the receipt of those vibrations by the body. For Pound, what is interesting is not that these vibrations and fluctuations in air pressure are heard as sound, but rather that there are multiple vibrations per second. His observations are not wrong, but his claims that there is a mathematical formula that will explain the structure of 'masterpieces' is a big leap.

Questioning what differentiates music from sound is a project that many composers were productively contemplating in the early twentieth century; notably Schoenberg, who wrote of the 'emancipation of dissonance'.[54] Jean-Jacques Nattiez considers Wagner's Tristan chord as an earlier exploration of the demarcation between music and sound, quoting Luciano Berio, who 'pointed out that the Tristan chord, at the time of its creation (1859), was nothing but "noise"' because its dissonance 'could not be countenanced by contemporary harmonic conventions'.[55] For Epstein, this is Pound's project, too – at least by the time he is writing *Antheil and the Treatise on Harmony*. But when Pound specifically discusses music as 'pure rhythm', he does not differentiate it from sound more broadly, such as speech, or what one might consider 'mere noise'. Since it is only 'masterpieces' that will abide by the rule of absolute rhythm, the theory only serves as a way of differentiating between poor and excellent music, not music and 'mere noise'.

In *Antheil and the Treatise on Harmony*, Pound extends his ideas about 'absolute rhythm' into an argument that there is one law that governs the spatial (tonal) and temporal (rhythmic) elements of music, by contending that a specific 'time-interval' should decide the organisation of musical pitch:

> The element most grossly omitted from treatises on harmony up to the present is the element of TIME. The question of the time-interval that must elapse between one sound and another if the two sounds are to produce a pleasing consonance or an interesting relation, has been avoided. (*EPM* 296)

For Pound, attention should be paid to notes sounded sequentially in compositions, rather than notes sounded at the same time. Chords or 'static' (*EPM* 297) harmony ought to be completely abandoned, and replaced with an approach to harmony that considers the relationships between consecutive notes, decided by mathematical formulae.

Pound's emphasis on 'TIME' should be read in the context of the modernist preoccupation with it. Pound strives to modernise his thought by moving away from the aesthetics of French Symbolism, towards discourses informed by science and maths. Bryony Randall has explored the changed relationship with time in daily life after industrialisation in modernist writing, while Mary Ann Gillies and Michael Whitworth have investigated how modernist writers engaging with time drew on Henri Bergson's concept of *durée*, and Einstein's scientific advances that replaced Newtonian time with Einsteinian space-time.[56] Pound's interest in finding a rule that joins the spatial and temporal elements of music shows him to be enmeshed in discussions about the relationship between time and space. He seeks validation from those with scientific knowledge when he says (in his usual cryptic style): 'Author of a work on Einstein approved the treatise; thought it ought to be longer' (*EPM* 301), and draws parallels between music and physics when he says: 'Antheil is extremely sensitive to the existence of music in time-space. The use of the term "fourth dimension" is probably as confusing in Einstein as Antheil' (*EPM* 262).

Pound frames his theory as scientific by claiming it will perform an incredible service to music through mathematics, but his engagement with science and maths is both minimal and vague. He asserts his ideas without fully explaining them or providing evidence for his assumptions. A particular chord progression, he says, is '*probably* perfectly sound. I mean from the point of view of mathematics' (*EPM* 298, my emphasis), but the mathematical evidence is not given, and the example seems to display gaps in his knowledge rather than supporting his ideas. For Margaret Fisher, Pound exhibits a 'breezy dismissal of the need to explain the mathematics behind the theory . . . An alternative perspective is that Pound maintained a taciturnity bordering on the occult and a cloaking of Great Bass in the kind of mystery that surrounded masterpieces'.[57] Even if this was the case, Pound's ambiguity sits strangely beside his assertion that his ideas can be verified with mathematical rules, and his writing fails to adhere to his own strict standards for precision and clarity. Without explaining what he means by 'the mathematics of these relations', Pound declares:

> If I can only get the mathematics of these relations so complicated that composers will become discouraged; give up trying to compose by half-remembered rules and really listen to sound, I shall have performed no inconsiderable service to music. (*EPM* 304)

Antheil and the Treatise on Harmony does not provide any new rules that composers could utilise, despite claiming they exist. The text is really a provocative way of advocating new forms and styles of composition that do not conform to harmonic systems which, Pound argues, have been causing musical stagnation. Composers, he says, have 'rotted their melodies by trying to find schemes which "harmonize" according to a concept of "harmony" in which the tendency to lifelessness was inherent' (*EPM* 300). His main claim is thus a very simple one: composers should avoid clichéd or archaic musical styles, and be attentive to sound. The half-formed mathematical explanations he ventures might seem unnecessary to make this point – one might feel that few composers or musicians would disagree with his sentiment. They must, though, be understood as part of Pound's attempt to modernise his thought and aesthetic judgements, and assert himself as an expert, in line with Gourmont's conviction about the precision of great artworks and artists.

Pound's next move is to disassociate himself wilfully from other composers who had been developing new music – such as Schoenberg, whom he dismisses without explanation as 'lacking in interest' (*EPM* 297) – and other music theorists, asserting his difference from his contemporaries in the same way that he wished to distance himself from association with the poetry of the previous century. 'Harmony in Bach's time was a vigorous and interesting matter' (*EPM* 297), but Joseph Corfe's nineteenth-century *Thorough Bass Simplified* (*EPM* 297) is dismissed. Margaret Fisher notes that Pound had a 'distaste' for 'popular composition manuals' such as those of Ernst Friedrich Richter, which Fisher suggests could be due to Richter's popularity: the 25th English edition of *Manual of Harmony* was published in 1912, and Richter's books were 'brief and to the point' (not unlike Pound's short *Antheil and the Treatise on Harmony*).[58] Pound lauds the achievements of writers, musicians and artists of centuries ago, but the more recent are dismissed as Pound strives to assert the uniqueness of his own ideas.

Antheil and the Treatise on Harmony is part of Pound's complex renegotiation with music, and continues the break that is so clearly articulated in 'Mauberley': it views music in mathematical and visual terms, not in relation to '"the sublime" / In the old sense'.[59] This is particularly apparent from the way Pound promotes Antheil's music. For Pound, Antheil's 'Ballet Mécanique' is the new music he has been looking for since the 'Vorticist Manifestos of 1913–14', which 'left a blank space for music' (*EPM* 253). Pound wants to champion the avant-garde, as well as distance himself from what he termed 'impressionist' music (*EPM* 38). Many composers, for Pound, were guilty of producing atmospheric, impressionist music that eats away at the senses rather than refining them, and makes accurate perception more difficult: Wagner 'produced a sort of pea-soup', while 'Debussy distilled it into a heavy mist, which the post-Debussians have dessicated [sic] into a diaphanous dust cloud' (*EPM* 255) – something imprecise, and impossible to get hold of. His commitment, informed by Gourmont, to conceive of music in visual terms continues when he says 'Let us say that chords are like colour' (*EPM* 255) and compares the music to a visual *presentation*: 'it is, or should be, as definitely a presentation or exhibition as if the performer were to bring out a painted picture and hang it before the audience' (*EPM* 269). Pound praises Antheil, who he says was doing something concrete with music by 'talking vaguely of "tuning up" whole cities', so that 'with the performance of the Ballet méchanique [sic] one can conceive the possibility of organizing the sounds of a factory' (*EPM* 315). Antheil's music, Pound claims, is relevant to the modern age by mimicking new technology, and avoids the mushiness of impressionism by focusing on rhythmic precision, achieving Gautier's hardness by simulating the hard sounds of the factory.

Pound's success in refashioning his idea of music to rid it of mass-mobilising affect is limited, because rhythmic vibrations of the body are affective too. Wyndham Lewis identifies this when he claims Pound and Antheil are interested in sensationalism, shock and spectacle. For Lewis, says Michael Coyle, the 'clamorings of the avant-garde were no less informed by a relentless attempt to "startle into credulity" than were the ubiquitous slogans of the marketplace'. Lewis 'denounced the Bergsonian glamorisation of sensation', saying 'The attempt to make sensation the "exclusive fact" of our existence threatened to engulf "western man" in the darkness of solipsism'.[60] While Pound is actively trying to avoid capitulation to musical sensation in one respect, Antheil's music and its violent vibrations offer a new kind of overwhelming affect very different from that which Pound finds dangerous in Debussy and Wagner, which he finds primarily dependent on an atmosphere created by melody.

'Great Bass'

In 'Great Bass' Pound elaborates on how measurements of time provide the substance for an absolute ordering system, or a 'main base' for all musical composition:

> Certain sounds we accept as 'pitch', we say that a certain note is do, re, mi, or B flat in the treble scale, meaning that it has a certain frequency of vibration.
>   Below the lowest note synthesized by the ear and 'heard' there are slower vibrations. The ratio between these frequencies and those written to be executed by instruments is OBVIOUS in mathematics. The whole question of tempo, and of a main base in all musical structure resides in use of these frequencies. (*GK* 73)

Pound's argument that more consideration ought to be given to frequencies that are not audible by humans is explained less cryptically in the earlier 'Machine Art' (1927–30), where he tries to clarify parts of *Antheil and the Treatise on Harmony*: 'I tried to point out in my brochure on Antheil that harmony as studied, the history of the scale, etc. had hitherto dealt with frequencies from 8 or 16 to the second, up to 36,000 per second'.[61] The 'main base', therefore, should be a frequency related to the lowest note, but lower than the human ear can hear. This develops into a claim that every piece should have the same tempo to match (in a fashion) the frequency of its 'lowest note':

> The 60, 72 or 84, or 120 is a BASS, or basis. It is the bottom note of the harmony. If the ear isn't true in its sense of this time-division the whole playing is bound to be molten, and doughy . . . Failing to hit the proper 'Great Bass', the deficient musician fumbles about OFF the gt. bass key as a poor singer fumbles about a little flat or a ¼ tone too high. (*GK* 233)

According to Pound, the lowest note of a piece of music should have a frequency that can function as a metronome mark. He also explains this more clearly in 'Machine Art', when he writes: 'instead of a key of C major, you will start with a related "Great Bass" key, you will take, say, 256 to the minute instead of to the second as your "tonic"' (*MA* 74). The frequency of a middle C is 256 Hz, and frequencies are measured in cycles per second, meaning that for 256 per minute, the frequency of the note below human hearing would be calculated by dividing by 60 to find the cycles per second. This comes to 4.2666. However, if we could hear it, this would be a pitch of C#, and this frequency is no longer related to the lowest note; it is a little more than a half-tone sharp – something that Pound is clearly against, as we can see from the analogy with the singer who should not be even '¼ tone too high'. Additionally, the existence of a 'Great Bass' relies on a 'bottom note of the harmony' to begin with, which seems to depend on the existing rules of functional harmony. Since the 'Great Bass' does not replace the harmonic structure of the piece, the '256 to the minute' does not function 'instead of a key of C major'. To arrive at Pound's 'main base' while keeping frequencies related to the lowest note (making the theory more coherent in its own terms) we could continue to divide a frequency by two to get the frequencies we are unable to hear.[62] For an A1 (110 Hz) we could divide 110 by two repeatedly, to get 55, 27.5, 13.75, 6.875, 3.475, 1.71875 and so on. Pound does not identify which of these numbers should then be used as the 'main base', but attempting to use any as a metronome mark would be difficult. One option would be to use 13.75 by playing to 137.5 BPM, or we could then multiply the smallest, 1.71875, by 60 to get 103.125 BPM. A 'Great Bass' of 137.5 or 103.125 beats per minute would be difficult to achieve.

'Great Bass' shows Pound extending his attempt to find an empirical way to judge 'good' music and musicians. To do this he constructs a rule so that the pitch frequency and tempo of a 'good' composition can be connected in a clearly observable and supposedly rational way. Pound makes assertions to master the idea of music and show his control of the topic: it is 'the deficient musician' who does not play music according to Pound's 'rule' (*GK* 234). Once again, Pound's aim is to manage and rationalise music, while also providing a methodology for measuring music's value that claims to be objective, in line with Gourmont's suggestions about discrimination and artistic hierarchy. 'Gourmont', explains Sherry, 'argues that proper artistic enjoyment relies on a "désintéressement" (*PS*, 193), the detachment that is a function of the visual distance so emphatically lacking among the musical masses'.[63] Since scientific and mathematical discourses seem to allow access to objective forms of knowledge, Pound puts his faith in these to explain how music works and distinguish between poor and excellent musicians.

Rhythm, Natural Hierarchy, Rational Ordering Systems and Fascism

Asserting that 'deficient' musicians do not abide by the rules of 'Great Bass' shows Pound working some of the more political aspects of Gourmont's thought into his conceptualisation of music and musical value. The ability to judge frequency and compose what Pound considers accomplished music rests on the ability to carefully discriminate between sounds: 'by listening to the sound' more carefully better compositions will be produced, since 'Some people have a sense of absolute frequency' (*EPM* 299, 305). For Pound, as for Gourmont, an individual's capacity for aesthetic judgement points to a natural hierarchy based on physiology. As Sherry has shown, these ideas have their roots in the original meaning of the term *idéologie*: 'an objective analysis of the social meaning of sense impressions', or the concept that ideas come from the experience of sensation.[64] Sherry traces this back to eighteenth-century post-revolutionary Paris, where a group of intellectuals were sceptical about the potential for the abstract ideals of liberty, fraternity and equality to provide the guidelines for effective social policies and governance. They turned instead to the body and sensation, arguing that faculties of perception and understanding should guide moral judgements.[65] These ideas had liberal beginnings, but would be taken up by reactionaries in the late nineteenth and early twentieth centuries, as arguments were made for the supremacy and deficiency of individuals based on physiological characteristics and – as Pound claims with his 'deficient' musician – faculties of aesthetic perception. Sherry's reading of Gourmont finds that 'Minds gifted with a superior intelligence should claim the rank of a preferred social class: Gourmont makes this suggestion insistently, but obliquely'.[66] Likewise, the musician who does not abide by the rule of 'Great Bass' is, for Pound, simply not naturally capable of creating valuable art.

Pound, like Gourmont, is an *idéologue* since he sees his own judgements verified by physiology and the natural world. When Pound describes rhythm as 'perhaps the most *primal* of all things known to us ... *basic* in poetry and music mutually' (*T* 23) he emphasises the importance of bodily sensation, universalises rhythm as something of fundamental importance and places himself at the top of a social hierarchy of people who can make these claims. He does this by reproducing elements of scientific discourses that seek to classify, explain and allocate levels of importance to different phenomena. Rhythm makes poetry essential. By describing rhythm as a basic element of poetry and as something primal, Pound can argue for poetry's fundamental importance to humanity. In his discussion of Henri Gaudier-Brzeska's sculpture he makes further claims about the 'primal' nature of his art, which are combined with disdain for individuals with inferior faculties of aesthetic perception:

> We turn back, we artists, to the powers of the air, to the djinns who were our allies aforetime, to the spirits of our ancestors. It is by them that we have ruled and shall rule, and by their connivance that we shall mount again into our hierarchy ... Modern civilisation has bred a race with brains like those of rabbits and we who are the heirs of the witch-doctor and the voodoo, we artists who have been so long the despised are about to take over control.[67]

Comparing people to rabbits and discussing hereditary degeneration will call up, for many contemporary readers, the dehumanising descriptions of Jewish people by the Nazis and their arguments for the Final Solution during the Second World War. These notions of primitivism, degeneration and eugenics were not unique to Pound, and have been explored in the work of modernists such as Woolf, Eliot and Yeats by Donald J. Childs.[68] For Michael Bell, 'despite its scholarly and scientific claims, the anthropology available to the generalisation of Conrad, Eliot, Joyce, Lawrence, Pound, and Yeats was still pre-scientific and based on premises that would be dismissed by the later discipline of social anthropology'.[69]

These discourses, which informed Pound's notion of aesthetic judgement as a marker of a natural social hierarchy and led him to prioritise the visual, obliquely inform his aesthetics and the musical theories of 'absolute rhythm' and 'Great Bass'. According to Sherry, we need to discuss in detail modernists' 'new standard of visual immediacy in words [that] led them to esteem (what they saw as) a superior directness in the political cultures of Nazism and fascism'.[70] As Sherry explains, 'for Pound, as for the *ideologues*, truth and value lie in the primary register of the human faculties', and this 'sensory and aesthetic experience – on which valid concepts rely – is the language of a new political gnosis'.[71] Pound values vital musical and rhythmic urges but thinks these have been lost to the modern man, while the intelligent – those at the top of the hierarchy – can appreciate the artistic achievements of the past:

> It is not intelligent to ignore that in Greece and in Provence the poetry attained its highest rhythmic and metrical brilliance at times when the arts of verse and music were most closely knit together, when each thing done by the poet had some definite musical urge or necessity bound up within it. (*LE* 91)

Pound's confidence in his ability to make these judgements, just like his ability to present the image, relies on his assurance in his own perceptions, and his ability to remove contradiction to arrive at universal truths.

In *Guide to Kulchur*, published in 1938 when Pound's involvement with Italian fascism began, Pound wants music to be a rational ordering system in the face of the complexities and incongruities he finds around him every day: 'the function of music is to present an example of order, or a less muddied congeries and proportion than we have yet about us in daily life' (*GK* 255). Clinging to the idea that things can be objectively and correctly described, he states:

> I mean or imply that certain truth exists. Certain colours exist in nature though great painters have striven vainly, and though the colour film is not yet perfected. Truth is not untrue'd by reason of our failure to fix it on paper. (*GK* 295).

Pound is interested in the singular truth of an object – certain truth and not truths – and throughout his writing he has a sense of surety that there is a world-outside, or thing-in-itself that can be correctly apprehended and accurately described through language. His attempts to do this through music fail, and the shortfalls of his claims can be seen in the tension between the grand claims he makes and the vague and allusive nature of his writing in his musical theories.

According to Frankfurt School theorists, who deal directly with the kind of thought that facilitates fascism in the immediate aftermath of the Second World War, this is a central problem with post-Enlightenment rationality. As Adorno puts it in a criticism that is not of Pound specifically, but of reductive and totalising thought processes:

> Instead of thinking out the inadequacies of the absolute claim, and thus qualifying his judgement more proficiently, the paranoiac insists on the unchanging element. Instead of going further by penetrating into the heart of the matter, the entire process of thought serves the hopeless purpose of particularized judgement.[72]

In Pound's case, this occurs when he does not fully explain his musical theories, when he points to that which is 'OBVIOUS' without evidencing his claim. The methodologies of Frankfurt School writers notice this problem, and seek strategies to avoid reductive modes of thought by contemplating the remainder left over from concepts that are understood through normalising or universalising means. Faced with the eradication of difference, Adorno focuses on the contradictions and inconsistencies that are papered over in a normalising society, and does so by abandoning closed types of systematic investigation. David Jeneman discusses Adorno's concern with the standardisation of human experience in relation to Paul Felix Lazarsfeld's sociological 'administrative research' into US radio. Giving only minimal categories for a response to radio shows, such as 'like' or 'dislike', schematises aesthetic sense and silences individual subjective responses. For Adorno, Jeneman says, 'this willingness of the social sciences . . . to "liquidate" its subjects, deriving "fixed" elements to a graph, was tantamount to a type of subject-murder'.[73] Adorno's texts and writing style rebel against the standardisation of commodities and mass-produced culture, standing 'in the face of the totalitarian unison with which the eradication of difference is proclaimed as a purpose in itself'. *Minima Moralia*'s 'disconnected and non-binding character of the book's form, [and] the renunciation of explicit theoretical cohesion' are techniques used to resist conceptual wholeness and instead embrace contradiction and fragmentation.[74] While this is a highly useful way of thinking about *The Cantos*, and particularly Canto LXXV, as I will explain in my final reading to come, in 'absolute rhythm' and 'Great Bass' Pound does away with difference by universalising rhythm as the only component of music to argue for mathematical laws that explain the beauty of artworks, which eradicates diversity, multiplicity and the role of context and interpretation to achieve his goals and avoid ambiguity about what music is, and which compositions are valuable.

Pound tries to iron out the complexity involved in explaining with language what music is and how it generates ideas and emotion. He reduces it to an essence that can be adequately described by language. The frustration that we see in Pound's approach to music is comparable to that which informs his fascism. For Herbert Marcuse, patterns of simplification and searching for absolute truths are recurrent and dangerous trends of post-industrial thought:

> The protest against the vague, obscure, metaphysical character of such universals, the insistence of familiar concreteness and protective security of common and scientific sense still reveal something of that primordial anxiety which guided the recorded origins of philosophic thought in its evolution from religion to mythology, and from mythology to logic . . . Particular things (entities) and events only appear in (and even as) a cluster and continuum of relationships, as incidents and parts in a general configuration from which they are inseparable; they cannot appear in any other way without losing their identity.[75]

In other words, Marcuse says that an anxiety about abstraction, embodied in the inability to fully grasp or explain the nature of fundamental concepts, is what has propelled philosophers. When Pound finds rhythm to be all that music comprises, music duly loses its identity as something distinct from or which consists only partly of rhythm. Pound's musical theories and his attempts to manage music fall into the trap Marcuse identifies: desiring a solid resolution to its vague, metaphysical character, he turns to simplifying theories that have the veneer of logic, but which are impossible to verify or refute because of their vagueness. 'Absolute rhythm' and 'Great Bass' are the result of Pound's intense dissatisfaction with his inability to describe what music offers poetry, which he believes is essential if he is to write poetry that can offer the aesthetic education that might improve and regenerate a decaying society. According to Paul Morrison, Pound's intense disappointment with contemporary politics and economics drives his desire for simple answers: 'Pound's fascism and anti-Semitism have their origins in a profound and potentially revolutionary dissatisfaction with the liberal settlement; the anticapitalist, antibourgeois fervour that motivates both need not have assumed the reactionary form it did'.[76] This is not merely an apology that seeks to preserve some semblance of good intention in Pound's original motivations. It identifies something important, but convenient to forget: fascism, however misdirected, often has its roots in a deep and perhaps justifiable discontentment – the same discontentment that can produce revolutionary, rather than reactionary, thought.

This frustration is everywhere in Pound's approach to music. Musical writing starts out as the key to elevated meaning in poetry for Pound, but since the musical is not graspable for 'direct presentation' and its essence cannot be easily identified, he seeks a way to rationalise and define it in his musical theories. As we have seen, these are highly speculative and problematic. The way Pound engages with music is the product of his anxiety about art's ability to accurately represent the world, when the world and daily concepts are in fact sites of unsettling obscurity.

It is significant, even if it is not inevitable, that in the 1930s he finds a compatible mode of thought in the proponents of fascism. His conviction that art and society are connected is an example of the 'rendering politics aesthetic' that Walter Benjamin associated with F. T. Marinetti, with whom Pound was well acquainted and who appears in Canto LXXII as a ghost promoting violent fascism.[77] According to Benjamin, fascism

> attempts to organise the newly created proletarian masses without affecting the property structure which the masses strive to eliminate. Fascism sees its salvation in giving these masses not their right, but instead a chance to express themselves. The masses have a right to change property relations; Fascism seeks to give them an expression while preserving property. The logical result of Fascism is the introduction of aesthetics into political life.[78]

In other words, fascism allows the expression of dissent without fundamentally altering the social structure, because it addresses only financial surfaces: money rather than labour and production. Equally, it treats race only as the expression of difference, instead of as a socially, economically and geographically constructed variable of a common humanity. A reliance on surface appearances and rejection of multiple ideas and possibilities is present – whilst also by no means an inevitable precursor – in Pound's writing on music much earlier than his documented involvement with fascist politics.

In that sense, the interesting question is not whether *The Cantos*, and especially *The Pisan Cantos*, are informed by Pound's fascism, but how changes in Pound's aesthetics prefigured and foreshadowed his fascism. Out of Pound's aesthetic preoccupation with clarity and directness which leads him to reductive simplifications, and his desire to regenerate art and society, comes a belief in natural hierarchies of individuals, and this makes hierarchical fascist thought possible. That aesthetics (in Pound's case) drive fascism is more significant than whether *The Cantos* contain overtly fascist statements, after Pound's allegiance to fascism is clear.

It is notable that the musical theories in *Antheil and the Treatise on Harmony* and *Guide to Kulchur* do not do much work connecting music to poetry. What music can offer poetry – once a core concern of Pound's – has slipped out of sight, as Pound strays from the original purpose of his study of music as he attempts to explain, rationalise and restrain it. There is a conflict between what Pound says in his tracts and theories, when he tries to explain music, and what he does in his poetry, which highlights the importance of issues of form. This conflict is staged in Canto LXXV, in which the form and inclusion of the music contrasts with what is communicated at the level of content in the lines of verse. In the remainder of this chapter, I want to read Canto LXXV two ways. First, informed by what we might find there if we look at its content through the lens of Pound's fascism, and his ideas about hierarchy and artistic genius. Second, I want to consider what we might find in Canto LXXV if we approach music as something that has escaped Pound's multiple attempts to rationalise it, and see it as an art form that injects multiplicity and contradiction into the poem. The inclusion of the score can be read as the artwork's assertion of its own materiality, interpretability and irreducibility.

Canto LXXV through Pound and *Paideuma*

Up until now I have mainly discussed the score in Canto LXXV, but the rest of the poem must also be addressed to appreciate its tension between form and content. Although Canto LXXV has capitulated in some respects to the incommunicability of music through language by giving us music in place of language, the verses that precede the score can shape its reception. The opening seven lines of verse offer a possible framework for contextualising and interpreting the score: they can be read as Pound's claim about an absolute standard by which true artistic genius and truth can be measured, and the continuing presence of divine truth and beauty in European culture across generations.

> Out of Phlegethon!
> Out of Phlegethon!
>   Gerhart
>   art thou come forth out of Phlegethon?
> with Buxtehude and Klages in your satchel, with the
> Ständebuch of Sachs in yr/luggage
> – not of one bird but of many (C LXXV/470)

The verses imagine Münch appearing out of Phlegethon – one of five rivers of the underworld in Greek mythology – carrying with him people and items that have influenced his musical score. The first is composer and organist Dieterich Buxtehude, whose baroque style influenced Bach.[79] Ludwig Klages was a philosopher and psychologist who specialised in handwriting analysis, and the *Ständebuch* book of trades was contributed to by Hans Sachs, a *Meistersinger* of Nuremberg on whose work Wagner also drew.[80] In addition to Münch's acclaimed intellectual and artistic references, the melody itself has a history of appropriation by genius. Pound sees the melody originating in the lost excellence of the troubadours, who influenced Janequin's interest in the accurate representation of natural sounds, prompting him to compose the melody that Francesco de Milano later rewrote. All these influences, he argues, can be found in Münch's violin line: 'by listening to the violin alone', Pound writes, 'we reach back to a period at least three centuries prior to Janequin, who was born towards 1475 and was published in the sixteenth century' (*EPM* 391).

For Pound, the true representation of birdsong in the different manifestations of the musical score is a recurring presence which has transcended culture, politics, time and space:

> Clément Janequin wrote a chorus, with words for the singers of the different parts of the chorus. These words would have no literary or poetic value if you took the music away but when Francesco da Milano reduced it for the lute the birds were still in the music. And when Munch transcribed it for modern instruments the birds were still there. They ARE still in the violin parts.[81]

Pound thought that although culture and art had long been in decline, certain artworks retained an enduring, universal truth. Pound's conviction that certain composers and works deserved to be celebrated and recuperated is evident from his work in Rapallo, where he organised concerts of 'forgotten' composers' works with Münch and Rudge.[82] Mark S. Byron summarises Pound's ideas about cultural decline in Europe:

> The decline of culture during the 'heavy era' (*GK* 230) coincides with the rise to prominence of northern Europe. The French Bourbon court is slated by Pound, and Tuscan culture is eclipsed by Napoleonic aggression (*GK* 263). The 'teutonic paideuma of the Leibniz-Bach episode' shines in the darkness of Europe and includes Handel, Goethe, and Beethoven (*GK* 230).[83]

The teutonic *paideuma* (i.e. the *paideuma* of the Teutons) that Pound refers to is the ancient German cultural memory, which he represents as informing Münch's score in Canto LXXV: the poem's speaker asks Münch if he has come out of the flaming river Phlegethon, carrying German cultural influences. When Münch reuses the ideas of Buxtehude and Klages, he pulls them out of obscurity and they are reborn from the flaming river of the dead. Münch's influences are instances of genius across the ages: artists and intellects who are able to say something precise and true – and therefore enduring – about the world.

Pound derives his idea of essential truths being reborn in a culture over generations from Frobenius, whom he met in 1929 and corresponded with throughout the 1930s. For Tony Tremblay,

> Frobenius's use of the term *paideuma* was derived from the Greek to mean the way in which culture, as teacher, imprints itself on man, whereas Pound used the word to imply the more mystical sense of a submerged complex of ideas of any given period, those that are, moreover, constantly in action. For Pound, *paideuma* is the template of culture that people carry inside them – including assumption, inherited biases, habits of thinking, logical defaults, and prejudices. A vital and undying energy always in the air, *paideuma* is opposite to ideology in that it is the people's wisdom and cannot be learned, though it is discernible by the method of close study of the natural scientist. Pound believed that *paideuma* was the innate intelligence that remained after all book learning was forgotten and that the study of the tangle of these ideas in literature, myth and history would reveal the active principles of an age.[84]

The 'natural scientist' who informed Pound's ideas was, as we have seen, Gourmont, and the 'innate intelligence' is limited to a select few, such as those who reproduce the score of *Le chant des oiseaux*, meaning there is again an explicitly political aspect of Pound's attribution of genius and excellence to the individuals referenced in Canto LXXV. While Pound borrows the term *paideuma* from Frobenius, this concept of recurrent genius had been in his thought since 1910: 'I find in Guido's "Place where I found people whereof each one grieved overly of Love," some impulse that has ultimate fruition in [Dante's] Inferno V' (*T* 19). In Cavalcanti's verses, for Pound, is an 'impulse' – a primary and truthful urge – that reasserts itself in Dante's inferno. In Pound's own version of *paideuma*, 'one of the rights of the masterwork is the right of rebirth and recurrence' (*GK* 250). By including the score in Canto LXXV, Pound places himself in a series of superior artists who are keeping the essence of the birdsong alive in artworks, validating his own work as a masterpiece by recognising Münch's musical masterpiece, and becoming the next stage in the chain of transmission.

Münch's violin part is not merely mimetic for Pound – it *is* the thing that it describes or imitates. He writes in 'Machine Art' that music should not be a representation of the nightingale (*MA* 72): 'in music there is representation of the sole matter wherein music can be "literally" representative, namely sound. Thus the violinist reading Janequin's music transposed said: a lot of birds, not one bird alone' (*GK* 152–3). It is many birds because it is the essence of birdsong, and not just one instance of it, that Pound finds captured in the score. The difference between a poor imitation and the thing itself is a judgement Pound is confident he can make, based on his notion of aesthetic judgement and hierarchy from Gourmont: interpreting the score and hearing the music requires visual discrimination and skill. Canto LXXV prioritises the visual by offering an instance of precise, direct presentation, and it avoids the emotional pull of aural, affective sound. In line with Gourmont's conviction about the supremacy of the optical sense, in Canto LXXV the eye and the mind must do the work of producing the sound. Following Gautier's exhortation to work in mediums that offer resistance, the score resists facile transformation into sound, requiring musical sight-reading ability or a musical performance. Pound makes hearing the music dependent on visual perception, limiting understanding of the music to those at the top of the hierarchy.

When Pound was awarded the Bollingen Prize for *The Pisan Cantos* in 1949, and the *New York Times* ran the story under the headline 'Pound, in Mental Clinic, Wins Prize for Poetry Penned in Treason Cell', the Bollingen judges were forced to construct a defence of the award given to an indicted and self-confessed fascist.[85] Karen Leick has investigated how articles by Robert Hillyer in the *Saturday Review of Literature* caused a public controversy by accusing the judges of anti-Semitism and fascism, and claiming T. S. Eliot was an unpatriotic expatriate who had orchestrated the prize in an act of authoritarianism.[86] The judges, according to Ronald Bush, 'fell back on formalist criteria of poetic value and helped to forge a mandarin, politically conservative "New Criticism" that would dominate the next two decades of literary discourse'.[87] *The Pisan Cantos* were widely interpreted as Pound's prioritisation of the aesthetic by New Critics who sought to promote literary modernism as an apolitical, formalist movement: to claim art as a space apart from the mounting political and ideological pressures of the Cold War.[88] Hugh Kenner's *The Pound Era* is indicative of the successful attempt to reconstruct Pound – who was widely considered treasonous by the general public even though he was never convicted – as a canonical aesthetic genius.[89]

Examining the contents of Münch's satchel shows the limitations of attempts to claim aesthetic transcendence and separation from politics in *The Pisan Cantos*. Ludwig Klages wrote a 1944 tract on rhythm and was a philosopher of handwriting analysis, expression and graphology, but he was also an anti-Semite whose philosophy has been analysed as influential 'pre-Nazi rhetoric' in its essentialising, totalitarian approach to politics and ideology.[90] Michael Golston has identified that 'as early as 1900, Klages foregrounds issues of rhythm, race, pulse and blood in his writing', claiming that the rhythms of handwriting can tell him something racial about an individual: 'he formulates the body as a rhythmical phenomenon deeply implicated in physiological, biological, cultural, and cosmic rhythms'.[91] We have seen the importance Pound placed on rhythm, and he too connected rhythm to biology and race, claiming that composers of Bach's era 'thought of music as travelling rhythm going through points of barriers of pitch and pitch combinations. They had this concept in their blood, as the oriental has his raga and his tala' (*EPM* 297). Pound sets up an essential difference between the 'oriental' and the Western musician, so that his interest in the supposedly apolitical aesthetic in Canto LXXV reveals itself as an assertion of the genius of a particular, Western European tradition that is based on biological differences.

More recently, as scholarly methodologies have returned to a concern with historical and material conditions after the New Historicist turn in the 1990s, *The Pisan Cantos* have been read as demonstrating penance and remorse. For Mark Byron, Canto LXXV

> provides an opportunity to show remorse for [Pound's] errant ways – his support for the Fascist regime, and his enthusiastic criticism of the economic system he judged responsible for the cycle of warfare – and to redeem himself through the expression of beauty in his art. Pound is framed as a figure of stoical belief in the divine, glimpsed at in art and in nature.[92]

Like the New Critics, Byron sees *The Pisan Cantos* turning away from the political commentary and historical narrative that have dominated the preceding series – although Byron departs from the New Critical method by arguing that Pound is self-consciously attempting to position himself as an aesthete led astray by the pursuit of divine beauty. Less convincing is Byron's claim that Pound is apologising for his 'errant ways', since it is widely documented that Pound retained his commitment to fascism. On his return to Italy after his release from St. Elizabeths, a psychiatric hospital, in 1958, before stepping off the boat in Naples, Pound gave the fascist salute.[93] *The Pisan Cantos* continue to be read for evidence of Pound's remorse, with Canto LXXXI most often read as contrite:

>   Pull down thy vanity
> Thou art a beaten dog beneath the hail,
> A swollen magpie in a fitful sun,
> Half black half white
> Nor knowst'ou wing from tail
> Pull down thy vanity
>   How mean thy hates
> Fostered in falsity,
>   Pull down thy vanity, (C LXXXI/541)

Interpreting these lines as evidence of Pound confessing his wrongdoing is problematic, since it is not clear who is being asked to 'pull down' their 'vanity'. Is this Pound's conversation with himself in his open-air cell at Pisa, where he is 'a beaten dog', isolated and exposed to the 'hail' and 'sun'? Are these lines evidence of Pound's sudden change of heart about fascism – 'hates' that he now considers 'fostered in falsity', with his indictment and incarceration the result of his 'vanity'? The difficulty in attributing a speaker or subject to these lines makes it tricky to speculate about who is vain and wrong: is it Pound, his guards, Italian fascists, his American indictors, or someone else? Even if we read Pound as the speaker of these lines, they could show defiance towards his captors: foolish Americans who do not know 'wing from tail' and ought to 'pull down thy vanity'. In the same sequence, the rebellious claim in Italian, 'non casco in ginnocchion' ('I will not fall on my knees') occurs twice (*C* LXXIV/447, LXXVII/493).

The tantalising ambiguity of snippets of *The Pisan Cantos* means great difficulty is involved in judging whether they demonstrate defiance or penitence. They have a mysterious and puzzling quality that encourages critical approaches that seek to clarify obscure passages – often with biographical details. After the impersonal documentary style of 'The China Cantos' and 'The Adams Cantos', the return to the lyric I in *The Pisan Cantos* encourages the sequence to be read as deeply personal and confessional. For Jason M. Baskin, *The Pisan Cantos* 'are the remnants of the embodied actions – memory, speech and perception – that constitute Pound's "person"', so that the sequence shows Pound returning to issues of subjectivity, which is not 'lyrical transcendence predicated on the isolation of an individual consciousness' but the acknowledgement of the importance of 'social relation'.[94] In Baskin's analysis, *The Pisan Cantos* shifts its focus away from historical grand narratives to acknowledge the importance of personal relationships and daily interactions: evidence of a softer and more sentimental Pound. Yet this redemptive reading is based on seeing Pound as the orchestrator of all the meanings in his text, and runs into difficulties when we acknowledge that Pound's aesthetics of optical prioritisation and his *paideuma*, which permeate the sequence, are deeply politicised and hierarchical. While Canto LXXV is intensely personal in its references to Münch and his score that was played by Rudge in Rapallo, Pound's ideas about hierarchies of individuals who produce true and enduring art – ideas that drive his fascism – are also deeply embedded in this poem. In order to find positive potential in *The Pisan Cantos*, we must look past our desire to pardon or condemn Pound, for the places where the poetry refuses to be reduced to a single statement. The form contradicts the kind of hierarchical and reductive thought Pound was capable of and demonstrated in his essays, letters and articles. There are numerous fault lines, contradictions and ruptures in his hierarchical aesthetic judgements, which, as we have seen, are produced by a coldly rational mode of thought that seeks to justify racial superiority and hierarchy. In Pound's writing on music, these ruptures are particularly apparent.

Canto LXXV: Reading Otherwise

There is a countercurrent running in Pound's thought about music that does not seek to do the reductive work of rationalising its effects through language or mathematics, and this offers another perspective through which to approach the score of *Le chant des oiseaux* in Canto LXXV. In 'How to Read', which T. S. Eliot's footnote claims was written in 1927 or 1928, Pound writes that musical writing has an enhanced level of meaning that is unachievable by words alone. This musical writing is not just rhythmic: it is 'wherein the words are charged, over and above their plain meaning, with some musical property, which directs the bearing or trend of that meaning' (*LE* 25). In 'How to Read', an idea of music as transcendent of linguistic meanings that cannot be explained as 'pure rhythm' is still lingering in Pound's thought (*LE* 25). Pound describes musical writing as containing a force tending often to lull, or distract the reader from the exact sense of the language. It is poetry on the borders of music and music is perhaps the bridge between consciousness and the unthinking sentient or even insentient universe. (*LE* 26)

This appeal to music as distinct from the rational is different from the controlling mathematical and empirical tactics used to explain it in 'absolute rhythm' and 'Great Bass', where Pound seems to have abandoned the connection between music and poetry. In 'How to Read', though, musical writing is reconnected to Pound's poetics as that which lulls the reader into an aesthetic trance, in which they are unable to use rationality to make sense of words and their somatic effects.

Even in *Guide to Kulchur*, where 'Great Bass' champions rhythm as a universal ordering principle for music, Pound is not consistent in applying a coldly mathematical approach to judge music's value. He claims that an increase in 'narrative sense' (which seems to mean for him the linguistic communication of rational ideas) has led to a decrease in the musical, emotive aspect of poetry: Pound identifies 'a gain in narrative *sense* from 1600 to 1900', but finds that there were '*tones* that went out of English verse' at the same time (*GK* 294, emphasis added). Pound affiliates language with sense and order, prizing clarity and precision, but he also acknowledges that there is something else that he wishes to bring to his poetry – an emotive or 'tonal' element, which he tries to ground in music. For Pound, 'Art hangs between chaos on one side and mechanics on the other' (*EPM* 47). If the arrival at narrative 'sense' has been at the expense of the 'tonal' or 'musical' elements, then the above quotation could be applied to the opposing requirements Pound outlines in his Imagist principles: we can associate directness of expression and economy of language with mechanics, while the musical, tonal and emotive aspects are chaos. Pound's desire to combine order and the chaotic, or the rational and irrational, shows his attempt to include the entirety of a concept that also includes its opposite, or the paradoxical totality that is at once absence and presence, order and chaos, logic and emotion.

Pound's contradictory and fragmented approach to music is a complex negotiation with competing arguments about what music is. Is it a base, mass producer of non-critical emotion, or a transcendent art form? Is it an important way of connecting aesthetics with the empirical world via felt vibrations and Pythagorean mathematics? Or is it primarily an abstract art form, in contrast to the direct presentation of the visual? Does it transcend lexical communication, offering access to a world of feeling beyond language? Is it a democratic, universal language? Is it an art form of purity and unity of form and content, and direct communication? All these intractable questions are in play in Pound's work, and in his discussions of music; all inform Canto LXXV. The inclusion of the score gestures to what cannot be communicated through language. We now know – thanks to the publication of Pound's *Posthumous Cantos* – that Pound wrote several drafts of material in Italian for Canto LXXV that were abandoned at Pisa, in favour of the sparse seven lines of verse and the musical score.[95] With the abandonment of these Italian drafts, all of them longer than the final one – and coming after Canto LXXIV, which is long and highly verbose – Canto LXXV seeks an escape from language, trying a different form of communication.

Canto LXXV presents the paradox of music through music: the score is visually present, but aurally absent. The visuals are immediately accessible but the musical sound is deferred, and understanding it requires a further transformation by requiring conscious, linguistic explanation. While the visual difference of text and musical notation are accentuated by their proximity, the repetition of syllables with open vowels, 'out' and 'art' – '*Out* of Phlegethon! / *Out* of Phlegethon, / Ger*hart*! *Art* thou come forth . . .' – reminds us that texts, like scores, can be converted into sound. We are encouraged to recognise the continuity as well as the difference between words and music. Canto LXXV heightens our awareness of the interconnectedness of image, text and music, all functioning as systems of signs gaining meaning from their points of resemblance as well as distinction. Canto LXXV presents us with 'created and uncreated' sound fitting the 'decreation' technique that Wallace Stevens finds in *The Pisan Cantos*. For Stevens, these poems are 'making pass from the created to the uncreated', and the uncreated beseeches us to interpret it actively and create from the rubble, engaging us with the 'precious portents of our own powers'.[96] In other words, our interpretation must meet the score and the catalogue of history we are given in Münch, Klages, Buxtehude, the *Ständebuch* of Sachs and Janequin. It is neither the artwork nor the artist, but what the artwork is met with that produces its meaning. The poem carries out Adorno's observation that 'art awaits its own explanation', rather than simply containing suggestions about universal or enduring truths that can be uncovered by attending to Pound.[97]

The form and genesis of the text work against Pound's attribution of individual genius to particular historical figures because the circumstances of its production required so much collaboration. *The Cantos* as a whole gains its meaning from things outside itself: different texts, histories, languages and images, and in *The Pisan Cantos* and Canto LXXV others create the very marks on the page. Mark Byron provides an excellent discussion of the circumstances of *The Pisan Cantos*' composition, which were begun during the start of the Second World War but finished in the US Army detention centre at Pisa, where Pound was held awaiting indictment for charges of treason between 24 May and 16 November 1945. For two and a half weeks Pound was held in an open-air cage, before being moved to a medical tent. Only on 18 September did he gain correspondence privileges, and began to send pencil manuscripts of what would become *The Pisan Cantos* to his wife Dorothy and daughter Mary, who forwarded them to his publishers.[98] For Canto LXXV, these instructions were given after the seven lines of verse:

> (HERE FOLLOWS the music of Gerhart's Jannequin [sic], as I think printed in Townsman, Canzone degli Ucelli [sic]. Probably have to be reduced in size as Townsman's page larger than usual page size.)[99]

Pound refers to the January 1938 edition of *Townsman* in which the score was published, followed by his article 'Janequin, Francesco Da Milano' (*EPM* 434–5). Canto LXXV lays no claims to be the work of one individual, as the material circumstances of its production show. Pound's scraps of manuscript were transmitted from Pisa to Dorothy to Pound's publishers, while Dorothy searched for a copy of the 1938 *Townsman* so that the score could be included in the published work. She wrote to James Laughlin on 16 December 1945: 'the pages are as I received them. I don't know whether the censor bagged some. I am hunting for Gerhardt Münch's music. If I find I will enclose'.[100] Olga Rudge, too, was looking for the music, so that T. S. Eliot and James Laughlin received copies from Olga and Dorothy respectively at the end of December.[101]

Acknowledging the collaboration involved in producing Canto LXXV provides another way of reading the poem's claims about individual genius, by noticing what is left out. When Münch emerges triumphant from the flaming river of the underworld accompanied by men and artefacts of genius, only their achievements are narrated, while those who might have informed, facilitated or transmitted their art are omitted. Arguably, all published writing relies on collaborative effort – this is also the case elsewhere in *The Cantos*, when Pound translates texts and draws on historical narratives. In Canto LXXV that always-present but often-hidden group work is especially visible due to the visual difference of the score.

The materiality and collaborative effort behind art is reinforced in Canto LXXV, even though it also advocates looking beyond the material and immediate to assert the transcendence of art and genius across time and space. The handwritten score requires that we acknowledge the labour that has gone into its production on an immediate, material level.

The score, and the handwriting that differs from the typed text, breaks the frame of poetry, preventing us from seeing it as an autonomous or natural artwork. On a conceptual level, the poem encourages contemplation of the long history of ideas and reformulations that contribute to any artwork, as they contribute to Münch's score. Yet the presence of the score reveals the artificiality of the 'naturalness' of these supposedly autonomous and transcendent artworks, the sense of which is derived from their apparent unity and totality, which is really the result of socially and historically situated labour. For Adorno, although an artwork is constructed in a rational world, through technical manipulation of its material it can seem or seek to transcend the boundaries of the rational, and this is one of the ways that an artwork can have value and utopian potential:

> In art the subject exposes itself, at various levels of autonomy, to its other, separated from it and yet not altogether separated. Art's disavowal of magical practices—its antecedents—implies participation in rationality. That art, something mimetic, is possible in the midst of rationality, and that it employs its means, is a response to the faulty irrationality of the rational world as an overadministered world.[102]

In moving towards fragmentation and abstraction of meaning, modernist art forms reject the myth that art can represent the nature that society has in fact repressed and rejected. That 'nature' which the totalising work purports to represent is in fact only the construction of 'nature' as otherness by a society that is distancing nature through labour. Modernist literature acknowledges the labour involved in its production and forgoes attempts at the illusion of naturalness by rejecting realism and identifiable narrative or poetic structures. Canto LXXV is contradictory, since it claims that art can successfully imitate nature or achieve true beauty, by taking as its subject the 'essence' of the birdsong transmitted through history, but it also lends itself the appearance of difference rather than normality or naturalness, and draws attention to the rational labour involved in its production.

Music seemed to offer something crucial – a pure way of communicating – that Pound was unable to find elsewhere. For Pound, 'music is perhaps the bridge between consciousness and the sentient or even unthinking universe' (*LE* 26). Here, music promises to connect concepts that are reliant on their opposites: music offers to bond conscious and unconscious thought, or perhaps even thought and non-thought. Music is riddle-like for Pound, and in his long engagement with it he tries to decipher its riddle. It says something that he feels he understands, but which he cannot explain in language. Language seemed to Pound to contain direct, rational meaning, but was also paradoxically an arbitrary system of symbols and signs mediating the real. Further, Pound thought language had been damaged through overuse, and that this was having dire social effects. As Pound strives to get out of closed ways of thinking, music is often his answer. William Carlos Williams explains what Pound was trying to do when he says the poet was moving 'away from the word as symbol toward the word as reality'.[103] While Pound never has full confidence that the word can be the thing that it describes, he spends a long time trying to take it close via music: to make something unique – a luminous detail – out of musical language that shows something new. In Canto LXXV this dilemma is demonstrated, rather than resolved or explained. Providing a musical score *and* the absence of the musical sound, Canto LXXV reaches towards a totality and accepts the impossibility of providing one.

Pound had long been asking questions that have preoccupied philosophers about what music is, how it creates meaning and how those meanings can be expressed in language. In his attempts to understand music he grapples with the nature of absolutes, the insufficiency of linguistic communication and the immediate yet perpetually deferred way of making meaning that music offers. Much work is required to create meaning out of the score in Canto LXXV: it must be turned into sound, and it must be explained using language if it is to be discussed. The creation of meaning from the score depends on the reader, and interpretative activities that go on outside the poem and extend past its composition. While Pound's musical theories attempted to reduce music to an essence and formula, by Canto LXXV he has terminated this effort. Music has offered and withheld things from Pound throughout his negotiations with it, and in Canto LXXV the inclusion of the score represents that struggle and contradiction through its visual presence and aural absence. Pound shows the labour involved in artistic production through the score's transmission between different artists who searched for the birdsong and the absent presence of music, knowing that meaning is always perpetually deferred. Canto LXXV demonstrates that artworks often want to represent things that are held just out of reach, and beyond our understanding.

When the Bollingen Prize was awarded to *The Pisan Cantos* in 1949, William Barrett asked in the *Partisan Review*, 'how is it possible, in a lyric poem, for technical embellishment to transform vicious and ugly matter into beautiful poetry?'[104] At the level of content, there is plenty of material to read Canto LXXV as an affirmation of fascist politics, and this is also true of other parts of *The Cantos*. But there is an internal conflict between the referential content in the seven lines of verse and what the musical score communicates formally about the failed desire to harness truth and beauty, the collaboration required to produce the artwork and the interpretation that it beseeches. By analysing the history and ideas contributing to Pound's understanding of music, we can appreciate the significance of the musical score in Canto LXXV, which combines image, music and text in a paradoxical and intermedial capitulation to the ineffable separateness of music. Canto LXXV registers the insufficiency of quotidian, rational language and reaches towards music as an auxiliary dimension through which something new might be communicated.

Notes

1. Robert Hillyer, 'Treason's Strange Fruit: The Case of Ezra Pound', *The Saturday Review of Literature*, 11 June 1949. Robert Hillyer, 'Poetry's New Priesthood', *The Saturday Review of Literature*, 18 June 1949.
2. Stuart Y. Macdougal, 'Provençal Literature', in Demetres P. Tryphonopoulos and Stephen J. Adams, eds, *The Ezra Pound Encyclopedia* (London: Greenwood Press, 2005), p. 244.
3. Rachel Blau DuPlessis, 'Propounding Modernist Maleness: How Pound Managed a Muse', *Modernism/modernity* 9.3 (2002), 395. See also A. Walton Litz, 'Florence Farr: A "Transitional Woman"', in Maria DiBattista and Lucy McDiarmid, eds, *High and Low Moderns: Literature and Culture 1889–1939* (New York: Oxford University Press, 1996), p. 87. Richard Ellmann, *Yeats: The Man and the Masks* (London: Faber & Faber, 1961), p. 133.
4. Florence Farr, *The Music of Speech* (London: Elkin Mathews, 1909).
5. Plato, *The Republic: Book 1* (London: Penguin, 1955), pp. 93–5.
6. Gioseffo Zarlino, *Istitutioni harmoniche* ([1558] New Haven, CT: Yale University Press, 1968), pp. 21–2.
7. Bruno Nettl, *The Study of Ethnomusicology: Twenty-nine Issues and Concepts* (Champaign, IL: University of Illinois Press, 1983), pp. 132, 210.
8. See Chapter 1, 'Histories of Musical Transcendence', pp. 30–7.
9. Ezra Pound, 'I Gather the Limbs of Osiris X', *The New Age* 10.15 (8 February 1912), 343–4, https://library.brown.edu/pdfs/1140814100327734.pdf (last accessed 7 August 2020).
10. Ezra Pound, 'I Gather the Limbs of Osiris XI', *The New Age* 10.16 (15 February 1912), 369–70, https://library.brown.edu/pdfs/1140814101805980.pdf (last accessed 7 August 2020).
11. Daniel Katz, 'Ezra Pound's Provincial Provence: Arnaut Daniel, Gavin Douglas, and the Vulgar Tongue', *Modern Language Quarterly* 73.2 (2012), 177. There is a more detailed discussion about problems with modernism's claim to 'make it new' in Chapter 5, 'Modernism Today', p. 207.
12. Ezra Pound, 'The Encounter', in *Selected Poems and Translations*, ed.

Richard Sieburth (London: Faber & Faber, 2010), p. 42. Originally published in Ezra Pound, *Lustra* (London: Elkin Matthews, 1916).
13. Ezra Pound, 'The Encounter', in *Selected Poems and Translations*, p. 53.
14. K. K. Ruthven, *Guide to Ezra Pound's 'Personæ'* (Berkeley, CA: University of California Press, 1969), p. 147.
15. Ezra Pound, 'I Gather the Limbs of Osiris II', *The New Age* 10.6 (7 December 1911), 130–1, https://library.brown.edu/pdfs/1140814082593168.pdf (last accessed 7 August 2020).
16. Ezra Pound, 'I Gather the Limbs of Osiris IX', *The New Age* 10.13 (25 January 1912), 297–9, https://library.brown.edu/pdfs/114081409614388.pdf (last accessed 7 August 2020).
17. Stanley J. Coffman Jr, 'Imagism and Symbolism', in *Imagism: A Chapter for the History of Modern Poetry* (Norman, OK: University of Oklahoma Press, 1951), pp. 74–103. Sherry, *Modernism and the Reinvention of Decadence*, pp. 156–9. Edmund Wilson provided a critical account of statements by Verlaine and Mallarmé in *Axel's Castle: A Study in the Imaginative Literature of 1870–1930* ([1931] London: Collins, 1961), pp. 12–20.
18. Stéphane Mallarmé, 'Crisis in Poetry', in *Selected Prose Poems, Essays and Letters*, trans. Bradford Cook (Baltimore: Johns Hopkins University Press, 1956), p. 42.
19. Ezra Pound, *Gaudier-Brzeska* ([1916] New York: New Directions, 1960), p. 84.
20. Sherry, *Ezra Pound, Wyndham Lewis and Radical Modernism*, pp. 43–90, 141–86, 180–5.
21. Rémy de Gourmont, *Natural Philosophy of Love*, trans. Ezra Pound (London: Boni & Liveright, 1922). See also Kathryne V. Lindberg, *Reading Pound Reading: Modernism after Nietzsche* (Oxford: Oxford University Press, 1987), p. 136.
22. Gourmont, *Natural Philosophy of Love*, pp. 188–9.
23. Ibid. p. 50.
24. Rémy de Gourmont, *Esthétique de la langue française* (Paris: Mercure de France, 1916), pp. 315–16. Cited and translated in Sherry, *Ezra Pound, Wyndham Lewis and Radical Modernism*, p. 21.
25. Sherry, *Ezra Pound, Wyndham Lewis and Radical Modernism*, p. 4.
26. Ibid. pp. 1–23.
27. Ibid. p. 5.
28. Ibid. p. 5.
29. See the discussion of Pythagoras in Chapter 1, 'Histories of Musical Transcendence', p. 30.
30. Sherry, *Ezra Pound, Wyndham Lewis and Radical Modernism*, p. 5.
31. Ibid. p. 23.
32. Richard Sieburth, *Instigations: Ezra Pound and Rémy de Gourmont* (Cambridge, MA: Harvard University Press, 1978). Sherry, *Ezra Pound, Wyndham Lewis and Radical Modernism*, p. 5.
33. Sherry, *Ezra Pound, Wyndham Lewis and Radical Modernism*, p. 22. Gourmont, *Esthétique de la langue française*.
34. Julien Benda, *Belphegor*, trans. S. J. I. Lawson (New York: Payson and Clarke, 1929), p. 144.

35. Sherry, *Ezra Pound, Wyndham Lewis and Radical Modernism*, p. 17.
36. Wyndham Lewis, *Time and Western Man*, ed. Paul Edwards ([1927] Santa Rosa, CA: Black Sparrow Press, 1993), p. 61.
37. Ezra Pound, TL (carbon) of letter to Dr. Louis Berman n.d. [1922], New York Public Library, Berg Collection, James Sibley Watson/The Dial Papers 1920–1972, B7199281. Quoted by Kimberley Kyle Howey in 'Ezra Pound and the Rhetoric of Science, 1901–1922' (2009: unpublished PhD thesis submitted to University College London).
38. Pound, *Gaudier-Brzeska*, pp. 84, 17.
39. Ethan Lewis, 'Imagisme', in Ira B. Nadel, ed., *Ezra Pound in Context* (Cambridge: Cambridge University Press, 2010), p. 274.
40. Sherry, *Ezra Pound, Wyndham Lewis and Radical Modernism*, p. 51. Sieburth, *Instigations*, pp. 5, 12, 173.
41. Reed Way Dasenbrock, *The Literary Vorticism of Ezra Pound and Wyndham Lewis* (Baltimore: Johns Hopkins University Press, 1985), p. 93.
42. Ezra Pound, 'Vorticism' (1914), in *Gaudier-Brzeska*, p. 89.
43. Weir, *Decadence and the Making of Modernism*, p. 35.
44. Théophile Gautier, *Émaux et camées*, ed. Claudine Gothot-Mersch (Paris: Gallimard/Poésie, 1981), p. 149.
45. Ezra Pound, 'The Hard and the Soft in French Poetry', *Poetry* 11.5 (February 1918), 264–71. Reprinted in *Ezra Pound's Poetry and Prose*, vol. 3 (London: Garland, 1991), p. 55.
46. Ezra Pound, 'James Joyce: At Last the Novel Appears', *Egoist* 4.2 (February 1917), 21–2. Reprinted in *Ezra Pound's Poetry and Prose*, vol. 2 (London: Garland, 1991), p. 187.
47. Epstein, *Sublime Noise*, p. 101.
48. T. S. Eliot, 'T. S. Eliot Talks about his Poetry', in *The Poems of T. S. Eliot: Collected and Uncollected Poems*, vol. 1, ed. Christopher Ricks and Jim McCue (London: Faber & Faber, 2015), p. 458.
49. Ezra Pound, 'Hugh Selwyn Mauberley', in *Selected Poems 1908–1969*, p. 99.
50. Rebecca Beasley, *Theorists of Modern Poetry: T.S. Eliot, T.E. Hulme, Ezra Pound* (Abindgon: Routledge, 2007), p. 32.
51. Ezra Pound, 'Hugh Selwyn Mauberley', in *Selected Poems 1908–1969*, p. 98.
52. Erin E. Templeton, 'Ezra Pound, George Antheil and the Complications of Patronage', in Robert P. McParland, ed., *Music and Literary Modernism* 2nd edn (Newcastle-upon-Tyne: Cambridge Scholars, 2009), p. 71.
53. Dmitri Tymoczko, *A Geometry of Music: Harmony and Counterpoint in the Extended Common Practice* (Oxford: Oxford University Press, 2011), p. 28.
54. Arnold Schoenberg, 'Opinion or Insight', in *Style and Idea*, p. 263.
55. Nattiez, *Music and Discourse*, p. 46.
56. Bryony Randall, *Modernism, Daily Time and Everyday Life* (Cambridge: Cambridge University Press, 2007). Mary Ann Gillies, *Henri Bergson and British Modernism* (Montreal: McGill-Queen's University Press, 1996). Mary Ann Gillies, 'Bergsonism: "Time Out of Mind"', in David Bradshaw, ed., *A Concise Companion to Modernism* (Oxford: Blackwell, 2003),

pp. 95–115. Michael Whitworth, *Einstein's Wake: Relativity, Metaphor, and Modernist Literature* (Oxford: Oxford University Press, 2001).
57. Margaret Fisher, *The Transparency of Ezra Pound's Great Bass* (Emeryville, CA: Second Event Art Publishing, 2013), https://read.amazon.co.uk/?asin=B00EBXO1WK (last accessed 3 August 2018).
58. Fisher, *The Transparency of Ezra Pound's Great Bass*. Ernst Friedrich Richter, *Manual of Harmony: A Practical Guide to its Study Prepared Especially for the Conservatory of Music at Leipzig*, ed. Alfred Richter, trans. Theodore Baker (New York: G Schirmer, 1912).
59. Pound, 'Hugh Selwyn Mauberley', in *Selected Poems 1908–1969*, p. 98.
60. Michael Coyle, *Ezra Pound, Popular Genres, and the Discourse of Genre* (University Park, PA: Pennsylvania State University Press, 1995), p. 160.
61. Ezra Pound, *Machine Art and Other Writings: The Lost Thought of the Italian Years*, ed. Maria Luisa Adrizzone (Durham, NC: Duke University Press, 1996), p. 73.
62. Daniel Albright also suggested a way of applying the 'Great Bass' theory that is based around dividing the lowest note by two, but he offers it as an explanation rather than an alternative, perhaps because he was not aware (since he does not refer to it) of Pound's other explanation in 'Machine Art'. Albright writes: 'eventually the concert A can be divided into something measured not in cycles per second, but in cycles per minute; and then it becomes a rhythm, a ticktick on a metronome, not a sound'. Albright also notes that 'Karlheinz Stockhausen devised a similar analysis of the relation of pitch to rhythm while composing *Gruppen* [1958]'. Albright, *Untwisting the Serpent*, p. 163.
63. Sherry, *Ezra Pound, Wyndham Lewis and Radical Modernism*, pp. 21–2.
64. Ibid. p. 9.
65. Ibid. pp. 9–11.
66. Ibid. p. 22.
67. Ezra Pound, 'The New Sculpture', in *Ezra Pound's Poetry and Prose*, vol. 1, p. 222.
68. Donald J. Childs, *Modernism and Eugenics: Woolf, Eliot, Yeats, and the Culture of Degeneration* (Cambridge: Cambridge University Press, 2007).
69. Michael Bell, 'Primitivism: Modernism as Anthropology', in Peter Brooker, Andrzej Gasiorek, Deborah Longworth and Andrew Thacker, eds, *The Oxford Handbook of Modernisms* (Oxford: Oxford University Press, 2010), p. 354.
70. Sherry, *Ezra Pound, Wyndham Lewis and Radical Modernism*, p. 7.
71. Ibid. p. 71.
72. Adorno and Horkheimer, *Dialectic of Enlightenment*, pp. 194–5.
73. Jeneman, *Adorno in America*, p. 6.
74. Adorno, *Minima Moralia*, p. 18.
75. Herbert Marcuse, *One Dimensional Man* ([1964] Abingdon: Routledge, 2003), p. 211.
76. Paul Morrison, *The Poetics of Fascism: Ezra Pound, T. S. Eliot, Paul de Man* (Oxford: Oxford University Press, 1996), p. 4.
77. Walter Benjamin, 'The Work of Art in the Age of Mechanical Reproduction', in *Illuminations*, trans. Hannah Arendt (New York: Schocken Books, 1969), p. 234.

78. Ibid. p. 241.
79. Kerala J. Snyder, *Dieterich Buxtehude: Organist in Lübeck* (Rochester, NY: University of Rochester Press, 2007), pp. 104–5.
80. See for example Nitzan Lebovic, *The Philosophy of Life and Death: Ludwig Klages and the Rise of a Nazi Biopolitics* (New York: Palgrave Macmillan, 2013). See Hans Sachs, *The Book of Trades (Ständebuch)*, ed. Jost Amman (New York: Dover, 1973); Dieter Borchmeyer, *Drama and the World of Richard Wagner* (Princeton, NJ: Princeton University Press, 2003), p. 183.
81. Ezra Pound, *ABC of Reading* (New York: New Directions, 1960), p. 54.
82. Programmes of these concerts, published in *Il Mare*, are reprinted in *EPM* 418–28.
83. Mark S. Byron, 'European History: The Enlightenment', in Demetres P. Tryphonopoulos and Stephen J. Adams, eds, *The Ezra Pound Encyclopedia* (London: Greenwood Press, 2005), p. 108.
84. Tony Tremblay, 'Frobenius, Leo (1873–1938)', in Demetres P. Tryphonopoulos and Stephen J. Adams, eds, *The Ezra Pound Encyclopedia* (London: Greenwood Press, 2005), pp. 126–7.
85. 'Pound, in Mental Clinic, Wins Prize for Poetry Penned in Treason Cell', *New York Times*, 20 February 1949. See also Ira B. Nadel, ed., *The Cambridge Companion to Ezra Pound* (Cambridge: Cambridge University Press, 1999), p. xxix.
86. Karen Leick, 'Ezra Pound v. *The Saturday Review of Literature*', *Journal of Modern Literature* 25.2 (2001–2), 19–37.
87. Ronald Bush, 'Modernism, Fascism, and the Composition of Ezra Pound's *Pisan Cantos*', *Modernism/modernity* 2.3 (1995), 69.
88. Michael Coyle and Roxana Preda, 'A Prize Fight and Institutionalisation, 1948–1951', in *Ezra Pound and the Career of Modern Criticism: Professional Attention* (Rochester, NY: Camden House, 2018), pp. 1–23. Jason M. Baskin, *Modernism Beyond the Avant-Garde: Embodying Experience* (Cambridge: Cambridge University Press, 2019), p. 72.
89. Hugh Kenner, *The Pound Era* (Berkeley, CA: University of California Press, 1971).
90. Werner Wolff claimed that 'rhythm has been considered as the main problem of graphic expression and Ludwig Klages put it into the center of his graphological system'. Werner Wolff, *Diagrams of the Unconscious, Handwriting and Personality in Measurement, Experiment and Analysis* (New York: Grune and Stratton, 1948), p. 69. See also Ludwig Klages, *Rhythmen und Runen* (Leipzig: Johann Ambrosius Barth, 1944), and Lebovic, *The Philosophy of Life and Death*, p. 6.
91. Michael Golston, *Rhythm and Race in Modernist Poetry and Science: Pound, Yeats, Williams, and Modern Sciences of Rhythm* (New York: Columbia University Press, 2007), p. 118.
92. Mark S. Byron, 'A Defining Moment in Ezra Pound's *Cantos*: Musical Scores and Literary Texts', in Michael J. Meyer, ed., *Rodopi Perspectives on Modern Literature: Literature and Music* (Amsterdam and New York: Rodopi, 2002), p. 165.
93. Nadel, ed., *The Cambridge Companion to Ezra Pound*, p. xxix. Andrei

Guruianu and Anthony Di Renzo, *Dead Reckoning: Transatlantic Passages on Europe and America* (Albany, NY: SUNY Press, 2016), p. 197.
94. Baskin, *Modernism Beyond the Avant-Garde*, pp. 96, 88.
95. Ezra Pound, *Posthumous Cantos*, ed. Massimo Bacigalupo (Manchester: Carcanet, 2015), pp. 98–9, 108–9, 112–17, 201–3.
96. Wallace Stevens, 'The Relations between Poetry and Painting', in *The Necessary Angel: Essays on Reality and the Imagination* (New York: Vintage, 1951), pp. 175–6.
97. Adorno, *Aesthetic Theory*, p. 353.
98. Byron, 'A Defining Moment in Ezra Pound's *Cantos*', p. 162.
99. Pound's typescript for Canto LXXV, quoted in Byron, 'A Defining Moment in Ezra Pound's *Cantos*', p. 162. Byron's helpful note reads: 'this typescript derives from the Ezra Pound Collection in the Beinecke Rare Book and Manuscript Library at Yale University: YCAL (Yale Collection of American Literature) MSS 43, Box 76, Folder 3393. Other typescripts contain small variations in wording, but the same composition scheme adheres: the poetic matter is followed by a blank space or a signal to leave such a space for the music. See YCAL MSS 43, Box 76, Folders 3394 and 3397; and Box 77, Folder 3404'.
100. Dorothy Pound to James Laughlin, 16 December 1945, James Laughlin Collection, Beinecke Rare Book and Manuscript Library, Yale University, cited in Byron, 'A Defining Moment in Ezra Pound's *Cantos*', 162.
101. Byron, 'A Defining Moment in Ezra Pound's *Cantos*', p. 162.
102. Adorno, *Aesthetic Theory*, pp. 69–70.
103. William Carlos Williams, 'Excerpts from a Critical Sketch: A Draft of XXX Cantos by E. P.', in *Selected Essays* (New York: Random House, 1954), p. 107.
104. William Barrett, 'Comment: A Prize for Ezra Pound', *Partisan Review* (April 1949), 344–7.

Chapter 4

Sylvia Townsend Warner, Ideology and Marxist Aesthetics

Sylvia Townsend Warner explores the possibilities for writing after high modernist formal innovation. Warner's texts show that the artwork still has the potential to contemplate complex ideas through narratives that analyse ideology, social interaction and the function of art. Warner worked as a professional musicologist between 1916 and 1928, so her references to music must be approached as extremely well informed and significant. Writing in 1927 about Beethoven, she uses characteristically straightforward language to construct a sophisticated argument about the value of music: 'Even when the music seems to be saying nothing in particular, or something rather foolish, there can be no doubt for the hearer that whatsoever is said, is meant'.[1] This statement, written the year after Warner published her first novel, is indicative of the ideas she brings to her fiction. She identifies that Beethoven's music is celebrated for its sincerity and authenticity, with 'no doubt for the hearer' about its meaning; yet the vagueness and variability of 'seems' and 'whatsoever is said' identifies that this is likely to be different for each individual. Music necessitates and masks the role of individual interpretation required to extract meanings from it, which are attributed and variable although they seem integral and absolute. This is the source of music's interest and value for Warner. Her writing is attentive to the forces that imperceptibly shape music and its interpretations, from the material conditions of money and education to abstract concepts of transcendence and universality.

Warner's fiction contains nuanced conceptualisations of ideologies and how they can operate through music. She published a huge amount of writing between 1926 and 1978, and she often explores issues of ideology and identity that came to be theorised in the middle of the twentieth century by Raymond Williams, Theodor W. Adorno and Louis Althusser. Her short story 'The Music at Long Verney' investigates the relationships between wealth, culture and identity, showing that ideologies are at work in places where they are not readily acknowledged, such as people's music preferences. Ideologies, in Warner's fiction, are not oppressive sets of ideas, but subtly inform identities and have a dynamic relationship with material conditions. Education and wealth produce ideologically constituted subjects in varied and unpredictable ways, and the new experiences or environments in which she places her characters can prompt recognition of the ideological aspects of previously unexamined beliefs. Her second novel, *Mr Fortune's Maggot*, imagines the consequences when Timothy Fortune's foundational ideologies are challenged by his experience of a different culture. Warner draws on her musicological expertise in *Mr Fortune's Maggot* to evaluate the appropriation by Christian religious discourses of Pythagorean and mathematical explanations of music, which she represents as shaping identities that rely on thinking that Western thought and aesthetics are universal. The novel explores how musical education and aesthetics affect perceptions of beauty and order, participating in ideologies of cultural, racial and religious hierarchy.

These two texts show Warner's enduring interest in money and ideology, and we should view her political allegiances against this background. Warner joined the Communist Party of Great Britain in 1935, and was under MI5 surveillance between 1935 and 1955. A letter from Valentine Ackland in Warner's MI5 file acknowledges the receipt of their membership cards, and apologises that 'we' – Warner and Ackland – 'are so isolated' in Chaldon, the rural location in Dorset where they lived.[2] Despite that location, Warner was an active member of the Party. She ran her local branch of the Left Book Club and travelled to Spain during the Civil War to work as a medical auxiliary.[3] Warner's interest in Marxist thought comes through in her 1948 novel *The Corner That Held Them*, which is about a convent but focuses on its finances and the work that is required to keep it running. By bringing issues of money and production into the foreground, the novel encourages a historical materialist approach to the past, claiming that to understand a society and its culture we must analyse the means through which it sustains itself.

Although preoccupied with money and labour, *The Corner That Held Them* does not easily map on to the line established at the 1934 Soviet Writers Congress by Comintern (the international branch of the Communist Party that set directives on how to help advance communism) about how art produced by Communist Party members should work to reveal social inequalities and divisions. While Maroula Joannnou contends that Warner 'permits her characters no sanctuary from the materiality of existence', I argue that she shows the limitations of explaining human life and music in material terms alone.⁴ In Warner's fiction culture and art are materially grounded, but experiencing aesthetic beauty can also open up new ways of thinking and prompt people to act differently. The most transformative experience Henry Yellowlees has in *The Corner That Held Them* is hearing a completely new kind of music for the first time, yet the texts from which he sings are purchased by a chaplain instead of food for his leper colony (*CH* 264). In Warner's fiction the cultural importance of musical transcendence is complicated by and comes into conflict with the conditions of its production and reception.

Warner's writing – especially *The Corner That Held Them* – should be considered part of a British Marxist literary tradition that can be productively compared with the philosophical thought of the Frankfurt School, which Tyrus Miller finds 'particularly adapted to enrich our understanding of the twentieth-century modernist' artwork.⁵ In the later parts of this chapter, I put Warner's thought into dialogue with Christopher Caudwell, whose complex Marxist aesthetic went unappreciated for some time (while Warner's remains unacknowledged). For Warner, music and art have the utopian potential to change how individuals understand, relate to and act in the world – issues seen by Caudwell and theorised extensively by Adorno – while this potential is often frustrated and thwarted by poverty and material conditions.

Although it is unusual to include a chapter on Warner next to Joyce and Pound, this is not the first attempt to discuss her alongside canonised writers. David James has sought to compare Warner's writing with T. S. Eliot's aesthetics of depersonalisation, arguing that an 'implicit striving for a separation of author from artwork' was a 'quintessential component of her aesthetic aspirations for narrative fiction'.⁶ Warner's narration is certainly hard to pin down: it is not always clear who is speaking or thinking because she so often switches focalisation, and her narrators cannot be fixed to one perspective because they use a variety of registers that flit from serious to humorous, scathing to tender. Yet, as James shows, it is difficult to fully reconcile her writing with an Eliot-like impersonality. Unlike James, I want to show that Warner's value is not in a partial adherence to an established high modernist aesthetic, but in the different complexity offered by her texts. In Warner's fiction the resettlement and reconfiguration of ideas is apparent, not modes of abrupt formal alteration or clear confrontation with traditions. Her writing also participates – along with other 1930s writers like Storm Jameson, as James notes and Jan Montefiore argues – in recuperating a rigorous form of realism suitable to address the pressing social issues of the interwar period, responding to what many saw as a retreat from political issues in high modernist writing.[7] Warner's texts are acutely aware of the material conditions in which music is produced and received, but they also explore how aesthetic experiences can work on people without their knowledge, transmitting values or abstract concepts that shape a person's thinking. Warner's fiction addresses and critically handles issues of musical transcendence, aesthetic autonomy and universality, exploring the functions, value and limitations of these concepts in human life and social interactions.

Warner, Musicologist

This chapter requires a more grounded approach than the previous two to explain the significance of biographical details about Warner's life that are not widely known. An account of Warner's education and professional career, which she began as a musicologist, can help us to appreciate the depth of knowledge she brings to her writing. Warner's initial education was informal, since women were unable to attend Harrow school where her father taught history, which was also where the family lived. She studied music in an unofficial capacity with Percy Carter Buck, then a young teacher at Harrow who would be Professor of Music at the University of London by 1925, receiving a knighthood for services to music in 1937.[8] Although married, in 1913 he and Warner began a romantic relationship that would last for seventeen years. By 1928 Warner considered herself Buck's intellectual equal, regardless of his many titles and accolades. Referring to their secret romantic relationship, she wrote in her diary in 1928 of a 'niggling conviction that love is impossible between equals. One must have a little condescension or a little awe'.[9] Buck's many credentials, afforded by the greater educational and professional opportunities for men, did not appear to intimidate or inspire any jealousy in Warner.

Warner also studied Tudor notation with eminent musicologist Richard Terry. Lynn Mutti has pointed out how significant it was for him to take a female pupil.[10] Richard Searle cites Terry praising Warner's 'first class intellect' as 'brilliant' and 'genius'.[11] Terry was editor-in-chief of the *Tudor Church Music* project when it began in 1916, which helps to explain Warner's appointment to the editorial board, although her biographer Claire Harman writes that the job was 'so timely and fortunate for Sylvia that it is hard to believe that Percy Buck did not engineer it'.[12] Warner wrote in her diary that she knew she was given the editorial position on *Tudor Church Music* despite there being candidates 'with as good or better qualifications', showing she was aware of the limited employment opportunities for women in fields where men could achieve more qualifications.[13]

Between 1916 and 1928 Warner earned a small salary working on the editorial board preparing the Oxford University Press editions of *Tudor Church Music*, which were funded by the Carnegie Trust. This involved collecting the fifteenth- and sixteenth-century manuscripts of composers including Thomas Tallis, William Byrd, Robert White and John Taverner, and editing them into publishable form.[14] The manuscripts were often incomplete and had to be transcribed from Tudor to modern notation so that they could be read by contemporary musicians. If the musical knowledge required for an invitation to work on *Tudor Church Music* was considerable, it was nothing compared to that which Warner acquired during the twelve years the project ran. She did the majority of the travelling to cathedrals, libraries and archives where the manuscripts were located, which Harman puts down to the fact that she was the only member of the editorial team who 'had no family to be inconvenienced', as well as the only woman.[15]

Warner discusses the importance and complexity of the editorial choices she made in detail in an article, 'Doubting Castle', published in *Music and Letters* (1924). She writes that an editor 'must pick his way through a morass where it is very easy to go wrong, and quite impossible to feel sure of going right'.[16] Despite describing her own work, she uses the male pronoun through the essay, which anticipates her readership and acknowledges the male-dominated workplace and academe. There are some fascinating observations in this essay, where we can see Warner has already developed clear ideas about the value of art and her approved methods of analysis. Warner advocates a historicist approach to understanding artworks, and rejects the idea of universal or absolute value: 'No artist's work has purely absolute value. It is conditioned by time and place'.[17] There is also an intense suspicion of what she calls 'blind faith', which she says is both an 'ingrained flaw of character' and a form of 'mental laziness'.[18] Warner's attentiveness to context, history and detailed analysis, which is evident in her fiction, was developed during her work as a musicologist, which made Warner into a rigorous editor, music theorist and historian.

Warner was also a proficient composer, and Harman suggests that her plans to study with Arnold Schoenberg were prevented by the outbreak of the First World War.[19] Very little of her music still survives, but Richard Terry described Warner's compositions as 'remarkable' in May 1919.[20] Warner writes in her diary about hearing her version of sixteenth-century composer Robert White's music performed, saying it was 'entertaining to hear my added cantus part careering about that roof . . . Hearing *my* version, done for them, incorporating both 4 and 8 pt versions absolutely clinched my conviction that the 4 pt is an adaptation'.[21] Warner claims the version, which was in the fifth volume of *Tudor Church Music*, as her own, acknowledging the high level of control and judgement she had in her editorial work. But she also says it was 'done for them' (the singers) indicating that her work was not just an academic or archival study, but primarily for those who would perform and hear the music.

Warner began to write fiction towards the end of her work on *Tudor Church Music*, and her first novel, *Lolly Willowes*, is about the limitations on women's lives in the 1920s. The title character, Laura, who is expected to tolerate a life of servitude and dependency in her elder brother's household because she does not marry, comments: 'Women have such imaginations, and lead such dull lives'.[22] Warner, thanks in part to *Tudor Church Music*, did not have a dull life. Still, the conditions of her education, affected positively by her father's position and access to other educators at Harrow, but limited by her sex, seem to have produced in Warner someone minutely attentive to the social and economic conditions in which people acquire knowledge, and how this shapes their identity and the options available to them. These issues come into play in her late and so far little discussed short story, 'The Music at Long Verney'.

'The Music at Long Verney'

'The Music at Long Verney' uses subtly shifting narrative focalisation, combined with references to the economic conditions of music production and reception, to explore the ideological underpinnings of aspects of identity often considered deeply personal, like musical taste. The story is about social, economic and cultural change: landowners Oliver and Sibyl Furnival rent out the manor house they have lived in 'forever' and move to the gamekeeper's cottage because 'the cost of living was going up' and the upkeep of the large house 'was a drain on their income' (*MLV* 5, 4). Arriving from London to rent the house, businessman Anthony Simpson and his family are of the newly wealthy middle class who have made their money through trade: 'One of those companies he's a director of makes weed killer' (*MLV* 11). Anthony thinks he understands how class and culture operate. He assumes that a taste for classical music is synonymous with wealth and landownership, but people's preferences are more complicated than he imagines.

Anthony has the money to rent Long Verney, but he also feels he must demonstrate specific cultural tastes:

Anthony put on a Monteverdi record. He still hadn't found the right music for Long Verney. So far, Handel had fitted in best – but Handel fits in anywhere. A great deal of Chopin must have been played in the house at one time. But what house hadn't had Chopin played in it? It ought to be something more homegrown: Arne, perhaps. Best of all, maybe, the counterpoint music of the Church of England: Greene, Pelham Humfrey, Battishill. He must find records, and if there were none, commission some. He liked the house well enough to intend on a longer lease, so it would be worthwhile taking a little trouble. Music and finance were his interests. He had an exquisite ear for both. Oliver and Sibyl had a gramophone too, with records of Noel Coward and Duke Ellington. (*MLV* 10)

Anthony is preoccupied with inhabiting the house as it 'ought' to be inhabited and so he 'fits in': he does this by trying to find the 'right' music, and by 'fill[ing] the house with ballet dancers, opera singers, photographers and intellectuals' in a bid to display how cultured he is (*MLV* 12). Anthony considers a wide range of composers, from the Baroque (Handel) to Romantic (Chopin) as well as British examples beginning with Thomas Arne, a composer for theatre though best known for 'Rule Britannia'.[23] An inspection of these composers reveals the royal, aristocratic and bourgeois circumstances of music production, showing how producing and accessing culture is linked to the possession of wealth. Handel and Chopin especially exemplify the success made possible by patronage and connections among high society. King George I was a patron of Handel, and the royal children were the composer's pupils in the 1720s. Donald Burrows notes that Handel held the title of 'music master' to the king, and benefited from several high-profile patrons, including Queen Anne, who 'granted him an annual pension of £200, apparently in return for undefined services'.[24] Chopin's connections among the Polish aristocracy, where he was brought up and educated, enabled him to play in the prestigious Paris salons,[25] although he also earned large parts of his income from concerts attended by the newly wealthy middle classes in France and Vienna.[26] By the end of 'The Music at Long Verney', Anthony is trying to recreate the world of late-eighteenth-century aristocratic patronage, inviting musicians from London to play in the hall. He finally chooses the music of Haydn who, as Pierpaolo Polzonetti has shown, composed prolifically and circulated around European capitals as the beneficiary of the House of Esterhazy.[27]

Warner's fiction is acutely aware of music as produced and received within relationships of power, and represents Anthony's musical taste as formed within ideology: a way of thinking that makes sense of the world and validates identity, in this case sustaining a belief in a connection between wealth and particular kinds of music. Anthony is representative of the bourgeois business class, and Warner works with a notion of ideology that can be illuminated with the theories of Frankfurt School Marxist theorists – especially Adorno and Horkheimer, for whom ideology has a specific function in capitalist modernity. When the economic value of a commodity is no longer connected to its use value, exchange value becomes abstract and requires ideological support. 'Ideology', Adorno and Horkheimer write, 'is split into the stubborn photograph of the world and the naked lie about its meaning'.[28] Ideology is a combination of observable reality (or, more accurately, a perspective on observable reality stubbornly masquerading as objective fact, like a photograph which might appear to be a faithful reproduction but in which choices have inevitably been made about perspective, inclusion and exclusion) and an attribution of meaning to that reality, which works because it appears to be rooted in truth. Terry Eagleton summarises Adorno's thinking on ideology thus: 'Commodity exchange effects an equation between things which are in fact incommensurable, and so, in Adorno's view, does ideological thought'.[29] In other words, ideological thought is that which differentiates between things and ascribes value, when that value requires ideological support. It functions by creating false equivalences, similar to the false comparisons by which exchange value is differentiated in a marketplace where use value is no longer applicable. As such, it provides ways to evaluate objects as well as ways of thinking or living, all of which contribute to identity. Since the subject's identity relies on ideological support for ascribing value to things that are consumed, ideology becomes a form of binary thinking that validates or confers otherness.

In Warner's story, music's value for Anthony is largely in the identity it allows him to perform, to inhabit his new home in the 'right' way. Despite this performative element, Warner does not give the sense that his preferences are wrong or false: this is not a vulgar conceptualisation of ideology as false consciousness. His ideas about music are ideological in the sense that they work with unexamined ideas about the right music for Long Verney, which are based in logical observations about past conditions of music production that contained some truth, but to which he attributes the same meaning in the present, when those conditions no longer apply. His ideas about music and class do not supplant his aesthetic appreciation: rather, his aesthetic appreciation is represented as conditioned by what he believes appropriate. Anthony acts out what he believes is the correct behaviour, so that Warner shows how ideologies can perpetuate themselves by producing subjects who act according to them.

When small details are reported in 'The Music at Long Verney', it is unclear whether they are factual snippets imparted by a detached narrator, or focalised through Anthony, so that the narration recreates the way that simple observations which could be understood as facts might equally be perspectives coloured by ideology. When the narrator tells us 'Music and finance were his interests', this seems quite straightforward. Yet right after, when we learn 'He had an exquisite ear for both' this seems more like Anthony's opinion of himself. Since the word 'exquisite' does not make sense in that context, the language Anthony uses to assert his connoisseurship shows the limitations of his perception of himself as educated and refined (*MLV* 10). That this word is relayed, with its connotations of affectation and pretentiousness, instead of any suggestion that his ear is skilled or knowledgeable, unsettles any sense of a benevolent or impartial narrator, prompting reconsideration of the first statement. While seemingly imparting simple information, the narration shows how Anthony homogenises 'music and finance' as 'interests' that serve the utilitarian function of preserving his identity as someone with economic success and exceptional taste, of which he has the first but not the second.

A wealthy businessman attempting to properly occupy his new stately home by listening to 'Rule Britannia' and Haydn is an amusingly pompous image, and his contemplation of a classical (in the broad sense) repertoire is underscored with a final gesture towards the extent of his affectation: the Furnivals listen to 'records of Noel Coward and Duke Ellington' (*MLV* 10). Together with the economic changes that prompt the Furnivals to rent out Long Verney, their preferred music signals changes in who culture is produced by – no longer only wealthy and well-connected white men, but black and openly homosexual men too. Ellington's jazz was popular among white audiences in the same era as Jim Crow violence before the civil rights movements in the USA, and Harvey G. Cohen has argued that this popularity 'subverted and undercut racial stereotypes, changing the possibilities for black Americans in the mass media'.[30] Noel Coward's theatre has been described by John Lahr as an 'essentially homosexual comic vision', and Alan Sinfield argues that Coward 'holds homosexuality at the brink of public visibility'.[31] The Furnivals' musical taste highlights how dated Anthony's ideas are, and the different tastes and ways of living that are obscured for his ideologically constituted subjectivity.

Notions of cultural capital – to use a term connected with the thought of Pierre Bourdieu, which refers to the material and economic value of cultural knowledge – are invoked and challenged by Warner's story, since the straightforward connections Anthony makes between music and class are too basic. For Bourdieu, cultural knowledge acquired through education in the home or at school is valuable in a similar way to property, because it is acquired monetarily and can be converted into other kinds of capital.[32] Anthony associates Long Verney with a certain style of music by assuming those who lived there in the past had tastes that matched the kinds of culture they were financially able to access. Owners of estates like Long Verney would have been able to attend classical concerts and host their own, while access to music for the eighteenth- and nineteenth-century working class would have been limited, particularly in rural areas before radios were affordable. Jonathan Rose notes that 'For most working people, Sunday School offered the only opportunity for serious musical education'. In the latter half of the nineteenth century there were some 'free Sunday evening concerts', but these were primarily in larger cities and towns.[33] Bourdieu does not claim a thoroughly rigid affinity between the possession of cultural capital and class, explaining the variables and problems that prevent a direct correlation, but he does notice broad trends. He identifies 'the very close relationship linking cultural practices (or the corresponding opinions) to educational capital (measured by qualifications) and, secondarily, to social origin (measured by father's occupation)', concluding that 'differences in cultural capital mark the differences between the classes'.[34] In other words, social classes have particular cultural tastes, and the tastes of one generation may correspond to those of the previous generation, if they have a similar economic and social status.

Anthony broadly expects the inhabitants of Long Verney to prefer classical music, but Oliver and Sibyl do not conform to his expectations. Their musical preferences are related to their confidence in their own choices because of their social status and isolation at Long Verney: both factors are related to their wealth, but more intricately than as the result of economic means alone. The 'impermeably self-righteous' Furnivals are so established that they do not have the same insecurities as Anthony, and even after renting out their house to the Simpsons, they are so confident that when walking in the woods 'They had no sense of trespass. Their woods. Their house' (*MLV* 11, 13). Oliver and Sybil do not enjoy the Haydn quartet when Antony invites them inside to listen to it: they sit 'waiting for the music to end' (*MLV* 13). Although they impose on the Simpsons they are 'Immune to any consideration of awkwardness', just as they are immune to any social expectations about what music they should enjoy. Oliver is content to admit that 'The music was far above my head' (*MLV* 17–18), and is completely unaffected by this knowledge, since that which is out of his reach or understanding does not concern him.

A change in narration contributes to the sense of confusion among the group as they listen to the music together. In preceding parts of the story, the narration is focalised through particular characters: from the perspective of the Furnivals and the circumstances that lead them to rent out the house, or the Simpsons as they settle in. When they all finally meet, short sentences shifting between the perspectives of the Furnivals, the musicians and the Simpsons heighten the sense of fragmentation and lack of mutual understanding:

> Oliver flicked a glance at Sibyl. The players attacked the allegro vivace. They're overdoing it, thought Anthony. His evening had been ruined; the joy with which he had listened to the first movement was irreparably past recall. What am I to say, what am I to say? Thought Naomi. (*MLV* 17)

'What am I to say?' sums up the difficulty of communicating the meeting, in which nobody understands each other or is aware of the complex preconceptions they each hold. Anthony misreads Oliver's reaction to the music because of his assumption about the universal relation between living in a large house and enjoying Haydn. Expecting Oliver to be an expert, Anthony inwardly criticises the performance as 'overdone' because of Oliver's glance, when an *allegro vivace* is by definition fast and lively, and Oliver has no idea whether the musicians are playing well or not.

Anthony treats a taste for classical music as a universal marker of wealth, but Warner shows that this association is based on economic conditions that have altered. This is what Raymond Williams describes as a 'residual' culture: a value that is 'lived and practised on the basis of the residue – cultural as well as social – of some previous social formation'.[35] While the economic means required to access music (and the kinds of music available) change, the traditions produced by economic conditions from the past also become reified, so that both affect the ways in which individuals' subjectivities are constructed and contribute to layers of experience and attitudes to culture.

'The Music at Long Verney' complicates models of a determined base and a determining superstructure by showing the diverse cultural practices that exist at a given moment. This is part of Raymond Williams's project in *Culture and Materialism*, and Warner explores similar issues through fiction.[36] She shows that the relationships between the superstructure and base are complicated and unpredictable in a way that often goes unrecognised. Music is part of superstructural relations as a cultural practice with a relationship to the economic base. While the base is the 'real social existence of man', in Williams's phrase, or 'the specific activities of men in real social and economic relationships', the common understanding of a superstructure has been 'the reflection, the imitation or the reproduction of the reality of the base in the superstructure in a more or less direct way', and the story shows that superstructural relations are 'never in practice either uniform or static'.[37] Anthony understands that people's access to culture can be determined by their economic means, but he does not understand that that those connections are continually shifting – even though as an emerging businessman he is an example of how social formations alter.

Anthony's ideas are not wrong or meaningless, though – they are very meaningful to him, since he believes in the validity of his choices. Ideologies are not simply abstract, imposed thoughts: if this were the case, they could be easily disregarded. Anthony believes in the authenticity and inviolable nature of his musical preferences. He is confident that his judgements are 'exquisite', and thinks no further about his choices or ideas. This is clear when he asks, 'But what house hadn't had Chopin played in it?' which both shows his ignorance and signifies the extent of his interpellation within ideology. The kind of music likely to be played in 'most' households is starkly different from that which Anthony imagines or assumes, showing how he constructs his own reality by considering only the musical tastes and habits he assumes wealthy people to have had. As Jonathan Rose points out, most (working-class) houses would not have had Chopin played in them. Increasingly, households would have had pianos in them, but not necessarily individuals who could play Chopin, afford lessons or buy Chopin manuscripts.[38] The question 'But what house hadn't had Chopin played in it?' is rhetorical: it appears obvious to Anthony, but it is really only the recognition of what he is capable of believing in his particular subject position, showing that he cannot think outside of the world of the wealthy and privileged. In Althusser's words, Anthony thinks 'That's obvious! That's right! That's true!' when he thinks about Chopin and his own musical choices, but really these are examples of the extent to which he is constituted by ideology.[39] Or, as Adorno and Horkheimer phrase it, 'Ideology becomes the systematic proclamation of what is': it is the assertion of things that seem to be true, through which ideas about the world become naturalised.[40]

Mr Fortune's Maggot

'The Music at Long Verney' is a useful introduction to ideology in Warner's texts, but her second novel, which shows the impact of being forced to question the ideologies that contribute to an individual's identity, offers a more serious investigation of the topic. Warner was still working on the *Tudor Church Music* project when *Mr Fortune's Maggot* was published in 1927: her established musicological profession was overlapping with the literary career that was just beginning. Warner's specialist knowledge of music informs the novel's critique of the colonial enterprise through the failure of Timothy Fortune's religious mission on the island of Fanua. Warner knows that music is intimately connected to religious practice, and implicated in justifications for colonialism and imperialism on the grounds of religious, technological and cultural supremacy. The novel's narration shows ideology at work in almost every assumption, interpretation, thought and utterance made by her characters.

Gillian Beer has written that if *Mr Fortune's Maggot* had been published 'fifty years later, it would be read as a post-colonial text', and now it usually is.[41] For Young-Hee Kwon the text explores the fate of imperial masculinity in late colonialism, while Gay Wachman has read the novel biographically as an example of lesbian 'crosswriting', and as a primitivist text that envisages a simpler, more remote way of living.[42] While Rod Edmond calls the novel a 'beautifully ironized' depiction of the colonial enterprise, Howard J. Booth argues that there is more at stake in the story than the end of empire account that has so far been discussed.[43] For Booth, the novel shows time – 'in its Western, colonial sense' – giving way, and recognises that 'the end of Empire does not only involve a readjustment to life within European borders but a questioning of everything including structures of thought, gendered identities and what life is for'.[44] Booth's argument can be extended by exploring music and mathematics as particular 'structures of thought' examined by the novel. They are central to Timothy's understanding of the world, as they are to Western European rationality. Through music and mathematics, *Mr Fortune's Maggot* shows what is at stake in the failure of the colonial enterprise: the (in)ability to maintain the superiority of Western rationality itself.

Mr Fortune's Maggot builds on the history of supposed civilising missions among the so-called native savages during European exploration of the South Pacific in the eighteenth and nineteenth centuries. Timothy, a former bank clerk, follows his call from God to the fictional South Pacific island of St Fabien, before embarking on his own mission to the tiny remote island of Fanua. Edmond has explored the history of colonialism in the South Pacific, and the ways in which religious missionaries transformed the lives of native populations. By the mid-nineteenth century, he writes, 'western traders and missionaries had done their best, which is now often seen as their worst': 'the material culture of South Sea islanders was stripped, the missionaries transformed their lifeways. The more heavily an island was colonized, the more demoralized it became'.⁴⁵ In a reversal of the historical narrative, it is the coloniser who loses faith in Warner's novel. Timothy converts no one, and eventually believes that the Fanuans are 'best as they are' (*MFM* 202). He comes to this conclusion after Lueli's attempted suicide, which prompts Timothy to question the benefits of the Western education he has tried to enforce on him. The implications of Timothy's perspective reach into every corner of life: judgements and ideas that had seemed stable are unsettled, from the value of Western knowledge to how each day should be lived.

Attitudes to music are singled out as markers of cultural difference at the start of the novel. The archdeacon warns Timothy that the Fanuans 'are like children, always singing and dancing, and of course immoral . . . Singing and dancing! No actual harm in that, of course, and no doubt the climate is responsible' (*MFM* 3–4). The Fanuans' response to music, 'singing and dancing', sits between assertions that they are 'like children' and 'of course immoral' in the archdeacon's sentence, showing the difficult space the islanders inhabit in his thought: they exhibit a joyful attitude to music which is childlike, with connotations of innocence, but they are also heathens. He does not recognise the contradiction in his own statement, or the rigidity and illogical nature of his conviction that although the islanders are like innocent children, they must be immoral because they are not Christians.

The archdeacon's dialogue contains references to a range of religious, aesthetic and scientific discourses that were closely connected and often mutually reinforcing at the start of the twentieth century. In his disapproval of the Fanuans' musical culture, Warner shows how Christian approaches to music as sacred and spiritual were becoming intertwined with discourses of natural history. Edmond notes the significance of these ideas in the colonies: while differences between other cultures were first understood in religious terms, 'by the eighteenth century, religiously framed colonialism was being replaced by natural history as the basis for constructing otherness'.⁴⁶ Differences between cultures began to be understood as the result of biological variations that were responsible for greater intelligence and industry that produced more advanced and morally superior civilisations. For the archdeacon, the Fanuans' response to music is evidence of their innate inferiority, echoing claims by Julien Benda and Remy de Gourmont about music as a vulgar art form, whose influence on Ezra Pound I discussed in Chapter 3.⁴⁷ Benda and Gourmont claimed that immediate bodily responses to music are base and vulgar because they bypass the intelligence. For these writers, Vincent Sherry says, 'true intelligence follows the physics of the eye, which actively analyzes' while 'aural debility characterizes the mental processes of the demotic masses'.⁴⁸ Sherry has shown that these ideas are integral to Pound's and Lewis's aesthetics and their radical politics, contributing to their arguments about natural hierarchy: 'whereas sympathy is the debased habit of the common folk, members of a body swayed to music, detachment is the rank and privilege of an aristocratic class'.[49] Being physically and emotionally moved by music (as opposed to intellectually stimulated) was the mark of inferior people, while being analytical and discriminatory was an indicator of superiority. The archdeacon is represented as adhering to very simple versions of these ideas when he associates vital, physical responses to music such as dancing with immorality, and characterises the Fanuans as a race of people with the intellectual ability of children.

Mr Fortune's Maggot subtly registers the impact of scientific approaches to justifying cultural supremacy on religious discourses. While the sciences and natural history made great changes to what is known about the world, *Mr Fortune's Maggot* shows that the benefits of rational observation, judgement and discrimination are limited if not extended to all ideas – in other words, if some judgements are taken for granted and remain rigid, such as racial hierarchy or the transcendent nature of Western religious music. For the archdeacon and Timothy, music should be a form of divine communication, but *Mr Fortune's Maggot* works against discourses of music as sacred, and separate from materiality. One of the only luxury items Timothy allows himself to take to Fanua is a harmonium, which he uses in his first of many (unsuccessful) religious demonstrations designed to 'convert' the islanders:

> Mr. Fortune sat down to his harmonium and sang and played through a hymn. His back was to the islanders, he could not see how they were taking it. But when, having finished the hymn and added two chords for the Amen, he turned round to announce the collect, he discovered that they had already dispersed. (*MFM* 15)

The two chords added for the Amen are an example of music's centrality to religious ritual: this is the plagal cadence (the passage from the subdominant to the dominant chords, or chords IV–I) which schoolchildren are still taught to recognise today through familiarity because of its use at 'Amen'.[50] Music is an integral part of religious codes, embedded within religious service and persisting in popular cultural knowledge. The customary hush of the congregation that Timothy expects as he prepares the collect, however, is instead the silence of his congregation's absence. The contrast between his expectations and the reality shows the entirely different responses that one phenomenon can produce, troubling the notion of any absolute or enduring truth. Timothy cannot see that this behaviour is culturally dependent: his traditions and rituals have produced someone unable to imagine other responses. The hymn, which to Timothy is part of a sacred tradition – he even forbids 'whistl[ing] tunes that had any especially sacred associations' (*MFM* 71) – is merely dull to the islanders, who quietly disappear.

The harmonium is an example of technologies that were specifically developed and marketed for transporting Western culture and music to the colonies, where they were frequently used because they were portable and suitable for outdoor use. In 1862, a 'Colonial Pianoforte' described as 'especially adapted for exportation to the Colonies' was repeatedly advertised in *The London Review*.[51] In an 1857 letter from a mission in the South Atlantic island of St Helena, a missionary wrote that the colonisers are 'anxiously desirous of contributions towards an Harmonium' for their church.[52] Arthur Ord-Hume has provided a history of the harmonium's production, and Robert F. Gellerman has explored the use of these instruments in missions in Africa.[53] Harmoniums featured in the 1851 Great Exhibition and the 1867 Paris Exhibition: huge-scale events in Britain and France where world cultures, artefacts and technologies were put on display.[54] At these exhibitions people from the colonies could be viewed alongside objects and inventions. Jeffrey A. Auerbach notes that the exhibitions may have been designed to show the 'unity and togetherness of the human community', but despite any positive intentions they also served a very different function: recruiting and transporting people from the colonies to perform their native rituals for European onlookers created a spectacle of the racialised other.[55]

The harmonium and Timothy's music are not benign offerings, but assertions of Western values. When Timothy tries to play a duet with Lueli, this moment of attempted cooperation contains a darker desire for sameness and submission. In narration focalised through Timothy, we learn how he understands Lueli's music:

> As for the duet plan it was not feasible, for the harmonium was tuned to the mean tone temperament and Lueli's pipe obeyed some unscientific native scale; either alone sounded all right, but in conjunction they were painfully discordant. Finding it impossible to convert Lueli's pipe, Mr. Fortune next essayed to train his voice to Christian behaviour. (*MFM* 70)

The 'mean tone temperament' of Timothy's harmonium is a Western tuning method. This Western tuning and the harmonic series are based on early Pythagorean mathematical observations that particular sounds (more specifically, wavelengths) that adhere to each other are produced by the application of mathematical ratios to materials.[56] For example, the application of the ratio 2:1 on a string produces frequencies according to that ratio, which we hear as octaves.[57] The history of music's relationship to ancient Western thought and its scientific explanation underpin Timothy's belief in the superiority of the tuning system to which he has become accustomed: it must be better than Lueli's 'unscientific' and 'native scale'. Timothy's interpretation of Lueli's music is ideological in the sense that he demonstrates binary thinking. He views differences he encounters negatively to protect his belief in the superiority of his own culture – which, after all, is why he has travelled to Fanua to convert the islanders. Timothy cannot recognise that the disparity between the way he describes his own tuning system and Lueli's is not a truth, but the manifestation of his assurance in the supremacy of Western traditions and the inferiority of his pupil's – something that the pipe as the material manifestation of Lueli's culture rebels against, refusing to be converted.

Musical knowledge contributes to Timothy's sense of superiority, but it is also paradoxically central to his idea of universality: that which can transcend cultural and linguistic difference. When he switches subjects, teaching Lueli geometry instead, he still conceptualises universality in musical terms. He believes Lueli will learn 'accurate thoughts, thoughts in just intonation, coming together like unaccompanied voices coming to a close' (*MFM* 168). When contemplating the mathematical knowledge he possesses, 'Mr Fortune began to think of himself possessing an universal elixir and charm', and he thinks, 'If only, if only I could teach him to enjoy an abstract notion! If he could once grasp how it all hangs together, and is everlasting and harmonious, he would be saved' (*MFM* 169, 176). For Timothy, 'accurate thoughts' are those which come 'together like unaccompanied voices coming to a close' in 'just intonation'. The common language supposedly available in mathematics is couched in musical metaphors of correct sounds and harmoniousness, so that universality and the musical seem inseparable for Timothy. He continues to impose his idea of a universal language on Lueli, where really this is the imposition of his own ideologies.

Warner's writing can appear straightforward, but its subtle suggestiveness is an important part of how it works. Her passing references to a rich selection of philosophies, histories and intellectual traditions mean that the reader who recognises them is implicated in acknowledging their function and significance. What David James calls her fiction of impersonality, I prefer to describe with the term Leo Bersani uses for Joyce's fiction, when he calls it 'perspectivally shifty'.[58] While in Joyce's writing the complexity is very much obvious and on the surface, in Warner's fiction we do not find an overt show of skill. The shifting focalisation of her narrative registers the provisional nature of perspective itself. At the same time, for attentive readers, Warner's texts eke out the ideological underpinnings of individual perception: especially when they are contradictory, self-serving or outright damaging to others.

Through a narrative form that switches between different perspectives, which are often difficult to attribute to a character or narrator, the novel shows us the contradictions and problems with the interpretative frameworks used to argue for cultural and religious superiority. Warner shows how far Timothy's desires, interests and preferences are constructed by his education within Western ideology, and reveals the drawbacks to his education, which prevents him from appreciating other forms of music: 'Mr. Fortune, in spite of his superior accomplishments, his cultivated taste, and enough grasp of musical theory to be able to transpose any hymn into its nearly related keys, was not so truly musical as Lueli' (*MFM* 69). The sentence begins with the narrator commenting on Timothy, but observations about his 'cultivated taste' and 'grasp of musical theory' are in his language and reflect his sense of his own 'superior accomplishments'. The final clause, however, cannot be attributed to him since he certainly does not acknowledge that he is 'not so truly musical as Lueli'. The final clause changes the meaning of the preceding clauses: his accomplishments are not simply superior, and what Timothy understands as his 'cultivated taste' is in fact a narrowing of the kind of music he can appreciate. It is not 'in spite' of his musical training that he cannot understand Lueli's music, as Mr Fortune might think: it is rather because of his education that he is not so truly musical as Lueli.

For Nigel Rigby, 'Timothy's rigid adherence to a regimented European musical form is part of the symbolic structure of the novel, in which mathematics stands for European rationality'.[59] Warner connects culture with the imperial processes of which it was manifestly a part, and encourages us to imagine ways in which Western value systems that claim universality, such as tonality and mathematics, are limited and limiting to thought, producing individuals who are unable to appreciate difference. Timothy cannot be balanced or open-minded about Lueli's music, because to admit that it has value would be to question the validity of all the choices he has made in his life. He conceives of his whole life as leading up to the moment when he achieves his first 'convert' on Fanua, thinking, 'He had waited, but after all not for long. The years in the bank, the years at St. Fabien, they did not seem long now' (*MFM* 19). Their musical abilities provide 'a curious study in contrasts' (*MFM* 68) for Timothy, in which his own music must come out on top for him to retain his sense of self. Christianity provides Timothy with a framework for navigating the world and daily life, and he believes his own choices about what is good and bad are verified by God. He imagines with satisfaction how in Christian salvation 'the chaff is blown away, the true grain lies still and adoring' (*MFM* 15) and has no doubt that he is part of the true grain. The pastoral imagery makes palatable a somewhat merciless belief in God's judgement: that the righteous will be easily and unflinchingly separated from those who will presumably experience eternal damnation. The metaphor is based on the proclamation of John the Baptist in Matthew 3.10–12: 'He will baptize you with the Holy Spirit and fire. His winnowing-fork is in his hand, and he will clear his threshing-floor and will gather his wheat into the granary; but the chaff he will burn with unquenchable fire.'[60] This harrowing metaphor, still using chaff and grain but adding the threat of being burned 'with unquenchable fire', shows how Timothy also censors and represses the more aggressive parts of the Bible, remembering a version with a more gentle separation and hierarchy. Still, Timothy's beliefs are constructed around simple and unforgiving binaries, so that when he is presented with difference, such as Lueli's music, he has no choice but to maintain that his own music is better to avoid invalidating his existing worldview and calling everything he knows into question.

Timothy's inability to concede the validity of Lueli's music betrays the single-mindedness that makes him want to destroy Lueli's idol. The violence in John the Baptist's proclamation returns in Timothy's recommendation to Lueli: 'You must destroy your idol. You had better burn it' (*MFM* 116). When Lueli refuses Timothy subjects him to a tirade of 'commanding, reasoning, expostulating, explaining, persuading, threatening' (*MFM* 117). Shortly afterwards, an earthquake begins. The wind comes into the hut 'like an actual angry presence' (*MFM* 119). The weather and the island rebel against Timothy's domineering behaviour:

> He felt the earth give a violent twitch under his feet as though it were hitting up at him, and he was thrown to the ground. There was a noise of rending and bellowing, the lamp gave a last frantic leap, again he felt the ground buffet him like the horns of a bull, and then with a crash and a spurt of fire the roof of the hut caved in.
>
> At the same moment he felt something large and heavy topple across his body.
>
> He could not move and he could not think. He saw flames rising up around him and heard the crackle of the dried thatch. Again the ground began to quiver and writhe beneath him, and suddenly he knew what was happening – an earthquake!
>
> The bulk that lay on top of him was the harmonium. He was pinned beneath it – presently the flames would reach him and he would be burned to death. (*MFM* 119).

The island punishes Timothy for threatening Lueli. It is as though the ground were beating him, 'hitting up at him', 'like the horns of a bull'. It is not the idol but Timothy who risks being 'burnt to death', as though he needs punishment for worshipping a false god. Then, it is specifically the harmonium that pins him to the ground. His musical education restricts his capacity for appreciating Lueli's music, and the harmonium as the physical manifestation of Western ideology restricts his movements and holds him down to receive his punishment.

Timothy does not interpret events in this way. The destruction of the harmonium only leads Timothy to teach Lueli his version of universal beauty through geometry instead. After a gruelling morning of geometry, 'A few minutes before noon the height of the tree was discovered to be fifty-seven foot nine inches' (*MFM* 184). This knowledge seems to pain Lueli rather than bring him joy. Lueli is already depressed, since his idol was destroyed in the earthquake, but the geometry – symbolic of the imposition of Western rationality – is the event immediately before he tries to drown himself. He 'turned his eyes to the tree and looked at that. A sort of shadowy wrinkle, like the blurring on the surface of milk before it boils, crossed his face' and in a 'sleep-walking fashion he turned and went down towards the bathing pool', where he holds himself under the water (*MFM* 185).

Mr Fortune's Maggot offers no suggestions for a course of action, no alternative or better way of living. After Lueli's attempted suicide Timothy loses faith in the superiority of his own ideas and is completely undone. He notes that the 'calm joy of mathematics' had 'failed him' (*MFM* 201), and he realises that his nature is bound up with a will to erode difference: if he does not leave the island, if

> he stayed on, flattering himself with the belief that he had learnt his lesson, he would remember for a while no doubt; but sooner or later, inevitably he would yield to his will again, he would begin to meddle, he would seek to destroy. (*MFM* 200)

With the loss both of his religious beliefs and of his conviction about the supremacy of Western versions of maths and music, 'he did not seem to have an idea left. Everything that was real, everything that was significant, had gone down with the island of Fanua and was lost forever' (*MFM* 249). Losing faith in one's values and beliefs, in this case, is not progressive, but the loss of everything that is real. It is in these terms that Warner does not offer an alternative to ideology, here or in her later novels: it is enough to show the intricacies of how it works. (Or all one can do, because to create an alternative within the same available framework is not really an alternative at all.) Music offers a unique space for exploring how values and tastes are materially shaped, since it often claims to be separate from economic and political ideas, but in *Mr Fortune's Maggot* it is the cornerstone of Timothy's belief system, without which he has nothing. As Booth claims, the novel is about much more than the end of empire: it considers broader questions about the morality of Western modes of thought, and acknowledges how difficult it is to imagine an alternative.[61] The way that Warner calls into question the universality of Western rationality in *Mr Fortune's Maggot* prefigures her membership of the Communist Party and her Marxism, which informs her later Marxist novels.

The Corner That Held Them

Warner clearly engages with Marxist ideas about work, class, money and revolution in her 1936 novel *Summer Will Show*, but the way *The Corner That Held Them* is rooted in Marxist thought is much less obvious. In *The Corner That Held Them* the ways music functions in economic and cultural life are fluctuating and unpredictable. At times the aesthetic provides such enjoyment that characters feel they momentarily transcend their poverty or escape their mundane lives, but music also constantly participates in the material world by taking part in product exchanges and negotiations. Warner's investigation of the material conditions of existence in *The Corner That Held Them* can be illuminated by reading the novel alongside sections of Marx's *Grundrisse*, as well as comparing and contrasting Warner's writing with contemporary British Marxist writers and intellectuals, such as contributors to the *Left Review*.

Warner's expert musical knowledge also informs *The Corner That Held Them*, which charts the fortunes of an isolated English convent called Oby. The novel has no protagonist. Instead, it documents the experiences of many who live at or encounter the convent over a two-hundred-year period, from its founding in the late twelfth century through to the late fourteenth century. The principal concerns of the novel are historical change and finance: it is 'entirely taken up with their money difficulties', as Warner wrote in a 1942 diary entry.[62] References to music's social functions and transcendence first appear when a scholar arrives at the Oby nuns' wicket for alms, and the narrative places the philosophical basis for music's association with the divine into a practical, human encounter. For the 'wandering scholar' music is an example of God's order and design in the world, but he also uses it in a material exchange, so that it occupies both spaces at the same time:

> In 1194 a wandering scholar, very old and shrill, came begging for a meal . . . he talked to the wicket-nun about the properties of numbers . . . he explained to them about the Proportion of Diapason, the perfect concord which is at once concord and unity, and showed them how, by placing the bridge of the

monochord so as to divide the string into a ratio of one and two, the string will sound the interval of the octave. Thus, he mumbled, was the nature of the Godhead perceptible to Pythagoras, a heathen; for it lies latent in all things. He sat on a bench in the sun, but overhead the wind howled, tormenting the willows along the Hog Trail and clawing the thatch, and the nuns could scarcely hear the demonstration of how the Godhead sounded to Pythagoras. It was really no loss, for his hand, shaking with cold and palsy, had failed to place the bridge correctly, and the diapason of the Trinity was out of tune. (CH 12–13)

The scholar refers to the mystical and holy significance given to 'perfect' musical intervals that accord with specific continuities and perfect ratios in mathematics. The diapason is the 'perfect' octave, an interval between two notes, one with double or half the other note's frequency. Although little evidence of Pythagoras's life from primary sources remains, this discovery is credited to him most notably by Iamblichus, a prominent Neoplatonist philosopher.[63] Donald C. Benson explains that 'the frequency ratio of every Pythagorean interval is a ratio between a power of two and a power of three . . . the Pythagorean requirement [is] that all intervals be associated with ratios of whole numbers'.[64] The mathematical harmonic series used today is based on these early observations about music, which noticed that if a string is divided (as the scholar says) 'into a ratio of one and two, the string will sound the interval of an octave'.[65] This means that comparable sounds are produced by materials of proportionally comparable mathematical ratios. For example, if a note has a frequency of 200 Hz, an octave above it will have a frequency of 400 Hz, and the octave below a frequency of 100 Hz: all ratios of 2:1. Mathematical philosophies contemplate the possibilities of the existence of numbers, infinites and immutable facts, so that they often engage questions of ontology and existence – similar metaphysical questions to those contemplated in philosophies of logic not associated with the mathematical, as Bertrand Russell and Paul Bernays have discussed.[66] The association of whole numbers with God that the scholar refers to is echoed in the language still used to describe whole numbers, or integers, in mathematics, which are often referred to as 'natural numbers'.[67]

The relationship between the ratios, sound and 'the Godhead' (or Godliness) is reliant on a form of Neoplatonic Idealism which considers the universe to be coherently (or harmoniously) ordered according to a specific principle or idea, and the logical organisation of phenomena in the natural world is considered proof of the existence of a primary principle, such as a God, or Absolute. Scholars such as John Findlay and Pauliina Remes have noted the influence of Neoplatonism on early Christianity.[68] Remes writes that it 'deeply influenced those Christians who had theoretical, theological or philosophical interests. Indeed, in many places the Neoplatonic approach was the only one available to a student committed to theoretical studies'.[69] For Franchino Gaffurio, author of among the earliest and most significant treatises on music theory, musical and mathematical proportions were connected specifically with divine questions of universal order. Cristle Collins Judd writes that:

> among the most important early printed treatises in terms of their influence on the sixteenth century were the writings of Franchino Gaffurio. His three most significant treatises, *Theorica musicae* (1492), *Practica musicae* (1496) and *De harmonia musicorum instrumentorun opus* (1518) ... provided a complete study in theoretical and practical music.[70]

Leslie Blasius notes that *Theorica Musicae* includes chapters entitled 'The mathematical foundations of proportion' and 'The derivation of musical interval from proportion', while *De harmonia* finishes with the chapter 'Mode and the correlation of music with the universal order', and 'closes with the resonances of musical systems with the virtues, the senses, and the cosmological structure of the world ... Hence, the great synthetic project of music theory is ... dependent on the sanction of neo-Platonic idealism'.[71]

Aspects of humanity and daily life that do not fit into perfect mathematical orders are at the forefront of *The Corner That Held Them*. The mathematics the scholar refers to may be 'perfect', but the material conditions that he has to contend with – his hand, the cold and the instrument – are not. The weather and the scholar's elderly body eclipse the coherence that is theoretically available in the world. The existence of God 'lies latent in all things', but it is 'things' that frustrate the scholar's attempt to demonstrate the work of God. The wind, we are told, 'howled' and 'clawed at the thatch' so that the nuns cannot hear the out-of-tune octave. The idea of a godly, transcendent music is ever present in the Oby nuns' holy rituals and the novices' training, yet it is also always in the hands of ordinary human beings, and affected by their daily concerns: economic, material or spiritual.

Warner's considerable academic knowledge of music and mathematics is discernible in this brief scene, which is an example of the subtle difficulty of her writing. She was an expert in the history of music theory, having contributed to an edition of *The Polyphonic Period Part 1: Method of Musical Art, 330–1400* by H. E. Wooldridge. The mathematical explanation of the diapason that reappears in the scholar's demonstration in *The Corner That Held Them* is discussed in chapter 1 of *The Polyphonic Period*. Warner's diary entries indicate that she had significant responsibility towards the work: at least a full chapter and the checking of the typescript. On 2 May 1929 she records that she was 'Then home to finish Wooldridge chap iii', and on 30 September she 'spent the evening putting positively the last finishing touches to positively the last t.s. of Wooldridge'.[72] The chapter for which Warner was responsible was 'The Materials of Polyphony, continued: Greek Music in the Latin Church', which discusses 'early Christian music' and decides that 'the similarity between the first Christian music and the Greek contemporary practice was complete as regards the technical basis', meaning that early Christian music was derived from Greek music and uses many of the same scales as its basis.[73] It is not widely acknowledged that Warner carried out this editing: she did it informally with Percy Buck, who alone is credited as the editor of the second edition. Richard Searle writes that Warner appears to have written and revised work on music that Buck was in charge of editing, but this is among the only published acknowledgment of her labour.[74]

Despite her lack of public recognition, Warner's job as a musicologist gave her financial independence: something that many women did not achieve at that time. Claire Harman has found that the *Tudor Church Music* project paid Warner £150 per year, or £3 a week.[75] Richard Overy can help us to understand the value of this wage today:

> in the inter-war years an average worker might take home between £2 and £3 a week in wages. Journalists and writers might make £10 to £15 a week. The wealthier middle and upper-middle classes, if they had also inherited wealth, might have an annual income of anything over £1000.[76]

Warner's was a relatively small salary for skilled work, then, but she also received an allowance of £100 from her mother, who controlled the family finances after the death of her father in 1915. Harman writes, 'Sylvia's annual income came to £160 after the rent had been paid'.[77] This enabled her to live in London independently at the age of twenty-five. It is perhaps unsurprising, given the role music played in her financial life, that in Warner's texts music is always connected to the economic concerns of her characters.

Marxism

Warner claims that she began *The Corner That Held Them* 'on the purest Marxian principles, because I was convinced that if you were going to give an accurate picture of the monastic life, you'd have to put in all their finances'.[78] In other words, even life in a convent – which claims to be devoted to spirituality, and shut off from the world – is centrally concerned with sustaining itself economically and materially. Warner's Marxism sits within the context of the increasing popularity of Marxist ideas among British left intellectuals in the 1930s. Janet Montefiore, Andy Croft and Valentine Cunningham have explored literary responses to Britain's economic problems and the ascendency of fascism in Germany and Italy.[79] As Overy explains, 'the notion that capitalism was in a state of physical, possibly fatal decay became embedded in popular perception of the economic system' during the 1930s.[80] British intellectual Marxists who were members of the Communist Party of Great Britain partially took their lead from Soviet Russia and the political Marxism of Lenin and the Bolshevik Russian Revolution. Alarmed by the spread of fascism in Europe during the 1930s, the Comintern changed its strategy. As research by Jonathan Haslam, John Callaghan, Ben Harker and Hugh Dalton has shown, the Comintern became more inclusive from 1935, encouraging the formation of 'Popular Fronts' outside the USSR in which Communists could operate, and the Popular Front in Britain was organised in opposition to the government's appeasement policy towards Nazi Germany.[81] Ben Harker notes that in Britain, 'the Popular Front turn ushered in a well-documented rapprochement between Communists, intellectuals and the broader national culture'.[82] *Left Review* was set up as 'the organ of the Writers' International' (the intellectual branch of Comintern) in Britain, and produced literary criticism in response to the fascist governments in Europe during the 1930s.[83] For *Left Review* editors and contributors, writing and criticism was an essential part of the attempt to internationalise communism and prevent the spread of fascism. This group of revolutionary British writers was, according to David Margolies, 'born out of the spirit of the Popular Front – or Peoples' Front, as it was known in Britain – which had been organised to stop fascism'.[84] The Left Book Club was organised by Victor Gollancz as a way to promote the Popular Front – a movement in which Warner and Ackland were deeply involved, founding their local Readers and Writers Club in affiliation.[85] The two historical novels Warner wrote in the 1930s – *Summer Will Show* (1936) and *After the Death of Don Juan* (1938) – are considered by critics to be political commentaries and anti-fascist texts.[86]

Warner was extremely well connected among the British intellectual Marxist community. She had close links with the *Left Review*, a pioneer of Marxist criticism in the 1930s, and with its editors. Margolies writes that 'there was not yet any Marxist literary criticism in English – they were creating it'.[87] According to Harman, Warner was 'frequently in contact with Edgell Rickword' – a founder member whom she visited at the magazine's headquarters in 1937 – 'and full of suggestions' for the magazine and the Party 'on which she hoped he might act'.[88] Tom Wintringham, who was a close friend to Warner in the 1930s, was a prominent CPGB member and an editor of *Left Review*. He was responsible for Warner's active involvement in the Spanish Civil War in 1936, requesting that she and Ackland travel to Barcelona to work for a Red Cross unit. Warner met Wintringham in May 1935, and over the summer he and his wife Kitty were regular visitors to Warner and Ackland's home in Chaldon, Dorset.[89] Warner would have been aware of Wintringham's book, *The Coming World War* (1935), which cites the Preface to the second British edition of Marx's *Capital* when explaining how capitalism – 'markets, rates of profit, monopolies, competition, poverty "caused by plenty," tariffs, class power' – was producing an environment in which war was inevitable.[90]

Since Warner doesn't elaborate on what beginning a text on 'Marxian' principles means to her, we can consider the texts by Marx she would have had access to. Warner was under MI5 surveillance from 1935 to 1955 due to her activities in the Communist Party, and a police report in Warner's file from 1952 finds it noteworthy that Warner and Ackland 'do possess some literature appertaining to socialism', although they do not say what.[91] Much of Marx was not immediately published in English, but an English translation of *Capital* had been available since 1887, with later versions published in 1903 and 1930.[92] Another text Warner could have read is the Preface to *A Contribution to the Critique of Political Economy* (1859), which contains the following passage:

> In the social production of their means of existence men enter into definite, necessary relations which are independent of their will, productive relationships which correspond to a definite stage of development of their material productive forces. The aggregate of these productive relationships constitutes the economic structure of society, the real basis on which a juridical and political superstructure arises, and to which definite forms of social consciousness correspond. The mode of production of the material means of existence conditions the whole process of social, political and intellectual life. It is not the consciousness of men that determines their existence, but, on the contrary, it is their social existence that determines their consciousness.[93]

'This classic statement' by Marx, writes Margolies, was widely known: it 'served fruitfully as the basis for much Marxist literary criticism' produced in the 1930s and published in *Left Review*.[94] The passage argues that individual consciousness, rather than being biologically determined or the result of some spiritual essence, is produced by labour and material conditions. *The Corner That Held Them* encourages acknowledgement that this has long been the case by setting the novel in the medieval period, beseeching a broader perspective on contemporary problems by demonstrating that the uneven distribution of materials and money has long caused inequality, showing that such issues are not merely specific to the present day. In *The Corner That Held Them*, the idea that social existence produces consciousness is refracted through a utopian lens, because Warner suggests that if this is the case, then consciousness is not fixed or static, but can be altered by new experiences, including new forms of art.

The Corner That Held Them is a Marxist text. Like the British Marxist theorist of the 1930s Christopher Caudwell, Warner maintained that art could help people imagine a different and better life; that it could fulfil a utopian function. Caudwell claimed that art can produce an 'emotional adaptation' in people: in other words, art can positively change the way people think and relate to the world.[95] Warner – writing after the defeat of the Republic in Spain and the Second World War, and changes in the Communist Party's line on the role of art – shows how this is often complicated and thwarted by the material conditions of existence.

Like other writers who were Communist Party members, Warner responded to Party guidelines on how to write to advance the socialist cause. At the 1934 Soviet Writers Congress, Andrei Zhdanov said that writers could 'Actively help to remold the mentality of people in the spirit of socialism. Be in the front ranks of those who are fighting for a classless society'.[96] British left-wing writing was varied in its methods and aims, and Margolies has explored the debates of the time with respect to how novels and criticism could be at once political and retain artistic value.[97] Still, much of this writing gained a poor reputation as didactic engagement with the contemporary class struggle. Valentine Cunningham claims that Socialist Realism 'helped to slow down literary experimentation and to smash up modernism especially in the novel, thus pushing the novel back beyond Henry James into the arms of nineteenth-century bourgeois naturalism'.[98] It has taken some time to rescue the writing of Warner and others from being swept along by this generalisation. Warner's writing is considerably more nuanced than some British Marxist writers wanted. Charles Madge, for example, writing in 1937, said 'If the novelist has any function in our age, it is to delineate the relationship of an individual to his class, on the basis of scientific materialism'.[99] For Montagu Slater, the 'Life' that writers should introduce the proletariat to 'equals *the* class struggle'.[100] Here, life is nothing but the struggle for equality on material terms, to achieve the necessities of life. Warner's two novels written during the 1930s – *Summer Will Show* and *After the Death of Don Juan* – are now read as thoughtful political commentaries rather than working to a formula of what the novel should be.

The Corner That Held Them comes from a different moment than that which Caudwell was writing in, during the years before his death in the Spanish Civil War, aged just twenty-nine. It comes after the horrors of the Second World War, and with the narrowing range of artistic possibility from successive controversies over the role of art within the British Communist Party that Ben Harker has addressed in his research.[101] The so-called Soviet Literary Controversy – which was discussed in Britain in *Modern Quarterly* between 1946 and 1947 – saw an increasingly hardline stance taken by the Soviet Union about what constituted good literature and criticism. Under the editorship of John Lewis, the journal became increasingly critical of writing that was not doing the ideological work of advancing socialism. *The Corner That Held Them* thus intervenes at a significant moment for British Marxist thought.

The ways in which the material focus of *The Corner That Held Them* is Marxist can be analysed by considering the processes of exchange and distribution in the novel alongside 'The General Relation of Production to Distribution, Exchange, Consumption' from the *Grundrisse*.[102] This was among the first drafts, written between 1857 and 1859, of material that would become *Capital*, but a partial English translation did not appear until 1904, with a full one appearing only in 1971.[103] The passage I quote below was unavailable to Warner, so I am not claiming she was directly influenced by this work.[104] The extract is particularly succinct, making it useful for a brief exploration of how *The Corner That Held Them* works with some of Marx's key claims about production and exchange:

> Production yields goods adapted to our needs; distribution distributes them according to social laws; exchange distributes further what has already been distributed, according to individual wants; finally, in consumption, the product drops out of the social movement, becoming the direct object of the individual want which it serves and satisfies in use.[105]

Although here Marx begins with production, moves through distribution and exchange, and ends with consumption, elsewhere he explains the absence of clear beginning and end points to this process: 'production is at the same time also consumption', since 'the individual who develops his faculties in production is also expending them', and 'consumption is directly also production', because 'in nutrition ... man produces his own body'.[106] Marx further clarifies different manifestations of distribution by explaining that 'before distribution means distribution of products, it is, first, a distribution of the means of production' which in a pre-industrial society is primarily the land: 'no production [is] possible without an instrument of production, even if that instrument is only the land'.[107] Since *The Corner That Held Them* details the distribution of land and materials during the set-up of Oby, these conditions are represented as essential for understanding the lives of the characters throughout the novel. When Brian de Retteville founds the convent in commemoration of his dead wife Alianor, he distributes the means of production (in this case, land and property) to the nuns: 'the site chosen was a manor called Oby' and 'all Alianor's fortune he gave to its endowment, and made a will leaving it half his own property' (*CH* 6). Brian also has to provide the nuns with the means to acquire some items by exchange, because they are not directly available from the land or they require extra labour: he must provide timber annually from elsewhere on his estate, plus the labour to cover its transportation, as well as money with which they can purchase wine (*CH* 8). Marx's opening to his essay on production – 'to begin with, the question under discussion is *material production*' – is equally apt as an assessment of the questions Warner's text immediately raises.

The novel begins with what Warner called 'all their finances', but it is equally concerned with spiritual and emotional needs. Brian de Retteville thinks:

> There was land, and water, and a population of serfs, not many but enough; there were buildings and outbuildings, a fish-pond, an excellent dovecote. What more could holy women desire?
>
> Negotiations with the house in France which was to supply his first batch of nuns enlarged his notions of what holy women desire. The abbess, a notable woman of business, sent him a long list of requirements . . . a good relic; books for the altar and for account-keeping; the complete furniture for the convent priest's chamber . . . a litter; tin porringers with lids to them; and a ring for the prioress. (*CH* 8)

Brian understands life's requirements in the most basic material terms, but the abbess lists objects of tradition and status like the ring and relic alongside timber and pots. Brian's inability to see the complexity of human need is significant: it is part of his intellectually limited, cruel and emotionally stunted character. He is also unable to show any love for his wife until she is dead, which is what prompts him to found the convent in her memory, so that Warner begins not only by detailing the distribution of the means of production, but with Brian's complex motivations: his guilt and belated attempt to express his repressed love for his wife. For Warner, the movement of money and things is bound up with people's emotional and spiritual needs, as well as with their material needs.

Warner's writing does not straightforwardly work to reveal clear class divisions or argue for socialism. Along with other women writers of the

1930s, as Janet Montefiore has argued, she effectively utilises the unfashionable form of the historical novel.[108] *The Corner That Held Them* is set in the medieval period before modern classes and social structures came into being. By setting the novel in the past, Warner encourages us to look beyond the specific circumstances of the present moment to think about the kinds of structures that perpetuate uneven distribution of wealth. Her writing asks us to consider how religion and art can support and challenge the iniquities of capital. The novel makes a fascinating intervention in the debates of the time: it holds up the utopian potential of art, but shows too how material conditions and life's vicissitudes (like illness or external events) inform an unfolding history.

Christopher Caudwell makes for an interesting comparison with Warner: he struggled to be taken seriously as a Marxist thinker, while Warner's significance is yet to be fully demonstrated. Caudwell's writing was criticised for being too idealistic in the so-called Caudwell Controversy, which took place in contributions to *Modern Quarterly* between 1950 and 1951. In the 1970s, when the New Left moved towards a more rigorous, continental Marxism, Terry Eagleton and Perry Anderson dismissed Caudwell again. In 1976, Eagleton wrote in the *New Left Review* that there was 'little, except negatively to be learned from him'.[109] E. P. Thompson famously found a residuum of interest in Caudwell, and Stan Smith and Christopher Pawling, among others, have undertaken further reclamation. Pawling sees in Caudwell's writing a concern 'to foster an intelligent debate about literary theory and aesthetics, rather than just promoting a "politics through literature" version of literary criticism'.[110] Smith argues that in Caudwell's writing there is 'a rationale for art as something more than a vehicle of ideology', which is absent from much British Marxist writing of the 1930s.[111] For Thompson, Caudwell was a 'premonitory sign of a more sophisticated Marxism' that would develop after the 1960s.[112] By reading Warner with Caudwell, I want to make a similar case for her.

Caudwell's utopian thought sees art as something that can alter people's awareness of the world and what constitutes reality. Art, he said, exhibits 'a reality which though secondary is yet higher and more complex' and 'only by means of this illusion can be brought into being a reality which would not otherwise exist'.[113] Art should not merely show people the true state of their current existence – it is not only for revealing contemporary class divisions and inequalities to improve the conditions of existence in the terms already available to people. For Caudwell,

> The value of art to society is that by it an emotional adaptation is possible. Man's instincts are pressed in art against the altered mould of reality, and by

a specific organisation of the emotions thus generated, there is a new attitude, an *adaptation*.[114]

Caudwell sees reality as a mould – or a way of thinking – which can be changed with effort, and when prompted. The important emotional effects of art can help people come to a new and different view of the world. By 'emotional', Caudwell refers to a change that is not coldly intellectual, or entirely rational. The aim is not just to reveal reality or material conditions, but to imagine something beyond it – a utopian possibility.

For Warner as for Caudwell, art can produce illusions through which great things can be imagined, and both writers' convictions about the possibilities of art to positively expand people's thinking can be compared to later Marxist theorists like Adorno. Though he comes from a very different Marxist tradition, is not precisely the same and uses different terminology, he shares with Warner and Caudwell an interest in the utopian possibilities of art. For Adorno, art does not exist as a copy of the world but as an 'apparition' through which our knowledge of the world can be altered:

> Artworks are images as apparition, as appearance, and not as a copy. If through the demythologization of the world consciousness freed itself from the ancient shudder, that shudder is permanently reproduced in the historical antagonism of subject and object. The object became as incommensurable to experience, as foreign and disconcerting, as mana once was.[115]

Adorno argues that artworks are distinct from reality, though they exist in relation to it. The 'shudder' for Adorno is the registration of separation from nature that comes with consciousness. It is the awareness of something lost, and gained. It is the history of mankind, from which mankind wishes to free itself, for which art holds out the possibility. The successful artwork shows the object and experience as foreign, and as terrifying as mana – a supernatural being. Through artworks historically constituted, mythologies and ways of understanding the world can be challenged, and different realities can be imagined.

In one scene in particular, *The Corner That Held Them* investigates the complex intersection of art's claims to aesthetic transcendence through music, which has the capacity to achieve this utopian emotional adaptation, while Warner also represents how material conditions and events can suddenly, indeed violently, thwart that possibility. Towards the end of the novel, the bailiff at Oby, Henry Yellowlees, is travelling to collect money owed to the convent. He stops off for the night at a leper house run by a chaplain who has a love of music, and has acquired manuscripts of a new style of music, the *ars nova*. This was new and innovative music, incorporating two or more polyphonic and rhythmically diverse vocal parts. Henry sings the three-part music with the chaplain and a leper called John, and it has a profound impact on him:

> If *Triste loysir* had seemed a foretaste of paradise, the Kyrie was paradise itself. This was how the blessed might sing, singing in duple measure that ran as nimbly on its four feet as a weasel running through a meadow, with each voice in turn enkindling with the others, so that the music flowed on and was continually renewed. And as paradise is made for man, this music seemed made for man's singing; not for edification, or the working out of an argument, or the display of skill, but only for ease and pleasure, as in paradise where the abolition of sin begets a pagan carelessness, where the certainty of Christ's countenance frees men's souls from the obligations of Christian behaviour, the creaking counterpoint of God's law and man's obedience. (CH 262)

Henry is awakened to a new sense of himself through the music which has a utopian effect: his ideas about what is possible in the world are broadened when he hears this completely new music. It seems to be a taste of paradise – something so beautiful it is not of this world, and it enables him to imagine freedom from religion and the rules that govern everyday life.

This music was radically new in fourteenth-century England. The chaplain explains that 'most of the things in this book are in the *Ars nova* style. This Kyrie by Machault, for instance . . .' (CH 261). Originating in France, *ars nova* (meaning 'new technique' but also commonly thought of as 'new art') refers to the style of music developed between 1310 and 1375 by composers and poets such as Guillaume de Machault (or Machaut, 1300–77), the composer of the chaplain's Kyrie.[116] *Ars nova* was produced during a time of rapid change in musical styles and notation: it was both rhythmically and harmonically innovative, incorporating two or more polyphonic and rhythmically diverse vocal parts, as Henry notices – a development made possible by new systems of musical notation that allowed these complex forms to be written down, as Nicolas Bell has explained.[117] The chaplain has acquired these music books from France, presumably at great expense and very quickly, since this part of the novel takes place between 1374 and 1377 (CH 239). The three singers are acutely affected by the music, and the chaplain remarks, 'I tell you, there has never been such music in the world before' (CH 262). The chaplain, the bailiff and the leper singing together provides a way for them to share an experience in a world in which they would otherwise have no common ground, and in which John's illness would usually prevent him from social interaction with anyone but other lepers: the other lepers, who take no part in the singing, remain nameless and undifferentiated.

John the leper's ability to sing with them, however, only goes so far in undoing the social division created by his poverty and illness: the promise of transcending boundaries that Henry imagines when he hears the music is not fulfilled. John stands apart from Henry and the chaplain, singing 'by rote' away from the music books (*CH* 262). The separation between the singers reflects the music's structure: the beautiful new harmonies and rhythms are reliant on a new degree of difference between each vocal part, compared with the earlier plainchant style on which *ars nova* is an elaboration.[118] Their mutual delight is reliant on their separate parts, in other words a degree of difference and separation, so that in the structure of the music lies the truth that they cannot fully transcend the boundaries of their social positions. The practice of singing even reinforces the division between John and the others in visible spatial terms: 'he stationed himself at the further end of the room; it was clear that he knew his place as a dog does' (*CH* 261). Despite noticing this, Henry continues to see socially transcendent capacity in the music: he thinks 'how many an hour these two must have spent together ... perhaps they bent over the same music-book, their love of music overcoming the barrier between life and death-in-life' (*CH* 262). Henry imagines the music to have a more positive social function than it does in reality, so that he can justify his own enjoyment of it.

While art can be utopian for Warner, she critiques the idea that it can be used to promote one political position because of the range of ways the same piece of art can be received by different individuals. The *ars nova* that has enriched Henry's experience is also part of a tangible social injustice. The lepers accuse the chaplain of spending money on music books instead of food, leaving them hungry. This stacks up when we know that the music was made possible by new systems of notation that allowed these complex forms to be written down, during a time when paper was expensive. Even John, who enjoys singing, admits 'it is true, there was often nothing to eat', while Henry notices that 'if the food given to a guest were so bad the food given to the lepers must be worse' (*CH* 273, 262). In Henry's absence the lepers revolt and murder the chaplain. John recounts what happened when Henry returns:

> They set on us while we were singing. We were singing, we did not hear them come. They had armed themselves, some with sticks, some with bones. They struck him down and beat him, and one of them thrust a bone into his mouth and down his gullet, and worked it to and fro till his gullet split and the blood ran out. (*CH* 272)

The chaplain's preoccupation with the aesthetic when people are going hungry shows how art can appear a frivolous luxury when there are pressing material needs to be met. The same piece of music that helps Henry to imagine a better world also contributes to this violent uprising. Just as the allure of the music has caused the chaplain to neglect the needs of the lepers and provoke their anger, so the singing masks the approaching violent crowd. The gruesome act of rebellion is targeted precisely at the part of the body that is used for singing and eating.

As Henry realises after his experience with the chaplain and the leper colony, the same phenomenon can mean different things to individuals inhabiting a variety of subject positions. Henry thinks, 'for each one of us lives in his microcosm, the solidity of this world is a mere game of mirrors, there can be no absolute existence for what is apprehended differently by all' (*CH* 276). Warner's writing considers the effect of music's aesthetic beauty on individuals and the way those effects interconnect with poverty and illness. Despite the horrible murder, Henry is so overwhelmed by *ars nova* that he achieves a sense of comradeship with John because of their experience singing together, and he improves John's material existence by helping him. After the leper house has been burned down, the chaplain is dead and John is destitute, Henry 'threw to the leper what food he had' and took him to Killdew where 'he would be well cared for' (*CH* 274). Henry is transformed by the music, from someone who has limited and practical aspirations to someone who takes pleasure in helping others achieve a better life. He begins by considering 'a future in which he would clear up the nun's tangle at Oby' (*CH* 242) as an improvement on his limited lot. By the end of the novel, he is willing to help the disadvantaged and able to articulate a rapturous experience of music that improves his quality of life despite his poverty. We might consider how Warner's representation of music's value is informed by her own experience. Looking back on her life to the time when she was working on *Tudor Church Music* in 1918, living on her small salary in London, she remembered the significance of her musical work against her relative poverty: 'from time to time I felt hungry, and in winter I often felt cold. But I never felt poor'.[119] Music played a supporting economic role in her life, but had a sustaining spiritual role too.

In Warner's texts, and in particular *The Corner That Held Them*, the value of art lies not just in its ability to awaken people to social injustices in order to reorganise society. Warner identifies that while food and shelter are indeed necessities, people need more than physical things. Art has a function in and of itself because when people experience it, it adds value to their lives and is able to enlarge their notions of how it is possible to live. While for some British Marxist writers, life was nothing but the struggle for equality on material terms to achieve the necessities of life, in *The Corner That Held Them* music offers something other than basic necessities: a utopian potentiality. However, the novel keeps open the way that this utopian potential can always flip over into being only an illusory escape from the material world. After the chaplain's death,

> Henry and the leper sat on the grass, the leper sitting a dozen paces away, but near enough to prompt Henry in the bass part of *Triste loysir* until he could sing it steadily enough for the tenor part to be added. They sang it three times through, and if in the beginning Henry remembered the chaplain, from whose stinking body the chill of evening had now swept off the flies, by the third repetition nothing remained but the delight of the two voices answering and according. (*CH* 274)

Singing forms a connection between Henry and John, which we can see as solace from worldly horrors. However, the move in the middle of this passage to the chaplain's dead body complicates this: is this transcendence or simply the creation of an environment which makes it possible to forget violence, like the falling temperature that leads the flies to retreat from the corpse?

Warner's *The Corner That Held Them* retains a space for the utopian potential of art, something seen by Christopher Caudwell and extensively theorised by Adorno, but she also demonstrates a keen sense of how this can be complicated and potentially thwarted by the manifold immanent possibilities thrown up by the material conditions of existence. Music, in Warner's fiction more broadly, is a significant part of human identity, tradition and aspiration. It can inspire humane actions but also has the potential to provoke violence when one's beliefs or material existence are threatened. Warner's claim that music is not reducible to a single argument and can fulfil a variety of functions is a nuanced statement about the full complexity of human existence, its squalor and splendour, and the excellent and terrible powers of art, which are rooted not only in its connections with the material world, but also in its power to surprise, inspire emotion and enrich lived experience.

Notes

1. Sylvia Townsend Warner, 'Ludwig Van Beethoven', in *With the Hunted*, ed. Peter Tolhurst (Norwich: Black Dog Books, 2012), p. 182.
2. Letter from Valentine Ackland to the Communist Party, 4 January 1935 (London, 2006), KV/2/2337, National Archive. Claire Harman also writes that 'in the spring of 1935 both women [Warner and Valentine Ackland] were admitted into the Communist Party'. Claire Harman, ed., *The Diaries of Sylvia Townsend Warner* (London: Chatto & Windus, 1994), p. 93.
3. Claire Harman, *Sylvia Townsend Warner: A Biography*, 2nd edn (London: Minerva, 1991), pp. 152–6.

4. Maroula Joannou, 'Preface', in Gill Davies, David Malcolm and John Simons, eds, *Critical Essays on Sylvia Townsend Warner, English Novelist 1893–1978* (Lewiston, NY: The Edwin Mellen Press, 2006), p. iii.
5. Miller, *Modernism and the Frankfurt School*, p. 147.
6. David James, 'Realism, Late Modernist Abstraction, and Sylvia Townsend Warner's Aesthetics of Impersonality', *Modernism/modernity* 12.1 (2005), 112.
7. Janet Montefiore, *Men and Women Writers of the 1930s: The Dangerous Flood of History* (London: Routledge, 1996), pp. 141–4.
8. Harman, *Biography*, p. 22.
9. Harman, ed., *Diaries*, p. 86.
10. Lynn Mutti, 'That Odd Thing, a Musicologist', *Journal of the Sylvia Townsend Warner Society* (2013), 25.
11. Richard Searle, 'Sylvia Townsend Warner and *Tudor Church Music*', *Journal of the Sylvia Townsend Warner Society* (2011), 71, 73, 74.
12. Harman, *Biography*, p. 38.
13. 24 September 1958, The Diaries of Sylvia Townsend Warner, 38 vols, 1927–78, in The Sylvia Townsend Warner and Valentine Ackland Collection, Dorset County Museum.
14. Oxford University Press Archives: CP/ED/001034 (390 items, 1916–20); CP/ED/001035 (535 items, 1920–52).
15. Harman, *Biography*, p. 43.
16. Sylvia Townsend Warner, 'Doubting Castle', *Music and Letters* 2 (1924), 157–8.
17. Ibid. 157.
18. Ibid. 158.
19. Harman, *Biography*, p. 26.
20. Richard Terry quoted in Hilda Andrews, *Westminster Retrospective: A Memoir of Sir Richard Terry* (London: Oxford University Press, 1948), p. 134.
21. Harman, ed., *Diaries*, p. 38.
22. Warner, *Lolly Willowes*, p. 234.
23. Todd Gilman, *The Theatre Career of Thomas Arne* (Lanham, MD: University of Delaware Press, 2013), pp. 2, 565.
24. Donald Burrows, *Handel* (Oxford: Oxford University Press, 1994), p. 94, and also pp. 220, 166, 36, 147.
25. Andreas Ballstaedt writes that when Chopin was performing 'the salon had become a mark of social status whose exclusive character helped distinguish higher ranks within the new money from the lower middle classes i.e. the petite bourgeoisie'. Andreas Ballstaedt, 'Chopin as Salon Composer in Nineteenth-Century German Criticism', in John Rink and Jim Samson, eds, *Chopin Studies 2* (Cambridge: Cambridge University Press, 2006), p. 22.
26. Jim Samson has detailed Chopin's 'association with the salon' and aristocratic society, while also noting that concert-giving and audiences were changing in the nineteenth century, with concerts increasingly attended by the wealthy middle classes, proving musicians with another form of income aside from patronage. Jim Samson, 'Myth and Reality: A Biographical Introduction', in Jim Samson, ed., *The Cambridge Companion to Chopin*

(Cambridge: Cambridge University Press, 1992), pp. viii, 2. See also Janet Ritterman, 'Piano Music and the Public Concert, 1800–1850', in Samson, ed., *The Cambridge Companion to Chopin*, p. 16.
27. Pierpaolo Polzonetti, 'Haydn and the Metamorphoses of Ovid', in Mary Hunter and Richard Will, eds, *Engaging Haydn: Culture, Context and Criticism* (Cambridge: Cambridge University Press, 2012), p. 214.
28. Adorno and Horkheimer, *Dialectic of Enlightenment*, trans. John Cumming, p. 147.
29. Terry Eagleton, *Ideology: An Introduction* (London: Verso, 1991), p. 126.
30. Harvey G. Cohen, 'Duke Ellington and "Black, Brown and Beige": The Composer as Historian at Carnegie Hall', *American Quarterly* 56.4 (2004), 1004.
31. John Lahr, *Coward the Playwright* (London: Bloomsbury, 1982), p. 66. Alan Sinfield, 'Private Lives/Public Theatre: Noel Coward and the Politics of Homosexual Representation', *Representations* 36 (1991), 58.
32. Pierre Bourdieu, 'Cultural Reproduction and Social Reproduction', in Richard K. Brown, ed., *Knowledge, Education and Cultural Change: Papers in the Sociology of Education* (London: Tavistock Publications, 1973). Pierre Bourdieu, *Distinction* ([1979] London: Routledge, 1999), p. 1.
33. Jonathan Rose, *The Intellectual Life of the British Working Classes* (Reading: Cox & Wyman Ltd., 2001), pp. 196–8.
34. Bourdieu, 'Cultural Reproduction and Social Reproduction', pp. 5, 61.
35. Raymond Williams, *Culture and Materialism* ([1980] London: Verso, 2005), p. 45.
36. Ibid. p. 44.
37. Ibid. pp. 33, 34, 32.
38. See Rose, *The Intellectual Life of the British Working Classes*, pp. 197, 198. For alterations in musical taste and consumption in the nineteenth century more broadly, see William Weber, 'Mass Culture and the Reshaping of European Musical Taste, 1770–1870', *International Review of the Aesthetics and Sociology of Music* 8.1 (1977), 6–7.
39. Louis Althusser, *On Ideology* ([1971] London: Verso, 2008), p. 46.
40. Theodor W. Adorno and Max Horkheimer, *Dialectic of Enlightenment*, trans. Gunzelin Noeri ([1944] Stanford, CA: Stanford University Press, 2002), p. 118. In this instance, I prefer Noeri's translation to John Cumming's, which reads, 'It becomes a vigorous and prearranged promulgation of the status quo'. Adorno and Horkheimer, *Dialectic of Enlightenment*, trans. John Cumming, p. 147.
41. Gillian Beer, 'The Centrifugal Kick', in Maroula Joannou, ed., *Women Writers of the 1930s: Gender, Politics and History* (Edinburgh: Edinburgh University Press, 1999), p. 82.
42. Young-Hee Kwon, '*Mr Fortune's Maggot* and the De-Masculinization of the Victorian Imperial Romance', *Literature Interpretation Theory* 18 (2007), 303–23; Gay Wachman, *Lesbian Empire: Radical Crosswriting in the Twenties* (New Brunswick, NJ: Rutgers University Press, 2001). Jane Garrity also reads the novel in terms of lesbian crosswriting in *Step-daughters of England: British Women Modernists and the National Imaginary* (Manchester: Manchester University Press, 2003), pp. 144–7.

43. Rod Edmond, *Representing the South Pacific: Colonial Discourse from Cook to Gauguin* (Cambridge: Cambridge University Press, 1997), p. 265.
44. Howard J. Booth, 'Colonialism and Time in *Mr Fortune's Maggot*', *Literature Compass* 11.12 (2014), 750.
45. Edmond, *Representing the South Pacific*, pp. 9–10.
46. Ibid. pp. 8–10.
47. See Chapter 3, 'Remy de Gourmont', p. 7.
48. Sherry, *Ezra Pound, Wyndham Lewis and Radical Modernism*, p. 21.
49. Ibid. p. 19.
50. See William Duckworth, who notes that 'the plagal cadence is most familiar as the Amen ending of a hymn'. William Duckworth, *Cengage Advantage Books: A Creative Approach to Music Fundamentals* (Boston: Cengage Learning, 2009), p. 212. See also Steven Porter who explains 'a plagal cadence is a IV–I progression. It is familiar as the "Amen" sung at the end of many hymns'. Steven Porter, *The Harmonization of the Chorale: A Comprehensive Workbook Course in Harmony* (New York: Excelsior Publishing, 1987), p. 10.
51. *The London Review and Weekly Journal of Politics, Literature, Art, and Society*, vol. 5, July–December (London, 1862), 4 October, vii; also 13 September, vi.
52. 'St. Helena.– (Extract of a letter from Lady Ross to a Lady in England)', in *The Colonial Church Chronicle and Missionary Journal* (London: Rivingtons, 1857), p. 320.
53. Arthur W. J. G. Ord-Hume, *Harmonium: the History of the Reed Organ and its Makers* (London: David & Charles, 1986), p. 88; Robert F. Gellerman, *The American Reed Organ and the Harmonium* (Vestal, NY: The Vestal Press, 1996), p. 134.
54. *Official Catalogue of the Great Exhibition of the Works of Industry of All Nations*, 2nd edn (London: Spicer Brothers; W. Clowes & Sons, 1851), pp. 67, 209, 228, 241. *Catalogue of the British Section: Paris Universal Exhibition of 1867* (London: Spottiswoode & Company, 1867), pp. 60, 88, 289.
55. Jeffrey A. Auerbach, *The Great Exhibition of 1851: A Nation on Display* (New Haven, CT and London: Yale University Press, 1999), p. 159.
56. Maor, *The Pythagorean Theorem*, p. 19.
57. Daniel D. Bonar, Michael J. Khoury, Jr and Michael Khoury, eds, *Real Infinite Series* (Washington, DC: Mathematical Association of America, 2006), p. 66. Ron Larson and Bruce Edwards note that 'in music, strings of the same material, diameter, and tension, whose lengths form a harmonic series, produce harmonic tones'. Ron Larson and Bruce Edwards, *Calculus of a Single Variable*, 9th edn (Belmont, CA: Cengage Learning, 2006), p. 621.
58. Bersani, *The Culture of Redemption*, p. 158.
59. Nigel Rigby, 'The South Seas, Sexuality and Modernism', in Howard J. Booth and Nigel Rigby, eds, *Modernism and Empire* (Manchester: Manchester University Press, 2000), p. 236.
60. See also 3 Luke 1:20. *The Holy Bible, New Revised Standard Version: Containing the Old and New Testaments* (Cambridge: Cambridge University Press, 1994).

61. Booth, 'Colonialism and Time in *Mr Fortune's Maggot*', 750.
62. Harman, ed., *Diaries*, p. 117.
63. Iamblichus, *On the Pythagorean Way of Life*, trans. John Dillon and Jackson Hershbell (Atlanta: Scholars Press, 1991), p. 115. See also Iamblichus, *Iamblichus: On the Pythagorean Life*, trans Gillian Clarke (Liverpool: Liverpool University Press, 1989), p. 51, and Walter Burkert, *Lore and Science in Ancient Pythagoreanism*, trans. E. Minar (Cambridge, MA: Harvard University Press, 1972), p. 375.
64. Donald C. Benson, *A Smoother Pebble: Mathematical Explorations* (Oxford: Oxford University Press, 2003), p. 56.
65. See Bonar et al., eds, *Real Infinite Series*, p. 66: 'Indeed, for each integer n the string can vibrate so that n arcs are formed, and the wavelength will be 1/n times the wavelength for the first harmonic. In this way the series of reciprocals relates to harmonics and harmonies'. See also Larson and Edwards, *Calculus of a Single Variable*, p. 621: 'In music, strings of the same material, diameter, and tension, whose lengths form a harmonic series, produce harmonic tones'.
66. Bertrand Russell, *Introduction to Mathematical Philosophy* ([1919] New York: Cosimo, 2007), p. 202. Paul Bernays, 'On Platonism in Mathematics', in Paul Benacerraf and Hilary Putnam, eds, *Philosophy of Mathematics: Selected Readings* (Cambridge: Cambridge University Press, 1964), p. 262.
67. Andrew D. Irvine, ed., *Philosophy of Mathematics* (Oxford: Elsevier, 2009), p. 11: 'Start with the natural numbers, the whole numbers, 0, 1, and so on.'
68. John N. Findlay, 'Neoplatonism and Western Christian Man', in R. Baine Harris, ed., *Neoplatonism and Contemporary Thought: Part Two* (New York: SUNY Press, 2002), p. 298.
69. Pauliina Remes, *Neoplatonism* (Berkeley, CA: University of California Press, 2008), p. 2.
70. Cristle Collins Judd, *Reading Renaissance Music Theory: Hearing with the Eyes* (Cambridge: Cambridge University Press, 2000), p. 17.
71. Leslie Blasius, 'Mapping the Terrain', in Thomas Christensen, ed., *The Cambridge History of Western Music Theory* (Cambridge: Cambridge University Press, 2002), pp. 31, 34.
72. Harman, ed., *Diaries*, p. 35.
73. H. E. Wooldridge, *The Polyphonic Period Part I: Method of Musical Art 330–1400*, ed. Percy Carter Buck (Oxford: Oxford University Press, 1929), pp. 26, 29.
74. Searle, 'Sylvia Townsend Warner and *Tudor Church Music*', 85. For Warner's relationship with Buck, see Harman, *Biography*, p. 24.
75. Harman, *Biography*, p. 40.
76. Richard Overy, *The Morbid Age: Britain Between the Wars* (London: Allen Lane, 2009), p. xv.
77. Harman, *Biography*, p. 40.
78. Claire Harman, ed., 'Sylvia Townsend Warner 1893–1978: A Celebration', *PN Review* 8.3 (1981), 23, 36.
79. Montefiore, *Men and Women Writers of the 1930s*, p. 15. Andy Croft, *Red Letter Days* (London: Lawrence & Wishart, 1990). Valentine

Cunningham, *British Writers of the Thirties* (Oxford: Oxford University Press, 1988).
80. Overy, *The Morbid Age*, p. 53.
81. Jonathan Haslam, 'The Comintern and the Origins of the Popular Front 1934–1935', *The Historical Journal* 22.3 (September 1979), 682–4. John Callaghan and Ben Harker, eds, *British Communism: a Documentary History* (Manchester: Manchester University Press, 2011), pp. 125–45. Hugh Dalton, 'The "Popular Front"', *The Political Quarterly* 7.4 (October 1936), 488.
82. Ben Harker, '"The Trumpet of the Night": Interwar Communists on BBC Radio', *History Workshop Journal* 75.1 (2013), 83.
83. Janet Batsleer et al. note that 'it was not until 1934 that a British section of what had by then become the Writers' International was formed in Britain. The founding of this section was the culmination of a process set in motion by the second International Conference of Proletarian and Revolutionary Writers, held at Charkob in November 1930'. Janet Batsleer, Tony Davies, Rebecca O'Rourke and Chris Weedon, eds, *Rewriting English* (London: Routledge, 2013), pp. 60, 58. See also David Margolies, 'Introduction', in David Margolies, ed., *Writing the Revolution: Cultural Criticism from 'Left Review'* (London: Pluto Press, 1998), p. 9. There were debates about how best to write for the proletariat, stop fascism and internationalise communism, as I will explain in more detail later in this chapter.
84. Margolies, ed., *Writing the Revolution*, p. 4.
85. Harman, *Biography*, p. 152.
86. Warner, *After the Death of Don Juan*; *Summer Will Show*. Janet Montefiore describes *Summer Will Show* and *After the Death of Don Juan* as 'anti-fascist' texts, and argues against George Orwell in 'Outside the Whale' who sees anti-fascist writing as all inevitably crass. Montefiore, *Men and Women Writers of the 1930s*, pp. 16, 142. Warner herself claimed that *After the Death of Don Juan* is 'a parable or allegory, or what you will, of the political chemistry of the Spanish War'. See Harman, *Biography*, p. 175. Barbara Brothers considers *Don Juan* to be a contemporary political allegory that maps eighteenth-century Spain onto 1930s Spain, saying that Warner 'depicts [in the historical novel] the social and political turmoil that prevented the Spanish republic of 1931 from becoming stable enough to withstand the fascists within and outside Spain'. Barbara Brothers, 'Writing Against the Grain: Sylvia Townsend Warner and the Spanish Civil War', in Mary Lynn Broe and Angela Ingram, eds, *Women's Writing in Exile* (Chapel Hill, NC: University of North Carolina Press, 1989), p. 353. Chris Hopkins, however, disagrees with the 'simplification of past and present' in Brothers's analysis, arguing that 'The novel makes considerable effort to tell dual histories, in which the two histories remain separate'. Chris Hopkins, *English Fiction in the 1930s* (London: Continuum, 2006), pp. 103–4.
87. Margolies, ed., *Writing the Revolution*, p. 4. In Margolies's point about a new 'movement' of Marxist, specifically literary criticism notwithstanding, he neglects to mention late-nineteenth-century Marx-inflected critical writings by William Morris, for example, *Signs of Change* (London: Longmans, 1896). There were also other genres of text available that dealt directly with Marxist ideas, although not in the form of literary criticism,

such as J. A. Hobson's *Imperialism* (London: George Allen & Unwin, 1902). The connection between societal problems produced by capitalism and war was to become central to the ideology of Writers' International members and other intellectual members of the Communist Party during the 1930s. Overy explains that this book 'gave a firm intellectual foundation to the connection between capitalism and war', and notes the presence of 'war-mania' during the 1930s and the focus on the effects of capital in society as a contributing, or the main, factor. Overy, *The Morbid Age*, pp. 188–9, 184.
88. Harman, *Biography*, p. 172.
89. Ibid. pp. 141, 144, 153.
90. Tom Wintringham, *The Coming World War* (London: Lawrence & Wishart, 1935), p. 12.
91. Letter from Dorset Constabulary to Superintendent D. Blakeman, 10 December 1952, KV/2/2338, National Archive.
92. Karl Marx, *Capital*, trans. Samuel Moore and Edward Aveling (Moscow: Progress Publishers, 1887). Karl Marx, *Capital: A Critical Analysis of Capitalist Production*, trans. Friedrich Engels (London: Lawrence & Wishart, 1903). Karl Marx, *Capital*, trans. Eden Paul and Cedar Paul (London: J. M. Dent & Sons, 1930).
93. Emile Burns, ed., *A Handbook of Marxism* (London: Victor Gollancz, 1935), pp. 371–2. This book contains translations of sections of work by Marx and commentary by Burns.
94. Margolies, ed., *Writing the Revolution*, p. 1.
95. Christopher Caudwell, *Studies in a Dying Culture* (New York: Dodd Mead, 1958), p. 77.
96. A. A. Zhdanov, 'Soviet Literature – The Richest in Ideas, the Most Advanced Literature' [speech], in Maxim Gorky et al., eds, *Soviet Writers' Congress, 1934: The Debate on Socialist Realism and Modernism in the Soviet Union* (London: Lawrence & Wishart, 1977), p. 19.
97. Margolies, ed., *Writing the Revolution*, pp. 7–8.
98. Cunningham, *British Writers of the Thirties*, p. 299.
99. Charles Madge, *Left Review* 3.3 (April 1937), 183, reprinted in Margolies, ed., *Writing the Revolution*, p. 10.
100. Montagu Slater, *Left Review* 1.5 (January 1935), 128, reprinted in Margolies, ed., *Writing the Revolution*, p. 33.
101. Ben Harker, 'Politics and Letters: The "Soviet Literary Controversy" in Britain', *Literature and History* 24.1 (2015), 41–57. Ben Harker, '"Communism is English": Edgell Rickword, Jack Lindsay and the Cultural Politics of the Popular Front', *Literature and History* 20.2 (2011), 16–34.
102. Karl Marx, *Grundrisse*, ed. and trans. David McLellan (London: Macmillan, 1971), p. 22.
103. Ernst Theodor Mohl writes that 'the publication of Marx's 1857–9 manuscript began in Germany, on the pages of *Die Neue Zeit* [*The New Times*], with two partial publications by Karl Kautsky: the "Introduction" (Marx 1903) and "Carey and Bastai" (Marx 1904)'. Ernst Theodor Mohl, 'Germany, Austria and Switzerland', in Marcello Musto, ed., *Karl Marx's Grundrisse: Foundations of the Critique of Political Economy 150 Years Later* (London: Routledge, 2008), p. 189.

104. The *Handbook of Marxism* that Warner could have had access to indicates that '*Capital* was the completion of the detailed analysis of capitalism which Marx had already begun in his earlier works, especially *The Critique of Political Economy*'. Burns, ed., *A Handbook of Marxism*, p. 373.
105. Marx, *Grundrisse*, p. 22.
106. Ibid. pp. 23–4.
107. Ibid. pp. 30, 19.
108. Montefiore, *Men and Women Writers of the 1930s*, pp. 142–3.
109. Terry Eagleton, 'Raymond Williams: An Appraisal', *New Left Review* 95 (1976), 3.
110. Christopher Pawling, 'Revisiting the Thirties in the Twenty-First Century: the Radical Aesthetics of West, Caudwell, and Eagleton', in Anthony Shuttleworth, ed., *And in Our Time: Vision, Revision, and British Writing of the 1930s* (London: Associated University Presses, 2003), p. 50. See also Christopher Pawling, *Christopher Caudwell: Towards a Dialectical Theory of Literature* (London: Macmillan, 1989), p. 163, and Leonard Jackson, *The Dematerialisation of Karl Marx* (London: Longman, 1994), pp. 127–8.
111. Stan Smith, 'Balancing Accounts: Caudwell, Eagleton and English Marxism', *Critical Survey* 7.1 (1995), 78.
112. E. P. Thompson, 'Christopher Caudwell', *Critical Inquiry* 21 (1995), 305.
113. Christopher Caudwell, *Illusion and Reality: A Study of the Sources of Poetry* (London: Macmillan, 1937), p. 30.
114. Caudwell, *Studies in a Dying Culture*, p. 77.
115. Adorno, *Aesthetic Theory*, p. 110.
116. Anne Walters Robertson, *Guillaume de Machaut and Reims: Context and Meaning in His Musical Works* (Cambridge: Cambridge University Press, 2002), p. 4. Nicolas Bell, 'Signs of Change from *ars antiqua* to *ars nova* in Polyphonic Music of the Early Fourteenth Century', in Nils Holger Petersen, Claus Cluver and Nicolas Bell, eds, *Signs of Change: Transformations of Christian Traditions and Their Representations in the Arts, 1000–2000* (Amsterdam: Rodopi, 2004), pp. 363–72. Anna Zayaruznaya, *The Monstrous New Art* (Cambridge: Cambridge University Press, 2002), p. 266.
117. Bell, 'Signs of Change', p. 363.
118. Bell explains that *ars nova* was 'a vocal piece for two, three or four different voice-parts, based on a portion of plainchant'. Bell, 'Signs of Change', p. 363.
119. Sylvia Townsend Warner, *Scenes of Childhood and Other Stories* (London: Chatto & Windus, 1981), p. 138. See also Harman, *Biography*, p. 40.

Chapter 5

Music and Twenty-first-century Modernism

This book has argued for the value of a specific methodology – the application of continental philosophies of music to literary engagements with music – that moves away from simple formalism to provide greater understanding of the political implications of aesthetic forms. If, as Adorno claims, analysing art is valuable because it can provide what Hegel calls 'a revelation of truth' about the web of social forces and historical ideas in and through which it was produced,[1] the aesthetic can be political because it can disclose things about the social world that otherwise would be difficult to see. Perceiving aspects of the world anew can make different ways of thinking and living possible. Adorno's method of materially and historically informed formal analysis can be used to investigate the real-world implications of seemingly abstracted things like literary and musical forms, discourses of musical transcendence and notions of aesthetic purity. With this methodology I have analysed music's role in Pound's pursuit of artistic perfection, which leads him to advocate aesthetic *and* social hierarchies,[2] and explored how celebrating the indeterminacy and complexity of musical meaning helps Joyce and Warner to promote critical engagement with aesthetic abstraction *and* social differences. The way music is used in literature can formally articulate and endorse different social worlds.

Modernist writers wanted their texts to have an impact on the world, and there is a consensus that effective criticism must do the same today: it must 'both interpret and speak to the world', as Dipesh Charkrabarty claims.[3] Or, as Catharine Stimpson writes, it must 'live in and work for our century'.[4] Joyce, Pound and Warner are no longer of our century, but the problems of language and ideology they debate through music and modernist forms are still relevant. Novelists today continue to use music and literature to ask how art and politics inform each other, and are still deeply influenced by the notions of musical transcendence this book has evaluated. Richard Powers's Man Booker Prize longlisted novel

Orfeo (2014) is one example: its topics are twentieth-century politics, music and science, but Powers also relies heavily on notions of musical transcendence. Another example of twenty-first-century musico-literary interaction is Paul Griffiths's *let me tell you* (2008), a modernist project novel that returns to musically inspired methods of formal innovation to consider how ideology operates through language. Since contemporary writers continue to ask what can be achieved by combining literary and musical forms, and to debate the value of linguistic meaning against the communicative capacity of music, the methodology I have offered in this book offers a purchase on matters we have not yet found our way out of.

This final chapter unpacks the politics of Powers's and Griffiths's very different novels, to initiate the use of my approach for analysing musical themes and forms in further contemporary writing.[5] *Orfeo* tracks the life of a composer and is set in post-9/11 USA where anxieties about terrorism are rife. The novel contains detailed descriptions of pieces of music, including an account of Olivier Messiaen's *Quatuor pour la fin du temps*, which was composed and premiered in a prisoner-of-war camp during the Second World War. With stories such as these, *Orfeo* reminds us of the political and material realities of music production, but the novel also paradoxically frames music as a world apart from politics, and a place where eternal truths can be found. *Orfeo*'s conservative attitude to music is bolstered by a conservative family politics and valorisation of totalising structures that is reinforced through the novel's form as well as the music it endorses. An approach to music and modernism that considers the politics of form and aesthetics can illuminate the extent of *Orfeo*'s conservatism: something that critics to date – who have focused either on form or on politics – have been unable to see.

Orfeo engages with modernism at the level of content by making modernist music its topic, while *let me tell you* does so at the level of form by using a writing constraint that draws on modernist techniques and aims. The novel is narrated by Ophelia from Shakespeare's *Hamlet* and uses only the words spoken by her in the play. Griffiths's writing constraint can be compared with Arnold Schoenberg's twelve-tone compositions that are considered the height of modernist musical experimentation. Schoenberg restricts the tones available to the composer to break the habits of functional harmony, and Griffiths limits the range of words he draws on to break habitual language use. *let me tell you* uses a form inspired by modernist music and a literary movement indebted to modernism to reflect on how far our use of language is ever free, combining musical techniques and the novel form to explore the ideological nature of language and thought. *let me tell you* was adapted into a prize-winning song cycle by acclaimed Danish composer Hans Abrahamsen, demonstrating an ongoing dialogue between music and literature that is having a significant impact in the contemporary art world.

My method of analysis offers an angle of vision from which the politics of *Orfeo* and *let me tell you* can be viewed. Understanding the political aspects of the music drawn on by Griffiths and Powers for their topics and forms helps to identify the kinds of worlds these texts advocate and construct through their use of music. Both texts are products of authors for whom there is still much to be extracted from modernist music, but while *Orfeo* merely has characters who talk about modernist music, *let me tell you* can be considered a modernist novel. This distinction tells us something about how and why a novel can be considered modernist today, which in turn provides a view on debates about the temporality of modernism and its apparent recurrence in recent years: if modernism was a product of the conditions of the first half of the twentieth century, why are writers returning to modernist music and methods of formal innovation today?

Orfeo

Powers is widely considered an explosive contemporary writer, but *Orfeo*'s narrative trajectory restores its main character's childhood beliefs about the universal, timeless beauty of music of the classical period, demonstrating a conservative and recuperative nostalgia that has been obscured by the novel's formal complexity and its use of controversial up-to-date topics like DNA modification and terrorism. *Orfeo* takes us on a chronological journey through shifts in Western classical and avant-garde music, which it frames as the ground on which debates about the nature and value of art take place. The novel represents musical change as occurring at an accelerated pace during the twentieth century, as notions of aesthetic beauty rooted in tonality and tightly ordered forms give way to dissonance and noise, before order returns in the form of recuperative tonality. We experience these changes through the eyes and ears of composer Peter Els, whose lifetime's musical education begins with a childhood bewitched by the apparently timeless beauty of Mozart and music of the classical period. As a teenager he is introduced to Mahler's ambiguous proto-modernism, and in his twenties receives a university education that covers atonality and conceptual art. Els attends the first performance of John Cage's chaotic, immersive performance piece *Musicircus* in 1967, and watches the interactions between Karlheinz Stockhausen, the Beatles and Luciano Berio trouble the boundaries between the popular and avant-garde. By the close of the novel Els has listened to Anthrax's heavy metal and contemplated the pros and cons of live music streaming.

These transformations in music send Els on an ideological and emotional journey, during which he changes his beliefs about what art is and eventually changes them back again. The young Els has a passion for classical music because it seems to articulate a truth that can 'peel away the lie of daily life'.[6] Mozart's *Jupiter* transports him to a 'purer world' beyond the banality of everyday existence: it feels like a hand that 'scoops Peter up and lifts him high above the blocked vantage of his days'.[7] Peter initially believes two powerful and connected things about music: it is otherworldly, from a 'distant planet' and separate from the drudgery of the human world;[8] at the same time, he has a Schopenhauerian belief that music is the metaphysical essence of human emotion and experience.[9] He interprets Mahler's *Kindertotenlieder* as incredible for their ability to capture 'the sound of false recovery', the 'precise signature of doubt and hope', and even tries to notate the sound his girlfriend makes during orgasm.[10] The young Peter Els believes in music's metaphysical power to communicate the essence of experience and emotion.

Powers's novel is invested in accentuating how shocking and damaging modernist atonality can be for people who are deeply moved by classical music and functional harmony. At university, Els asks his prestigious composition teacher, 'Isn't the point of music to move listeners?' His mentor answers, 'No, the point of music is to wake listeners up'.[11] Through the disbelieving eyes and ears of the young composer, Powers has us watch the appreciation of beautiful, emotionally charged art among the cultured classes give way to the widespread intellectual approval of music that shocks and requires critical engagement. Els is devastated by this shift, because his beliefs about what it means to be human are bound up with his faith in the timeless beauty of classical music, which seems to demonstrate the ahistorical nature of human emotions and promises to reveal the truth of the human soul. We have seen tonality wield a similar ideological power in Warner's *Mr Fortune's Maggot*, where God's divine order and design seem nowhere more evident, for Timothy Fortune, than in musical harmony and mathematics. But while Warner views the beauty perceived in Western meantone temperament as culturally and historically contingent, rather than a universal truth, in *Orfeo* Powers recuperates tonality and functional harmony as the true and enduring.[12]

Beauty versus ugliness

To arrive at this conclusion, *Orfeo* sees Els – who is always in search of the perfect music – embark on a Faust-like journey for musical truth.

Els struggles to decide between the contrasting ideologies that seem to be posited by tonality and atonality. Is the beauty of tonal music evidence that it contains metaphysical, emotional and spiritual truths? Or is that a sham: should music be dissonant and jarring to wake people up to ideology? Although Adorno is mentioned by name just once in *Orfeo*, Els is unmoored by a notion that is thoroughly Adornian: that the kind of aesthetic beauty available in tonality might be a consolatory fantasy instead of natural and universal. Until his university education, Els believes – similar to practitioners of 'art for art's sake' – that art serves humanity by being beautiful and stirring the emotions. Els's desire to make music that pleases everyone suggests a Kantian belief in the universal nature of beauty: the 'judgement of taste', Kant writes, 'must involve a claim to validity for all men'.[13] The position advocated by Els's composition teacher – that art should 'wake people up' – is a simplified version of Adorno's attitude to art, for whom notions of beauty are not universal but socially produced, and have social consequences beyond providing pleasurable experiences. By the end of the novel Els returns to his Kantian beliefs about art, but to appreciate the politics of this position we must understand Adorno's arguments against Kant's notions of universal beauty.

For Adorno, aesthetic beauty and its cultural consumption have contributed to forming a world in which much is wrong. Notions of beauty have become so established that they appear natural and contribute to the suppression of critical independent thought. In *Aesthetic Theory*, Adorno writes: 'Terror itself peers out of the eyes of beauty as the coercion that emanates from form; the concept of the blinding glare of beauty articulates this experience.'[14] Here, beauty pleases people by relegating the non-beautiful beyond its realms. In other words, to experience pleasure from beauty, the awful and unpleasant must be absent. Beautiful forms silence and banish terror, which becomes like a spectre, haunting and repressed, peering out from behind the eyes of the beautiful object. The formal qualities that characterise the beautiful are recast by Adorno as a terrible sort of coercion that forces thought into uncritical acceptance of beautiful forms. To describe beauty as blinding also articulates the dangers of overpowering and instantaneous responses to art that preclude critical engagement with the world, blinding the subject to the true – and non-beautiful – conditions of their existence. As I discussed in Chapter 2, Adorno's claims about the true conditions of existence are rooted in the Marxist concepts of alienation and exploitation, and the emptiness that is perpetuated through the fulfilment of manufactured needs that are met by capitalist overproduction and mass culture.[15] These aspects of Adorno's thought underpin

Charles B. Sumner's explanation of why Adorno values the ugly, rather than the beautiful:

> In working out his theory on the relationship between art and society, Adorno takes de-humanisation as a social fact, and he sees beauty as an affirmative consolation for the de-humanisation registered by socio-political interest and suppressed in judgements of taste. Accordingly, he emphasises the potential for aesthetic dissonance and ugliness to reject this consolation and heighten socio-political interest. This heightened interest might then actually move us to confront particular forms of de-humanisation and thereby effect positive social change. [16]

The social fact of 'de-humanisation' refers to the damaged subjectivities produced by the social conditions of modernity. As we have seen in *Aesthetic Theory* and as Sumner identifies here, for Adorno beauty is like a consolation prize that distracts from the iniquities of social conditions. Instead, Adorno argues for the benefit of art that is ugly (because it can express an otherwise unseen truth about the awful condition of the modern subject) and dissonant (because it can articulate the contradictions of capitalist mass culture), because art that produces dissatisfaction rather than comfort might stoke the desire for social change. In Chapter 3 of *Aesthetic Theory*, 'On the Categories of the Ugly, the Beautiful, and Technique', Adorno implicitly reviews Kant's notion of aesthetics as the philosophical theory of beauty by examining the validity of ugliness, especially in 'modern art':

> Dissonance is the technical term for the reception through art of what aesthetics as well as naïveté calls ugly. Whatever it may be, the ugly must constitute, or be able to constitute, an element of art ... In modern art, the weight of this element [the ugly] increased to such a degree that a new quality emerged.[17]

For Adorno, the naive understanding of ugliness is art that lacks skill or beauty. Instead, ugliness is often the result of formal qualities better described as dissonance: aspects of form that prevent the artwork from being explained through existing frameworks for perceiving and understanding the world. That ugliness has been largely excluded from discussion of aesthetics is demonstrative of the blindness to varied forms of art caused by a focus on beauty. Els demonstrates this focus and associated Kantian beliefs about art during his youth, before his ideas are challenged by the dissonance of modern music. For Adorno, ugliness can be found in modern painting, poetry and prose – the examples he cites in *Aesthetic Theory* are 'The anatomical horror in Rimbaud and Benn, the physically revolting and repellent in Beckett'[18] – but the dissonance of atonal music (what he calls New Music) is the most salient example. New Music, for Adorno, situates itself counter to aesthetic norms, rejecting the consolation and illusory comfort of the beautiful to reveal the truth of the isolated, alienated modern subject, paving the way for the dissatisfaction required to desire social change.

Recuperating a version of the past

Orfeo has Els consider whether modernist music has this positive potential, but ultimately answers no. The novel treats modernist music as a temporary aberration, after which the public and intellectuals alike return to appreciating emotionally charged tonality. Towards the end of the novel, Els experiences tonality's beauty as a truth he had foolishly mistaken for old-fashioned. As he listens to a piece of music that cycles through musical techniques developed centuries ago, including melodic inversion, which he describes as 'the oldest trick in the book', a realisation 'hits Els like the naked truth'.[19] The techniques from which he tried to distance himself as an unwilling disciple of the avant-garde are revealed as the timeless and universal foundations of the perfect music he has always searched for:

> He sits here, years too late, knowing everything. Music has turned out to be the very thing he was taught to scorn. All his fellow composers have scattered on the winds of changing taste. But the young are still here, still in a hurry for transcendence, still willing to trade Now for something a little more durable ...[20]

Tonality reasserts itself as 'everything', while composers who have diverged from it were merely following 'changing tastes'. Modernist and experimental music is roundly and swiftly dismissed as a passing fad, while a form of 'transcendence' (a term discussed at length in Chapter 1) specifically equated with tonality is reasserted as a universal and ahistorical truth, different from the transient 'Now'. The novel does not seek to complicate this idea: this is an important realisation for Els at a climactic moment in the novel that forms a crucial stage of the narrative resolution.

The piece of music that convinces Els of the timeless beauty of tonality is Steve Reich's 'Proverb', which repeats Wittgenstein's phrase 'How small a thought it takes to fill a whole life' as it cycles through a range of established musical devices, including inversion and augmentation.[21] Els identifies that the piece is modelled on *ars antiqua*, the name given to European medieval music of the thirteenth century originating in Paris.[22] Reich's 'Proverb' is described as containing 'just enough passing dissonance to reassure listeners that it had heard the rumours about the previous [twentieth] century', but Els interprets the piece's collapse 'back into ars antiqua' as confirmation that 'the millennium-long search for novel harmonies' is 'a search now done'.[23] For Els, 'Proverb' demonstrates that music has exhausted itself and ended up back where it started: the truth of music is available in old styles and devices, not briefly fashionable modernist forms. Yet despite Els being a highly educated composer and lifelong student of music, the knowledge of medieval music in the novel is limited. A brief investigation can show us the limitations of the novel's assertions about the eternal relevance of *ars antiqua*, which do not reflect the radical nature of a style of music that was revolutionary in its time, and constantly changing.

Ars antiqua is the precursor to *ars nova*, which is present in Warner's *The Corner That Held Them*, as discussed in Chapter 4. *Ars antiqua* (old art) was the name given to complex polyphonic music produced in thirteenth-century Paris by intellectual and ecclesiastical communities. The name distinguishes it from fourteenth-century *ars nova* (new art), which had an even greater degree of rhythmic and melodic complexity. While only sacred music (performed in churches) was notated on expensive manuscript paper during this time, the polyphonic motets (pieces of music comprising several parts with words) that came to dominate *ars antiqua* and *ars nova* are said to have been influenced by secular music, as are their use of refrains, which are widely considered to have originated in troubadour music. The practice of notation, which required education, time and expensive materials, contributed to the dominance and reach of *ars antiqua* and *ars nova* by facilitating its teaching and transmission.[24] In Chapter 4, I examined Warner's acknowledgement in *The Corner That Held Them* that *ars nova* is the product of specific material conditions, connected to the availability of manuscript paper on which the complex music could be notated. Warner historically and materially situates *ars nova*, but she also has the music appear transcendent to certain characters.[25] The bailiff Henry Yellowlees is overwhelmed by its beauty, while the starving lepers are uninterested in the music's aesthetic value. Warner identifies that a person's ability to experience art as beautiful or transcendent can be linked to their economic and material security: to the lepers the music is just evidence of money wasted on expensive French manuscripts that could have been spent on food, while for the bailiff the music is a beautiful interlude during a moment of enjoyable rest. In *The Corner That Held Them* we see that music is a material product, but we also see its capacity to stir the emotions of Henry Yellowlees in a way that feels otherworldly. Warner knows that music can feel transcendent and universal, but that variations in poverty, education, free time and power mean it is rarely experienced in the same way by all.

Warner illuminates complications and contradictions in what art is, how it is created and the ways it is experienced. *Orfeo* is quite a different novel, because it tries to offer a clear statement about what art is. In *Orfeo* recent art forms – specifically modernism and the mid-twentieth-century avant-garde – either fade away or become commoditised, while much older forms like *ars antiqua* strike Els as eternally relevant. Powers does not ask what would make Els feel that this music has all the answers. Nor does the novel examine the many reasons why a well-educated man – who has long idealised European classical music that was also produced predominantly by educated men – might be open to seeing transcendence in the European music of the past that is still listened to today. Els, who is reaching the end of his life and has always wanted to leave a legacy, might be attracted to the observation that the music and ideas of people long dead but similar to him are still having an impact on the world, because he too hopes to leave a trace after his death. The novel reinforces Els's convictions about what music is because it does not question them by considering the formation of his tastes and beliefs. Because *Orfeo* is largely focalised through the idealistic and intellectually limited Els, it does not consider the nuances and materiality of older art forms, or the ways in which they were viewed at the time. *Ars antiqua* is far from a unified or simple style of music. As Edward H. Roesner has explained, it used three main techniques: organum and conductus, the use of which declines steadily as the thirteenth century progresses, and motet, which eventually became dominant.[26] The names given to the music of the high Middle Ages (which were used at the time and are still used today) shift from *ars antiqua* (old art) to *ars nova* (new art) and *ars subtilior* (subtler art), demonstrating the development seen by intellectual and musical communities in which innovation and progress were desired and considered positive. *Orfeo* praises *ars antiqua*, but its attempt to claim eternal authority for older art forms while casting experimental music aside does not reflect the radical spirit of the innovators of the high Middle Ages or the music they produced. The music of the thirteenth century is offered as evidence of a longstanding musical truth in a novel that fails to contemplate how radical *ars antiqua* was at the time. As a result of this narrow view, *Orfeo* cannot contemplate how twentieth-century music might be approached in the future, and writes it off as a passing fad.

Reinforcing established aesthetics and ways of living

In *Orfeo* even the most loyal disciples of the avant-garde eventually reject it and succumb to the allure of tonality's apparently timeless transcendence. Conceptual performance artist Richard Bonner often condescends to Els for believing in 'beauty': 'You're a masterpiece guy, aren't you? Gimme that old-time religion. People getting fragged in your living room, and you're still trying to sweet-talk beauty into a quickie.'[27] Bonner demonstrates a suspicion of beauty that is a simplified version of Adorno's criticisms, claiming it distracts from the ugliness of real events. Eventually, though, Bonner finds that his once-shocking art has been commoditised – turned into 'the next consumer-friendly dose of distraction for people who're bored by halftime spectacles'[28] – and responds by asking Els to co-write an opera. Bonner 'laid out what he wanted for the opera. He'd spent his entire life fleeing from narrative, and now he discovered, to his surprise, that it might not be too late to embrace the kind of storytelling that the world craved'.[29] Very specific elements of aesthetic and artistic history are framed here as revelatory truth and ahistorical desire. Bonner has realised that certain formal qualities are universal: the 'world' wants narrative and tonality, irrespective of culture, and the 'craving' comes from within, bypassing logic or reason, suggesting something natural and unavoidable. It is significant that at this moment the narration becomes difficult to attribute to a particular character. While an account of what Bonner says to Els, it is not reported speech. The narrator summarises and clarifies with an omniscience that rises above the confusion to tell us concisely of Bonner's lifelong mistakes and 'surprise' at his change of heart.

Implicit in all this is the idea that modernist music inexplicably decided to give people what they never really wanted, which is a rather simple and banal way of pushing much twentieth- and twenty-first-century music aside. Such a claim is only really possible because contemporary discourse about art music is so impoverished. It would be impossible, for example, to claim that experimental forms of twentieth-century literature or visual art are entirely devoid of value. A novel purporting to be cutting-edge could not claim that James Joyce wrote unnecessary books, and that we should again start writing like Chaucer, Austen or Dickens. It would be equally difficult to promote a return to Romantic landscape painting by claiming that nobody really likes Vincent Van Gogh, Damien Hirst or Banksy. Yet Powers does feel he can claim that twentieth-century music was a mistake. It's remarkable that Powers decides to have an omniscient narrator write off vast quantities of experimental music like this, in a novel that goes to such lengths to cast itself as intensely up to date by making Twitter central to its formal innovation, using terrorism as controversial subject matter and including news reports of recent real-world events.

Powers's narration often switches focalisation, but the result is very different from Warner's shifting focalisation discussed in Chapter 4. Warner uses the technique to show us the complexities or contradictions in her characters' thinking, and to reveal the limitations of their perspectives. *Orfeo* is largely focalised through Els but often slips into omniscience, summarising thoughts or speech and even informing us of characters' unconscious desires. When Els hears Reich's 'Proverb' in a café, the narrative voice works hard to support Els's conviction that everyone believes in and desires the timeless beauty of tonal music. When an unnamed woman leaves the café we are told that 'She, too, will die wanting things she won't even be able to name'.[30] Is this Els projecting his notions of life and desire onto her? Or is an omniscient narrator telling us something about this woman even she doesn't yet know, as a way of supporting the idea that Els has finally figured it all out? The ambiguity of the narrative voice makes it impossible to attribute the sentence solely to Els's limited perspective. With sleight of hand, the narrative reinforces the notion that the kind of art Els now values could satisfy this woman's desires, should she only realise it. This is indicative of Powers's narration, which regularly offers wise-sounding summaries while masking the extent of the narrator's intervention and guidance by making it difficult to judge the source of the voice. It is notable, too, that the narrative voice is unswervingly masculine: we do not hear from female characters in *Orfeo*, who only exist as satellites of Els. We never get any sense of what Clara, Maddy or Sara are thinking, outside what they say to Els and his interpretation of their behaviour.

Since *Orfeo* is primarily focalised through Els and requires us to be interested in what happens to him, a close engagement with modernist music is framed as a damaging experience. We watch Els's long and difficult journey back to certainty about the universality of tonality and, significantly, this goes hand in hand with a renewed conviction about the primary importance of family life. Els abandons his family to devote his life to a search for musical truth. He needs to find out if classical or modernist music is 'true' music, and is unable to allow them both to stand: he requires a singular truth. In order to write 'experimental music' with Richard Bonner, Els 'left a wife' and 'abandoned a daughter': 'For nothing, for music, for a chance to make a little noise in this world. A noise that no one needed to hear'.[31] Experimental music is completely unnecessary in *Orfeo*, but the 'trivial tune' that Els writes shortly before the break-up of his family, which uses 'all the rules from Intermediate Theory', is a 'total delight' and hyperbolically described as the kind of music that 'might even have saved lives'.[32] A clear binary is set up: an easy, pleasant tune is life-giving, but difficulty and dissonance ruins lives. By the end of the novel, Els believes that experimental music caused him to make the mistake of abandoning tonality and his family, and that he should have stayed at home because the world doesn't need any new music. His ideological return to tonality paves the way for the reconciliation that provides the narrative resolution, which reaffirms the importance of the family. He is able to apologise to his ex-wife – saying that he 'never should have left you and Sara for music', since it turns out the perfect music was already out there anyway – and reconciles with his daughter in the novel's closing scene.[33] *Orfeo* constructs a world where new music is not required because tonal music is true and enduring, and when Els sees this he realises that attending to his family would have been a better use of his time. The novel offers us a society that already has everything it needs, where no changes to social traditions like the family or established forms of art are required.

Orfeo is a recuperative and nostalgic text that holds up longstanding aesthetics and ways of living as right and true. We are provided with a positive view of the family, since the novel ends by framing it as the right choice, while tonality and *ars antiqua* are proclaimed the location of musical truth. And just as *Orfeo* offers a limited account of *ars antiqua*, it offers a simple version of the family. Problems with the nuclear family have long been recognised: its patriarchal nature, its enforcement of rigid and unequal gender roles, and the way that laws and social privileges benefiting the family unit limit freedom and opportunities for women or anyone not heterosexual or who does not live in a nuclear family household. In the latter half of the twentieth century feminist theorists built on observations made by Marx and Engels about the economic and social disadvantages the patriarchal family imposes on women, and society as a whole, since it safeguards the uneven distribution of wealth by ensuring that accumulated capital and property are retained within families by being transmitted down the male line of inheritance.[34] Simone de Beauvoir identified much greater, far-reaching social consequences for women expected to live in patriarchal family units.[35] In *The Anti-Social Family* Michelle Barrett and Mary McIntosh recorded an array of difficulties experienced by women living in nuclear families, such as isolation and the pressures of normalised unpaid domestic labour. They also note the power of the family as an ideology, pointing out the considerable role of the media in framing the family as the most desirable and widespread way of living, despite the fact that at the time of their writing in 1982, nuclear families accounted for only a third of households.[36] The ideas of Marx, Engels and de Beauvoir informed Shulamith Firestone's calls for the abolition of the traditional family and sex differences in 1970, which she identified as the basis of inequality and oppression. Firestone also connected sex oppression with race oppression by identifying that both gendered and racial hierarchies rely on discourses about the biological superiority of men and white people, and biology-as-destiny.[37]

Firestone's abolitionist calls were renewed in 2019 by Sophie Lewis, whose *Full Surrogacy Now: Feminism Against Family* argues for the abolition of the nuclear family to make way for more egalitarian, communal and fulfilling ways of living. Lewis uncovers a very different picture of family life than the idealised one we find in *Orfeo*. She points out that families and households are not always havens: domestic abuse and child abuse take place in the home, while gay and trans people can experience the pressure to emulate heterosexual, cisgendered family role models as ideological violence.[38] Reviewing this writing on the family illuminates the narrowness and intense conservatism of *Orfeo*'s approach to family life. None of the problems with the family that have long been observed by others arise in the novel because of the narrative and character choices made by Powers. Writing a novel from the perspective of a character like Els prevents Powers from having to deal with difficulties connected to gender, sexuality or race. In addition, Els doesn't have any friends with non-normative identities to broaden his horizons, and for his own part experiences only artistic and romantic challenges. The disruption to the Els household relies on a well-worn, highly gendered cliché: the incompatibility of the male artistic genius with family life. There are also numerous aspects of Els's identity, tastes and desires that Powers chooses not to cover. Els is driven by an artistic passion, for sure, but what about the patriarchal ideologies that might explain why his aesthetic goals seem superior to the drudgery of domestic responsibility, or how easily he is able to obtain complete independence to pursue them? What about Els's obsession with there being a singular, ultimate truth about music that means that he thinks only one of the limited forms he identifies – classical tonality or modernist dissonance – must be 'true'? Powers's novel never wonders how this obsession with neatness, order and singularity might be unsurprising in a character who encounters very little complexity and plurality in life, or among the identities and experiences of the people he knows.

Modernist music as terrorism

Powers frames modernist music as responsible for Els's problems, not Els's dogged, selfish pursuit of singular truth. Modernist music prompts Els to abandon what we are told is the true locus of meaning – the family – and even accidentally turns him into a terrorist. Without his family Els is lonely and unoccupied in old age, so he reignites a passion for science as a hobby. After modifying bacterial DNA with a code derived from reducing a piece of music to a series of numbers (the novel is hazy on the details) he accidentally produces a dangerous strain and is pursued by the police as a bio-terrorist. When the police arrive at his house, they fail to notice all the texts by modernist composers, who wrote 'battle manuals that agitated for all-out assault on the general public over the last hundred years. Boulez's *Orientations*. Schoenberg's *Harmonielehre*. Messiaen's *Technique de mon langage musical*' – these are really responsible for the composer's accidental terrorism, the text implies, though the police cannot see it.[39] Els directly blames modernist music for making him a terrorist: 'I wanted music to be the antidote to the familiar. That's how I became a terrorist.'[40] The sentence quoted is from a Twitter account – @Terrorchord – set up by Els to frame his biological accident as an intentional piece of terrorism and performance art, so we can't be certain that Els is genuine: he could be trying to shock his audience. Even so, desiring newness and difference of the kind found in unfamiliar, dissonant music has deadly consequences in *Orfeo*, which frames deviating from the familiar – whether the family or tonality – as a mistake and a dangerous enterprise.

There is no aspect of Els's identity that is not conservative: he is a white, educated, heterosexual male who believes his musical preferences are the location of universal truth. Experiencing so much changing music during his life is confusing and distressing, making him want to 'break free of time and hear the future', to 'tunnel into forever through the walls of Now'.[41] True music, he thinks, will be as relevant in the future as it is now, so he believes that finding true music will provide access to the transcendent truths of the future and all time. Paradoxically, though, in *Orfeo* that 'future' is eventually arrived at through rejecting the innovations of the twentieth century and returning to the musical traditions of the more distant past. Even Els's cutting-edge science experiment is really another way of validating a much older strain of thought: it is an attempt to create a new 'music of the spheres'.[42] By encoding DNA with musically derived numbers, Els tries to give music a physical presence and ensure it has real-world consequences: he wants music to affect a biological organism that is part of the order and fabric of the physical world.

Els initially wants to make music that is beautiful for everyone – 'one slight noise that might delight you all'[43] – but having failed to do this, he seeks the universal another way: by writing 'Tunes for forever, for no one'.[44] Els's DNA 'music', which will be audible to nobody, instead of wonderful to everybody, shows his enduring interest in universality and totalising forms. Yet he has to reduce a piece of music to a series of numbers in order to 'programme' it into the DNA. 'Does it hurt to know that any piece of music, however sublime, can be turned into a unique large number?' Els asks.[45] Yet after this process, music is longer recognisable as music, and it certainly lacks the affective capacity that Els values above all. In Chapter 3, we saw something similar happen with Pound, who also searches for essences and tries to turn music into numbers, whereby it is becomes not-music and lacks the communicative qualities that drove him to engage with music in the first place.[46] In *Orfeo*, similarly to what happens in Pound's thought, the search for an essence results in a reduction that divests music of its complexity. For Cristina Iuli the novel is about the 'failures of Els' (the biggest of which is his reduction of music to data) and his poor attempts to 'fix' things into place. Iuli argues that Els is wrong to conflate mathematics and music, or music and the world, and she argues that the novel critiques his failed attempts to find essences and impose symmetry on the world.[47] Els is certainly a tragic hero, but even if we are encouraged to be critical of his choices and see his flawed obsession with finding music's essence as the reason for his downfall, the novel still demonises modernist music, which is guilty of causing Els's confusion about what art is and should be that drives him to seek its essence.

Myth and totalising forms

Aside from the references to modernist music, *Orfeo*'s most ostensible engagement with modernism is its mythic underpinning – a very modernist technique in what is otherwise a very anti-modernist novel. The novel's title encourages us to read Els as a modern-day Orpheus and foregrounds the connection between music and tragedy. According to the Greek myth, Orpheus's music was powerfully, universally affective: he was able to charm animals, plants and rocks. In other words, Orphic music moves everything, from living things to inanimate objects.[48] In the myth of Orpheus, as in so many discourses since, harmony in the musical sense is associated with the concept of harmony – as in order and connection – more broadly, since music is framed as uniquely capable of achieving connections with all things. Music holds out the possibility of a commonality, or shared understanding between things in the world that appear otherwise unconnected. Despite his power, Orpheus's story is tragic because his wife Eurydice dies the day after their wedding. His music gains him access to the underworld and the opportunity to rescue her, but he makes the mistake of looking back as she follows him out, which he was instructed not to do. She is pulled back down, and he has to return without her.

Els wants to create music with the Orphic power to move people and the physical world, and to overcome death by being universally beautiful and so transcending time and space. Els is also referred to as the 'Bio-hacker Bach' on the news while he is evading arrest, and his amateur bio-hacking, which tries to encode music into cells, attempts to bridge the gap between art and life: to transcend the boundaries between the human and the natural by giving music's transcendence a material form. Trying to explain his genetic project to Maddy, the narrator-Els says, 'Four billion years of chance had written a score of inconceivable intricacy into every living cell'.[49] Els's biological experiments are based on his conviction about the connection between art and the physical world, but this connection is asserted weakly through metaphorical language and rhetoric. For Els, life becomes music simply through the use of the word 'score' to describe the structure of cells. Els's way of thinking erodes the differences between things and simplifies the complexities in the world around him. Orpheus's decline begins when he loses Eurydice – the loss of a kind of perfection – while Els declines after the loss of Maddy and Sara, due to his search for aesthetic perfection: 'And that is the curse of a life spent looking for transcendence: nothing real will ever suffice'.[50] Els's pursuit of musical transcendence is his fatal flaw, but the novel also paradoxically advocates for classical music's transcendence, as we have seen. In *Orfeo*, it seems that life is only cursed for those who are wrong about the established location of truth and transcendence.

The novel's valorisation of classical music, tonality and traditional family life are formally reinforced by the novel's structure, which offers the wholeness and totality advocated at the level of content.[51] The narrative comprises Els's whole life: there are three narrative timelines that merge in the closing pages, moving between Els's present, flashbacks to his past and short snippets from his future, going some way to demonstrating the novel's commitment to totalities. At the end of the novel, the short snippets – which are in a different font and encased by lines to ensure they stand out – are identified as tweets from the account @Terrorchord, set up after Els's meeting with Bonner during his flight from the police. When the three narratives finally merge, the novel replicates the sense of divine order and formal coherence that Els admires in music. Reich's 'Proverb' is constructed of sections that 'weave together so seamlessly it's clear they were shaped from the start solely for this reunion', and Mozart's *Jupiter* lays 'down a foundation for all the developments to come' in 'its first few notes'.[52] *Orfeo* also introduces three component parts – three narratives – that are united at the end. The novel thus frames itself as similar to 'Proverb', which sparks Els's awakening to the eternal relevance of tonality, and *Jupiter*, which is present at the beginning and end of Els's musical journey. *Orfeo* tells us which aesthetic forms are timelessly beautiful, and replicates them, claiming the same status for itself.

Orfeo *and musico-literary criticism*

Critics have noticed the novel's keen interest in music, its preoccupation with wholeness and completion, its formal complexity and interest in politics. So far, there has been no analysis of how the novel's use of music contributes to its conservatism. *Orfeo*'s overt references to music and its complex form have produced criticism that seeks to validate the novel in line with the claims it makes about itself, by examining how it might replicate particular kinds of musical structures. (We saw the same problem in the criticism of Joyce's 'Sirens' discussed in Chapter 2.)[53] Miriam Fernandez-Santiago compares *Orfeo* with music by building on Jay Labinger's argument that Powers's earlier novel, *The Gold Bug Variations*, emulates musical form because it 'resonate[s] with Neo-Baroque aesthetics'. Fernandez-Santiago argues that 'Labinger's list of structural and thematic features can also fit a description of *Orfeo*',[54] which is significant because the 'isomorphic arrangement of themes, voices, plot nodules, and characters, as well as of puns, allusions, and biographical, textual, intertextual and extratextual (historical) parallelisms' – which can be compared with Neo-Baroque aesthetics – 'confers the novel with a labyrinthine, polycentric structure that however suggests (and challenges the reader to find or construct) a complex, coherent – though elusive – whole'.[55] For Fernandez-Santiago, elements of the Orpheus myth – specifically Orpheus's musical connection with the natural world, which seems to transcend the limits of the human – are given a present-day setting in *Orfeo*. She argues, though, that representations of Orpheus charming the natural world in painting are often typically 'anthropocentric', which undermines the music's claim to transcendence. *Orfeo*, she continues, dramatises the attempt to resolve this paradox: to be transcendent, and to remain of this world.[56] *Orfeo*, for Fernandez-Santiago, offers the reader the material to solve this problem: the novel 'appeals to each reader's responsible contribution to its completion, asking more questions than it gives answers, but leading the tune towards love and belief'.[57] In this reading, *Orfeo* is full of contradictions and unresolved questions, and recruits the reader as an active participant to fill in its gaps. But this is not the case, as we have seen. Attention to the way the novel handles music, and the way it is structured, shows that this text is much less open than it might appear, and promotes an identifiably conservative aesthetics and politics.

Criticism that compares musical and narrative forms often fails to do more than point out similarities, without explaining why those similarities matter. In other words, there is often no clear pay-off. A. Elisabeth Reichel also exemplifies this approach. She wants to identify *Orfeo*'s use of 'structures and techniques that are commonly associated with another medium, namely music' and 'sets out to investigate what precisely the forms and functions of these musical components are'.[58] Some similarities are drawn between *Orfeo* and Monteverdi's opera *L'Orfeo*, but this is a dead end: she concludes that 'Despite a large number of parallels, a one-to-one correspondence between the opera and the novel does not exist'.[59] The point of the analysis is unclear, and so is the reason for undertaking it in the first place, since the novel does not explicitly reference Monteverdi's opera. Next, the presence of music at the level of form and content is said to be significant, but this is never justified: 'it is this double presence of music that renders the macrostructural musical elements in Powers's novels particularly noteworthy'.[60] Tracing thin similarities between musical and literary forms is commonly considered as an end in itself. Reichel concludes that the novel says a number of different things about music, and suggests that 'readers, too, may re-evaluate the functions and meanings of music'.[61]

This kind of criticism does not 'live in and work for our century'. Neither Reichel nor Fernandez-Santiago can tell us anything about why the musical forms or themes matter; neither has any way of judging the significance of the aesthetics they comment on. *Orfeo*'s engagement with music is assumed to be a positive feature, showing that discourses about music's positive aesthetic potential have such an enduring power that they are rarely approached critically and historically, even in scholarship on musico-literary form. Fernandez-Santiago and Reichel both argue that the novel celebrates multiplicity by exploring varied musics and forms, but their claims contradict something else they both notice: the novel's celebration of wholeness and universality, which Fernandez-Santiago directly discusses, and which is implicit in Reichel's claims about the novel's musicality at the level of form and content. How can a novel celebrate multiplicity and its opposite, universality, at the same time? The answer is that it doesn't. Different musics and ideas are certainly present in *Orfeo*, but they are not all given the same weight or value. These analyses fail both to notice *Orfeo*'s critique of modernist music and to see that advocating Western tonality as the location of universal beauty makes *Orfeo* a deeply conservative text.

We need a critical approach to music and ways of discussing the interactions between aesthetics and politics if we are to extract something of value from formally complex novels like *Orfeo*. As we have seen, the novel's complexity tends to be written off simply as the demonstration of different ideas, with no discussion of the ways they are framed. *Orfeo* acknowledges how integral to a person's sense of self their musical preferences can be, but ultimately recommends conservative attitudes of change avoidance, because Els comes to believe his life would have been better if he had stuck to functional harmony and family life. Despite *Orfeo*'s claims to newness through references to science and terrorism, Powers relies on discourses about the transcendence of classical music to validate conservative aesthetics and ways of living.

let me tell you

Griffiths's decision to intentionally restrict the language available to him is reminiscent of the writing constraints used by Oulipo practitioners – a group of literary innovators who are invariably discussed in relation to modernism – in France during the 1960s and 1970s.[62] *let me tell you* could hardly be a more different novel. It has a female narrator – a reimagined Ophelia from *Hamlet* – and is interested in the work of challenging, rather than reinforcing, assumptions and common practices. Paul Griffiths uses a writing constraint, limiting himself to the 483 words spoken by Ophelia in Shakespeare's play. The choice to use a constraint is indebted to French Oulipo practitioners: a group founded in Paris in November 1960 by novelist Raymond Queneau and mathematician François Le Lionnais, who used formal rules and constraints to produce different and unusual literature. For example, Georges Perec's novel *A Void* (1969) excludes the letter e, and the mystery around the absence of the letter – and the theme of absence more generally – is key to the story.[63] A piece of writing that excludes one or more letters is called a lipogram, but the void in Perec's novel goes further than a single letter. He is unable to use the French words for mother, father or family (*mère, père, famille*) so that under the writing constraint direct references to these significant relationships are impossible. Another Oulipian work is Raymond Queneau's *Exercises in Style*, which retells a story ninety-nine times using different literary techniques as a way of exploring what is produced when writing the same events in different ways. The group's name is derived from an acronym of the phrase *Ouvroir de littérature potentielle*, which roughly translates as 'workshop of potential literature', and as this name suggests, the writers were interested in thinking about what writing could become instead of what it already was, and sought rules that would force unusual ways of writing and produce defamiliarising effects.[64] Similarly, Griffiths's formal choice makes any word not spoken by Ophelia in *Hamlet* unavailable for use in *let me tell you*. This type of constraint can affect a story's content by preventing the author from referring directly to certain people or things, and it can also preclude a variety of grammatical constructions due to the unavailability of particular words. Unlike *Orfeo*, *let me tell you* is not interested in reinforcing established notions of beauty, art or value – it is not even interested in using everyday words or common expressions.

Using such limited language presents a number of challenges and opportunities to Griffiths, who combines the writing constraint with the task of creating a more detailed narrative and history for Ophelia, who has limited dialogue in Shakespeare's play. For example, Ophelia uses the word 'them' but not 'they' in *Hamlet*, which makes a common way of referring to more than one person impossible in *let me tell you*. Instead, alternatives must be found, like 'he and she'. Griffiths is forced to make what he can out of the material at hand, instead of being directed by how he might usually plan, write or think. While 'he and she' is a functional substitution for 'they', it is an unusual way to speak. The absence of 'they' forces a solution that gives Ophelia's narrative a whimsical tone and contributes to forming a slight eccentricity in her character. As we can see, a writing constraint can do more than simply limit the author: it can be productive, generating a way of writing that deepens a character in a manner that might not otherwise have been considered – and which appropriately develops her original character, which is mysterious and troubled in *Hamlet*. Another example is the absence of 'mother' from Ophelia's vocabulary in *Hamlet*, which has a significant impact on the story Griffiths is able to write for her. He uses the word 'she' instead, which affects the novel's content because such an impersonal way of referring to a parent cannot help but communicate a difficult relationship, which Griffiths then has to construct. The absence of the word 'mother' helps to spur the development of a psychologically complex childhood for Ophelia, in which the mother is emotionally and often physically absent, resulting in a lack of intimacy and trust between parent and child.

As these examples show, when writing with a restricted corpus the starting point must be what is possible to construct with the words available, instead of an idea or plotline. In an interview (of which I make much use in the following discussion) Griffiths describes how this 'way of writing can unlock something otherwise unavailable' since 'phrases and sentences will seem to form themselves without a writer's volition'.[65] His claim shares much with T. S. Eliot's advocacy of using rhythm instead of pre-existing ideas to drive or 'bring to birth the idea' of a poem – as discussed in this book's introduction.[66] Eliot claims he looks to rhythm to avoid quotidian language use, while Griffiths intentionally restricts his available vocabulary to escape routine ideas and phrases. Griffiths had originally intended to write a novel using all of the words from *Hamlet* only once, but found that he could 'say almost anything with this stock of words' and chose Ophelia's limited dialogue to impose more stringent rules on what it was possible to say.[67] Peter Kirwan points out a further strategy that increases the unfamiliarity of the writing: 'Griffiths avoids extended collocations derived from the play, resisting individual moments of overt quotation'.[68] 'Collocation' is a term used in linguistic analysis to refer to words commonly located together in a text or collection of texts. Since Shakespeare's plays are widely known, avoiding arrangements of words from the plays that could appear familiar helps to ensure that *let me tell you* is as different from *Hamlet* as possible. Using the avoidance of collocations as an additional restriction also ensures that Griffiths does not fall back – even unconsciously – on easily accessible or well-known sentences and grammatical constructions. Kirwan's essay 'Mis/Quotation in Constrained Writing' is the only critical discussion I have found of this novel so far, and although he does not make an explicit connection between the text and modernist music of the kind I make below, he does find that the words in Griffiths's 'limited corpus recur insistently and musically'.[69]

Modernist, musical formal innovations

let me tell you is the product of a musicologist who turns to literature, inspired by methods of formal innovation that are both modernist and musical, to examine the rules and ideologies that govern everyday language use. To explain his desire to write in order to make 'overt what in other writing we don't notice', Griffiths quotes serialist and electronic composer Milton Babbitt: 'Everyone works according to the rules; I would just prefer to know what mine are'.[70] Griffiths's voluntary constraint is reminiscent of the self-imposed restriction of the twelve-tone compositional method used by Babbitt and originally developed by Arnold Schoenberg, which was also intended to make the creative process more challenging. Schoenberg wrote that 'composing with twelve tones . . . does not facilitate composing; on the contrary, it makes it more difficult', because it generates unusual problems that require unusual solutions.[71] Very limited combinations of notes are possible when composing with a twelve-tone row, which sets the range of tones and their relationship for the duration of the piece. It is not possible to use the rules of functional harmony – which Schoenberg regarded as a different kind of constraint – to structure compositional development when using twelve-tone technique.[72] Innovative formal methods become necessary to generate progression or produce and release tension. Schoenberg claimed that 'The restrictions imposed on a composer by the obligation to use only one set [of twelve tones] in a composition are so severe that they can only be overcome by an imagination which has survived a tremendous number of adventures'.[73] Similarly, Griffiths found using a restricted corpus of words 'hugely useful in forcing solutions beyond the obvious and immediate'.[74] His claim that 'writing under deliberate constraint can also be, paradoxically, a liberation' is a sentiment that underpins Schoenberg's technique as well as his own.[75]

In *let me tell you*, a modernist emphasis on form is used, Griffiths says, 'to find things you could never have found any other way': to achieve new ways of writing and thinking.[76] For Griffiths, 'All verbal communication is constrained', whether 'by the nature and traditions of the language' or the environment in which someone speaks.[77] Writing under a constraint reveals the ordinarily unacknowledged reliance on particular words and grammatical constructions. Griffiths describes it as a 'delusion' to say we ever use language 'freely', and that writing 'normally' is only to write under the rules and restrictions we are most accustomed to, and which have become 'invisible'.[78] This comes close to a discussion of how ideologies work through everyday language – something that is also, as we have seen, at the back of modernist formal innovation, prompting the desire to write and think otherwise, for which they often draw on music's non-linguistic and non-referential mode of communication.

Deciding to find new ways of restricting the material available to the artist requires, first of all, recognising that rules and constraints are involved in all systems of language and composition – something Schoenberg considered significant when he was composing in the early twentieth century, as did Babbitt during his career that spanned the mid- to late twentieth century, and which Griffiths considers significant still. A similar observation was driving the literary experiments of the French Oulipian novelists, as we have seen. Acknowledging the limitations of everyday language was also crucial for a number of British writers between the 1960s and 1980s. In *British Avant-Garde Fiction of the 1960s* (2019), writing constraints are identified as key to Brigid Brophy's methods for departing from realism, and to many novels by Christine Brooke-Rose.[79] Brooke-Rose has often used specific grammatical constraints – one thinks especially of *Between* (1968), *Thru* (1975) and *Amalgamemnon* (1984). In *Between*, she gives her narrator no name, never uses the word 'I' (except in dialogue), nor the verb 'to be'. In *Amalgamemnon* she attempts to write entirely in the future tense, so that nothing strictly happens in the novel, which has the effect of leaving open an array of possible futures. In *Invisible Author: Last Essays*, Brooke-Rose begins her discussion of constraints she has used in her novels by identifying some of the innumerable 'invisible constraints' that are present whenever language is used, which go unseen because they have become second-nature to readers and writers.[80] Constraints are intended to alter the writing process and the resultant texts, so it follows that using them can produce formally unusual literature. Brooke-Rose notes that she has been called 'anti-realist' by critics who claim that deviating from the conventions of realism precludes engagement with the real world. Such criticism fails to recognise literary realism as a specific set of rules and constraints, and is part of what Brooke-Rose calls an 'old dispensation that regarded reality as pre-existent and merely to be "captured" by the artist', instead of something that is actively being constructed in both realist and non-realist works.[81] For critics who claim Brooke-Rose is anti-realist, the core issue is which writers are accurately representing the world, or who is accessing the truth of reality, where reality is considered something objective that can be accurately accessed and described. Formally experimental artists – whether before or after the modernists – are engaged in challenging aesthetic traditions that have come to seem natural, as well as the world those naturalised forms purport to accurately represent. Formalism, then, can challenge entrenched ways of seeing the world, while realism has been rejected by novelists who wish to avoid extant notions of what the world is like by adhering to established narrative, plot or character conventions.

Griffiths shares with Brooke-Rose (and with Schoenberg) a conviction that what appears familiar, pleasant or normal is not necessarily natural, right or true. For all three, commonplace ways of arranging words or tones contain an array of rules and restrictions that have become invisible by virtue of being so familiar. This is a very different notion from the one that underpins *Orfeo*, which promotes the familiar structures of the family and classical music as truthful and correct. As we have seen in our analysis of beauty and ugliness in relation to *Orfeo*, perceptions of art as beautiful or pleasant often rely on familiarity with specific formal qualities, which also means that art which seems beautiful can be more easily understood, while art that is formally unusual can be experienced as difficult and unpleasant. This further illuminates a key difference between *Orfeo* and *let me tell you*. *Orfeo*, despite its formally innovative aspects, functions as a plot-driven, realist novel: conflict and uncertainty are eventually resolved and the value of established aesthetics and living arrangements is finally reinforced. *let me tell you* is not seeking to fulfil those conventions; it makes a different set of narrative choices, attempting to make Ophelia's well-known story unfamiliar in content and form. Both novelists are working in established traditions – realism for Powers and an array of formalist experimentation for Griffiths – but the respective traditions are invested in very different work.

Dissonance and difficulty

I want now to discuss the functions and effects of Schoenberg's and Griffiths' similar type of formal constraints, starting with the ways that unfamiliar aesthetic forms produced with writing constraints are often considered difficult to read, listen to or enjoy. Adorno analysed Schoenberg at length and his observations can help to illuminate an approach to *let me tell you*. The serialist compositions Schoenberg produced using tone rows were his strategy for achieving atonality: the 'emancipation of dissonance' from tonality, and an archetypal formal modernist musical innovation.[82] Adorno, as discussed in Chapter 2, generates a social critique out of Schoenberg's formalism by analysing tonal relationships as analogous to social relationships.[83] I want to analyse Schoenberg from a different angle now, by considering the possible social effects of listening, and how listening might prompt reflection on the category of music and the consumption of artworks more broadly.

Listening to dissonant music offers a new frame of reference against which the harmonic and structural similarities of compositions that use functional harmony can be recognised, and against which the passivity of much everyday listening might be revealed. Lydia Goehr discusses the different ways Adorno and Schoenberg approach the difficulty of listening to serialism. Schoenberg hoped the listening public would eventually enjoy the music (albeit a different kind of enjoyment than that produced by familiarity, generated instead out of the effort required to follow and comprehend the music), while Adorno located the radicalism of atonality precisely in its capacity to shock, which prevents it from seeming pleasant or natural.[84] Atonality, which cannot be enjoyed or consumed in the same way as tonality since it aims to frustrate both the expectations created by functional harmony and the forms of enjoyment they provide, requires critical engagement with aesthetic traditions instead of passive consumption. Tonality, which appears familiar, pleasant and therefore 'natural', can be thrown into new relief through its contrast with atonality. To summarise Adorno's claims in 'Music and New Music' from *Quasi Una Fantasia*, the development of atonality (what Adorno calls 'New Music') shows us that music changes; it has changed in the past and will change again.[85] Tonal music, one might then note, has its own history of adaptation and rejection. Is, then, our perception of tonal music as 'natural' historically contingent? Might tonality only appear natural, merely as a condition of it being usual? As Goehr explains, Adorno is interested in using the music to 'pose questions to undermine our confidence in familiarity'.[86] The jarring dissonance of serialism's atonality discloses the extent of the standardisation enforced by tonality and familiar forms of functional harmony, which makes possible a critique of the culture industry's production of standardised material that promotes passive consumption. The value of atonality is not, therefore, in its ability to adapt the listening public to something new, as Schoenberg hoped, but to facilitate reflection on the historicity of what appears natural. This reflection is more valuable, for Adorno, than the idea that the listening public might simply get used to another kind of music. It follows that if our present condition is not natural, then it can be changed.

let me tell you has a comparable aim of prompting reflection on what appears natural, but addresses standard language usage rather than standard tonality. Reading the novel probably does not produce a shock comparable to the dissonance of atonal music (although Griffiths's method might strike some readers as very strange), yet the writing does have an unusual quality to it, and different reading practices are required to extract value from the work, just as different listening practices are required with atonality. There is an unsettling and Beckettian quality to much of the novel, which feels heavily stripped down due to the limited vocabulary. When Ophelia asks, 'Is the sun up? No. Then it must be night', this might be a statement of the obvious, or a reflection on the difficulty of seeing the simplest things clearly under the emotional duress she is experiencing towards the end of the novel.[87] Thought and language often break down in this text. In the closing paragraphs, Ophelia's impending death is foregrounded in the disintegration of her language: 'Snow. Now. No. O. This is me'.[88] From a four-letter word that means frozen water, Ophelia becomes a passing moment in time, then a negative or rejection, and finally zero or nothing, before declaring, 'This is me'. As these examples show, it is not possible to enjoy *let me tell you* in the same way as a plot-driven narrative in which obstacles are overcome in a story moving towards resolution and the restoration of order: we know Ophelia's story and its tragic ending already. There is, as one might expect, much repetition when using only 483 words, and the writing is often ambiguous, requiring considerable inference.

All these features mean that to extract value from the novel, it has to be approached with an awareness of its method; as an experiment with form that beseeches active participation instead of passive consumption. Accordingly, Griffiths does not keep his technique a secret. A short preface tells us: 'You will see, in what follows, what Ophelia has to say of her life'; 'all this Ophelia will speak in her own words, those words alone. She is like the rest of us; we all have no more than the words that come to us in the play'.[89] The preface is attributed to 'The King', but if we read 'the play' as metaphor for a life, the last clause gestures to Griffiths's conviction that all language use is constrained. Openly working under formal restraints is described by Griffiths as a method for 'demystifying the experience' of an artwork, and 'inviting the audience to engage with the work as an artifact'.[90] The reader is encouraged to acknowledge not only the unnaturalness of the artwork in question, but also the unnaturalness of apparently natural language, and by extension other art forms that have come to appear natural.

The form of *let me tell you* is part of a strategy intended to have real-world effects, resisting passive consumption and encouraging a reader's critical reflection on artistic forms and processes. Like so many modernist artworks, Griffiths's novel aims to transform its reader. Unlike Schoenberg, though, he is not waiting for the public to come round to his compositional method. The novel seeks to do what Adorno claims is radical about atonality: to prompt reflection on what appears natural and hold out the possibility that thought could be different. *let me tell you* explores something that Raymond Williams describes as integral to the modernist movement: 'the thesis of the non-natural status of language'.[91]

let me tell you is not a coldly formal exercise. It is often evocative and profound, reflects thoughtfully on the nature of language and self-reflexively refers to its own project. In her first sentence – 'So: now I come to speak' – it is though Ophelia is back from the dead, finally speaking after a long wait or hesitation, so that the novel opens by recognising its distance from the Shakespearean play to which it responds. Ophelia's declaration that 'My words may be poor, but they will have to do'[92] references the limited range of words, and using 'poor' as the descriptor is partially forced by the technique, since Ophelia does not have the option of 'limited' or 'few'. The recourse to 'poor', rather than being a drawback, opens up a range of meanings. Describing the words given to Ophelia by Shakespeare, and remobilised painstakingly by Griffiths, as 'poor' invites broader questions about how useful or sufficient language is for communicating – even in texts of great acclaim and longstanding cultural significance (as in *Hamlet*) or on occasions where an unusual level of thought has been used (as in *let me tell you*). Ophelia's character is developed when she describes her words as 'poor': she appears humble and anticipates the insufficiency of her narrative. Yet the sentence need not indicate that Ophelia really is a poor storyteller: it could tell us more about her capacity to reflect on the insufficiency of language for communicating her experience. Ophelia might fear she is unskilled, while in fact being deeply in tune with the suspicion of language driving the novel's form. The novel's opening manages to build Ophelia as a complex character, as well as prompting reflection on literary form and language.

The lines Ophelia speaks in *Hamlet* are relatively few, but much of her language is evocative and philosophical. Griffiths's use of that rich language, combined with his objective of imagining a full life for a tragic and contemplative character, produces a novel full of thoughtful and unusual meditations on memory, language, identity and authenticity:

> I know I have it in me to say things that are not so and have never been so, but that I wish had been so. There are, as well, things in my head that I cannot remember and will never remember. They are not in my memory; they are in me.
>
> But now and again words come to me as if it rained words in my head—words given me by some other, as if I had no hand in what I say, as if all I may do is give speech, let the words come and come, and go on and on, and whilst they go on I cannot say what I would truly wish to say. I may do nothing, held still by my own words—if they are my own. My words go on, but *I* cannot speak.[93]

When Ophelia declares that she can 'say things' that 'have never been so, but that I wish had been so', she contemplates the potential of language to bring new ideas and worlds into being. She thinks about the unconscious mind: things in her 'head' that she 'cannot remember', where repressed or forgotten ideas, linguistically figured, reside. By claiming that these ideas and potential are 'not in my memory' but 'in me', Ophelia suggests that identity is partially the result of the way language works on people without their conscious knowledge, rather than thought about rationally and retained as memory. Griffiths directly references his method of having Ophelia tell a new story using the words originally given to her by 'some other', who we know to be Shakespeare, but at the same time considers the wider difficulties of using a language system that pre-exists the individual to say things that feel authentic. Using language is like having 'no hand' in what it is possible to say, as though the words were already chosen, impeding genuine expression: 'what I would truly wish to say'. At other times in the novel, Ophelia reflects instead on the possibilities that remain, even within a constrained system of thought: 'when you look at your memory what you see is not quite yourself. You are more than your memory. You are all that you have been and could be'.[94] The book contemplates the potential of the individual and asks what ought to shape them, suggesting that one need not be constrained by perception or by past events, while demonstrating this by constructing out of Ophelia's past language a rich character with a fuller history and longer story. *let me tell you* is a return to modernist literary forms and topics through techniques informed by modernist music. It is evidence of an ongoing dialogue between music, literature and modernist formal techniques in contemporary writing, which shows that the need to use music to investigate ideology and language remains pressing.

Musical interactions with literature

The success of composer Hans Abrahamsen's opera let me tell you – named after and based on Griffiths's novel – shows that literary-musical interactions are still highly regarded in the contemporary art world. The opera, produced in collaboration with the soprano Barbara Hannigan, premiered with the Berlin Philharmonic in December 2013. In 2016 it won the Grawemeyer Award – one of the most prestigious awards for contemporary composition. The reception of the opera shows that longstanding ideas about music's ability to heighten the communicative capacity of language are still driving notions of musical value among prominent composers and critics. In an interview filmed for the Grawemeyer Award's website, Abrahamsen says that he was interested in Griffiths's attempt to give Ophelia – who is often manipulated in *Hamlet* and says relatively little – a new life with depth, and a history told in her own voice.[95] The title given to the Grawemeyer interview with Abrahamsen – 'Adding Emotional Depth and Nuance to Limited Words'[96] – reveals an attitude to the value of music that could be considered archaic for a contemporary music award. The language used to explain the opera's accomplishment rests on claims about music's emotional veracity. Could it be that these ideas are still common currency in the art world today? Or are notions about music's inherent truthfulness being approached as so widely accepted among the public that they are a suitable way to briefly justify a high-profile art award? Either way, the idea that music communicates the emotions clearly still has strong cultural purchase, and it entails an array of connected philosophical ideas: that music can tell us something about the nature of being human, and that it embodies essences which get to the core of conceptual thinking and abstractions. While critics – especially certain sociologists and analytic philosophers, as discussed in Chapter 1 – have been keen to highlight the problems with such notions, they must not be entirely cast aside when they are still significant and often unexamined forces that shape people's thinking. At the same time, uncritical recourse to ideas about musical transcendence can negate a variety of discourses around the materiality of art that have convincingly challenged notions of music's aesthetic purity in recent years.

The return by contemporary music to modernist writing in Abrahamsen's setting of *let me tell you* is not a one-off. György Kurtág's 2018 opera *Samuel Beckett: Fin de Partie* is based on Beckett's *Endgame* and employs modernist methods to generate ambiguous tonalities. Alex Ross writes that Anton Webern – that 'Schoenbergian purist' who sought to avoid traces of tonality – is a 'musical ghost who haunts' Kurtág's opera, which unites a modernist text with a modernist-inspired compositional style.[97] A further opera that takes a modernist text as its primary inspiration is Olga Neuwirth's adaptation of Virginia Woolf's *Orlando*, which was the first full work written by a woman to premiere at the Vienna State Opera in December 2019. The opera begins, as does the novel, in 1598, and it cycles through musical forms and styles from the full range of its historical setting – from Tudor polyphony to modern rock music – before it ends in December 2019.

Today's writers and composers continue to be fascinated by modernist texts and forms, and to find them useful. Although *Orfeo* and *let me tell you* demonstrate very different ways of engaging with music, they are indicative of an ongoing dialogue between words and music created by writers who still find much of value to be extracted from twentieth-century music, both formally and thematically. The interactions between music, literature and modernist formal innovation for which I have offered a methodology in this book are not relics of the past, but are reappearing in literature and music today. Yet while in *Orfeo*, modernism causes people to think too much, leading to isolation and dangerous political activity, *let me tell you* encourages critical and independent thought in its reader through the use of modernist forms, making a case for the continuing relevance of modernist techniques.

Modernism Today

My arguments – that modernism is still relevant and still being produced today – raise some questions. What does this mean for debates about what modernism is and when it took place? Does claiming that a twenty-first century text like *let me tell you* is modernist mean that modernism was not a response to social and political conditions specific to the turn of the twentieth century? Or does it mean that those conditions have not substantially changed? (That would be hard to argue, since social conditions have clearly altered quite dramatically in the last hundred years.) Alternatively, does it means that modernism refers to a range of formal techniques that can be employed with validity at any time? Or are today's artworks that can be called modernist simply returning to older techniques, thereby lacking the claims to newness that seem so important to the modernists of the late nineteenth and early twentieth centuries? And in that case, does it mean something different to be modernist in the twenty-first century, nearly one hundred years after the high modernism of the 1920s, after the late modernism of the 1950s and after the rise and fall of postmodernism? *let me tell you* is modernist because modernism is not a specific aesthetic category, nor is it tied to a specific moment in time: it is art that engages critically with ideology and with otherness at the level of form. This is the reason why modernist art is still being produced today, and why it is still relevant.

Increasingly it is argued that there has not been a return to modernism so much as a continuation of modernist aims and techniques. Many critics claim that attempts to extend, re-energise and redirect methods of modernist formal innovation and philosophical contemplation continued in France and Britain after so-called late modernism, offering support for the increasingly popular thesis that modernism did not simply end and give way to postmodernism. The Oulipo group are often described as sharing and developing modernism's commitment to formal innovation and philosophical contemplation. Cóilín Parsons calls Oulipo 'one of the twentieth century's (and late modernism's) great efforts to, among other things, find a via media between C. P. Snow's two cultures'.[98] Burhan Tufail connects modernism with Oulipo via French Symbolism when he describes Mallarmé as both 'proto-modernist' and 'proto-Oulipian'.[99] Julia Jordan's *Late Modernism and the Avant-Garde British Novel* (2020) examines the modernist inheritance of post-war experimental writing, including Oulipo.[100] The fact that Oulipo is discussed in conjunction with modernism demonstrates the difficulty of fully extricating writing from its inheritance – similar to the way that modernism is now recognised as a renegotiation with previous aesthetic practices, rather than a complete break.[101] Dennis Duncan's substantial archival study *The Oulipo and Modern Thought* (2019) does not directly mention modernism, but he does emphasise something that the group shares with modernism, which is its engagement with crucial philosophical issues of the time.[102] David James argues that modernism is 'the scene of an unfinished argument about the novel's critical and formal potentiality', and although he does not discuss Oulipo his description of modernism aligns with the Oulipo group's aim to be a 'workshop of potential literature'.[103]

Oulipo and other post-war experimental writing has seen a resurgence of popular as well as critical interest recently, making *let me tell you* part of a body of texts attentive to literary experimentation and formal complexity.[104] Yet even if we describe *let me tell you* in what might, at first glance, seem to be broader terms – as an experimental novel rather than a modernist or Oulipian novel – periodisation and categorisation do not become easier, because the term 'experimental' also has a periodic history. It is sometimes used to describe postmodern writing, and frequently used in conjunction with another term – the 'avant-garde' – that has military beginnings and sustained political connotations. As Kaye Mitchell points out in *British Avant-Garde Fiction of the 1960s* (2019), critics writing on 1960s fiction have had difficulty both deciding which word to use to define it and agreeing on what the word means:

> The editors of a recent *Routledge Companion to Experimental Literature* (2012) concede that they use 'avant-garde', 'innovation' and 'experiment' 'more or less interchangeably', while acknowledging that 'there are import nuances of difference in connotation, especially between experimental and avant-garde'; the latter 'begins its career in the military context, but then migrates to the political sphere', and 'aesthetic avant-gardism continues to be allied with political radicalism'.[105]

let me tell you certainly has a claim to political radicalism, but since avant-gardism also connotes being at the forefront of something, the 1920s and 1960s artworks that serve as inspiration for the novel's form mean that it cannot be considered straightforwardly new or trailblazing.

A text does not need to be unequivocally new or novel to be modernist. I have already argued that by analysing Joyce's, Pound's and Warner's uses of music, we can see that much older ideas about music's expressive potential are crucial to modernism, although they also contribute to modernist formal innovation and sit beside competing ideas about music as the product of material conditions and power relations. Associating modernism simply with newness is problematic. As Michael North has pointed out, the phrase 'make it new', which has become 'such common shorthand for modernist novelty', did not become widely used by the critical establishment until after Hugh Kenner referred to it in 1950.[106] Pound's essay collection *Make it New* was not published until 1934, and Mark Byron has shown that the phrase was neither Pound's nor new, but a translation of an inscription on the bathtub of Shang Dynasty Emperor Ch'eng T'ang (1766–1753 BCE). For Byron, 'The imperative to "Make It New" is simultaneously and purposefully ancient and modern as a call for the continual critical appraisal of one's aesthetic tools and methods'.[107] The 'it' in the modernist mantra *make it new* refers to the valuable art and ideas of the past, acknowledging the older materials and traditions that are being reused and remade.

Still, modernism's apparent claim to newness has been approached as a problem in need of a solution. By the mid-twentieth century modernism's heyday had passed and critics had begun to discuss it in the past tense. In 1960 Harry Levin asked 'What was Modernism?' and Maurice Beebe replied in 1974 with 'What Modernism Was'.[108] Raymond Williams change the 'what' to 'when' in his 1987 lecture 'When Was Modernism?' and discusses the difficulties posed by artworks that are getting older and older, but are still referred to as examples of 'modernism'. Williams interrogates the term 'modern', noting that it came into general usage in the late sixteenth century as synonymous with 'now', so that calling early-twentieth-century art forms 'modernist' means that the modern, paradoxically, seems stuck in the past.[109] For Williams, modernism was temporal and stylistic, with narrow limits set by a few professionals: an ideologically constituted category elevated and prioritised to the detriment of other forms of art and literature.[110] The aim of the New Modernist Studies, and this book's inclusion of Sylvia Townsend Warner and Paul Griffiths, is to address the limitations that strict date ranges and formalist value judgements have imposed on modernist studies by broadening the range of authors, topics, locations and methods included in work on modernism.

Williams's argument that modernism is destined to proclaim its newness while being stuck in the past has since been contested by claims that modernism never gave way to postmodernism and is still being produced. Modernism's return to centre stage is closely connected to widespread doubt about the validity of the postmodern as a discrete moment in time or a clear aesthetic category, as well as the identification of modernist styles, themes, forms and concerns in contemporary literature and culture. For Peter Osborne, modernism is a stylistic category, not a temporal one, and it is 'far from over'.[111] For Jacques Rancière 'there was no post-modern rupture',[112] while Andreas Huyssen writes that 'discourses of modernity and modernism have staged a remarkable comeback' in recent years, with 'much talk these days of modernity at large, second modernity, liquid modernity, alternate modernity, countermodernity, and whatnot'.[113] David Cunningham quotes this passage by Huyssen in the anthology *The Contemporaneity of Modernism* (2016), which asks whether the contemporary moment is a modernist moment.[114] In *Modernist Futures* (2012) David James writes that 'modernist commitments, principles and aesthetics continue to inform the contemporary novel'.[115] Critics are increasingly committed to showing that modernism is back – at least in modified form – if indeed it ever went away.

In any case, if we agree with Vincent Sherry in *Modernism and the*

Reinvention of Decadence (2014)[116] and Jessica Feldman in *Victorian Modernism* (2002),[117] modernism has it roots firmly in nineteenth-century literature, as much as its creators and commentators might have sought to obscure its indebtedness. This means that modernism does not just extend much further forwards out of the early twentieth century than was once argued, but much further backwards into the nineteenth century as well. Two anthologies – *Reconnecting Aestheticism and Modernism* (2016) and *Decadence in the Age of Modernism* (2019) – argue that the presence of decadence in twentieth-century writing has been neglected.[118] I have contributed to reconnecting modernism with its past by illuminating the musical histories and philosophies – including British Aestheticism, German Romanticism, medieval music, Plato and Pythagoras – referred to by Joyce, Pound and Warner as part of their efforts to provide fresh ways of engaging with the world. The problem of negotiating modernism's claims to newness today, when it has long ceased to be new, recede into the distance if we recognise that modernism was never entirely new anyway.[119]

Critics have sought to redefine modernism in a way that accounts or allows for its continuing relevance today. My main contention in this book – that music plays a crucial role in modernist challenges to rational thought – draws together arguments made by a number of critics who are seeking to explain modernism's persistence. For Gabriel Josipovici, modernism is not 'a style, like mannerism or impressionism', nor a 'period of art history, like the Augustan or the Victorian age', but a complex of recurring problems to which different artists find a range of solutions. Josipovici describes modernism as 'the coming into awareness by art of its precarious status and responsibilities'.[120] If modernism begins to realise its 'precarious status' it contains reflection on what art is, while the reference to 'responsibilities' claims modernism knows that art has an impact in the world, and a duty to affect thought and perception for the better. Josipovici argues that the problems modernism takes responsibility for addressing are connected to the secularism of Enlightenment rationality, which relies on empirical, scientific methods of discovering truth and is an age 'without access to the transcendental'.[121] It is no coincidence that modernist writers are drawn to discourses about music, which are laden with the promise of transcending language and rational thought. As I argued in the Preface to this book, I share Josipovici's conviction that modernism can be characterised as a response to the increasingly obvious limitations of reason, which modernists see as responsible for problems with – as well as improvements to – human life since the Enlightenment. Josipovici is scathing of today's celebrated British fiction writers, including Martin

Amis, Ian McEwen and Julian Barnes, who leave him 'feeling that I and the world have been made smaller and meaner' because they retreat into sentimental simplicity and fail to grapple with discussions about what art is, or what its responsibilities are.[122] Overall, he sees a narrowing, rather than an opening out, of ideas in their novels. Powers is a suitable addition to his list of writers who fail to enlarge our understanding of the world, because *Orfeo* promotes familiarity and advocates recuperating a romanticised notion of art and life. *Orfeo* doesn't tolerate the idea that what seems different, disturbing or unusual might have value. *let me tell you*, on the other hand, locates value precisely in what is strange and unusual, and uses a writing constraint to estrange the author from language and grammar in a way that seeks to generate reflection on aspects of language that are invisible and have become naturalised. This is what early-twentieth-century modernism shares with the modernism I argue is still being produced today: a rejection of nostalgia and commitment to engaging with difference and otherness.

Griffiths's novel is modernist if we agree with Michael North, who argues modernism is an engagement with critical problems and the past that has happened – and will continue to happen – multiple times, and in different ways. In 'The Afterlife of Modernism' (2019) North reconceptualises modernism in a way that explains why it can recur in the twenty-first century, as I am claiming, by seeing it as a process of continual regeneration, rather than unique to the early twentieth century.[123] The word 'afterlife' is indebted to a move made by Sherry in *Modernism and the Reinvention of Decadence*, which turns modernism's association with the new on its head, showing how we can also conceptualise it as the very old: if the term 'modern' comes from *modo* meaning 'now', the modern can also be thought of as the end of history, and as coming after everything else. It is both the newest time and the latest time, coming at the end of time. Sherry thus conceptualises modernism in the word 'aftermath': modernism being the product of the last days, after everything has already happened.[124] North develops on Sherry's 'aftermath' with his notion of 'afterlife' by arguing – along with Douglas Mao – that modernism's condition of belatedness continues to speak to our own.[125] The sense of coming after everything is something that every present moment has experienced, so that to be modern means to construct oneself in relation to, but also as distinct from, the past. For North, 'The modern, then, is not a single return to a classical past' but 'a constant renewal', and 'Its mode of recurrence does not involve a constant return of the same, for the simple reason that the past to which it returns is itself always changing'.[126]

We can see Griffiths engaging with and altering the past in *let me tell you* via its reimagining of *Hamlet*, its giving a life to Ophelia informed by contemporary understandings of gender and otherness, and in its Oulipian-inspired literary repurposing of Shoenberg's musical constraints. Griffiths recruits this collage of materials and ideas to address absences in textual artefacts, to respond to and repurpose innovations of the past, and to interrogate ideological aspects of language that are still in need of recognition today. For North, 'the drive for novelty is not so much an expression of the free and unconditioned status of modern beings as the opposite: a reaction against the sense that every possible way of life and art is worn out and used up'.[127] We can see the reaction North describes in Griffiths's attempt to refresh literary language in *let me tell you*, but not in *Orfeo*, which celebrates, rather than reacts against, the past and seeks to return to it, rather than to change anything.

Modernism has long been associated with a conscious effort to change something, even if it does not achieve a complete rupture. For Susan Stanford Friedman, modernism moves away from some forms and ideas, and towards the formation of alternatives, making it a contradictory 'phenomenon that signifies both the formation of hegemonies and their dissolution, the production of grand narratives and their dismantling'.[128] Modernism seems to hang between two connected yet conflicting states: it both creates and destroys for Friedman, just as Ezra Pound's use of the phrase *make it new* gestures to new art's reliance on the culture of the past. For Joseph Anderton this contradictory aesthetic is especially evident in late modernism, and is encapsulated by the word 'vegetating', which connotes being alive, but in a static, vegetative state. In Beckett and Kafka, and among their commentators, Anderton claims, vegetating becomes the accurate representation of living in modernity, so that for Adorno, 'vegetating life, which entails the decay of experience, the impairment of reflection and the immersion in cultural and philosophical ruins, is the malady of modernity'.[129] The preoccupation with 'vegetating' also explains why modernism has not gone away. Through its vegetating, late modernism 'formalizes the abortive but enduring kernel that exists within the spirit of modernism': 'self-preservation through prolific transformation' and a 'regenerative and therefore interminable quality'.[130] Anderton's claims are not simply about late modernism – in any temporal sense at least – since Kafka died in 1924. Like North, for whom modernism is a process of 'continual renewal', Anderton sees it as 'restlessly static, incomplete, residual and cyclic'.[131] In these formulations, modernism is characterised by oppositional forces.

Music recurs in modernist thought and experimentation because engaging with music is to engage with its oppositional qualities of directness and abstraction, which makes it particularly suitable for addressing the kinds of dual, contradictory concerns that preoccupy modernist texts as they attempt to unpick the limited binaries that structure rational thought. The modernist preoccupation with music is illuminated by critical claims about modernism's conflicting characteristics, since music has dual claims to directness and abstraction, to immediacy and perpetual deferral. Music appears direct because it seems to create meaning without pointing to things outside itself, unlike signifying language, sculpture or the visual arts (as Walter Pater famously claimed). Yet that same quality – the formal production of meaning – makes music abstract, because it has no linguistic or material referent. Equally, music seems immediate because it vibrates the body, while linguistic comprehension of its meaning can be the opposite: perpetually deferred. Anderton's language about the 'abortive but enduring' nature of modernism can be repurposed to explain music's role: music's meaning can seem enduring – to communicate human truths that bypass culture, time and space – but comprehending exactly what an abstract art form says can be an abortive exercise, similar to the way modernist writing often aims to transcend language, while acknowledging the impossibility of doing so.

A text or artwork that holds oppositional ideas in tension can be described as dialectical. C. D. Blanton argues that late modernism is dialectical in *Epic Negation: The Dialectical Poetics of Late Modernism* (2015), which takes Pound's characterisation of the epic as 'a poem including history' as a starting point from which to explore Pound's reliance on, and negation of, the epic tradition and history in the *Cantos*.[132] The requirement to offer a narrative of the past that can be securely departed from in an assertion of modernist difference means that Pound must rely on totalising narratives about history as something that can be understood and explained, yet at the same time Pound claims that the present moment, being different, requires his different poetics to make sense of a world in which grand narratives and hegemonies no longer hold. Blanton's title specifies late modernism's dialectical poetics, but he begins his discussion in 1922. Just as Anderton's argument is not limited to late modernism, I want to expand Blanton's claims about modernism's dialectical qualities through an awareness of the function of music in modernist texts.

Dialectical thinking is present in Joyce's exploration of music's dual claims to materiality and transcendence in 'Sirens', discussed in Chapter 2. Pound is working with the dialectic of abstraction and materiality from as early as the Imagist Principles of 1912, by trying to use music to achieve the direct communication of abstract emotions. Ultimately, though, where Joyce celebrates contradictions and revels in staging a dialectical debate, Pound often tries to resolve opposing forces into a hierarchy, and the dialectical poetics of the *Cantos* – its epic negation for Blanton; for me, its staging of absence and presence through music in Canto LXXV – is the result of his being unable to achieve that resolution, even though he desires it. Warner often shows us an idea and its opposite. We see the limitations of Timothy Fortune's belief in musical universality in *Mr Fortune's Maggot*, and the intricate relationship between the worldly and the heavenly in *The Corner That Held Them*, where the transcendence of music and the religious life of the convent rely on material items like manuscript paper, stone, firewood and grain. Griffiths, meanwhile, engages a dialectic by claiming that everyday language is beset by structures and patterns that constrain thinking, but employs a constraint to achieve a degree of freedom, so that *let me tell you* is both reliant on, and a negation of, regulatory constraints.

Modernism is oppositional, contradictory and dialectical because it is interested in contesting Enlightenment rationality, as described in this book's Preface. Like the reversal of Enlightenment progress narratives by Adorno and Horkheimer in *Dialectic of Enlightenment*, artists whom we call modernist challenge the notion that rational thought has only brought improvements, because they see social life as beset by an array of significant and worsening problems. Jürgen Habermas's essay 'Modernity: An Unfinished Project' (1981) offers a concise summary of Enlightenment rationality:

> The project of modernity as it was formulated by the philosophers of the Enlightenment in the eighteenth century consists in the relentless development of the objectivating sciences, of the universalistic foundations of morality and law, and of autonomous art, all in accord with their own immanent logic . . . Partisans of the Enlightenment such as Condorcet could still entertain the extravagant expectation that the arts and sciences would not merely promote the control of the forces of nature, but also further understanding of self and world, the progress of morality, justice in social institutions, and even human happiness.[133]

Habermas acknowledges that by the twentieth century, many believed that Enlightenment rationality had failed to deliver on its promise of increasing justice and human happiness through unswerving adherence to the self-contained laws of science and logic. Joyce, Pound, Warner and Griffiths are modernist because they draw on music to explore what cannot be put into words, as they seek to illuminate – and ultimately to overcome – the dominance of empirical, rational thought that has resulted from what Habermas calls 'the relentless development of the objectivating sciences' since the Enlightenment. Pound hopes mathematics and objective scientific methods might help him to create perfect art, but he also knows that much of importance remains out of the rational mind's reach. He is enthralled by Enlightenment methods of scientific observation, and yet he knows that the Enlightenment has failed because the health of art and society have long been in decline. Pound wants to recuperate a totality and engages with music because discourses about it contain an array of dialectical oppositions – absence and presence, directness and abstraction, materiality and transcendence – that he wants, but is unable to resolve, so that those contradictions and tensions permeate his writing. For Joyce, rational thought is problematic because it has not brought justice, but has justified physical and ideological colonial violence. Joyce celebrates indeterminacy, multiplicity and liminality, and finds music useful for generating textual forms that defy fixed hierarchies. For Warner, rational thought has resulted in rigid and limited ways of thinking, and it has failed to produce a society with adequate living standards and opportunities for everyone – especially the working class and women. Warner knows that music's elision of precise verbal meaning means that people's interpretations of it are freighted with ideological content that is often difficult to see.

Modernist artworks acknowledge the necessity of using rational thought and ideological language as they attempt to escape the problems of rational thinking and ideology. Modernist writers recognise the difficulty of their position, which necessitates using language to address the limitations of language. This is part of what Josipovici describes when he claims modernism is 'the coming into awareness by art of its precarious status and responsibilities'.[134] Modernist artworks know that they must address social problems, but that they must do so specifically through formal invention, because the concept of art that they have inherited is complicit in two connected tenets of Enlightenment rationality. The first is a notion of the beautiful as a specific category and the standard for judging the legitimacy of art, as theorised by Kant, for whom the 'beautiful constitutes another domain of validity, alongside those of truth and morality', according to Habermas.[135] The second tenet is aesthetic autonomy.[136] Kant's claim that judgements of beauty ought to be entirely disinterested constructs art as a bourgeois pastime, suitable for those with free time to dedicate to purely aesthetic contemplation, or the expert who can effectively articulate the reason for their judgement. To claim the aesthetic is autonomous has the effect – troubling to modernists – of limiting art's agency: if art is apolitical, and judged by its adherence to a standard of beauty which is universal and arrived at through disinterested contemplation, this means that art is rendered powerless and unable to produce any social change. This is why Adorno describes the reflective capacities of autonomous art as 'guilty' in *Aesthetic Theory*, and why he opens with the claim that 'It has now become self-evident, as far as art is concerned, that nothing is self-evident any more, either in art itself or in its relation to the whole, not even its right to exist'.[137] If autonomous art actively strives to serve no useful purpose, then its right to exist is called into question. If it is constructed as a separate sphere, distinct from law, politics or work, then its relation to life – to the whole – becomes uncertain. Both aesthetic autonomy and notions of the beautiful are areas where Enlightenment rationality operates by limiting art's agency, demarcating the range of valuable aesthetic experience and ultimately affecting what kinds of thought are possible.

We have seen that Adorno's analysis of the discourses of modernity includes a challenge to Kant's characterisation of beauty and the distinctive character of the aesthetic domain. That *Orfeo* ultimately returns to and endorses Kantian notions of true art as universally beautiful demonstrates that the novel cannot be called modernist in the terms this book has set out. In *Orfeo*, Els's attempt to overcome the distinction between art and life by injecting 'music' into cells has disastrous consequences, so that the novel ends by claiming that the aesthetic should have remained a domain apart from the material world, and apart from politics. *Orfeo* advocates returning to a Kantian Enlightenment understanding of beauty in its valorisation of classical music, and claims that the aesthetic ought to remain distinct from politics. Conversely, the form of *let me tell you* is driven by Griffiths's conviction about the capacity of art to affect thought and action, and the benefits of difficulty, unfamiliarity and dissonance – convictions that I argue he shares with modernist writers who are engaged in contesting familiar, rational forms of thought.

Politics, Aesthetics and Music

A growing body of work on everyday aesthetics is contesting the supremacy of the beautiful and recuperating experiences and categories that have been neglected by critics and philosophers examining primarily 'high' or 'fine' artworks.[138] John Dewey is a crucial early point of reference for the repudiation of the nineteenth-century relegation of 'aesthetics' to the realm of fine arts in Western culture. His 1932 lectures (now collected in *Art as Experience*) challenge the reduction in scope of aesthetics to beauty and sublimity.[139] More recently, Sianne Ngai has examined 'unprestigious' aesthetics in *Ugly Feelings* (2005) and *Our Aesthetic Categories: Zany, Cute, Interesting* (2015).[140]

Work on everyday aesthetics often reveals the organisation and validation of aesthetic categories as a political process happening through writing and discourse and in institutions where power operates. Jacques Rancière's oeuvre makes two claims that offer more depth to my arguments that music has a political role in modernist literature, which is still being produced today. The first claim is that the aesthetic and the political are always intertwined and mutually inform each other, because the organisation of the aesthetic (what can be seen, sensed, felt and thought) has political consequences, while politics is experienced aesthetically as an organised hierarchy of voices, ideas, spaces and things. Second, Rancière rejects claims that modernism is limited to the early twentieth century, because art does not arise from social conditions in a straightforward case of cause and effect. Rather, art and aesthetics exist in a dialectical relationship with the social because they inform ways of understanding and organising the world. This means that the aesthetic informs the social relations and historical events that take place and the ways they are understood, rather than simply being a product of those conditions.

Rancière is interested in twentieth-century challenges to high art and the aesthetic autonomy championed during German Romanticism. In *Aisthesis* (2013) he opens by observing that the 'darlings of the market' have encroached into the once 'venerable museums', apparently opposing the 'ethereal idealities of art'. This is not a tragedy, but an example of how art has 'ceaselessly redefined itself'.[141] Such redefinition is a feature of what we call modernism, which contains the conviction that 'the contemporary world is structured by a separation that must be abolished'.[142] The segregation of high art and the policing of the aesthetic functions to ideologically support a hierarchical society by instilling a sense of the normality and inevitability of hierarchy into the community. A new aesthetic sensibility, widened from focusing on fine art and beauty to include the practical, mass-produced, ugly or mundane in an attempt to overcome the distinction between art and life, signals a reconfiguration of the relationships between aesthetics and politics. The goal, for Rancière, is greater social equality, and this can be achieved through art that troubles or abolishes hierarchies. The elevation of the prosaic, industrial and vulgar to the status of art is indicative of a new *regime of art* formed during the twentieth century that he terms the 'aesthetic regime' (and which he distinguishes from the 'representative regime' and the 'ethical regime' of images) produced by the shifting *distribution of the sensible.*

These two italicised phrases are key to Rancière's arguments about how aesthetics and politics are connected. In 'The Distribution of the Sensible: Politics and Aesthetics' he argues that by analysing what a society prioritises aesthetically we can understand its values.[143] The distribution of the sensible refers to the arrangement of what can be aesthetically experienced or sensed, as well as the sensible arrangement of people and things in a particular culture. When certain aesthetic forms become prioritised, such as 'the theatre, the page, or the chorus', they form communities connected by shared experiences of watching, reading or listening.[144] People who experience similar aesthetic forms share a sense of what counts as aesthetic, and the structures of their aesthetic experiences affect what it is possible to sense, as well as the organisation of ideas, spaces and relationships. Joseph J. Tanke calls the distribution of the sensible Rancière's 'concept for the general allocation of bodies, voices, roles, and capacities at work within a given community'.[145] The distribution of the sensible is not only about what we might usually refer to as 'aesthetics': it refers to the organisation of everything that can be sensed and known, including people, so that the political organisation of a community is experienced aesthetically.

Rancière views the aesthetic autonomy championed under German Romanticism as one tenet of what he terms the representative regime of art, which established art's proper forms, and a hierarchy of genres and topics. The phrase 'regime of art' claims similarities between aesthetics and governments as systems of organisation, and suggests their codependency. Different regimes of art exert an influence on how people think and act, and on how societies are organised. In Ancient Greece, for example, Rancière claims that art was not relegated to a separate realm: there was no rift between fine art and the utilitarian objects produced through craft, while acting took place in non-specialist, public spaces rather than in a designated area, the theatre.[146] Later, though, 'the tragic stage would become the stage of visibility for an orderly world governed by a hierarchy of subject matter and the adaptation and manners of speaking to this hierarchy'.[147] Moving theatrical performances to the stage formally separates dramatic performance from everyday life, inscribing a hierarchy via aesthetic experience.

Visibility is a crucial issue for Rancière, who claims that politics is aesthetic because it 'revolves around what is seen and what can be said about it, around who has the ability to see and the talent to speak, around the properties of spaces and the possibilities of time'.[148] In other words, the organisation of what is seen, heard or experienced affects thoughts and actions, and social hierarchies are experienced aesthetically. Further, what counts as aesthetic in a particular moment affects what can be sensed, and aesthetic experiences become arranged in ways that affect the capacity to sense, think and act. Rancière encourages us to consider a number of questions. What counts as sensible in a particular culture or moment? What is deemed aesthetically relevant or significant in a particular context? Are there any transformations taking place that signal changes to what is valued aesthetically in a particular society?

Rancière argues against a view of history as a series of discrete, progressing moments. Instead, he sees a continual redistribution of the sensible and the formation of new aesthetic regimes that compete, interact and co-exist. Aesthetic forms and the kinds of sensible subjects they make possible undergo changes, providing different forms of organisation and ways of engaging with the world in their cultural moment. Modernism, for Rancière, challenged not only the regime associated with German Romanticism (that of aesthetic autonomy, with its separations and hierarchies) but also the political models of living that accompanied it. Crucially, modernism acknowledged that the aesthetic and political are interconnected, and this idea allows Rancière to make two claims for modernism. First, it is not a radical departure or seismic rupture, but part of ongoing redistributions of the sensible. Second, modernism is not simply self-conscious or self-reflexive art that acknowledges its status as art, but art that recognises the mutually informing relationship between art and life. In this formulation, modernism does not simply arise out of specific historical moments, because history (meaning social events and conditions) is not separate from the art that is produced in it: history is constructed aesthetically. Modernism's success was to recognise the aesthetic construction of history.

Since Rancière is interested in how aesthetic experiences affect people and inform their ideas and actions, he closes 'The Distribution of the Sensible: Politics and Aesthetics' by discussing not the formal characteristics of modernism but the type of subject with whom the modernist artwork tries to communicate. In Rancière's terms, it is the 'notion of the avant-garde' that 'defines the type of subject suitable to the modernist vision and appropriate, according to this vision, for connecting the aesthetic to the political'. To be modernist is to be avant-garde – as in, those forms of art that are at the forefront of politics – by producing art for 'the invention of sensible forms and material structures for a life to come'. To be modernist is to create aesthetic forms that do not necessarily please people in the moment that they are produced, but which offer 'innovative sensible modes of experience that anticipate a community to come'.[149] That is, modernist artworks look forward to a future in which new communities might be forged as a result of the aesthetic experiences they provide.

Rancière's model of the relationship between politics and aesthetics provides another way of arguing that modernism is not over, and helps to draw out the social effects and uses of pointedly formal texts like *let me tell you*. In Rancière's terms, a twenty-first-century artwork like *let me tell you* can be modernist because of the social effect its aesthetic form has the potential to produce. For Griffiths, what can currently be sensed and thought is not enough. His decision to use a writing constraint is driven by the desire to reveal and challenge the structures of everyday language, and by the conviction that aesthetic form can be used to escape patterns of language use and thought to produce new ideas and sensations. By being open about its use of a writing constraint, the novel requests a specific type of reader who is willing to engage with the novel's method, consider the reasons for that method and acknowledge the value of its defamiliarising effects. The novel anticipates the formation of a new subject and community of subjects who are willing to engage with the unfamiliar. Enjoyment is not necessarily required (in the way that Schoenberg anticipated a listening public who might finally enjoy serialism) but enough curiosity is needed to engage with what seems difficult because it is unusual. Modernist texts like *let me tell you* offer opportunities to engage with otherness and difference, rather than to retreat into what is already known and understood. The conservative politics of *Orfeo*, on the other hand, is visible in the numerous ways the novel feels no responsibility (to use a word crucial to Josipovici's definition of modernism quoted earlier) to change things, but recommends recuperating older systems for attributing aesthetic value and settling for the social formations that we already know. *Orfeo* rejects the work that modernist redistributions of the sensible require of people, which is to rethink beauty, the validity of relegating the aesthetic to a distinct realm, and the forms of social and political organisation like the family that accompany those aesthetic hierarchies.

Modernism exhibits dissatisfaction with the way the world is organised and does the political work of encouraging people to engage with otherness rather than returning to fixed, familiar forms and hierarchies. Understanding music is crucial to interpreting the politics of form in *Orfeo* and *let me tell you*. Reading *Orfeo* with a full understanding of musical and literary form shows that a text can have formally innovative elements, but not be modernist. Although Powers uses a musically inspired experimental form with three narrative strands, it only helps the novel to validate an aesthetic of wholeness and totality. The perspective of Peter Els further reinforces the superiority of older aesthetic forms such as classical music, and conventional family structures. *Orfeo* recuperates certainties and essences using a narrative focalised through a white, male central character and his male composer friends, and offers no narrative focalised through Els's girlfriend, wife, daughter or anyone occupying a marginal social position. Overall, Powers makes a case for the value of aesthetic autonomy and traditional notions of beauty through a character of the race, education and gender that has benefited most from the patriarchal, colonial world in which those hierarchies were developed and flourished. The novel recommends the world of the past, rather than a different life to come. Conversely, although *let me tell you* uses methods of formal innovation that build on established musical and literary devices, the novel is modernist because it uses them to encourage critical engagement with language, ideology, gender and marginalisation. The novel gives a voice to a female character who had little dialogue and an association with madness – that ultimate form of otherness – in *Hamlet*, using an experimental form driven by Griffiths' dissatisfaction with existing narratives: what has been said, how it has been said and by whom. Since otherness is central to the way *let me tell you* chooses to engage with the world at the level of content and form, the novel has the potential to create subjects able to act informed by an interest in what is aesthetically and socially marginalised.

Music remains crucial to today's modernist writers because it offers formal avenues to refreshing the language all texts must use by helping to elide its habitual structures, and by facilitating contemplation of what is marginalised by hierarchical thinking and closed systems of rational thought. Music continues to appeal to writers interested in aesthetic form, the potential for non-linguistic communication and the paradoxical mysteriousness of how it communicates that seems transcendent of language, but reliant on the materiality of rhythm and vibration. As an example of a twenty-first-century modernist literary experiment, *let me tell you* bears out the claims about early-twentieth-century modernism in this book's Preface: modernist texts question the stronghold of post-Enlightenment rationality, and use formal innovation to spark alternative ways of thinking that might make possible new methods of addressing social problems. Music's potential to produce formally innovative writing with some of the ambiguity of music's non-lexical meaning remains appealing to writers invested in contesting rational thought and language. Modernism is not just the eschewal of tradition, or a set of established formal techniques, or an early-twentieth-century experiment, but the repeated attempt to break thought of its habits. Writing that is informed by an interest in music's irreducibility to simple statements looks forward to and tries to bring about communities interested in complexity and difference.

Notes

1. G. W. F. Hegel cited in Adorno, *Philosophy of Modern Music*, p. 3.
2. See also Chapter 3, 'Rhythm, Natural Hierarchy, Rational Ordering Systems and Fascism', p. 114, where I discuss Pound's more explicit connections between the aesthetic and the social in his arguments that superior and inferior members of the human race can be identified through the quality of their aesthetic production or sensibility.
3. Dipesh Chakrabarty, 'Where Is the Now?', *Critical Inquiry* 30 (Winter 2004), 458.
4. Catharine R. Stimpson, 'Texts in the Wind', *Critical Inquiry* 30 (Winter 2004), 425.
5. Further examples include Julian Barnes' *The Noise of Time* (London: Vintage, 2016), which uses a fragmented narrative form to reimagine the life of composer Dmitri Shostakovich for the general reader. Contemporary novels about music more broadly are common. Each short story in Kazuo Ishiguro's *Nocturnes* (London: Faber & Faber, 2009) is focused on music and musicians; in Nick Hornby's *High Fidelity* (London: Victor Gollancz, 1995) listening to music can prompt personal development. In 2015 Marlon James became the first Jamaican novelist to win the Man Booker Prize for his novel about Bob Marley, *A Brief History of Seven Killings* (New York: Riverhead Books, 2014); one theme of Zadie Smith's novel *Swing Time* (London: Penguin, 2016) is the popular music industry.
6. Richard Powers, *Orfeo* (London: Atlantic Books, 2014), p. 58.
7. Ibid. pp. 30, 18.
8. Ibid. p. 19.
9. For Schopenhauer's philosophy of music, see Chapter 1, 'Histories of Musical Transcendence', p. 30.
10. Powers, *Orfeo*, pp. 37, 66.
11. Ibid. p. 94.
12. See the discussion of meantone temperament in Chapter 4, '*Mr Fortune's Maggot*', p. 148.
13. Kant, *Critique of the Power of Judgement*, p. 72.
14. Adorno, *Aesthetic Theory*, p. 68.
15. See the discussion of Adorno in Chapter 2, 'Cyclops', p. 72.
16. Charles B. Sumner, 'Beauty be Damned: Why Adorno Valorizes Carrion, Stench, and Putrefaction', in Kelly Comfort, ed., *Art and Life in Aestheticism: De-Humanizing and Re-Humanizing Art, the Artist and the Artistic Receptor* (Basingstoke: Palgrave Macmillan, 2008), p. 178.
17. Adorno, *Aesthetic Theory*, p. 60.
18. Ibid. p. 61.
19. Powers, *Orfeo*, p. 250.
20. Ibid. p. 251.
21. Ludwig Wittgenstein, *Culture and Value*, ed. G. H. von Wright and Heikki Nyman, trans. Peter Winch (Chicago: University of Chicago Press, 1980), p. 50. See also the Composer's Notes for 'Proverb': 'The short text, "How small a thought it takes to fill a whole life!" comes from a collection of Wittgenstein's writing entitled *Culture and Value*. Much of

Wittgenstein's work is "proverbial" in tone and in its brevity. This particular text was written in 1946. In the same paragraph from which it was taken Wittgenstein continues, "If you want to go down deep you do not need to travel far".' Steve Reich, *Composer's Notes for 'Proverb'* (1995), https://www.boosey.com/pages/cr/catalogue/cat_detail?musicid=557 (last accessed 7 August 2020).

22. Powers, *Orfeo*, p. 248. Nicolas Bell, 'Signs of Change', pp. 363–72.
23. Powers, *Orfeo*, pp. 244, 248.
24. For a discussion of *ars antiqua* and *ars nova*, including the significance of notation and historical context, see Edward H. Roesner, ed., *Ars Antiqua: Organum, Conductus, Motet* (Abingdon: Routledge, 2009), pp. xi–xix. For developments between *ars antiqua*, *ars nova* and the later *ars subtilior* (meaning 'subtler art' or 'even more nuanced art') see Daniel Leech-Wilkinson, 'Ars Antiqua – Ars Nova – Ars Subtilior', in James McKinnon, ed., *Antiquity and the Middle Ages: From Ancient Greece to the 15th Century* (Eaglewood Cliffs, NJ: Prentice Hall, 1990), pp. 218–40. For discussions of the influence of the relationship between secular music and *ars antiqua*, see Mark Everist, 'The Rondeau Motete: Paris and Artois in the Thirteenth Century', *Music and Letters* 69 (1988), 1–22, and Dolores Pesce, 'Beyond Glossing: The Old Made New in *Mout me fu grief/Robin m'aime/Portare*' in *Hearing the Motet: Essays on the Motet of the Middle Ages and Renaissance* (Oxford: Oxford University Press), pp. 28–51. Everist's article and Pesce's chapter are available in Roesner, ed., *Ars Antiqua*.
25. For a discussion of *ars nova* and transcendence, see Chapter 4, '*The Corner That Held Them*', p. 157.
26. Roesner, ed., *Ars Antiqua*, p. xiii.
27. Powers, *Orfeo*, p. 137.
28. Ibid. p. 259.
29. Ibid. p. 262.
30. Ibid. p. 249.
31. Ibid. pp. 201, 211.
32. Ibid. pp. 208, 209.
33. Ibid. p. 301.
34. In *The Economic and Philosophic Manuscripts of 1844*, Marx described marriage as 'certainly a form of exclusive private property'. Karl Marx and Friedrich Engels, *The Economic and Philosophic Manuscripts of 1844 and the Communist Manifesto*, trans. Martin Milligan (New York: Prometheus Book, 1988), p. 100. In 'Origin of the Family, Private Property and the State' Engels wrote that monogamy and the patriarchal family have long functioned to protect male authority, capital and property, insisting that 'The rule of the man in his family, the procreation of children who could only be his, destined to be the heirs of his wealth – these alone were frankly avowed by the Greeks as the exclusive aims of monogamy'. Karl Marx and Friedrich Engels, *Marx and Engels: Selected Works* (London: Lawrence & Wishart, 1968), p. 502.
35. For de Beauvoir the discursive construction of women as physically and intellectually inferior to men to justify the patriarchal hierarchy on which the family rests has resulted in extensive limitations on women's rights, education, freedom and opportunities. Simone de Beauvoir, *The Second*

Sex, trans. Constance Borde and Sheila Malovany-Chevallier (London: Vintage, 2015).
36. Michelle Barrett and Mary McIntosh, *The Anti-Social Family* ([1982] London: Verso, 2015), p. 8.
37. Shulamith Firestone, *The Dialectic of Sex: The Case for Feminist Revolution* ([1970] London: Verso, 2015).
38. A key part of Lewis's argument is that pregnancy is an exceptionally taxing form of work and that equality is impossible without acknowledging gestation as labour, and the social reorganisation such a shift would require. Sophie Lewis, *Full Surrogacy Now: Feminism Against Family* (London: Verso, 2019).
39. Powers, *Orfeo*, p. 194.
40. Ibid. p. 186.
41. Ibid. pp. 4, 107.
42. For a discussion of Pythagoras and music of the spheres, see Chapter 1, 'Histories of Musical Transcendence', p. 30.
43. Powers, *Orfeo*, p. 255.
44. Ibid. p. 299.
45. Ibid. p. 194.
46. For a discussion of Pound's reduction of music to numbers, see Chapter 3, 'Pound's Musical Theories', p. 106.
47. Cristina Iuli, 'Dissonance, Data, and DNA: Aesthetics, Biopolitics and Transgenic Music in Richard Powers' *Orfeo*', in Stefan Herbrechter and Elisabeth Friis, eds, *Narrating Life: Experiments with Human and Animal Bodies in Literature* (Leiden: Brill, 2016), pp. 112, 94.
48. Orpheus myths can be found in Ovid's *Metamorphosis* Books 10–11, and Virgil's *The Georgics* Book 4. Orpheus's musical power to charm everything is referred to in Book 11 of Ovid's *Metamorphosis*, 'The Death of Orpheus'. Ovid, *Metamorphosis*, trans. David Raeburn (London: Penguin, 2004).
49. Powers, *Orfeo*, p. 299.
50. Ibid. p. 362.
51. See Chapter 2, 'Cyclops', p. 72; Chapter 3, 'Rhythm, Natural Hierarchy, Rational Ordering Systems and Fascism', p. 114.
52. Powers, *Orfeo*, pp. 253, 22.
53. See Chapter 2, '"Sirens" and Musical Form as Aesthetic Paradigm', p. 55.
54. Miriam Fernandez-Santiago, 'Of Language and Music: A Neo-Baroque, Environmental Approach to the Human, Infrahuman and Superhuman in Richard Powers' *Orfeo*', *Anglia: Zeitschrift für Englische Philologie* 137.1 (2019), 130.
55. Ibid. 131.
56. Ibid. 132.
57. Ibid. 145.
58. A. Elisabeth Reichal, 'Musical Macrostructures in *The Gold Bug Variations* and *Orfeo* by Richard Powers; or, Toward a Media-Conscious Audionarratology', *Partial Answers: Journal of Literature and the History of Ideas* 15.1 (2017), 84.
59. Ibid. 94.
60. Ibid. 94.

61. Ibid. 95.
62. Peter Consenstein, *Literary Memory, Consciousness and the Group Oulipo* (Amsterdam: Rodopi, 2002), pp. 99–111. Lauren Elkin and Scott Esposito, *The End of Oulipo?: The Attempt to Exhaust a Movement* (Winchester and Washington, DC: Zero Books, 2012). Daniel Cartwright, 'The Oulipo and Modernism: Literature, Craft and Mathematical Form' (2019: unpublished PhD thesis submitted to University of Westminster).
63. Georges Perec, *A Void*, trans. Gilbert Adair ([1969] London: Vintage, 2008).
64. Stanley Fertig, 'Raymond Queneau et l'art de la défamiliarisation', *Temps mêlés* 150 (1983), 43–51.
65. Veronica Scott Esposito, 'Ophelia in 483 Words: A Conversation with Paul Griffiths', *Music and Literature* 7 (2016), 11, 13.
66. T. S. Eliot, 'The Music of Poetry' in *Selected Prose of T. S. Eliot*, p. 114.
67. Esposito, 'Ophelia in 483 Words', 7.
68. Peter Kirwan, 'Mis/Quotation in Constrained Writing', in Julie Maxwell and Kate Rumbold, eds, *Shakespeare and Quotation* (Cambridge: Cambridge University Press, 2018), p. 251.
69. Ibid. p. 251.
70. Esposito, 'Ophelia in 483 Words', 13.
71. Schoenberg, *Style and Idea*, p. 233.
72. See also the discussion of Schoenberg's twelve-tone technique in Chapter 2, 'Cyclops', p. 72.
73. Schoenberg, *Style and Idea*, p. 233.
74. Esposito, 'Ophelia in 483 Words', 13.
75. Ibid. 11.
76. Ibid. 18.
77. Ibid. 11.
78. Ibid. 12.
79. See the following essays in Kaye Mitchell and Nonia Williams, eds, *British Avant-Garde Fiction of the 1960s* (Edinburgh: Edinburgh University Press, 2019): Len Gutkin, 'Brigid Brophy's Aestheticism: The Camp Anti-Novel', pp. 72–89; Stephanie Jones, 'Christine Brooke-Rose and the Development of Experiment', pp. 193–219.
80. Christine Brooke-Rose, 'A Writer's Constraints', in *Invisible Author: Last Essays* (Columbus, OH: Ohio State University Press, 2002), p. 37.
81. Ibid. p. 41.
82. Arnold Schoenberg, 'Opinion or Insight', in *Style and Idea*, pp. 258–64. See Dahlhaus, *Richard Wagner's Music Dramas*, p. 64.
83. Atonal music eschews the hierarchical tonal relationships of functional harmony – a system of musical organisation that has been produced within a hierarchical social formation – and replaces them with a different (albeit comparably rigid) system of rules that seeks to avoid tonal hierarchies and the dominance of a particular tone. In this way, Adorno argues, atonal music can be read as a formal rebellion against both the standardisation of functional harmony and the hierarchical society in which the established tonal system was produced.
84. For Adorno's analysis of Shoenbergian music's effect on the listener, see Lydia Goehr, 'Dissonant Works and the Listening Public', in Tom Huhne,

ed., *The Cambridge Companion to Adorno* (Cambridge: Cambridge University Press, 2004), p. 227.
85. Adorno, 'Music and New Music', in *Quasi Una Fantasia*, pp. 249–68.
86. Goehr, 'Dissonant Works and the Listening Public', pp. 230–1.
87. Paul Griffiths, *let me tell you* (Hastings: Reality Street, 2008), p. 121.
88. Ibid. p. 138.
89. Ibid. p. 7.
90. Esposito, 'Ophelia in 483 Words', 18.
91. Williams, 'When Was Modernism?', p. 50.
92. Griffiths, *let me tell you*, p. 8.
93. Ibid. pp. 11–12.
94. Ibid. p. 83.
95. Hans Abrahamsen, Grawemeyer Award for Music (2016), http://www.youtube.com/watch?v=tNL0OL0Ux_s&feature=youtu.be (last accessed 7 August 2020).
96. Music Composition Awards, Grawemeyer Awards website (2016), http://grawemeyer.org/music-composition/ (last accessed 7 August 2020).
97. Alex Ross, 'György Kurtág, with his Opera of "Endgame," Proves To Be Beckett's Equal', *The New Yorker*, 17 December 2018, https://www.newyorker.com/magazine/2018/12/24/gyorgy-kurtag-with-his-opera-of-endgame-proves-to-be-becketts-equal (last accessed 7 August 2020).
98. Cóilín Parsons, 'John Banville, Long Form, and the Time of Late Modernism', in Kathryn Conrad, Cóilín Parsons and Julie McCormic Weng, eds, *Science, Technology and Irish Modernism* (Syracuse, NY: Syracuse University Press, 2019), p. 275.
99. Burhan Tufail, '*Drosophila Ludens*: Oulipian Designs on Mallarmé', in Michael Temple, ed., *Meetings with Mallarmé* (Exeter: Exeter University Press, 1998), p. 143.
100. Julia Jordan, *Late Modernism and the Avant-Garde British Novel* (Oxford: Oxford University Press, 2020).
101. Jessica Feldman, *Victorian Modernism: Pragmatism and the Varieties of Aesthetic Experience* (Cambridge: Cambridge University Press, 2002). Sherry, *Modernism and the Reinvention of Decadence*. Bénédicte Coste, Catherine Delyfer and Christine Reynier, eds, *Reconnecting Aestheticism and Modernism: Continuities, Revisions, Speculations* (Abingdon: Routledge, 2017). Kate Hext and Alex Murray, eds, *Decadence in the Age of Modernism* (Baltimore: Johns Hopkins University Press, 2019).
102. Duncan describes Oulipian writers as 'A group, then, who are frequently in the company – both socially and intellectually – of the figures we now identify as the leading philosophers of their day', so that 'we can read a great deal of Oulipian writing – from the 1960s and 70s, at least – as a creative participation in a variety of prominent intellectual debates'. Dennis Duncan, *The Oulipo and Modern Thought* (Oxford: Oxford University Press, 2019), p. 5.
103. David James, *Modernist Futures: Innovation and Inheritance in the Contemporary Novel* (Cambridge: Cambridge University Press, 2012), p. 3.
104. An anthology entered the mass market in 2019. See Philip Terry, ed., *The Penguin Book of Oulipo* (London: Penguin, 2019).

105. Mitchell and Williams, eds, *British Avant-Garde Fiction of the 1960s*, p. 4.
106. Michael North, *Novelty: A History of the New* (Chicago and London: University of Chicago Press, 2012), p. 169.
107. Mark S. Byron, 'Bathtub Philology: Ezra Pound's Annotative Realism', *Archives and Manuscripts* 42.3 (2014), 258.
108. Maurice Beebe, 'Introduction: What Modernism Was', *Journal of Modern Literature* 3.5 (1974), 1065; Harry Levin, 'What was Modernism?', *The Massachusetts Review* 1.4 (1960), 609–30.
109. Raymond Williams, 'When Was Modernism?', in *The Politics of Modernism*, p. 32.
110. Williams is referring to methods of literary criticism and the version of the canon that dominated from the 1950s, largely due to F. R. Leavis in the UK, and through the New Criticism advanced by John Crowe Ransom, Allen Tate and Cleanth Brooks in the USA.
111. Peter Osborne, 'Modernity is a Qualitative, not a Chronological Category', *New Left Review* 1.192 (1992), 23–45. Peter Osborne, *Anywhere or Not at All: Philosophy of Contemporary Art* (London: Verso, 2013), p. 72.
112. Jacques Rancière, *Aesthetics and its Discontents*, trans. Steven Corcoran (Cambridge: Polity, 2009), p. 36.
113. Andreas Huyssen, 'Introduction: Modernism after Postmodernity', *New German Critique* 99 (2006), 1.
114. David Cunningham, 'Time, Modernism, and the Contemporaneity of Realism', in Michael D'Arcy and Mathias Nilges, eds, *The Contemporaneity of Modernism: Literature, Media, Culture* (Abingdon: Routledge, 2016), p. 49.
115. James, *Modernist Futures*, p. 1.
116. Vincent Sherry recovers modernism's decadent and symbolist inheritance, which was actively suppressed by artists and critics alike. He examines 'the partisan motives of particular critics' who 'exert extraordinary influence in developing ideological affiliations' for modernism and vigorously asserting its difference and newness. Sherry, *Modernism and the Reinvention of Decadence*, pp. 3–4.
117. Jessica Feldman aims to uncover the Victorian literary traits hidden within modernism, and modernist aspects of nineteenth-century figures like Dante Gabriel Rossetti and John Ruskin. Feldman identifies that categories and terminology are frequently fraught with complications, since 'Aestheticism, like Modernism, suffers from chronological disarray: some critics consider it a turn-of-the-century movement, others trace it back as far as the Pre-Raphaelites, John Ruskin, Théophile Gautier, and even John Keats'. Jessica Feldman, *Victorian Modernism: Pragmatism and the Varieties of Aesthetic Experience* (Cambridge: Cambridge University Press, 2002), p. 56.
118. Coste, Delyfer and Reynier, eds, *Reconnecting Aestheticism and Modernism*. Hext and Murray, eds, *Decadence in the Age of Modernism*.
119. Much like Sherry and Williams, who both see modernism as a constructed category that does various kinds of political and ideological work, Susan Stanford Friedman argues that modernism is both a useful and a prob-

lematic category, because it helps us to engage with the magnitude of the world and its past, but involves inclusions and exclusions that have political consequences. One consequence is the construction of modernism – as highbrow, intellectual and philosophical art – as a primarily Western and European product, contributing to longstanding colonial ideas about the superiority of the Western world. Susan Stanford Friedman, *Planetary Modernisms: Provocations on Modernity Across Time* (New York: Columbia University Press, 2015), pp. 36–7. Jade Munslow Ong has contested the assumption that if modernism happens outside Europe, it must happen after European modernism by showing that the novels of Olive Schreiner can be productively considered examples of nineteenth-century African modernism – a claim that involves rethinking both categories of modernism and modernity. See Jade Munslow Ong, *Olive Schreiner and African Modernism: Allegory, Empire and Postcolonial Writing* (London: Routledge, 2018).
120. Gabriel Josipovici, *Whatever Happened to Modernism?* (New Haven, CT and London: Yale University Press, 2010), p. 11.
121. Ibid. p. 68.
122. Ibid. p. 174.
123. Michael North, 'The Afterlife of Modernism', *New Literary History* 50.1 (Winter 2019), 91–112.
124. Sherry, *Modernism and the Reinvention of Decadence*, pp. 2, 61, 122–3.
125. Douglas Mao, 'Our Last September: Climate Change in Modernist Times', in Michael D'Arcy and Mathias Nilges, eds, *The Contemporaneity of Modernism: Literature, Media, Culture* (Abingdon: Routledge, 2016), p. 32.
126. North, 'The Afterlife of Modernism', 109.
127. Ibid. 96.
128. Stanford Friedman, *Planetary Modernisms*, p. 36
129. Joseph Anderton, 'Vegetating Life and the Spirit of Modernism in Kafka and Beckett', *Modernism/modernity* 26.4 (2019), 812.
130. Ibid. 824, 815.
131. Ibid. 815.
132. C. D. Blanton, *Epic Negation: The Dialectical Poetics of Late Modernism* (Oxford: Oxford University Press, 2015).
133. Jürgen Habermas, 'Modernity: An Unfinished Project' (1981), in Maurizio Passerin d'Entrèves and Seyla Benhabib, eds, *Habermas and the Unfinished Project of Modernity: Critical Essays on The Philosophical Discourse of Modernity* (Cambridge, MA; MIT Press, 1997), p. 45.
134. Josipovici, *Whatever Happened to Modernism?*, p. 11.
135. Habermas, 'Modernity: An Unfinished Project', p. 47.
136. The notion that art is separate from other areas of life arose in German Romanticism with the demarcation of the aesthetic as a specific domain and became formalised in the *art pour l'art* doctrine of the nineteenth century.
137. Adorno, *Aesthetic Theory*, pp. 225, 1.
138. See Yuriko Saito, *Everyday Aesthetics* (Oxford: Oxford University Press, 2008).
139. John Dewey, *Art as Experience* (London: Penguin, 2005).

140. Sianne Ngai, *Ugly Feelings* (Cambridge, MA: Harvard University Press, 2005) and *Our Aesthetic Categories: Cute, Zany, Interesting* (Cambridge, MA: Harvard University Press, 2015).
141. Jacques Rancière, *Aisthesis: Scenes from the Aesthetic Regime of Art*, trans. Zakir Paul (London: Verso, 2013), p. x.
142. Ibid. p. 62.
143. The original French title is *Le Partage du sensible: Esthétique et politique* (2000). It was published in English translation along with interviews and a glossary of terms as *The Politics of Aesthetics*.
144. Rancière, *The Politics of Aesthetics*, p. 10.
145. Joseph J. Tanke, 'Which Politics of Aesthetics?', in Scott Durham and Dilip Gaonkar, eds, *The Distributions of the Sensible* (Evanston, IL: Northwestern University Press, 2019), p. 79.
146. Rancière refers to this as the ethical regime of images, which predates the representative and aesthetic regimes, although the formation of a new regime does not mean the disappearance of the previous regime: they can all exist at the same time. Rancière, *The Politics of Aesthetics*, pp. 20–1.
147. Ibid. p. 13.
148. Ibid. p. 8.
149. Ibid. pp. 24, 25.

Bibliography

Abbott, Helen, *Between Baudelaire and Mallarmé: Voice, Conversation and Music* (Farnham: Ashgate, 2009).
Abrams, M. H., *The Mirror and the Lamp: Romantic Theory and the Critical Tradition* (Oxford: Oxford University Press, 1953).
Abrahamsen, Hans, 2016 Grawemeyer Award for Music, https://www.youtube.com/watch?v=tNL0OL0Ux_s&feature=youtu.be (last accessed 7 August 2020).
Adorno, Theodor W., 'On Popular Music', *Studies in Philosophy and Social Science* 9 (1941), 17–48.
Adorno, Theodor W., *Negative Dialectics*, trans. E. B. Ashton (New York: Seabury Press, 1973).
Adorno, Theodor W., 'On Popular Music', in Simon Frith and Andrew Godwin, eds, *On Record: Rock, Pop and the Written Word* (London: Routledge, 1990), pp. 301–14.
Adorno, Theodor W., 'Music, Language, and Composition', trans. Susan Gillespie, *The Musical Quarterly* 77.3 (1993), 401–14.
Adorno, Theodor W., *Alban Berg*, trans. Juliane Brand and Christopher Hailey (Cambridge: Cambridge University Press, 1994).
Adorno, Theodor W., *Aesthetic Theory*, ed. Gretel Adorno and Rolf Tiedemann, trans. Robert Hullot-Kentor (Minneapolis: University of Minnesota Press, 1997).
Adorno, Theodor W., *Quasi Una Fantasia*, trans. Rodney Livingstone ([1963] London: Verso, 1998).
Adorno, Theodor W., *Metaphysics: Concepts and Problems* (Stanford, CA: Stanford University Press, 2001).
Adorno, Theodor W., *Essays on Music*, ed. Richard Leppert, trans. Henry W. Pickford (New York: Columbia University Press, 2002).
Adorno, Theodor W., *Minima Moralia*, trans. Edmund Jephcott ([1948] London: Verso, 2005).
Adorno, Theodor W., *Philosophy of New Music*, trans. Robert Hullot-Kentor (Minneapolis: University of Minnesota Press, 2006).
Adorno, Theodor W., *Philosophy of Modern Music*, trans. Anne G. Mitchell and Wesley V. Blomster ([1947] London: Continuum, 2007).
Adorno, Theodor W. and Max Horkheimer, *Dialectic of Enlightenment*, trans. John Cumming ([1944] London: Verso, 1997).

Adorno, Theodor W. and Max Horkheimer, *Dialectic of Enlightenment*, trans. Gunzelin Noeri ([1944] Stanford, CA: Stanford University Press, 2002).

Albright, Daniel, *Untwisting the Serpent: Modernism in Music, Literature, and Other Arts* (Chicago: University of Chicago Press, 2000).

Allen, Stuart, 'Thinking Strictly Prohibited: Music, Language and Thought in "Sirens"', *Twentieth-Century Literature* 53.4 (2007), 442–59.

Althusser, Louis, *On Ideology* ([1971] London: Verso, 2008).

Anderton, Joseph, 'Vegetating Life and the Spirit of Modernism in Kafka and Beckett', *Modernism/modernity* 26.4 (2019), 805–27.

Andrews, Hilda, *Westminster Retrospective: A Memoir of Sir Richard Terry* (London: Oxford University Press, 1948).

Antliff, Mark, *Avant-Garde Fascism: The Mobilization of Myth, Art, and Culture in France, 1909–1939* (Durham, NC and London: Duke University Press, 2007).

Aristotle, *Complete Works of Aristotle, Vol. 2: The Revised Oxford Translation*, ed. Jonathan Barnes (Princeton, NJ: Princeton University Press, 1984).

Armstrong, Tim, *Modernism: A Cultural History* (Cambridge: Polity, 2005).

Aronson, Alex, *Music and the Novel: A Study in Twentieth-Century Fiction* (Totowa, NJ: Rowman and Littlefield, 1980).

Attali, Jacques, *Noise: The Political Economy of Music*, trans. Brian Massumi (Manchester: Manchester University Press, 1985).

Auerbach, Jeffrey J., *The Great Exhibition of 1851: A Nation on Display* (New Haven, CT and London: Yale University Press, 1999).

Ballstaedt, Andreas, 'Chopin as Salon Composer in Nineteenth-Century German Criticism', in John Rink and Jim Samson, eds, *Chopin Studies 2* (Cambridge: Cambridge University Press, 2006), pp. 18–34.

Barber, Cecil, 'Battle Music', *The Musical Times* 59.899 (1918), 25–6.

Barnes, Julian, *The Noise of Time* (London: Vintage, 2016).

Barrett, Michelle and Mary McIntosh, *The Anti-Social Family* ([1982] London: Verso, 2015).

Barrett, William, 'Comment: A Prize for Ezra Pound', *Partisan Review* (April 1949), 344–7.

Baskin, Jason M., *Modernism Beyond the Avant-Garde: Embodying Experience* (Cambridge: Cambridge University Press, 2019).

Batsleer, Janet, Tony Davies, Rebecca O'Rourke and Chris Weedon, eds, *Rewriting English* (London: Routledge, 2013).

Baudelaire, Charles, *Paris Spleen: Little Poems in Prose*, trans. Keith Waldrop (Middletown, CT: Wesleyan University Press, 2009).

Bauerle, Ruth H., ed., *Picking up Airs: Hearing the Music in Joyce's Text* (Urbana, IL: University of Illinois Press, 1993).

Baugh, Bruce, 'Left-Wing Elitism: Adorno on Popular Culture', *Philosophy and Literature* 14.1 (1990), 65–78.

Beasley, Rebecca, *Theorists of Modern Poetry: T.S. Eliot, T.E. Hulme, Ezra Pound* (Abingdon: Routledge, 2007).

Beauvoir, Simone de, *The Second Sex*, trans. Constance Borde and Sheila Malovany-Chevallier (London: Vintage, 2015).

Beckett, Samuel, *Disjecta: Miscellaneous Writings and a Dramatic Fragment*, ed. Ruby Cohn (New York: Grove Press, 1984).

Beebe, Maurice, 'Introduction: What Modernism Was', *Journal of Modern Literature* 3.5 (1974), 1065–84.
Beer, Gillian, 'The Centrifugal Kick', in Maroula Joannou, ed., *Women Writers of the 1930s: Gender, Politics and History* (Edinburgh: Edinburgh University Press, 1999), pp. 76–86.
Beerbohm, Max, *The Works of Max Beerbohm* (London: John Lane, The Bodley Head, 1896).
Bell, Michael, 'Primitivism: Modernism as Anthropology', in Peter Brooker, Andrzej Gasiorek, Deborah Longworth and Andrew Thacker, eds, *The Oxford Handbook of Modernisms* (Oxford: Oxford University Press, 2010).
Bell, Nicolas, 'Signs of Change from *ars antiqua* to *ars nova* in Polyphonic Music of the Early Fourteenth Century', in Nils Holger Petersen, Claus Cluver and Nicolas Bell, eds, *Signs of Change: Transformations of Christian Traditions and Their Representations in the Arts, 1000–2000* (Amsterdam: Rodopi, 2004), pp. 363–72.
Benda, Julien, *Belphegor*, trans. S. J. I. Lawson (New York: Payson and Clarke, 1929).
Benjamin, Walter, *Illuminations*, trans. Hannah Arendt (New York: Schocken Books, 1969).
Benson, Donald C., *A Smoother Pebble: Mathematical Explorations* (Oxford: Oxford University Press, 2003).
Bernays, Paul, 'On Platonism in Mathematics', in Paul Benacerraf and Hilary Putnam, eds, *Philosophy of Mathematics: Selected Readings* (Cambridge: Cambridge University Press, 1964).
Bersani, Leo, *The Culture of Redemption* (Cambridge, MA: Harvard University Press, 1990).
Blanton, C. D., *Epic Negation: The Dialectical Poetics of Late Modernism* (Oxford: Oxford University Press, 2015).
Blasius, Leslie, 'Mapping the Terrain', in Thomas Christensen, ed., *The Cambridge History of Western Music Theory* (Cambridge: Cambridge University Press, 2002), pp. 27–45.
Bonar, Daniel D., Michael J. Khoury, Jr and Michael Khoury, eds, *Real Infinite Series* (Washington, DC: Mathematical Association of America, 2006).
Booth, Howard J., 'Colonialism and Time in *Mr Fortune's Maggot*', *Literature Compass* 11.12 (2014), 745–53.
Booth, Howard J. and Nigel Rigby, eds, *Modernism and Empire* (Manchester: Manchester University Press, 2000).
Borchmeyer, Dieter, *Drama and the World of Richard Wagner* (Princeton, NJ: Princeton University Press, 2003).
Bourdieu, Pierre, 'Cultural Reproduction and Social Reproduction', in Richard K. Brown, ed., *Knowledge, Education and Cultural Change: Papers in the Sociology of Education* (London: Tavistock Publications, 1973).
Bourdieu, Pierre, *Distinction* ([1979] London: Routledge, 1999).
Bowie, Andrew, *Music, Philosophy and Modernity* (Cambridge: Cambridge University Press, 2009).
Bowie, Andrew, 'Romanticism and Music', in Nicholas Saul, ed., *The Cambridge Companion to German Romanticism* (Cambridge: Cambridge University Press, 2009), pp. 243–55.

Bowra, Cecil, *Greek Lyric Poetry: From Alcman to Simonides* (Oxford: Oxford University Press, 1961).
Boyle, Robert, '*Ulysses* as Frustrated Sonata Form', *James Joyce Quarterly* 2.4 (1965), 247–54.
Bradbury, Malcolm, 'What Was Post-Modernism? The Arts in and after the Cold War', *International Affairs* 71.4 (October 1995), 763–74.
Bribitzer-Stull, Matthew, *Understanding the Leitmotif: From Wagner to Hollywood Film Music* (Cambridge: Cambridge University Press, 2015).
Brooke-Rose, Christine, 'A Writer's Constraints', in *Invisible Author: Last Essays* (Columbus, OH: Ohio State University Press, 2002), pp. 36–52.
Brothers, Barbara, 'Writing Against the Grain: Sylvia Townsend Warner and the Spanish Civil War', in Mary Lynn Broe and Angela Ingram, eds, *Women's Writing in Exile* (Chapel Hill, NC: University of North Carolina Press, 1989).
Brown, Susan, 'The Mystery of the *Fuga per Canonem* Solved', *Genetic Joyce Studies* 7 (Spring 2007), https://www.geneticjoycestudies.org/articles/GJS7/GJS7brown (last accessed 7 August 2020).
Bucknell, Brad, *Literary Modernism and Musical Aesthetics: Pater, Pound, Joyce, Stein* (Cambridge: Cambridge University Press, 2001).
Budd, Malcolm, *Music and the Emotions* (London: Routledge, 1992).
Burkert, Walter, *Lore and Science in Ancient Pythagoreanism*, trans. E. Minar (Cambridge, MA: Harvard University Press, 1972).
Burns, Emile, ed., *A Handbook of Marxism* (London: Victor Gollancz, 1935).
Burrows, Donald, *Handel* (Oxford: Oxford University Press, 1994).
Bush, Ronald, 'Modernism, Fascism, and the Composition of Ezra Pound's Pisan Cantos', *Modernism/modernity* 2.3 (1995), 69–87.
Byron, Mark S., 'A Defining Moment in Ezra Pound's *Cantos*: Musical Scores and Literary Texts', in Michael J. Meyer, ed., *Rodopi Perspectives on Modern Literature: Literature and Music* (Amsterdam and New York: Rodopi, 2002), pp. 157–82.
Byron, Mark S., 'European History: The Enlightenment', in Demetres P. Tryphonopoulos and Stephen J. Adams, eds, *The Ezra Pound Encyclopedia* (London: Greenwood Press, 2005), p. 118.
Byron, Mark S., 'Bathtub Philology: Ezra Pound's Annotative Realism', *Archives and Manuscripts* 42.3 (2014), 258–69.
Callaghan, John and Ben Harker, eds, *British Communism: a Documentary History* (Manchester: Manchester University Press, 2011).
Carrier, David, *High Art: Charles Baudelaire and the Origins of Modernist Painting* (Philadelphia: Pennsylvania State University Press, 1996).
Cartwright, Daniel, 'The Oulipo and Modernism: Literature, Craft and Mathematical Form' (2019: unpublished PhD thesis submitted to University of Westminster).
Caudwell, Christopher, *Illusion and Reality: A Study of the Sources of Poetry* (London: Macmillan, 1937).
Caudwell, Christopher, *Studies in a Dying Culture* (New York: Dodd Mead, 1958).
Chakrabarty, Dipesh, 'Where Is the Now?', *Critical Inquiry* 30 (Winter 2004), 458–62.
Cheng, Vincent J., *Joyce, Race and Empire* (Cambridge: Cambridge University Press, 1995).

Childs, Donald J., *Modernism and Eugenics: Woolf, Eliot, Yeats, and the Culture of Degeneration* (Cambridge: Cambridge University Press, 2007).
Childs, Peter, *Modernism* (Abingdon: Routledge, 2008).
Clarke, David, 'Musical Autonomy Revisited', in Martin Clayton, Trevor Herbert and Richard Middleton, eds, *The Cultural Study of Music* (London: Routledge, 2003), pp. 159–70.
Clayton, Martin, Trevor Herbert and Richard Middleton, eds, *The Cultural Study of Music* (London: Routledge, 2003).
Cockroft, Eva, 'Abstract Expressionism, Weapon of the Cold War', in Francis Frascina, ed., *Pollock and After: the Critical Debate* (London: Psychology Press, 1985), pp. 125–35.
Coetzee, J. M., *The Lives of Animals* (Princeton, NJ: Princeton University Press, 1999).
Coetzee, J. M., *Elizabeth Costello* (London: Vintage, 2004).
Coffman Jr, Stanley J., *Imagism: A Chapter for the History of Modern Poetry* (Norman, OK: University of Oklahoma Press, 1951).
Cohen, Harvey G., 'Duke Ellington and "Black, Brown and Beige": The Composer as Historian at Carnegie Hall', *American Quarterly* 56.4 (2004), 1003–34.
Cole, David W., 'Fugal Structure in the Sirens Episode of *Ulysses*', *Modern Fiction Studies* 19.2 (1973), 221–6.
Collini, Stefan, *What Are Universities For?* (London: Penguin, 2012).
Consenstein, Peter, *Literary Memory, Consciousness and the Group Oulipo* (Amsterdam: Rodopi, 2002).
Cook, Nicholas, *The Schenker Project: Culture, Race, and Music Theory in Fin-de-siècle Vienna* (Oxford: Oxford University Press, 2007).
Cooper, John Xiros, ed., *T.S. Eliot's Orchestra: Critical Essays on Poetry and Music* (London: Garland, 2000).
Coste, Bénédicte, Catherine Delyfer and Christine Reynier, eds, *Reconnecting Aestheticism and Modernism: Continuities, Revisions, Speculations* (Abingdon: Routledge, 2017).
Coyle, Michael, *Ezra Pound, Popular Genres, and the Discourse of Genre* (University Park, PA: Pennsylvania State University Press, 1995).
Coyle, Michael and Roxana Preda, 'A Prize Fight and Institutionalisation, 1948–1951', in *Ezra Pound and the Career of Modern Criticism: Professional Attention* (Rochester, NY: Camden House, 2018), pp. 1–23.
Croft, Andy, *Red Letter Days* (London: Lawrence & Wishart, 1990).
Cunningham, David, 'Time, Modernism, and the Contemporaneity of Realism', in Michael D'Arcy and Mathias Nilges, eds, *The Contemporaneity of Modernism: Literature, Media, Culture* (Abingdon: Routledge, 2016), pp. 49–64.
Cunningham, Valentine, *British Writers of the Thirties* (Oxford: Oxford University Press, 1988).
Dahlhaus, Carl, *Richard Wagner's Music Dramas*, trans. Mary Whittall (Cambridge: Cambridge University Press, 1992).
Dahlhaus, Carl, *The Idea of Absolute Music*, trans. Roger Lustig (Chicago and London: University of Chicago Press, 1991).
Dallapiccola, Luigi, 'On the Twelve-Note Road', trans. Deryck Cook, *Music Survey* 4.1 (1951), 318–32.

Dalton, Hugh, 'The "Popular Front"', *The Political Quarterly* 7.4 (October 1936), 441–88.

Dasenbrock, Reed Way, *The Literary Vorticism of Ezra Pound and Wyndham Lewis* (Baltimore: Johns Hopkins University Press, 1985).

Davies, Gill, David Malcolm and John Simons, eds, *Critical Essays on Sylvia Townsend Warner, English Novelist 1893–1978* (Lewiston, NY: The Edwin Mellen Press, 2006).

Dayan, Peter, *Music Writing Literature: From Sand to Debussy via Derrida* (Aldershot: Ashgate, 2006).

Derrida, Jacques, *Of Grammatology*, trans. Gayatri Chakravorty Spivak (Baltimore: Johns Hopkins University Press, 1997).

Descartes, René, *The Philosophical Writings of Descartes*, trans. John Cottingham, Dugald Murdoch and Robert Stoothoff (Cambridge: Cambridge University Press, 1985).

Dewey, John, *Art as Experience* (London: Penguin, 2005).

DiBattista, Maria and Lucy McDiarmid, eds, *High and Low Moderns: Literature and Culture 1889–1939* (New York: Oxford University Press, 1996).

Duckworth, William, *Cengage Advantage Books: A Creative Approach to Music Fundamentals* (Boston: Cengage Learning, 2009).

Duncan, Dennis, *The Oulipo and Modern Thought* (Oxford: Oxford University Press, 2019).

DuPlessis, Rachel Blau, 'Propounding Modernist Maleness: How Pound Managed a Muse', *Modernism/modernity* 9.3 (2002), 389–405.

Eagleton, Terry, 'Raymond Williams: An Appraisal', *New Left Review* 95 (1976), 3–23.

Eagleton, Terry, *Ideology: An Introduction* (London: Verso, 1991).

Edmond, Rod, *Representing the South Pacific: Colonial Discourse from Cook to Gauguin* (Cambridge: Cambridge University Press, 1997).

Eliot, T. S., *The Music of Poetry: The Third W.P. Ker Memorial Lecture, 24th February 1942* (Glasgow: Jackson, Son & Co., 1942).

Eliot, T. S., *Selected Prose of T. S. Eliot*, ed. Frank Kermode (London: Harcourt Brace Jovanovich, 1975).

Eliot, T. S., *The Sacred Wood and Major Early Essays* (New York: Dover, 1998).

Eliot, T. S., *The Poems of T. S. Eliot: Collected and Uncollected Poems*, vol. 1, ed. Christopher Ricks and Jim McCue (London: Faber & Faber, 2015).

Elkin, Lauren and Scott Esposito, *The End of Oulipo?: The Attempt to Exhaust a Movement* (Winchester and Washington, DC: Zero Books, 2012).

Ellis, A., ed., *The Cambridge Cultural History*, vol. 1 (Cambridge: Cambridge University Press, 1991).

Ellmann, Richard, *James Joyce* (Oxford: Oxford University Press, 1983).

Ellmann, Richard, *Yeats: The Man and the Masks* (London: Faber & Faber, 1961).

Epstein, Josh, *Sublime Noise: Musical Culture and the Modernist Writer* (Baltimore: Johns Hopkins University Press, 2015).

Esposito, Veronica Scott, 'Ophelia in 483 Words: A Conversation with Paul Griffiths', *Music and Literature* 7 (2016), 9–20.

Everist, Mark, 'The Rondeau Motete: Paris and Artois in the Thirteenth Century', *Music and Letters* 69 (1988), 1–22.

Fahy, Thomas, 'The Cultivation of Incompatibility: Music as a Leitmotif in Dorothy Richardson's *Pilgrimage*', *Women's Studies* 29.2 (2000), 131–47.
Fanning, David, ed., *Shostakovich Studies* (Cambridge: Cambridge University Press, 2006).
Farr, Florence, *The Music of Speech* (London: Elkin Mathews, 1909).
Feldman, Jessica, *Victorian Modernism: Pragmatism and the Varieties of Aesthetic Experience* (Cambridge: Cambridge University Press, 2002).
Fernandez-Santiago, Miriam, 'Of Language and Music: A Neo-Baroque, Environmental Approach to the Human, Infrahuman and Superhuman in Richard Powers' *Orfeo*', *Anglia: Zeitschrift für Englische Philologie* 137.1 (2019), 126–46.
Fertig, Stanley, 'Raymond Queneau et l'art de la défamiliarisation', *Temps mêlés* 150 (1983), 43–51.
Fillion, Michelle, *Difficult Rhythm: Music and the Word in E. M. Forster* (Chicago: University of Illinois Press, 2010).
Findlay, John N., 'Neoplatonism and Western Christian Man', in R. Baine Harris, ed., *Neoplatonism and Contemporary Thought: Part Two* (New York: SUNY Press, 2002).
Firestone, Shulamith, *The Dialectic of Sex: The Case for Feminist Revolution* ([1970] London: Verso, 2015).
Fisher, Margaret, *The Transparency of Ezra Pound's Great Bass*, Studies in Ezra Pound's Music and Poetry: Duration Rhyme and Great Bass vol. 2 (Emeryville, CA: Second Event Art Publishing, 2013), https://read.amazon.co.uk/?asin=B00EBXO1WK (last accessed 3 August 2018).
Ford, Ford Madox, *Parade's End* ([1924] London: Penguin, 2002).
Forster, E. M., *A Room With a View* ([1908] London: Penguin Classics, 2000).
Frascina, Francis, ed., *Pollock and After: the Critical Debate* (London: Psychology Press, 1985).
Freedman, Jonathan, *Professions of Taste: Henry James, British Aestheticism, and Commodity Culture* (Stanford, CA: Stanford University Press, 1992).
Frith, Simon and Andrew Godwin, eds, *On Record: Rock, Pop and the Written Word* (London: Routledge, 1990).
Furness, Raymond, *Wagner and Literature* (Manchester: Manchester University Press, 1982).
Garrity, Jane, *Step-daughters of England: British Women Modernists and the National Imaginary* (Manchester: Manchester University Press, 2003).
Gautier, Théophile, *Émaux et camées*, ed. Claudine Gothot-Mersch (Paris: Gallimard/Poésie, 1981).
Gellerman, Robert, F., *The American Reed Organ and the Harmonium* (Vestal, NY: The Vestal Press, 1996).
Gilbert, Stuart, *James Joyce's 'Ulysses': A Study* (New York: Vintage Books, 1958).
Gillies, Mary Ann, *Henri Bergson and British Modernism* (Montreal: McGill-Queen's University Press, 1996).
Gillies, Mary Ann, 'Bergsonism: "Time Out of Mind"', in David Bradshaw, ed., *A Concise Companion to Modernism* (Oxford: Blackwell, 2003), pp. 95–115.
Gilman, Todd, *The Theatre Career of Thomas Arne* (Lanham, MD: University of Delaware Press, 2013).

Gödde, Christopher and Thomas Sprecher, eds, *Correspondence 1943–1955: Theodor W. Adorno and Thomas Mann*, trans. Nick Walker (Cambridge: Polity Press, 2005).

Goehr, Lydia, 'Schopenhauer and the Musicians: an Inquiry into the Sounds of Silence and the Limits of Philosophizing about Music', in Dale Jacquette, ed., *Schopenhauer, Philosophy and the Arts* (Cambridge: Cambridge University Press, 1996), pp. 200–28.

Goehr, Lydia, 'Dissonant Works and the Listening Public', in Tom Huhne, ed., *The Cambridge Companion to Adorno* (Cambridge: Cambridge University Press, 2004), pp. 222–47.

Golston, Michael, *Rhythm and Race in Modernist Poetry and Science: Pound, Yeats, Williams, and Modern Sciences of Rhythm* (New York: Columbia University Press, 2007).

Gourmont, Rémy de, *Esthétique de la langue française* (Paris: Mercure de France, 1916).

Gourmont, Rémy de, *Natural Philosophy of Love*, trans. Ezra Pound (London: Boni & Liveright, 1922).

Green, Robert, *Ford Madox Ford: Prose and Politics* (Cambridge: Cambridge University Press, 1981).

Griffiths, Paul, *let me tell you* (Hastings: Reality Street, 2008).

Grose, Kenneth H., *James Joyce* (London: Evans Bros., 1975).

Guruianu, Andrei and Anthony Di Renzo, *Dead Reckoning: Transatlantic Passages on Europe and America* (Albany, NY: SUNY Press, 2016).

Gutkin, Len, 'Brigid Brophy's Aestheticism: The Camp Anti-Novel', in Kaye Mitchell and Nonia Williams, eds, *British Avant-Garde Fiction of the 1960s* (Edinburgh: Edinburgh University Press, 2019), pp. 72–89.

Habermas, Jürgen, 'Modernity: An Unfinished Project' (1981), in Maurizio Passerin d'Entrèves and Seyla Benhabib, eds, *Habermas and the Unfinished Project of Modernity: Critical Essays on The Philosophical Discourse of Modernity* (Cambridge, MA: MIT Press, 1997), pp. 38–58.

Hamilton, William, *The British Aesthetic Movement* (London: Reeves & Tucker, 1882).

Hanslick, Eduard, *On the Musically Beautiful: A Contribution Towards the Revision of the Aesthetics of Music*, trans. and ed. Geoffrey Payzant from the 8th edn (1891) of *Vom Musikalisch-Schönen: ein Beitrag zur Revision der Ästhetik der Tonkunst* (Indianapolis: Hackett Publishing, 1986).

Harker, Ben, '"Communism is English": Edgell Rickword, Jack Lindsay and the Cultural Politics of the Popular Front', *Literature and History* 20.2 (2011), 16–34.

Harker, Ben, '"The Trumpet of the Night": Interwar Communists on BBC Radio', *History Workshop Journal* 75.1 (2013), 81–100.

Harker, Ben, 'Politics and Letters: The "Soviet Literary Controversy" in Britain', *Literature and History* 24.1 (2015), 41–57.

Harkness, Marguerite, *The Aesthetics of Dedalus and Bloom* (London: Associated University Presses, 1984).

Harman, Claire ed., 'Sylvia Townsend Warner 1893–1978: A Celebration', *PN Review* 8.3 (1981), 30–61.

Harman, Claire, *Sylvia Townsend Warner: A Biography*, 2nd edn ([1989] London: Minerva, 1991).

Harman, Claire, ed., *The Diaries of Sylvia Townsend Warner* (London: Chatto & Windus, 1994).
Haslam, Jonathan, 'The Comintern and the Origins of the Popular Front 1934–1935', *The Historical Journal* 22.3 (September 1979), 682–4.
Haslam, Sara, *Fragmenting Modernism: Ford Madox Ford, the Novel and the Great War* (Manchester: Manchester University Press, 2002).
Hegel, G. W. F., *Aesthetics: Lectures on Fine Art*, vol. 2, trans. T. M. Knox (Oxford: Clarendon Press, 1975).
Hegel, G. W. F., *The Phenomenology of Spirit*, trans. A. V. Miller (Oxford: Oxford University Press, 1977).
Herman, David, '"Sirens" after Schönberg', *James Joyce Quarterly* 31.4 (1994), 473–94.
Herring, Philip, *Joyce's Ulysses Notesheets in the British Museum* (Charlottesville, VA: University Press of Virginia, 1972).
Hext, Kate and Alex Murray, eds, *Decadence in the Age of Modernism* (Baltimore: Johns Hopkins University Press, 2019).
Hillyer, Robert, 'Treason's Strange Fruit: The Case of Ezra Pound', *The Saturday Review of Literature*, 11 June 1949, p. 12.
Hillyer, Robert, 'Poetry's New Priesthood', *The Saturday Review of Literature*, 18 June 1949, p. 7.
Hobson, J. A., *Imperialism* (London: George Allen & Unwin, 1902).
Homer, *Odyssey*, book XII, trans. E. V. Rieu (London: Penguin, 1991).
Hopkins, Chris, *English Fiction in the 1930s* (London: Continuum, 2006).
Horkheimer, Max, *Critical Theory: Selected Essays*, trans. Matthew O'Connell (New York: Continuum, 1986).
Hornby, Nick, *High Fidelity* (London: Victor Gollancz, 1995).
Howey, Kimberley Kyle, 'Ezra Pound and the Rhetoric of Science, 1901–1922' (2009: unpublished PhD thesis submitted to University College London).
Huguenin, Jean René, *A Place of Shipwreck*, trans. Sylvia Townsend Warner (London: Chatto & Windus, 1963).
Huyssen, Andreas, *After the Great Divide: Modernism, Mass Culture, Postmodernism* (Bloomington, IN: Indiana University Press, 1986).
Huyssen, Andreas, 'Introduction: Modernism after Postmodernity', *New German Critique* 99 (2006), 1–5.
Iamblichus, *Iamblichus: On the Pythagorean Life*, trans. Gillian Clarke (Liverpool: Liverpool University Press, 1989).
Iamblichus, *On the Pythagorean Way of Life*, trans. John Dillon and Jackson Hershbell (Atlanta: Scholars Press, 1991).
Irvine, Andrew D., ed., *Philosophy of Mathematics* (Oxford: Elsevier, 2009).
Ishiguro, Kazuo, *Nocturnes* (London: Faber & Faber, 2009).
Iuli, Cristina, 'Dissonance, Data, and DNA: Aesthetics, Biopolitics and Transgenic Music in Richard Powers' *Orfeo*', in Stefan Herbrechter and Elisabeth Friis, eds, *Narrating Life: Experiments with Human and Animal Bodies in Literature* (Leiden: Brill, 2016), pp. 92–113.
Jackson, Leonard, *The Dematerialisation of Karl Marx* (London: Longman, 1994).
James, David, *Modernist Futures: Innovation and Inheritance in the Contemporary Novel* (Cambridge: Cambridge University Press, 2012).
James, David, 'Realism, Late Modernist Abstraction, and Sylvia Townsend

Warner's Aesthetics of Impersonality', *Modernist/modernity* 12.1 (2005), 111–31.

James, Marlon, *A Brief History of Seven Killings* (New York: Riverhead Books, 2014).

Jameson, Fredric, *The Modernist Papers* (London: Verso, 2007).

Jay, Martin, 'What's New? On Adorno and the Modernist Aesthetics of Novelty', in Stephen Ross, ed., *Modernism and Theory: a Critical Debate* (London: Routledge, 2009), pp. 171–5.

Jeneman, David, *Adorno in America* (London and Minneapolis: University of Minnesota Press, 2007).

Joannou, Maroula, ed., *Women Writers of the 1930s: Gender, Politics and History* (Edinburgh: Edinurgh University Press, 1999).

Johnson, Jeri, 'Introduction', in James Joyce, *Ulysses* (Oxford: Oxford University Press, 1993).

Jones, Stephanie, 'Christine Brooke-Rose and the Development of Experiment', in Kaye Mitchell and Nonia Williams, eds, *British Avant-Garde Fiction of the 1960s* (Edinburgh: Edinburgh University Press, 2019), pp. 193–219.

Jordan, Julia, *Late Modernism and the Avant-Garde British Novel* (Oxford: Oxford University Press, 2020).

Josipovici, Gabriel, *Whatever Happened to Modernism?* (New Haven, CT and London: Yale University Press, 2010).

Joyce, James, *Chamber Music* (London: Elkin Matthews, 1907).

Joyce, James, *Letters of James Joyce*, vol. 1, ed. Stuart Gilbert (London: Faber & Faber, 1966).

Joyce, James, *Selected Letters of James Joyce*, ed. Richard Ellmann (London: Faber & Faber, 1975).

Joyce, James, *Ulysses: A Critical and Synoptic Edition*, prepared by Hans Walter Gabler, with Wolfhard Steppe and Claus Melchior, 3 vols (New York and London: Garland Publishing, 1984).

Joyce, James, *Occasional, Critical, and Political Writing* (Oxford: Oxford University Press, 2003).

Joyce, Stanislaus, *My Brother's Keeper: James Joyce's Early Years*, ed. Richard Ellmann ([1953] Boston: Da Capo Press, 2003).

Judd, Cristle Collins, *Reading Renaissance Music Theory: Hearing with the Eyes* (Cambridge: Cambridge University Press, 2000).

Kant, Immanuel, *Critique of Pure Reason*, ed. and trans. Paul Guyer and Allen W. Wood (Cambridge: Cambridge University Press, 1998).

Kant, Immanuel, *Critique of the Power of Judgement*, ed. Paul Guyer, trans. Paul Guyer and Eric Matthews (Cambridge: Cambridge University Press, 2000).

Katz, Daniel, 'Ezra Pound's Provincial Provence: Arnaut Daniel, Gavin Douglas, and the Vulgar Tongue', *Modern Language Quarterly* 73.2 (2012), 175–99.

Kenner, Hugh, *The Pound Era* (Berkeley, CA: University of California Press, 1971).

Kirwan, Peter, 'Mis/Quotation in Constrained Writing', in Julie Maxwell and Kate Rumbold, eds, *Shakespeare and Quotation* (Cambridge: Cambridge University Press, 2018), pp. 247–59.

Kivy, Peter, *Music Alone: Philosophical Reflections on the Purely Musical Experience* (Ithaca, NY and London: Cornell University Press, 1990).

Klages, Ludwig, *Rhythmen und Runen* (Leipzig: Johann Ambrosius Barth, 1944).
Knowles, Sebastian D. G., ed., *Bronze by Gold: The Music of Joyce* (London: Routledge, 1999).
Kozloff, Max, 'American Painting During the Cold War', in Francis Frascina, ed., *Pollock and After: the Critical Debate* (London: Psychology Press, 1985), pp. 107–25.
Kramer, Lawrence, *Music as Cultural Practice, 1800–1900* (Berkeley, CA: University of California Press, 1990).
Kurath, Hans, Sherman McAllister Kuhn and Robert E. Lewis, *Middle English Dictionary*, 25 vols (Ann Arbor, MI: University of Michigan Press, 2001).
Kwon, Young-Hee, '*Mr Fortune's Maggot* and the De-Masculinization of the Victorian Imperial Romance', *Literature Interpretation Theory* 18 (2007), 303–23.
Lahr, John, *Coward the Playwright* (London: Bloomsbury, 1982).
Laplanche, Jean and Jean-Bertrand Pontalis, *The Language of Psycho-Analysis*, trans. Donald Nicholson-Smith (London: Karnac Books, 1988).
Larson, Ron and Bruce Edwards, *Calculus of a Single Variable*, 9th edn (Belmont, CA: Cengage Learning, 2006).
Lawrence, D. H., *The Letters of D. H. Lawrence*, ed. George J. Zytaruk and James T. Boulton (Cambridge: Cambridge University Press, 1981).
Lawrence, D. H., *St. Mawr and Other Stories*, ed. Brian Finney (Cambridge: Cambridge University Press, 1983).
Lebovic, Nitzan, *The Philosophy of Life and Death: Ludwig Klages and the Rise of a Nazi Biopolitics* (New York: Palgrave Macmillan, 2013).
Leech-Wilkinson, Daniel, 'Ars Antiqua – Ars Nova – Ars Subtilior', in James McKinnon, ed., *Antiquity and the Middle Ages: From Ancient Greece to the 15th Century* (Eaglewood Cliffs, NJ: Prentice Hall, 1990), pp. 218–40.
Lees, Heath, *Mallarmé and Wagner: Music and Poetic Language* (Aldershot: Ashgate, 2007).
Leick, Karen, 'Ezra Pound v. The Saturday Review of Literature', *Journal of Modern Literature* 25.2 (2001–2), 19–37.
Leighton, Angela, *On Form: Poetry, Aestheticism, and the Legacy of a Word* (Oxford: Oxford University Press, 2007).
Leppert, Richard and Susan McClary, eds, *Music and Society: the Politics of Composition, Performance and Reception* (Cambridge: Cambridge University Press, 1987).
Levin, Harry, 'What was Modernism?', *The Massachusetts Review* 1.4 (1960), 609–30.
Levin, Lawrence, 'The Sirens Episode as Music: Joyce's Experiment with Prose Polyphony', *James Joyce Quarterly* 3.1 (1965), 12–24.
Lewis, Ethan, 'Imagisme', in Ira B. Nadel, ed., *Ezra Pound in Context* (Cambridge: Cambridge University Press, 2010), pp. 274–84.
Lewis, Sophie, *Full Surrogacy Now: Feminism Against Family* (London: Verso, 2019).
Lewis, Wyndham, *Time and Western Man*, ed. Paul Edwards ([1927] Santa Rosa, CA: Black Sparrow Press, 1993).
Leys, Ruth, 'The Turn to Affect: A Critique', *Critical Inquiry* 37.3 (Spring 2011), 434–72.

Lindberg, Kathryne V., *Reading Pound Reading: Modernism after Nietzsche* (Oxford: Oxford University Press, 1987).

Litz, A. Walton, *The Art of James Joyce: Method and Design in 'Ulysses' and 'Finnegans Wake'* (London: Oxford University Press, 1961).

Litz, A. Walton, 'Florence Farr: A "Transitional Woman"', in Maria DiBattista and Lucy McDiarmid, eds, *High and Low Moderns: Literature and Culture 1889–1939* (New York: Oxford University Press, 1996), pp. 85–90.

Lockyer, Rebekah, 'Ford Madox Ford's Musical Legacy: *Parade's End* and Wagner', *Forum for Modern Language Studies* 50.4 (2014), 426–52.

Lukács, Georg, *German Realists in the Nineteenth Century*, ed. Rodney Livingstone, trans. Jeremy Gaines and Paul Keast (Cambridge, MA: MIT Press, 1993).

McClary, Susan, *Feminine Endings* (Minneapolis: University of Minnesota Press, 1991).

Macdougal, Stuart Y., 'Provençal Literature', in Demetres P. Tryphonopoulos and Stephen J. Adams, eds, *The Ezra Pound Encyclopaedia* (London: Greenwood Press, 2005), p. 244.

McDowell, John, *Mind and World* (Oxford: Oxford University Press, 1994).

Magee, Bryan, *The Philosophy of Schopenhauer* (Oxford: Oxford University Press, 1997).

Mallarmé, Stéphane, *Selected Prose Poems, Essays and Letters*, trans. Bradford Cook (Baltimore: Johns Hopkins University Press, 1956).

Mann, Thomas, *The Story of a Novel: The Genesis of 'Doctor Faustus'*, trans. H. T. Lowe-Porter ([1947] Harmondsworth: Penguin, 1971).

Mao, Douglas, 'Our Last September: Climate Change in Modernist Times', in Michael D'Arcy and Mathias Nilges, eds, *The Contemporaneity of Modernism: Literature, Media, Culture* (Abingdon: Routledge, 2016), pp. 31–48.

Mao, Douglas, and Rebecca L. Walkowitz, eds, *Bad Modernisms* (Durham, NC and London: Duke University Press 2006).

Maor, Eli, *The Pythagorean Theorem: A 4,000-Year History* (Princeton, NJ: Princeton University Press, 2007).

Marcuse, Herbert, *One Dimensional Man* ([1964] Abingdon: Routledge, 2003).

Margolies, David, ed., *Writing the Revolution: Cultural Criticism from 'Left Review'* (London: Pluto Press, 1998).

Martin, Peter J., *Music and the Sociological Gaze* (Manchester: Manchester University Press, 2006).

Martin, Timothy Peter, *Joyce and Wagner: A Study of Influence* (Cambridge: Cambridge University Press, 1991).

Marx, Karl, *Capital*, trans. Samuel Moore and Edward Aveling (Moscow: Progress Publishers, 1887).

Marx, Karl, *Capital: A Critical Analysis of Capitalist Production*, trans. Friedrich Engels (London: Lawrence & Wishart, 1903).

Marx, Karl, *Capital*, trans. Eden Paul and Cedar Paul (London: J. M. Dent & Sons, 1930).

Marx, Karl, *Grundrisse*, ed. and trans. David McLellan (London: Macmillan, 1971).

Marx, Karl and Friedrich Engels, *The German Ideology* (London: Lawrence & Wishart, 1965).

Marx, Karl and Friedrich Engels, *Marx and Engels: Selected Works* (London: Lawrence & Wishart, 1968).
Marx, Karl and Friedrich Engels, *The Economic and Philosophic Manuscripts of 1844 and the Communist Manifesto*, trans. Martin Milligan (New York: Prometheus Books, 1988).
Miller, Andrew, *Greek Lyric: An Anthology in Translation* (Indianapolis: Hackett Publishing, 1996).
Miller, Tyrus, *Modernism and the Frankfurt School* (Edinburgh: Edinburgh University Press, 2014).
Millington, Barry, *The New Grove Guide to Wagner and His Operas* (Oxford: Oxford University Press, 2006).
Mills, John, ed., *Psychoanalysis at the Limit: Epistemology, Mind, and the Question of Science* (Albany, NY: SUNY Press, 2004).
Milton, John, *The Poetical Works of John Milton*, vol. 2, ed. H. Darbishire (Oxford: Clarendon Press, 1955).
Mitchell, Kaye and Nonia Williams, eds, *British Avant-Garde Fiction of the 1960s* (Edinburgh: Edinburgh University Press, 2019).
Mohl, Ernst Theodor, 'Germany, Austria and Switzerland', in Marcello Musto, ed., *Karl Marx's Grundrisse: Foundations of the Critique of Political Economy 150 Years Later* (London: Routledge, 2008), pp. 189–201.
Moi, Toril, *Sexual/Textual Politics* (Abingdon: Routledge, 1992).
Montefiore, Janet, *Men and Women Writers of the 1930s: The Dangerous Flood of History* (London: Routledge, 1996).
Morris, William, *Signs of Change* (London: Longmans, 1896).
Morrison, Paul, *The Poetics of Fascism: Ezra Pound, T. S. Eliot, Paul de Man* (Oxford: Oxford University Press, 1996).
Moss, Gemma, '"A Beginning Rather Than an End": Popular Culture and Modernity in D. H. Lawrence's *St. Mawr*', *Journal of D. H. Lawrence Studies* 4.1 (December 2015), 119–39.
Moss, Gemma, 'Music in E. M. Forster's *A Room With a View* and *Howards End*: The Conflicting Presentation of Nineteenth-Century Aesthetics', *English Literature in Transition* 59.4 (2016), 493–509.
Moss, Gemma, 'Music, Noise and the First World War in Ford Madox Ford's *Parade's End*', *Modernist Cultures* 12.1 (2017), 59–77.
Moss, Gemma, 'Classical Music and Literature', in Anna Snaith, ed., *Literature and Sound* (Cambridge: Cambridge University Press, 2020), pp. 92–113.
Munslow Ong, Jade, *Olive Schreiner and African Modernism: Allegory, Empire and Postcolonial Writing* (London: Routledge, 2018).
Musto, Marcello, ed., *Karl Marx's Grundrisse: Foundations of the Critique of Political Economy 150 Years Later* (London: Routledge, 2008).
Mutti, Lynn, 'That Odd Thing, a Musicologist', *Journal of the Sylvia Townsend Warner Society* (2013), 17–34.
Nadel, Ira B., ed., *The Cambridge Companion to Ezra Pound* (Cambridge: Cambridge University Press, 1999).
Nadel, Ira B., ed., *Ezra Pound in Context* (Cambridge: Cambridge University Press, 2010).
Nash, John, 'Newspapers and Imperialism', in Howard J. Booth and Nigel Rigby, eds, *Modernism and Empire* (Manchester: Manchester University Press, 2000), pp. 175–96.

Nattiez, Jean-Jacques, *Music and Discourse: Towards a Semiology of Music*, trans. Carolyn Abbate (Princeton, NJ: Princeton University Press, 1990).

Nettl, Bruno, *The Study of Ethnomusicology: Twenty-nine Issues and Concepts* (Champaign, IL: University of Illinois Press, 1983).

Nettl, Bruno, *The Study of Ethnomusicology: Thirty-one Issues and Concepts* (Champaign, IL: University of Illinois Press, 2005).

Ngai, Sianne, *Ugly Feelings* (Cambridge, MA: Harvard University Press, 2005).

Ngai, Sianne, *Our Aesthetic Categories: Cute, Zany, Interesting* (Cambridge, MA: Harvard University Press, 2015).

Nietzsche, Friedrich, *The Birth of Tragedy*, trans. Douglas K. Smith, Oxford World's Classics (Oxford: Oxford University Press, 2000).

Nietzsche, Friedrich, *The Birth of Tragedy Out of the Spirit of Music*, ed. Michael Tanner, trans. Shaun Whiteside (London: Penguin, 2003).

Nolan, Emer, *James Joyce and Nationalism* (London: Routledge, 2002).

North, Michael, *The Political Aesthetic of Yeats, Eliot and Pound* (Cambridge: Cambridge University Press, 1991).

North, Michael, *Novelty: A History of the New* (Chicago and London: University of Chicago Press, 2012).

North, Michael, 'The Afterlife of Modernism', *New Literary History* 50.1 (Winter 2019), 91–112.

Ord-Hume, Arthur W. J. G., *Harmonium: the History of the Reed Organ and its Makers* (London: David & Charles, 1986).

Osborne, Peter, 'Modernity is a Qualitative, not a Chronological Category', *New Left Review* 1.192 (1992), 23–45.

Osborne, Peter, *Anywhere or Not at All: Philosophy of Contemporary Art* (London: Verso, 2013).

Overy, Richard, *The Morbid Age: Britain Between the Wars* (London: Allen Lane, 2009).

Ovid, *Metamorphosis*, trans. David Raeburn (London: Penguin, 2004).

Parsons, Cóilín, 'John Banville, Long Form, and the Time of Late Modernism', in Kathryn Conrad, Cóilín Parsons and Julie McCormic Weng, eds, *Science, Technology and Irish Modernism* (Syracuse, NY: Syracuse University Press, 2019), pp. 264–82.

Pater, Walter, *Appreciations: With an Essay on Style* ([1901] London: Macmillan, 1924).

Pater, Walter, *The Renaissance: Studies in Art and Poetry*, ed. Donald L. Hill (Berkley, CA: University of California Press, 1980).

Pawling, Christopher, *Christopher Caudwell: Towards a Dialectical Theory of Literature* (London: Macmillan, 1989).

Pawling, Christopher, 'Revisiting the Thirties in the Twenty-First Century: the Radical Aesthetics of West, Caudwell, and Eagleton', in Anthony Shuttleworth, ed., *And in Our Time: Vision, Revision, and British Writing of the 1930s* (London: Associated University Presses, 2003), pp. 11–20.

Perec, Georges, *A Void*, trans. Gilbert Adair ([1969] London: Vintage, 2008).

Perils, Alan D., 'Beyond Epiphany: Pater's Aesthetic Hero in the Works of Joyce', *James Joyce Quarterly* 17.3 (1980), 272–9.

Pesce, Dolores, 'Beyond Glossing: The Old Made New in *Mout me fu grief/Robin m'aime/Portare*', in *Hearing the Motet: Essays on the Motet of the Middle Ages and Renaissance* (Oxford: Oxford University Press), pp. 28–51.

Plato, *The Republic: Book 1* (London: Penguin, 1955).
Plato, *Phaedro*, ed. and trans. David Gallop (Oxford: Oxford University Press, 1993).
Poirier, Richard, 'Pater, Joyce, Eliot', *James Joyce Quarterly* 26.1 (1988), 21–35.
Polzonetti, Pierpaolo, 'Haydn and the Metamorphoses of Ovid', in Mary Hunter and Richard Will, eds, *Engaging Haydn: Culture, Context and Criticism* (Cambridge: Cambridge University Press, 2012), pp. 211–39.
Porter, Steven, *The Harmonization of the Chorale: A Comprehensive Workbook Course in Harmony* (New York: Excelsior Publishing, 1987).
Pound, Ezra, 'I Gather the Limbs of Osiris II', *The New Age* 10.6 (7 December 1911), 130–1, https://library.brown.edu/pdfs/1140814082593168.pdf (last accessed 7 August 2020).
Pound, Ezra, 'I Gather the Limbs of Osiris IX', *The New Age* 10.13 (25 January 1912), 297–9, https://library.brown.edu/pdfs/114081409614388.pdf (last accessed 7 August 2020).
Pound, Ezra, 'I Gather the Limbs of Osiris X', *The New Age* 10.15 (8 February 1912), 343–4, https://library.brown.edu/pdfs/1140814100327734.pdf (last accessed 7 August 2020).
Pound, Ezra, 'I Gather the Limbs of Osiris XI', *The New Age* 10.16 (15 February 1912), 369–70, https://library.brown.edu/pdfs/1140814101805980.pdf (last accessed 7 August 2020).
Pound, Ezra, *Lustra* (London: Elkin Matthews, 1916)
Pound, Ezra, 'James Joyce: At Last the Novel Appears', *Egoist* 4.2 (February 1917), 21–2.
Pound, Ezra, 'The Hard and the Soft in French Poetry', *Poetry*, 11.5 (February 1918), 264–71.
Pound, Ezra, *The Letters of Ezra Pound: 1907–1941*, ed. D. D. Paige (London: Faber & Faber, 1951).
Pound, Ezra, *The Translations of Ezra Pound*, ed. Hugh Kenner (London: Faber & Faber, 1953).
Pound, Ezra, *Literary Essays*, ed. T.S. Eliot (London: Faber & Faber, 1954).
Pound, Ezra, *ABC of Reading* (London: New Directions, 1960).
Pound, Ezra, *Gaudier-Brzeska* ([1916] New York: New Directions, 1960).
Pound, Ezra, *The Letters of Ezra Pound to James Joyce*, ed. Forrest Read (London: New Directions, 1967).
Pound, Ezra, *Guide to Kulchur* ([1938] New York: New Directions, 1970).
Pound, Ezra, *Selected Poems 1908–1969* (London: Faber & Faber, 1977).
Pound, Ezra, *Ezra Pound and Music: The Complete Criticism*, ed. R. Murray Schafer (London: Faber & Faber, 1978).
Pound, Ezra, *Ezra Pound's Poetry and Prose*, ed. Lea Baechler, A. Walton Litz and James Longenbach, 11 vols (London: Garland, 1991).
Pound, Ezra, *Machine Art and Other Writings: The Lost Thought of the Italian Years*, ed. Maria Luisa Ardizzone (Durham, NC: Duke University Press, 1996).
Pound, Ezra, *The Cantos of Ezra Pound* (New York: New Directions, 1996).
Pound, Ezra, *Selected Poems and Translations*, ed. Richard Sieburth (London: Faber & Faber, 2010).
Pound, Ezra, *Posthumous Cantos*, ed. Massimo Bacigalupo (Manchester: Carcanet, 2015).

Powers, Richard, *Orfeo* (London: Atlantic Books, 2014).
Proust, Marcel, *By Way of Saint-Beuve*, trans. Sylvia Townsend Warner ([1958] London: Hogarth Press, 1984).
Rancière, Jacques, *Aesthetics and its Discontents*, trans. Steven Corcoran (Cambridge: Polity, 2009).
Rancière, Jacques, *Aisthesis: Scenes from the Aesthetic Regime of Art*, trans. Zakir Paul (London: Verso, 2013).
Rancière, Jacques, *The Politics of Aesthetics*, ed. and trans. Gabriel Rockhill (London: Bloomsbury, 2013).
Randall, Bryony, *Modernism, Daily Time and Everyday Life* (Cambridge: Cambridge University Press, 2007).
Read, Richard, 'Art Criticism versus Poetry: an Introduction to Adrian Stokes's "Pisanello"', in E. S. Shaffer, ed., *Comparative Criticism Volume 17: Walter Pater and the Culture of the Fin-de-Siècle* (Cambridge: Cambridge University Press, 1995), pp. 133–60.
Reed, T. J., 'The "Goethezeit" and its Aftermath', in Malcolm Pasley, ed., *Germany: A Companion to German Studies* (London: Methuen, 1972), pp. 493–553.
Reich, Steve, *Composer's Notes for 'Proverb'* (1995), https://www.boosey.com/pages/cr/catalogue/cat_detail?musicid=557 (last accessed 7 August 2020).
Reichal, A. Elisabeth, 'Musical Macrostructures in *The Gold Bug Variations* and *Orfeo* by Richard Powers; or, Toward a Media-Conscious Audionarratology', *Partial Answers: Journal of Literature and the History of Ideas* 15.1 (2017), 81–98.
Reid, Susan, *D.H. Lawrence, Music and Modernism* (Basingstoke: Palgrave Macmillan, 2019).
Remes, Pauliina, *Neoplatonism* (Berkeley, CA: University of California Press, 2008).
Richardson, Dorothy, *Pilgrimage 1: Pointed Roofs, Backwater, Honeycomb* ([1921] London: Virago, 1979).
Richter, Ernst Friedrich, *Manual of Harmony: A Practical Guide to its Study Prepared Especially for the Conservatory of Music at Leipzig*, ed. Alfred Richter, trans. Theodore Baker (New York: G. Schirmer, 1912).
Rigby, Nigel, 'The South Seas, Sexuality and Modernism', in Howard J. Booth and Nigel Rigby, eds, *Modernism and Empire* (Manchester: Manchester University Press, 2000), pp. 224–48.
Ritterman, Janet, 'Piano Music and the Public Concert, 1800–1850', in Jim Samson, ed., *The Cambridge Companion to Chopin* (Cambridge: Cambridge University Press, 1992), pp. 11–31.
Robertson, Anne Walters, *Guillaume de Machaut and Reims: Context and Meaning in His Musical Works* (Cambridge: Cambridge University Press, 2002).
Roesner, Edward H., ed., *Ars Antiqua: Organum, Conductus, Motet* (Abingdon: Routledge, 2009).
Rose, Jonathan, *The Intellectual Life of the British Working Classes* (Reading: Cox & Wyman Ltd., 2001).
Ross, Alex, 'György Kurtág, with his Opera of "Endgame," Proves To Be Beckett's Equal', *The New Yorker*, 17 December 2018, https://www.newyor

ker.com/magazine/2018/12/24/gyorgy-kurtag-with-his-opera-of-endgame-proves-to-be-becketts-equal (last accessed 13 August 2020).

Ruskin, John, *Modern Painters*, 5 vols (London: Smith, Elder & Co., 1843–60).

Russell, Bertrand, *Introduction to Mathematical Philosophy* ([1919] New York: Cosimo, 2007).

Ruthven, K. K., *Guide to Ezra Pound's 'Personæ'* (Berkeley, CA: University of California Press, 1969).

Sachs, Hans, *The Book of Trades (Ständebuch)*, ed. Jost Amman (New York: Dover, 1973).

Sadie, Stanley, ed., *The New Grove Dictionary of Opera*, 2nd edn (London: Oxford University Press, 1992).

Said, Edward, *Musical Elaborations* (New York: Columbia University Press, 1991).

Saito, Yuriko, *Everyday Aesthetics* (Oxford: Oxford University Press, 2008).

Samson, Jim, *The Cambridge Companion to Chopin* (Cambridge: Cambridge University Press, 1992).

Schlegel, Friedrich, *Kritische Schriften und Fragmente 1–6* (Paderborn: Schöningh, 1988).

Schoenberg, Arnold, *Letters*, ed. Erwin Stein, trans. Eithne Wilkins and Ernst Kaiser (Berkeley, CA: University of California Press, 1964).

Schoenberg, Arnold, *Style and Idea: Selected Writings of Arnold Schoenberg*, ed. Leonard Stein, trans. Leo Black (London: Faber & Faber, 1975).

Schopenhauer, Arthur, *The World as Will and Representation*, vol. 1, ed. Judith Norman, Alistair Welchman and Christopher Janaway (Cambridge: Cambridge University Press, 2011).

Scotto, Robert M., '"Visions" and "Epiphanies": Fictional Technique in Pater's *Marius* and Joyce's *Portrait*', *James Joyce Quarterly* 11.1 (1973), 41–50.

Searle, Richard, 'Sylvia Townsend Warner and *Tudor Church Music*', *Journal of the Sylvia Townsend Warner Society* (2011), 69–88.

Shapiro, David and Cecile Shapiro, 'Abstract Expressionism: the Politics of Apolitical Painting', in Francis Frascina, ed., *Pollock and After: the Critical Debate* (London: Psychology Press, 1985), pp. 135–53.

Shepherd, John, 'Towards a Sociology of Music Styles', in Avron Levine White, ed., *Lost in Music Culture: Style and the Musical Event* (London: Routledge, 1987), pp. 56–76.

Sherratt, Yvonne, *Adorno's Positive Dialectic* (Cambridge: Cambridge University Press, 2002).

Sherry, Vincent, *Ezra Pound, Wyndham Lewis and Radical Modernism* (Oxford: Oxford University Press, 1993).

Sherry, Vincent, *Modernism and the Reinvention of Decadence* (Cambridge: Cambridge University Press, 2014).

Shockley, Alan, *Music in the Words: Musical Form and Counterpoint in the Twentieth-Century Novel* (Farnham: Ashgate, 2009).

Shuter, William F., 'Heraclitus, Hegel and Plato', in *Rereading Walter Pater* (Cambridge: Cambridge University Press, 1997), pp. 61–77.

Sieburth, Richard, *Instigations: Ezra Pound and Rémy de Gourmont* (Cambridge, MA: Harvard University Press, 1978).

Sinclair, May, 'The Novels of Dorothy Richardson', *The Egoist* 5.4 (1918), 57–9, https://modjourn.org/issue/bdr522839/ (last accessed 7 August 2020).

Sinfield, Alan, 'Private Lives/Public Theatre: Noel Coward and the Politics of Homosexual Representation', *Representations* 36 (1991), 43–63.
Smith, Don Noel, 'Musical Form and Principles in the Scheme of Ulysses', *Twentieth Century Literature* 18.2 (1972), 79–92.
Smith, Stan, 'Balancing Accounts: Caudwell, Eagleton and English Marxism', *Critical Survey* 7.1 (1995), 76–81.
Smith, Zadie, *Swing Time* (London: Penguin, 2016).
Snarrenburg, Robert, *Schenker's Interpretive Practice* (Cambridge: Cambridge University Press, 2005).
Snyder, Kerala J., *Dieterich Buxtehude: Organist in Lübeck* (Rochester, NY: University of Rochester Press, 2007).
Solis, Ted, ed., *Performing Ethnomusicology: Teaching and Representation in World Music Ensembles* (Berkeley, CA: University of California Press, 2004).
Spinks, Lee, *James Joyce: A Critical Guide* (Edinburgh: Edinburgh University Press, 2009).
Stanford Friedman, Susan, *Planetary Modernisms: Provocations on Modernity Across Time* (New York: Columbia University Press, 2015).
Stevens, Wallace, 'The Relations between Poetry and Painting', in *The Necessary Angel: Essays on Reality and the Imagination* (New York: Vintage, 1951).
Stimpson, Catharine R., 'Texts in the Wind', *Critical Inquiry* 30 (Winter 2004), 434–9.
Subotnik, Rose Rosengard, *Deconstructive Variations: Music and Reason in Western Society* (Minneapolis: University of Minnesota Press, 1996).
Sultan, Stanley, 'The Sirens at the Ormond Bar: "Ulysses"', *University of Kansas City Review* 26.2 (1959), 83–92.
Sumner, Charles B., 'Beauty be Damned: Why Adorno Valorizes Carrion, Stench, and Putrefaction', in Kelly Comfort, ed., *Art and Life in Aestheticism: De-Humanizing and Re-Humanizing Art, the Artist and the Artistic Receptor* (Basingstoke: Palgrave Macmillan, 2008), pp. 178–88.
Surette, Leon, *The Birth of Modernism: Ezra Pound, T. S. Eliot, W. B. Yeats and the Occult* (Montreal and London: McGill-Queens University Press, 1993).
Sutton, Emma, *Virginia Woolf and Classical Music: Politics, Aesthetics, Form* (Edinburgh: Edinburgh University Press, 2013).
Symonds, John Addington, *Essays Speculative and Suggestive* (London: Chapman and Hall, 1893).
Tanke, Joseph J., 'Which Politics of Aesthetics?', in Scott Durham and Dilip Gaonkar, eds, *The Distributions of the Sensible* (Evanston, IL: Northwestern University Press, 2019), pp. 79–96.
Templeton, Erin E., 'Ezra Pound, George Antheil and the Complications of Patronage', in Robert P. McParland, ed., *Music and Literary Modernism*, 2nd edn (Newcastle-upon-Tyne: Cambridge Scholars, 2009), pp. 65–84.
Terry, Philip, ed., *The Penguin Book of Oulipo* (London: Penguin, 2019).
Thompson, E. P., 'Christopher Caudwell', *Critical Inquiry* 21 (1995), 305–53.
Thompson, M. Guy, 'The Role of Being and Experience in Freud's Unconscious Ontology', in John Mills, ed., *Psychoanalysis at the Limit: Epistemology, Mind, and the Question of Science* (Albany, NY: SUNY Press, 2004), pp. 1–30.

Thornton, Weldon, *Allusions in Ulysses: An Annotated List* (Chapel Hill, NC: University of North Carolina Press, 1968).
Tindall, William York, 'Joyce's Chambermade Music', *Poetry* 80.2 (1952), 105–16.
Tremblay, Tony, 'Frobenius, Leo (1873–1938)', in Demetres P. Tryphonopoulos and Stephen J. Adams, eds, *The Ezra Pound Encyclopedia* (London: Greenwood Press, 2005), pp. 126–7.
Tryphonopoulos, Demetres P., and Stephen J. Adams, eds, *The Ezra Pound Encyclopedia* (London: Greenwood Press, 2005).
Tufail, Burhan, '*Drosophila Ludens*: Oulipian Designs on Mallarmé', in Michael Temple, ed., *Meetings with Mallarmé* (Exeter: Exeter University Press, 1998), pp. 143–59.
Tymoczko, Dmitri, *A Geometry of Music: Harmony and Counterpoint in the Extended Common Practice* (Oxford: Oxford University Press, 2011).
Virgil, *Georgics*, trans. Peter Fallon (Oxford: Oxford University Press, 2009).
Wachman, Gay, *Lesbian Empire: Radical Crosswriting in the Twenties* (New Brunswick, NJ: Rutgers University Press, 2001).
Waddell, Nathan, *Moonlighting: Beethoven and Literary Modernism* (Oxford: Oxford University Press, 2019).
Wagner, Richard, *Gesammelte Schriften und Dichtungen*, 10 vols (Leipzig: Siegel, 1907).
Wagner, Richard, *Three Wagner Essays*, trans. Robert L. Jacobs (London: Eulenburg Books, 1979).
Wagner, Richard, 'Beethoven', in *Music in European Thought: 1851–1912*, ed. Bojan Bujic (Cambridge: Cambridge University Press, 1988), pp. 65–6.
Wagner, Richard, *Wagner on Music and Drama*, trans. H. Ashton Ellis (New York: Da Capo Press, 1988).
Wagner, Richard, *Richard Wagner's Prose Works*, vol. 1, *The Art-Work of the Future and other Works*, trans. William Ashton Ellis (Lincoln, NE: University of Nebraska Press, 1993).
Wagner, Richard and Franz Liszt, *Correspondence of Wagner and Liszt*, ed. Francis Hueffer (New York: Haskell House, 1897).
Warner, Sylvia Townsend, 'Doubting Castle', *Music and Letters* 2 (1924), 155–68.
Warner, Sylvia Townsend, *The Espalier* (London: Chatto & Windus, 1925).
Warner, Sylvia Townsend, *Time Importuned* (New York: Viking Press, 1928).
Warner, Sylvia Townsend, *Some World Far From Ours and Stay Corydon, Thou Swain* (London: Elkin Matthews, 1929).
Warner, Sylvia Townsend, *Elinor Barley* (London: Cresset Press, 1930).
Warner, Sylvia Townsend, *A Moral Ending and Other Stories* (London: William Jackson, 1931).
Warner, Sylvia Townsend, *Opus 7* (London: Chatto & Windus, 1931).
Warner, Sylvia Townsend, *More Joy in Heaven* (London: Cresset Press, 1935).
Warner, Sylvia Townsend, *Museum of Cheats* (London: Chatto & Windus, 1947).
Warner, Sylvia Townsend, *The Cat's Cradle Book* (London: Chatto & Windus, 1960).
Warner, Sylvia Townsend, *King Duffus and Other Poems* (Wells: Clare, Son & Co, 1968).

Warner, Sylvia Townsend, *The Innocent and the Guilty* (London: Chatto & Windus, 1971).
Warner, Sylvia Townsend, *A Garland of Straw* ([1943] Freeport, NY: Books for Libraries Press, 1972).
Warner, Sylvia Townsend, *Kingdoms of Elfin* ([1977] Harmondsworth: Penguin, 1979).
Warner, Sylvia Townsend, *Scenes of Childhood and Other Stories* (London: Chatto & Windus, 1981).
Warner, Sylvia Townsend, *After the Death of Don Juan* ([1938] London: Virago, 1989).
Warner, Sylvia Townsend, *T. H. White: A Biography* ([1967] Oxford and New York: Oxford University Press, 1989).
Warner, Sylvia Townsend, *Mr Fortune's Maggot* ([1927] London: Virago, 2000).
Warner, Sylvia Townsend, *The Salutation* ([1932] Horam: Tartarus, 2000).
Warner, Sylvia Townsend, *The Music at Long Verney* (London: Counterpoint, 2001).
Warner, Sylvia Townsend, *Summer Will Show* ([1936] New York: New York Review of Books, 2009).
Warner, Sylvia Townsend, *A Spirit Rises* ([1962] London: Faber & Faber, 2011).
Warner, Sylvia Townsend, *A Stranger with a Bag* ([1966] London: Faber & Faber, 2011).
Warner, Sylvia Townsend, *The Flint Anchor* ([1954] London: Virago, 2011).
Warner, Sylvia Townsend, *Lolly Willowes* ([1926] London: Virago, 2012).
Warner, Sylvia Townsend, 'Ludwig Van Beethoven', in *With the Hunted*, ed. Peter Tolhurst (Norwich: Black Dog Books, 2012).
Warner, Sylvia Townsend, *The Corner that Held Them* ([1945] London: Virago, 2012).
Warner, Sylvia Townsend, *The True Heart* ([1929] London: Virago, 2012).
Warner, Sylvia Townsend, *Winter in the Air* ([1955] London: Faber & Faber, 2013).
Warner, Sylvia Townsend and Valentine Ackland, *Whether a Dove or a Seagull* (London: Chatto & Windus, 1934).
Warner, Sylvia Townsend and Alan Reynolds Stone, *Boxwood* ([1957] London: Chatto & Windus, 1960).
Weaver, Jack W., *Joyce's Music and Noise: Theme and Variation in his Writings* (Gainesville, FL: University of Florida Press, 1998).
Weber, William, 'Mass Culture and the Reshaping of European Musical Taste, 1770–1870', *International Review of the Aesthetics and Sociology of Music* 8.1 (1977), 5–22.
Weir, David, *Decadence and the Making of Modernism* (Amherst, MA: University of Massachusetts Press, 1995).
Whittall, Arnold, *Serialism* (Cambridge: Cambridge University Press, 2008).
Whittall, Arnold, 'Leitmotif', in Stanley Sadie, ed., *The New Grove Dictionary of Opera*, 2nd edn (London: Oxford University Press, 1992), p. 1137.
Whitworth, Michael, *Einstein's Wake: Relativity, Metaphor, and Modernist Literature* (Oxford: Oxford University Press, 2001).

Williams, Raymond, *Culture and Materialism* ([1980] London: Verso, 2005).
Williams, Raymond, *The Politics of Modernism: Against the New Conformists*, ed. Tony Pinkney ([1989] London: Verso, 2007).
Williams, William Carlos, *Selected Essays* (New York: Random House, 1954).
Wilson, Edmund, *Axel's Castle: A Study in the Imaginative Literature of 1870–1930* ([1931] London: Collins, 1961).
Wintringham, Tom, *The Coming World War* (London: Lawrence & Wishart, 1935).
Witen, Michelle, *James Joyce and Absolute Music* (London: Bloomsbury, 2018).
Witkin, Robert W., *Adorno on Music* (London: Routledge, 1998).
Wittgenstein, Ludwig, *Culture and Value*, ed. G. H. von Wright and Heikki Nyman, trans. Peter Winch (Chicago: University of Chicago Press, 1980).
Wolf, Werner, *The Musicalization of Fiction: A Study in the Theory and History of Intermediality* (Amsterdam: Rodopi, 1999).
Wolff, Werner, *Diagrams of the Unconscious, Handwriting and Personality in Measurement, Experiment and Analysis* (New York: Grune and Stratton, 1948).
Wooldridge, H. E., *The Polyphonic Period Part I: Method of Musical Art 330–1400*, ed. Percy Carter Buck (Oxford: Oxford University Press, 1929).
Woolf, Virginia, *The Essays of Virginia Woolf, Vol 4: 1915–28*, ed. Andrew McNeille (London: Hogarth Press, 1984).
Wordsworth, William and Samuel Taylor Coleridge, *Lyrical Ballads and Other Poems* (Hertfordshire: Wordsworth Editions, 2003).
Wurth, Kiene Brillenburg, *The Musically Sublime: Indeterminacy, Infinity, Irresolvability* (New York: Fordham University Press, 2009).
Yeats, W. B., *Essays and Introductions* (London: Macmillan, 1961).
Zarlino, Gioseffo, *Istitutioni harmoniche* ([1558] New Haven, CT: Yale University Press, 1968).
Zayaruznaya, Anna, *The Monstrous New Art* (Cambridge: Cambridge University Press, 2002).
Zhdanov, A. A., 'Soviet Literature – The Richest in Ideas, the Most Advanced Literature' [speech], in Maxim Gorky et al., eds, *Soviet Writers' Congress, 1934: The Debate on Socialist Realism and Modernism in the Soviet Union* (London: Lawrence & Wishart, 1977).
Zimmerman, Nadya, 'Musical Form as Narrator: The Fugue of the Sirens in James Joyce's *Ulysses*', *Journal of Modern Literature* 26.1 (2002), 108–18.

Musical Score

Tudor Church Music. John Taverner, William Byrd, Peter Philips, Thomas Weelkes, Orlando Gibbons, Thomas Tomkins, Thomas Morley, Robert White, George Kirby, Richard Farrant, John Mundy, Christopher Tye, Thomas Hunt, Adrian Batten, John Sheppard, John Dowland, Osbert Parsley, John Bull, Michael East, Thomas Caustun and John Hilton, ed. Percy Buck, Edmund H. Fellowes, A Ramsbotham, Richard Runciman Terry and Sylvia Townsend Warner, 10 vols (London: Oxford University Press, 1922–9).

Works without Authors

Catalogue of the British Section: Paris Universal Exhibition of 1867 (London: Spottiswoode & Company, 1867).

Music Composition Awards, Grawemeyer Awards website (2016) http://grawemeyer.org/music-composition/ (last accessed 7 August 2020).

Official Catalogue of the Great Exhibition of the Works of Industry of All Nations, 2nd edn (London: Spicer Brothers; W. Clowes & Sons, 1851).

The Colonial Church Chronicle and Missionary Journal (London: Rivingtons, 1857).

The Holy Bible, New Revised Standard Version: Containing the Old and New Testaments (Cambridge: Cambridge University Press, 1994).

The London Review and Weekly Journal of Politics, Literature, Art, and Society, vol. 5, July–December (London, 1862).

Archives

National Archive: KV/2/2337.

Oxford University Press Archives: CP/ED/001034, CP/ED/001035.

The Ezra Pound Collection at the Beinecke Rare Book and Manuscript Library at Yale University.

The Sylvia Townsend Warner and Valentine Ackland Collection, Dorset County Museum: The Diaries of Sylvia Townsend Warner, 38 vols, 1927–78.

Index

Aaronson, Alex, 2
Abbott, Helen, 35
Abrahamsen, Hans, 180, 206–7
Abrams, M. H., 51
absolute music, xiii–xiv, 32
absolute rhythm, Pound's theory, 90, 93, 95, 105–6, 107–12, 115, 117–18, 126
abstract expressionism, 16
Ackland, Valentine, 138, 161–2
Adorno, Theodor W., 10
  aesthetic autonomy, 216
  on 'art as apparation', 167
  beauty vs ugliness, 183–5
  challenge to Kant, 217
  charges of elitism, 40–1
  concern with the standardisation of human experience, 117
  critique of Stravinsky, 43
  critiques of, 40–3
  dialectical thinking, 42
  dissonance, 75, 184
  on ideology, 144
  mentioned in *Orfeo*, 183
  modernism, 13–16
  on music, xvi, 60, 67
  musicology, 13, 37–44
  on rationality, 116
  rejection of synthesis, 74–5
  'truth-content' of an artwork, 75
  on twelve tone technique, 76–7
  value of atonality, 202–3
  value of ugliness, 184
Adorno's Positive Dialectic (Sherratt), 43
aesthetic autonomy, 23–5, 140, 216–20, 222
aesthetic avant-gardism, and political radicalism, 209
aesthetic beauty, Wagner's dissonance as challenge to, 3
Aesthetic Theory (Adorno), 15, 183–4, 216
aesthetics
  as a discipline, 23
  everyday aesthetics, 217–18
  and fascism, 118–19
  German Romantic emphasis, 31
  influence on modernist literature, 51
  Joyce's engagement with Aestheticism, 51
  Kant on aesthetic contemplation, 31, 35
  mathematics and, 30–1
  and modernism, xi, 3, 34, 180, 210, 220
  and music, 217–22
  Orfeo and, 187–91
  and politics, 10, 62, 88, 220
  Pythagorean connection between logic and, 30
  Rancière on the policing of aesthetic categories, 62
affect, 27–8, 111–12
After the Death of Don Juan (Warner), 161, 163
'The Afterlife of Modernism' (North), 212
Aisthesis (Rancière), 218
Albright, Daniel, 16, 42–3, 103–4
alienation, 11, 75, 183
Allen, Stuart, 70
Althusser, Louis, 137
Amalgamemnon (Brooke-Rose), 200
Amis, Martin, 211–12
analytic philosophy, empirical approaches to music in, 28–9

Ancient Greece, 24, 38, 51, 219
Anderson, Perry, 166
Anderton, Joseph, 213–14
Antheil, George, 73, 90, 109, 111–12
Antheil and the Treatise on Harmony (Pound), 11, 90, 103, 105–7, 110–12, 119
anthropology of music, 25
The Anti-Social Family (Barrett & McIntosh), 190
Antliff, Mark, xii
appearance, thing-in-itself vs, 31
Aristotle, 30–1
Armstrong, Tim, xi
Arne, Thomas, 143
Aronson, Alex, 41
ars antiqua, 185–7
ars nova, 167–70, 186–7
ars subtilior, 187
art
 ability to accurately represent the world, 118
 capacity of language to articulate value of, 106
 capacity to address social problems, 33
 as means of maintaining bourgeois ideologies, 32
 morality and, 32, 35
 origination of aesthetic autonomy, 23
Art as Experience (Dewey), 217
art pour l'art doctrine, xiv, 32, 35
atonality, 76, 182, 184, 203
 vs tonality, 202
 value of, 203
Attali, Jacques, xv
Auerbach, Jeffrey A., 152
avant-garde
 literature, 209
 music, Joyce's interest in, 73
 relationship to politics and aesthetics, 220

Babbitt, Milton, 199–200
Ballet Mécanique (1924), 104
Barber, Cecil, xiv
Barnes, Julian, 212
Barrett, Michelle, 190
Barrett, William, 130
Baudelaire, Charles, 34–5
Baugh, Bruce, 41
beauty
 Kant on the universal nature of, 183
 as product of genius, 24
 vs ugliness, 182–5
Beauvoir, Simone de, 190
Beckett, Samuel, 81, 184, 207, 213
Beebe, Maurice, 210
Beer, Gillian, 149
Beerbohm, Max, 51
Beethoven, Ludwig van, 137
Bell, Michael, 115
Benda, Julien, 37, 99–101, 150
Benjamin, Walter, 118
Benson, Donald C., 158
Bergson, Henri, 37, 100, 109
Berio, Luciano, 108, 181
Berman, Louis, 101
Bernays, Paul, 158
Bersani, Leo, 16, 71
Between (Brooke-Rose), 200
birdsong, musical representation, 89–90, 120, 122, 129
The Birth of Tragedy: Out of the Spirit of Music (Nietzsche), 3, 34
Blanton, C. D., 215
Blasius, Leslie, 159
Blast magazine, 102
the body, music's effect, 1, 36–7, 214
Bolshevik Russian Revolution, 161
Booth, Howard J., 149
Bourdieu, Pierre, 145–6
Bowie, Andrew, xv, 14, 28–9, 65
Boyle, Robert, 55
Bradbury, Malcolm, 15–16
Bribitzer-Stull, Matthew, 65
The British Aesthetic Movement (Hamilton), 35
British Aestheticism, xiii, 3, 22–3, 34–5, 49, 211
 influence on Joyce, 49
British Avant-Garde Fiction of the 1960s (Mitchell & Williams), 200, 209
Brooke-Rose, Christine, 200–1
Brophy, Brigid, 200
Brown, Susan, 55
Buck, Percy Carter, 140, 160
Bucknell, Brad, 3, 14, 17, 34, 55–6, 63
Burnt Norton (Eliot), 1–2
Buxtehude, Dietrich, 120
Byron, Mark, 123, 127, 209

Cage, John, 181
Callaghan, John, 161
Canto LXXV (Pound)
 as affirmation of fascist politics, 130

dialectical thinking, 215
  knowledge required from the audience, 105
  and *Paideuma*, 119–25
  presentation and content, 89
  reading otherwise, 125–31
The Cantos (Pound), 103, 105, 117, 119, 127, 214–15
Capital (Marx), 162, 164
Carr, Helen, 91
Caudwell, Christopher, 139, 163–4, 166–7, 171
Caudwell Controversy, 166
Cavalcanti, Guido, 91–2, 101
censorship, political, 24
Chakrabarty, Dipesh, 179
Chamber Music (Joyce), 49, 50–5, 81
Le chant des oiseaux (Janequin), 89–90
Cheng, Vincent J., 79
Childs, Donald J., 115
Chopin, Frédéric, 148
Clarke, David, 80
class *see* social class
classical music, as outlet for self-reflection, 6
Coetzee, J. M., xii
Coffman, Stanley, 96
Cohen, Harvey G., 145
Cold War, modernist art, 16
Cole, David, 55
Coleridge, Samuel Taylor, 51
Collini, Stefan, 27
colonialism, 11, 13, 81, 216, 222
  Warner's commentary, 148–57
The Coming World War (Wintringham), 162
Comintern, 161
communism, 10, 13, 16, 138, 157, 161–4
Communist Party of Great Britain, 10, 138, 161
consciousness, 3, 34, 37, 64–5, 126, 129, 162–3, 167
conservatism, 180, 187–91, 196, 221
The Contemporaneity of Modernism (Cunningham), 210
A Contribution to the Critique of Political Economy (Marx), 162
Cook, Nicholas, 24
Corfe, Joseph, 111
The Corner That Held Them (Warner), 138–9, 157–60, 162–6, 167–71, 186, 215
Coward, Noel, 145

Coyle, Michael, 112
'Crisis in Poetry' (Mallarmé), 96
critical theory, xvi, 41
Critique of the Power of Judgement (Kant), 68
Croft, Andy, 161
cultural capital, 145–6
cultural regeneration, music as aid to, 3
Culture and Materialism (Williams), 147
The Culture of Redemption (Bersani), 16
Cunningham, David, 210
Cunningham, Valentine, 161, 163
'Cyclops' (Joyce)
  critics' efforts to resolve tensions, 79–80
  employment of fragmentation techniques, 72
  narrative style, 77, 79
  and Schoenberg's twelve-tone row, 72–3
  use of parody, 72, 78, 80

Dahlhaus, Carl, xiv–xv, 2, 31–2
Dallapiccola, Luigi, 73
Dalton, Hugh, 161
Daniel, Arnaut, 93
Dasenbrock, Reed Way, 102
Dayan, Peter, 34
Debussy, Claude, Pound's critique, 111
Decadence in the Age of Modernism (Hext & Murray), 211
decadent writing, Pound's criticism, 101
de-humanisation, 115, 184
The Delphinian Quarterly, 90
Derrida, Jacques, 34, 38–9
Descartes, René, xii, 38
Dewey, John, 217
Dialectic of Enlightenment (Adorno & Horkheimer), xii, 215
dialectical thinking
  Adorno's, 42
  Joyce's, 214
  Pound's, 214
  in 'Sirens', 214
  in texts or artworks, 214–15
  Warner's, 215
dialecticism
  in modernism, 13, 214–15
  in music, xvii, 39, 215–16
diapason, 157–9
Difficult Rhythm (Fillion), 16

dissonance
  in 'Cyclops' chapter of *Ulysses*, 72–81
  'emancipation of dissonance', 3
  in Joyce's work, 81
  in *let me tell you*, 202–6
  ratio and, 30
  relationship with ugliness, 184
  rise of early twentieth century music, 76
distribution of the sensible, 62, 218–19
'The Distribution of the Sensible: Politics and Aesthetics' (Rancière), 220
Doctor Faustus (Mann), xv, 41–2
Dolmetsch, Arnold, 91, 93
D'Orléans, Charles, 95
'Doubting Castle' (Warner), 141
Dujardin, Eduard, 63–4
Duncan, Dennis, 208
DuPlessis, Rachel Blau, 91
durée, Bergson's concept, 109

Eagleton, Terry, 144, 166
Eichendorff, Joseph, 51
Einstein, Albert, 109
Eliot, T. S., 1, 4, 104, 115, 125
  aesthetics of depersonalisation, 139
Ellington, Duke, 145
ellipses, Ford Madox Ford's use of, 7–8
Ellmann, Richard, 51
'emancipation of dissonance', 3
Emaux et Camées (Gautier), 102
emotion, music and communication of, 91–3
empiricism, 4, 27
'The Encounter' (Pound), 94
Endgame (Beckett), 207
Enlightenment rationality, 211, 215–17
epic, Pound's characterisation, 214
Epic Negation: The Dialectical Poetics of Late Modernism (Blanton), 214
Epstein, Josh, xiv, 3, 16, 17, 103
ethnomusicology, 25
eugenics, 115
Exercises in Style (Queneau), 197
Ezra Pound, Wyndham Lewis and Radical Modernism (Sherry), 90
Ezra Pound and Music (Schafer), 106

Fahy, Thomas, 5–6
the family, 190–2, 201, 221
Fanning, David, 59
Farr, Florence, 91

fascism
  Pisan Cantos as endorsement of, 88
  Pound's, 11–12, 119, 123–4
  rise of in Europe, xii, 161
Feldman, Jessica, 211
feminism, 190–1
Fernandez-Santiago, Miriam, 195–6
Fillion, Michelle, 16
Findlay, John, 158
Finnegans Wake (Joyce), 53
Firestone, Shulamith, 190–1
First World War, 8, 81
Fisher, Margaret, 110–11
Ford, Ford Madox, 7–8
formalism, 12, 24, 179, 201–2
Forster, E. M., 3
Four Quartets (Eliot), 1
fragmentation, 6, 8–9, 33, 50, 72, 74–5, 79–81, 117, 126, 129, 147
Francesco da Milano, 120
Frankfurt School, xi–xii, xvi, 10, 16, 116, 139, 144
Frankfurt School Marxism, 73
Freedman, Jonathan, 35
French Symbolism, 22–3, 34–5, 96, 109, 208
Friedman, Susan Stanford, 213
fuga per canonem, 12, 49, 55, 61
fugal structure, as basis of 'Sirens' chapter of *Ulysses*, 12, 49, 55–8; *see also* 'Sirens' (Joyce)
Full Surrogacy Now: Feminism Against Family (Lewis), 191
functional harmony, 40, 72, 74–7, 113, 180, 182, 197, 199, 202–3
Furness, Raymond, 59

Gaffurio, Franchino, 31, 159
Gaudier-Brzeska, Henri, 106, 115
Gautier, Théophile, 102–6
gender, 4–7, 13, 23, 149, 190–1, 213, 222
German Idealism, xiii
German Romanticism, xiv, 3, 22–3, 29, 31, 51, 211, 218–20
  Adorno and, 37
  influence on British thought, 35
Gesamtkunstwerk, Wagnerian concept, 9, 33, 65
Gilbert, Stuart, 55
Gillies, Mary Ann, 109
God, Descartes's description, 38
Goehr, Lydia, 34, 40, 202–3

Goethe, Johann Wolfgang von, 31, 51, 121
Gourmont, Rémy de, 37, 90, 114, 150
  influence on Pound, 97–102
'Great Bass', Pound's theory, 90, 93, 105–6, 110, 112–14, 115, 118, 126
Green, Robert, 9
Griffiths, Paul, 4, 17, 180, 197, 210
Grose, Kenneth H., 53
Grundrisse (Marx), 157, 164
Guide to Kulchur (Pound), 90, 106, 116, 119, 126

Habermas, Jürgen, 215–16
Hamilton, William, 35
Hamlet (Shakespeare), 197–8, 205–6, 213
De harmonia musicorum instrumentorun opus (Gaffurio), 159
Handel, George Frideric, 143
Hannigan, Barbara, 206
Hanslick, Eduard, 24
'The Hard and the Soft in French Poetry' (Pound), 103
Harker, Ben, 161
Harkness, Marguerite, 51
Harman, Claire, 140, 160
Harmonielehre (Schoenberg), 192
harmonium, and colonialism, 152
harmony, functional, 40, 72, 74–7, 113, 180, 182, 197, 199, 202–3
Haslam, Jonathan, 161
Haslam, Sara, 7, 75
Hauer, Joseph Matthias, 73
Haydn, Joseph, 143
Hegel, Georg Wilhelm Friedrich
  Adorno's challenge, 74
  lyric, 51–2
Herder, Johann Gottfried, 51
Herman, David, 50, 70, 73
Herring, Philip, 79
Hillyer, Robert, 88
Horkheimer, Max, xvi, 144
'Hugh Selwyn Mauberley' (Pound), 102, 104–6, 111
Huyssen, Andreas, 41, 210

The Idea of Absolute Music (Dahlhaus), 2
idealism, Kant's transcendental idealism, 31

ideology, xvi, 42, 179, 183, 206, 208, 216, 222
  Adorno and Horkheimer on, 144, 148
  aesthetic ideology of the artist, 25
  as false consciousness, 27, 144
  the family as, 190
  language and, 180
  Warner's exploration, 13, 137–8, 143–5, 149
'Image from D'Orléans' (Pound), 94–5
Imagism/Imagist principles, 54, 89–90, 92, 103, 126, 214
Des Imagistes (Pound), 54
In Search of Lost Time (Proust), xv, xvii
'infinite melody', Wagner's, 64
instrumental music, as pure form of communication, 31–2
The Interpretation of the Music of the XVIIth and XVIIIth Centuries (Dolmetsch), 93
Invisible Author: Last Essays (Brooke-Rose), 201
Istitutioni harmoniche (Zarlino), 92

James, David, 208, 210
James Joyce Quarterly, 51
Jameson, Fredric, 14
Jameson, Storm, 139
Janequin, Clément, 89, 120
Jay, Martin, 15
Jenemann, David, xvii, 41, 117
Joannnou, Maroula, 138
Johnson, Jeri, 64
Jordan, Julia, 208
Josipovici, Gabriel, 211–12, 216
Joyce, James
  aestheticism, 51
  Chamber Music, 50–5
  comparison of noise and music, 54–5
  comparison with Schoenberg's twelve-tone row, 72–4
  'Cyclops', 72–81
  democracy, 61–2, 67
  dialectical thinking, 214
  Dujardin's inspiration, 63–4
  early influence of British Aestheticism, 49
  Finnegans Wake, 53
  first published literary work, 50
  fugue/*fuga per canonem*, 12, 49, 55–8, 61
  Imagist context, 54

Joyce, James (*cont.*)
  interest in avant-garde music, 73
  leitmotif-like words and phrases, 64
  lyric, 54
  musical background, 11
  musical transcendence, 57
  nationalist discourse, 11
  Pater's influence, 36, 51
  politics, 10–11, 81
  polyphony, 55, 56–8
  A Portrait of the Artist as a Young Man, 51, 103
  Pound's review, 103
  'Sirens', 55–72
  song, 68–9
  stream-of-consciousness technique, 63
  Work in Progress, 81
  see also 'Cyclops'; 'Sirens'; *Ulysses*
Judd, Cristle Collins, 159
Jupiter (Mozart), 182

Kafka, Franz, 213
Kant, Immanuel
  Adorno's challenge, 217
  on aesthetic contemplation, 31, 35
  on beauty, 216
  critique of music, 36, 68
  on the status of music, 35–6
  thing-in-itself, appearance vs, 31
  on the universal nature of beauty, 183
Katz, Daniel, 93
Kenner, Hugh, 209
Kirwan, Peter, 199
Kivy, Peter, 28–9
Klages, Ludwig, 120
Kramer, Lawrence, 23
Kurtág, György, 207

Labinger, Jay, 195
Lahr, John, 145
language
  capacity to articulate value of art, 106
  modernism and, xi, xiii, 1, 7, 14, 22, 29, 35, 179–80, 197, 200, 204–6, 212–13, 216, 222
Late Modernism and the Avant-Garde British Novel (Jordan), 208
Laughlin, James, 128
Lawrence, D. H., 9–10
Lazarsfeld, Paul Felix, xvii, 117

Le Lionnais, François, 197
'Le Vers populaire' (Gourmont), 100
LeBon, Gustave, 100
Lees, Heath, 66
Left Book Club, 138, 161
Left Review, 157, 161–2
Leighton, Angela, 52
leitmotif
  Bribitzer-Stull's description, 65
  in Joyce's work, 59–60
  purpose, 59
  Wagner's use of, 59, 63–4
Leppert, Richard, 23–4
Les Lauriers sont coupés (Dujardin), 63–4
let me tell you (Abrahamsen), 206–7
let me tell you (Griffiths), 17, 180
  adaptation into song cycle, 180–1
  Beckettian quality, 203
  claim to political radicalism, 209
  comparison of Griffiths's and Schoenberg's writing constraints, 202
  comparison with *Orfeo*, 201–2, 207
  dissonance and difficulty, 202–6
  and early-twentieth-century modernism, 222
  engagement with and altering of the past, 212
  exploration of the non-natural status of language, 204
  innovations, 199–202
  literary-musical interaction, 206–7
  modernism, 180, 199–202, 221
  and relevance of modernism today, 207–17
  writing constraint, 180, 197–9, 213, 221
Levin, Harry, 210
Levin, Lawrence, 55
Lewis, Ethan, 102
Lewis, Sophie, 191
Lewis, Wyndham, 37, 100–2, 111–12
Leys, Ruth, 27
lipogram, 197
Lipps, Theodor, 100
listening public, 202–3, 221
Literary Modernism and Musical Aesthetics (Bucknell), 17
Litz, A. Walton, 55
live music streaming, 182
The Lives of Animals (Coetzee), xii
The Lives of Painters (Vasari), 23

Lockyer, Rebekah, 8
Lolly Willowes (Warner), 12, 142
Luening, Otto, 73
Lukács, Georg, 51
lyric
  Joyce's indebtness to, 54
  nineteenth century dominance, 51
  position in Hegel's aesthetic thought, 51–2

McClary, Susan, 23–4, 40
McDowell, John, 28–9
McEwen, Ian, 212
McIntosh, Mary, 190
'Machine Art' (Pound), 112–13, 122
Madge, Charles, 163
Make it New (Pound), 209
Mallarmé, Stéphane, xiv, 2, 34–6, 96, 99, 208
Mann, Thomas, 42
Manual of Harmony (Richter), 111
Mao, Douglas, 212
Maor, Eli, 30
Marcuse, Herbert, 117–18
Margolies, David, 161, 163
Marinetti, F. T., 118
marriage, Marx's description, 224n34
Martin, Peter J., 25–7
Martin, Timothy, 55, 63–4
mass culture, 41, 183
mathematics
  aesthetics and, 30–1
  investigating through music and art, xv
  mathematical basis of sound, 30
  music and, 158
  music-as-mathematics, 71
  Pound's musical theories and, 110
medieval music, 211
Messiaen, Olivier, 180
metaphysics
  Adorno's description, 38
  music as key to, 32
Miller, Tyrus, xi, 139
Millington, Barry, 59
Milton, John, x
Minima Moralia (Adorno), 75, 117
'Mis/Quotation in Constrained Writing' (Kirwan), 199
Mitchell, Kaye, 209
Modern Quarterly, 164
modernism
  Adorno on, 13–16
  aesthetics and, xi, 3, 34, 180, 210, 220
  association with a conscious effort to change something, 213
  classification and periodisation, xv, 115, 209
  crisis and, xi, 1, 4, 33
  as dialectical, 13, 214–15
  as driver of innovation, 14
  and fragmentation, 50, 72, 75, 129
  indebtedness to French symbolism's negotiations with music, 34
  Josipovici's description, 211
  and language, xi, xiii, 1, 7, 14, 22, 29, 35, 179–80, 197, 200, 204–6, 212–13, 216, 222
  and modernity, xii, 3, 14, 50, 72, 74–5, 210, 213
  nineteenth-century literary roots, 211
  North's reconceptualisation, 212
  Rancière's claims for, 220
  relevance in the twenty-first century, 207–17
  twenty-first-century approaches to, 180, 221–2
  vegetation of late modernism, 213
Modernism and the Frankfurt School (Miller), xi–xii
Modernism and the Reinvention of Decadence (Sherry), 210–12
Modernist Futures (James), 210
modernist literature
  influence of decadence and Aestheticism, 51
  recurring fragmentation themes, 75
  use of music in, 1
  as work of outsiders, 7
modernist music, framing of as terrorism, 191–3
modernist writing
  anti-establishment character, 7
  changed relationship with time, 109
  prominence of music in, xiii
  use of non-linguistic markers, 7
  Wagner's influence, 33
  as a window of time, 10
modernity, xi–xii, 3, 9–11, 14, 50, 53, 72, 74–5, 144, 184, 210, 213, 215, 217
'Modernity: An Unfinished Project' (Habermas), 215
Montefiore, Janet, 139, 161, 166
morality, relationship to art, 32, 35

Moritz, Karl Philip, 32
Morrison, Paul, 118
Mr Fortune's Maggot (Warner)
  commentary on colonialism, 150–2
  dialectical thinking, 215
  ideological power of tonality, 182
Münch, Gerhart, 89, 120
music
  absolute music, xiii–xiv, 32
  aesthetics and, 217–22
  as aid to cultural regeneration, 3
  anthropology of, 25
  beauty of, as product of genius, 24
  and communication of emotion, 91–3
  communicative capacity, x
  concerns about the emotional potential of, 37
  as dialectical, xvii, 39, 215–16
  differentiation from sound, xv, 67, 108–9
  dissonance and, 3; *see also* dissonance
  effect on the body, 1, 36–7, 214
  and the emotions, xiii–xiv, 38, 57, 59, 67, 92, 95–6, 99–101, 167, 183, 186, 206
  as expression of the "essence" of things, 2
  as form of divine communication, 151
  Joyce, Pound and Warner's view of, 11
  Joyce's comparison of noise and, 54–5
  Kant's critique, 36, 68
  Kivy on the meaninglessness of, 28–9
  as material product, xiv, 186
  measuring pitch, 108
  music-as-mathematics, 71
  non-referentiality, 3, 12, 14–15, 29, 31, 35, 44, 52, 200, 214
  novelists' concern with musical form, 3
  Pater's dictum about, 35–6
  rhythm as driver of poetic form, 1–2; *see also* rhythm
  song, x, 51, 69, 91, 98
  sound and, x, xiii, 12, 35, 114, 122, 127, 130; *see also* sound
  as a transcendent art form, 22; *see also* musical transcendence
  use of in literary modernism, 4
  vibrations and, xiii, 108, 112, 222

Music Alone (Kivy), 28
Music and Society (McClary & Leppert), 23
'The Music at Long Verney' (Warner), 137, 142–8
'The Music of Poetry' (Eliot), 1–2
The Music of Speech (Farr), 91
musical modes, Western, 92
musical transcendence
  in Adorno's thinking, 39
  the concept, xiv
  contemporary lack of appreciation, 22
  derivation of in Pater's thinking, 52
  as false ideology, 23, 27
  fugal or polyphonic form and, 58
  German Romantic origins, 31
  historical perspective, 23–5, 30–7
  impact of analysis on, 26–7
  in Joyce's work, 57
  non-referentiality and, 52
  in Powers' *Orfeo*, 180
  'Sirens' and critique of, 67–72
Musicircus (Cage), 181
musicology
  Adorno's approach, 13, 37–44
  New musicology, 23–9
  Schenker and formalism, 24
Mutti, Lynn, 140

Nash, John, 72–3, 79
nationalism, 11
Nattiez, Jean-Jacques, 25, 108
natural hierarchy, and fascism, 114–19
natural history, as basis for construction of otherness, 150
Natural Philosophy of Love (Gourmont), 90, 97
Nazi Germany, 24, 161
Neo-Baroque aesthetics, 195
Neoplatonic Idealism, 158–9
Nettl, Bruno, 25, 92
Neuwirth, Olga, 207
The New Age (journal), 93, 106
New Criticism, 16, 71, 123–4
New Left, 166
New Modernist Studies, 17, 210
New Music, 184
New Musicology, 23–5
Ngai, Sianne, 217
Nietzsche, Friedrich
  music as aid to cultural regeneration, 3

on the role of music in challenging social problems, 33–4
No More Parades (Ford), 8
noise, xiv, 54–5
Nolan, Emer, 79
non-referentiality of music, 3, 12, 14–15, 29, 31, 35, 44, 52, 200, 214
North, Michael, xii, 209, 212–13

Odyssey (Homer), comparison with Joyce's 'Sirens', 68–70
On the Musically Beautiful (Hanslick), 24
'Opinion or Insight?' (Schoenberg), 3
Ord-Hume, Arthur, 152
Orfeo (Powers), 17
   Adornian and Kantian themes, 183
   ars antiqua, 187, 190
   beauty vs ugliness, 182–5
   closing scene, 190
   comparison with *let me tell you*, 201–2, 207
   comparison with Monteverdi's opera *L'Orfeo*, 196
   conservativism, 180, 187–91, 196, 221
   dissonance and tonality, 181–2, 191
   framing of modernist music as terrorism, 191–3
   and Kantian notions of universal beauty, 217
   modernist content, 180
   and musico-literary criticism, 195–7
   mythic underpinning, 193–5
   recuperating a version of the past, 185–7
   subject matter, 180
   and tonality, 194
   and traditional family life, 194
   valorisation of classical music, 194
Orientations (Boulez), 192
Orlando (Woolf), 207
Ortega y Gasset, José, 37, 99–100
Osborne, Peter, 210
otherness, natural history as basis for construction of, 150
The Oulipo and Modern Thought (Duncan), 208
Oulipo group, 197, 208–9
Our Aesthetic Categories: Zany, Cute, Interesting (Ngai), 217
Overy, Richard, 160–1

Parade's End (Ford), 7–9
Parsons, Cóilín, 208
Pater, Walter, xiii, 35–6
   derivation of music's transcendence, 52
   influence on Joyce, 36, 51
patriarchy, 190
Pawling, Christopher, 166
perception, essence of emotion and, 3
Perec, Georges, 197
Perils, Alan D., 36
Persian modes, affective connotations, 92
Phaedro (Plato), 38
Pilgrimage (Richardson), 4–5, 63
The Pisan Cantos (Pound), 88, 103, 105, 119, 122–5, 127–8, 130
   Bollingen prize awarded to, 88, 122
Plato, 31, 211
   on musical modes, 92
   theory of forms, 38
Poirer, Richard, 36
politics
   aesthetics and, 10, 62, 88, 217–22
   and music, 217–22
   see also communism; fascism
The Polyphonic Period Part 1: Method of Musical Art, 330–1400 (Wooldridge), 159
polyphony, 55, 56–8, 207
Polzonetti, Pierpaolo, 143
A Portrait of the Artist as a Young Man (Joyce), 51, 103
postmodernism, 15, 208, 210
Pound, Ezra
   'absolute rhythm', 107–12
   Antheil and the Treatise on Harmony, 11, 90, 103, 105–7, 110–12, 119
   anti-Semitism, 98, 118
   Bollingen prize awarded to, 88, 122, 130
   The Cantos, 103, 105, 117, 119, 127, 214–15
   characterisation of the epic, 214
   commitment to conceive of music in visual terms, 111
   Des Imagistes, 54
   dialectical thinking, 214
   direct presentation, 90–7, 102
   disassociation from other composers, 110–11
   'The Encounter', 94
   eugenics, 115

Pound, Ezra (*cont.*)
  experiments with rhyme and metre, 94
  fascism, 11–12, 114–19, 123–4
  First World War and, 105–6
  'Great Bass' theory, 90, 93, 105–6, 110, 112–14, 115, 118, 126
  Guide to Kulchur, 90, 106, 116, 119, 126
  'The Hard and the Soft in French Poetry', 103
  'hard bits' of rhythm, 89, 103–4, 106
  'Hugh Selwyn Mauberley', 102, 104–6, 111
  ideologues, xiv, 114–15
  'Image from D'Orléans', 94–5
  Imagist principles, 90, 92, 95, 102, 126
  incarceration, 88
  influence of French thinkers, 37
  involvement with Italian fascism, 116
  on Joyce's poetry, 54
  limitations of language, 106
  'Machine Art', 112–13, 122
  Make it New, 209
  Mallarmé's influence, 36
  music and emotion, 91–3
  musical theories, 106–7
  music's effect on the body, 101
  politicisation of the aesthetic and, 107
  Rémy de Gourmont's influence, 97–102
  representation, 118
  rhythm, 89–90, 93–6, 103–4, 114–19
  Second World War, 128
  study of troubadour poets, 91
  symbolism and, 96–7, 101–2
  Théophile Gautier's inspiration, 102–6
  time, 109
  translations of Guido Cavalcanti's sonnets, 91
  vers libre, 93, 104
  'Vers Libre and Arnold Dolmetsch', 93
  see also The Pisan Cantos; Canto LXXV
Powers, Richard, 179–80, 212
Practica Musicae (Gaffurio), 31, 159
pregnancy, as labour, 225n38
Proust, Marcel, 3
'Proverb' (Reich), 185, 189
Purcell, Henry, x
Pythagoras, 30–1, 158, 211

Quatuor pour la fin du temps (Messiaen), 180
Queneau, Raymond, 197

race, 23, 98, 119, 123, 191, 222
  Gourmont on, 98
Rancière, Jacques, 62, 210, 218, 220–1
Randall, Bryony, 109
ratio, Pythagorean, 30, 158
rational ordering systems, and fascism, 114–19
rationality/rational thought, xiii, 6, 10, 14, 22, 29, 36, 95, 129, 211
realism, 139, 200–2
reason, xii, xvi, 16, 37, 99, 211
Reconnecting Aestheticism and Modernism (Coste, Reynier and Delyfer), 211
Reed, T. J., 31
regime of art, 218–19
Reich, Steve, 185
Reichel, A. Elisabeth, 196
Remes, Pauliina, 158
The Republic (Plato), 92
Revue wagnérienne (Dujardin), 64
rhythm
  absolute rhythm, 90, 93, 95, 105–6, 107–12, 115, 117–18, 126
  poetry and, 1–2, 115, 198–9
  Pound's 'hard bits' of rhythm, 89, 103–4, 106
  Pound's Imagist principles and, 90–1, 96
  race and, 123
  Yeats's use of, 52
Richardson, Dorothy, 4, 6, 63
Richter, Ernst Friedrich, 111
Rickword, Edgell, 161
The Rite of Spring (Stravinsky), 43
Roesner, Edward H., 187
Rogers, Margaret, 55
Romanticism, xiii
A Room with a View (Forster), 5
Rose, Jonathan, 146, 148
Ross, Alex, 207
Routledge Companion to Experimental Literature (Bray, Gibbons & McHale), 209
'Rule Britannia' (Arne), 143
Ruskin, John, 35
Russell, Bertrand, 158
Ruthven, K. K., 95

Sachs, Hans, 120
Said, Edward, 42
the salon, social class and, 172n25
Samuel Beckett: Fin de Partie (Kurtág), 207
Schafer, R. Murray, 106
Schenker, Heinrich, 24
Schlegel, Friedrich, xv
Schoenberg, Arnold, 3, 40, 72
  atonal music, 76
  'emancipation of dissonance', 108
  Joyce's awareness of, 73
  the listening public, 202–3, 221
  twelve-tone row, 50, 72, 199–200
Schopenhauer, Arthur, xiii, 2, 6, 14, 32–4, 58, 63, 92
  Wagner and, 63
Scotto, Robert M., 36
Searle, Richard, 140, 160
Second Viennese School, 3, 10
Second World War, xii, 115–16, 180
self-destruction, 10, 69
sexuality, 7, 191
Shepherd, John, 26
Sherratt, Yvonne, 43
Sherry, Vincent, xiv, 36, 51, 90, 96, 99–100, 102, 114–15, 150, 210, 212
Shockley, Alan, 40, 56
Sieburth, Richard, 102
simultaneity, 56–8, 61–2
Sinclair, May, 63
'Sirens' (Joyce)
  Adorno and the significance of how Joyce refers to music, 67
  Blazes Boylan's thematic material, 66
  comparison with Schoenberg's twelve-tone row, 73
  comparison with Sirens in the *Odyssey*, 68–70
  and critique of musical transcendence, 67–72
  effects of fugal structure, 61
  emulation of musical form, 58–62
  fugal structure debate, 55–8
  leitmotifs, 59–60
  stream-of-consciousness narrative, 65
  Wagner and, 62–7
Slater, Montagu, 163
Smith, Don Noel, 55
Smith, Douglas K., 3
Smith, Stan, 166
Snarrenburg, Robert, 24
Snow, C. P., 208

social anthropology, 115
social class, 5, 7, 40, 114, 142, 144–6, 151, 157, 163, 165–6, 216
  and the salon, 172n25
social problems
  art's capacity to address, 33
  role of music in challenging, 33–4
social relations, musical composition and, 37
Socialist Realism, 163
society, relationship between musical form and, 40
sociology, music and, 25–8
Solis, Ted, 25
song, x, 51, 69, 91, 98
Sorel, Georges, 100
sound
  affective power of, xiii, 37, 54
  effect on the body, 12, 68
  mathematical basis of, 30, 158
  and music, x, xiii, 12, 35, 114, 122, 127, 130
  music's differentiation from, xv, 67, 108–9
  rhythm and, 96, 106, 108
  sound waves, xiii, 103, 107–8
sound waves, definition, 108
Soviet Russia, 24
Soviet Writers Congress, 138, 163
Spanish Civil War, 138, 162
Spinks, Lee, 54
St. Mawr (Lawrence), 9–10
Stevens, Wallace, 127
Stimpson, Catharine, 179
Stockhausen, Karlheinz, 181
The Story of a Novel (Mann), 42
Stravinsky, Igor
  Adorno's critique, 43
  Pound's critique, 103
stream-of-consciousness, 63–5
Sublime Noise (Epstein), 16
Subotnik, Rose Rosengard, 41
Sultan, Stanley, 55
Summer Will Show (Warner), 157, 161, 163
Sumner, Charles B., 184
Surette, Leon, 4
Sutton, Emma, 16

Technique de mon langage musical (Messiaen), 192
Templeton, Erin E., 107
terrorism, framing of modernist music as, 191–3

Terry, Richard, 140–1
Testament (Villon), 104
Theorica Musicae (Gaffurio), 159
thing-in-itself
  appearance vs, 31
  music as the, xiii, 32–3, 58, 63
  music's potential for communicating, 35
  Pound's argument, 97, 116
Thompson, E. P., 166
Thorough Bass Simplified (Corfe), 111
Thru (Brooke-Rose), 200
time, modernist preoccupation with, 109
Time and Western Man (Lewis), 101
Tindall, William York, 53
'Tradition and the Individual Talent' (Eliot), 2
transcendence, musical *see* musical transcendence
Tristan chord, 108–9
Tristan und Isolde (Wagner), 3
Tufail, Burhan, 208
twelve-tone compositional technique, 42, 50, 72–7, 79–81, 199–200
  comparison with Griffiths' writing constraint, 180, 199
  Joyce's 'Cyclops' and, 72–81
Tymoczko, Dmitri, 108

ugliness, beauty vs, 182–5
Ugly Feelings (Ngai), 217
Ulysses (Joyce), xvii, 15
  critics' contradictory claims, 71
  exile and loneliness in, 80
  inspiration for 'interior monologue', 64
  modelling of 'Sirens' chapter, 12, 49
  narrative style, 72
  nationalist discourse, 11
  the *Odyssey* and, 73–4
  use of parody and pastiche, 53
  see also 'Cyclops'; 'Sirens'
universality, 77, 137, 140, 153–4, 157, 189, 192, 196, 215
Untwisting the Serpent (Albright), 16, 43

Vasari, Giorgio, 23
'Vers Libre and Arnold Dolmetsch' (Pound), 93
vibrations, xiii, 70, 100, 108, 112, 126, 222

Victorian Modernism (Feldman), 211
Viennese Classicism, 41
Virginia Woolf and Classical Music (Sutton), 16
A Void (Perec), 197
Vorticism, 102–3

Wachman, Gay, 149
Wagner, Richard, 3
  Gesamtkunstwerk, 9, 33, 65
  'infinite melody', 64
  influence on stream-of-consciousness, 63
  leitmotif, 59, 65
  Pound's critique, 111
  Schopenhauer's influence, 33
  and 'Sirens', 62–7
  Tristan chord, 108–9
  utopian thinking, 3–4, 9
Warner, Sylvia Townsend
  After the Death of Don Juan, 161, 163
  ars nova, 186
  career, 137
  and Christopher Caudwell's Marxist aesthetic, 139, 163, 166–7
  Communist Party membership, 138
  contribution to *The Polyphonic Period*, 159–60
  The Corner That Held Them, 138–9, 157–60, 162–6, 167–71, 186, 215
  critique of Beethoven, 137
  dialectical thinking, 215
  'Doubting Castle', 141
  education and professional career, 140–2
  exploration of superstructural relations, 147–8
  financial independence, 160
  First World War and, 141
  ideology in fiction of, 138, 143–5, 148–9
  involvement in the Peoples' Front of Britain, 161
  Left Book Club, 138, 161
  Left Review, 157, 161–2
  Lolly Willowes, 12, 142
  Marxism, 160–71
  and Marxist thought, 138
  MI5 surveillance, 138, 162
  Mr Fortune's Maggot, 138, 148–57
  'The Music at Long Verney', 137, 142–8

musical compositions, 141–2
musical transcendence and, 36
musicology, 140–2
music's role in the fiction of, 171
neglect by the critical establishment, 12–13
politics, 10, 13
published works, 13
realism, 139
relationship with Percy Carter Buck, 140
sexuality, 13, 149
Spanish Civil War and, 138, 162
study of music, 11
Tudor Church Music project involvement, 140–1, 148, 160
utopian thinking, 139, 167, 171
see also Mr Fortune's Maggot
Weaver, Harriet Shaw, 49, 56
Weaver, Jack W., 73
Webern, Anton, 207
Weir, David, 51, 102
What are Universities for? (Collini), 27
'What Modernism Was' (Beebe), 210
'What was Modernism?' (Levin), 210
'When Was Modernism?' (Williams), 210
White, Robert, 141

Whitworth, Michael, 109
Wilde, Oscar, 35
Williams, Raymond, 7, 137, 147, 204, 210
Williams, William Carlos, 130
Wind Quintet Op. 26 (Schoenberg), 77
Wintringham, Tom, 162
Witen, Michelle, 56
Wittgenstein, Ludwig, 185
Wolf, Werner, 56
Wolff, Janet, 23–4
women, social consequences of the patriarchal family unit, 190
Wooldridge, H. E., 159
Woolf, Virginia, 3, 5, 115, 207
  Wagner's influence, 64
Wordsworth, William, 51
Work in Progress (Joyce), 81
world music, 25
Worringer, Wilhelm, 100

Yeats, W. B., 4, 52, 91
Young-Hee Kwon, 149

Zarlino, Gioseffo, 92
Zhdanov, Andrei, 163
Zimmerman, Nadya, 55–7, 61

EU representative:
Easy Access System Europe
Mustamäe tee 50, 10621 Tallinn, Estonia
Gpsr.requests@easproject.com

www.ingramcontent.com/pod-product-compliance
Lightning Source LLC
Chambersburg PA
CBHW051605230426
43668CB00013B/1987